Sir John R. Hicks (from a portrait by Mark Wickham)

SIR JOHN R. HICKS:
Critical Assessments

Critical Assessments of Contemporary Economists

Forthcoming

Paul A. Samuelson
Milton Friedman
F.A. Hayek
Joseph Schumpeter

SIR JOHN R. HICKS
Critical Assessments

**Edited by John Cunningham Wood
and Ronald N. Woods**

VOLUME IV

ROUTLEDGE
London and New York

First published in 1989 by
Routledge
11 New Fetter Lane, London EC4P 4EE
29 West 35th Street, New York NY 10001

Selection and editorial matter © 1989 Routledge

Typeset in Times Roman by Leaper & Gard Ltd, Bristol, England
Printed and bound in Great Britain by Mackays of Chatham Ltd, Kent

British Library Cataloguing in Publication Data

Sir John R. Hicks: critical assessments. —
    (Critical assessments of
contemporary economists).
    Vol. 4
1. Economics. Theories of. Hicks, John,
1904–
I. Wood, John Cunningham   II. Woods,
Ronald N.
330.15′3

ISBN 0-415-01272-4

Library of Congress Cataloging-in-Publication Data

Sir John R. Hicks : critical assessments / edited by John Cunningham
    Wood and Ronald N. Woods.
        p.   cm. — (The Critical assessments of contemporary
    economists)
        ISBN 0-415-01272-4 (set)
        1. Hicks, John Richard, Sir, 1904-   . 2. Economists — Great
    Britain.   I. Wood, John Cunningham.   II. Woods, Ronald N.
    III. Series.
    HB103.H47S57   1989
    330′.092′4—dc19   88-23877

Contents

Abbreviations

A.E.	American Economist
A.E.J.	Atlantic Economic Journal
A.E.R.	The American Economic Review
B.E.R.	Bulletin of Economic Research
C.J.E.	Cambridge Journal of Economics
C.J.E.P.S.	The Canadian Journal of Economics and Political Science
D.Ec.	De Economist
Ec.	Econometrica
E.E.J.	Eastern Economic Journal
E.H.R.	Economic History Review
E.J.	Economic Journal
H.P.E.	History of Political Economy
I.E.J.	Indian Economic Journal
I.E.R.	International Economic Review
I.E.S.S.	International Encyclopedia of the Social Sciences
J.E.I.	Journal of Economic Issues
J.E.L.	Journal of Economic Literature
J.F.	The Journal of Finance
J.P.E.	Journal of Political Economy
J.P.K.E.	Journal of Post Keynesian Economics
K.K.	Kredit und Kapital
N.J.E.B.	Nebraska Journal of Economics and Business
O.E.P.	Oxford Economic Papers
P.F.Q.	Public Finance Quarterly
Q.J.E.	Quarterly Journal of Economics
R.E.S.	The Review of Economic Studies
S.A.J.E.	The South African Journal of Economics
S.E.J.	Southern Economic Journal
S.J.E.	Scandinavian Journal of Economics
Z.N.	Zeitschrift für Nationalökonomie

Hicks and Hollander on Ricardo: A Mathematical Note*†

K. Gordon

The model of Ricardo's economy that John Hicks and Samuel Hollander [1977] explored in this *Journal* laid to rest the notion that Ricardian models can be adequately constructed with the wage assumed to be at subsistence. The model in that paper dealt, for the most part, with an economy possessed of circulating capital only.[1] It examined the behavior of the wage and labor force as the economy approaches the stationary state. In the course of their investigation, Hicks and Hollander encountered the possibility that the wage and labor force might not approach stationary state levels in a smooth way, but might instead oscillate: the wage passing sometimes below subsistence, sometimes above it; the labor force increasing and decreasing. Such behavior, which Ricardo mentioned only briefly,[2] they named "the exception" [Hicks and Hollander, 1977, p. 358].

When such a possibility arises, it is natural enough to investigate the conditions that give rise to it. Hicks and Hollander did so and concluded that the approach to stationary state equilibrium will be smooth, provided only that "the elasticity of the marginal product curve must be greater than 1" [Hicks and Hollander, 1977, p. 356]. This note re-examines the model formally,[3] on the basis of Pasinetti's 1960 article. It shows that the Hicks–Hollander condition for non-oscillatory behaviour is sufficient, but not necessary.

I. The Model

Pasinetti's mathematical version of Ricardo's system examined an economy that produces two commodities — a wage good and a luxury good. His simpler, but essentially similar, one-commodity model presented in *Lectures on the Theory of Production* [1977] can be used to derive all the results that Hicks and Hollander obtained for the circulating-capital-only model. The system is summarized in the following five equations, using Pasinetti's notation with slight modifications: L for labor, w for the wage,

†Source: *Quarterly Journal of Economics*, Vol. 98 (4), November 1983, pp. 721–6.

and w^* for the subsistence wage. The output of the single commodity is denoted X, rent is R, and the mass of profit is P:

$$X = f(L); f(0) \geq 0; f'(0) > w^*; f''(L) < 0$$
$$W = wL$$
$$K = W$$
$$R = f(L) - Lf'(L)$$
$$P = X - R - wL.$$

Pasinetti's last two equations [1977, equations I.3.13 and I.3.14] have been omitted. They fixed the wage and the capital stock, which Hicks and Hollander treated as variable. In the case at hand, then, the wage and the rate of profit are related in the following way:

$$r = (f'(L) - w)/w$$

or, in the version used by Hicks and Hollander, $w = f'(L)/(1 + r)$.

II. The Dynamics

With the wage and the capital stock variable, the model becomes dynamic; its behaviour can be accounted for on strictly Ricardian principles. The population, hence the labor force, increase if the market wage exceeds the subsistence wage — this is the definition of subsistence. Any excess of profit over what Hicks and Hollander call "subsistence profit," and denoted P^* here,[4] leads to the accumulation of capital — this defines subsistence profit. Thus, the dynamics can be represented as

(1) $\dot{L} = Lg(w - w^*);\quad g(0) = 0;\quad g' > 0$

(2) $\dot{K} = \phi[Lf'(L) - wL(1 + r^*)];\quad \phi(0) = 0;\quad \phi' > 0;\quad r^* \geq 0.$

The system is in equilibrium[5] when $\dot{L} = \dot{K} = 0$, which obtains when $w = w^* = f'(L)/(1 + r^*)$. This equilibrium occurs at point E in Figure I, which reproduces, with identifying equations, the Hick–Hollander Figure I. Recalling that $K = wL$, equation (2) can be rewritten, and its new form, together with equation (1), make up a simultaneous system:

(3) $\begin{cases} \dot{L} = Lg(w - w^*) \\ \dot{w} = (1/L)\phi[Lf'(L) - wL(1 + r^*)] - wg(w - w^*). \end{cases}$

The plane depicted in Figure I then emerges as the phase plane for this system.

In general, the stability of the equilibrium (w^*, L^*), and the disequilibrium behavior of w and L, are examined by considering the disequilibrium behavior of (3).

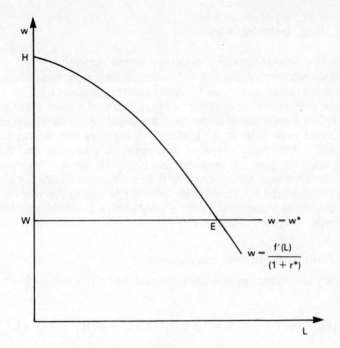

FIGURE I
[Hicks and Hollander, 1977, p. 354]

III. Behaviour Out of Equilibrium

Consider the relation between the mass of profit and growth of capital, $\dot{K} = \phi(P - P^*)$. This relation can be approximated using a Taylor's series to derive $\dot{K} = \phi'(0)(P - P^*)$, or

$$\dot{K} = (1 - h)(P - P^*); \quad 0 < h < 1,$$

where h is the portion of profit consumed when profit exceeds "subsistence." Under these assumptions, the rate of growth of the capital stock becomes

(4) $\qquad \dot{K}/K = (1 - h)(r - r^*).$

Equation (4) can be rearranged and combined with (1) to form system (5):

(5) $\qquad \begin{cases} \dot{L} = Lg(w - w^*) \\ \dot{w} = [1 - h][f'(L) - w(1 + r^*)] - wg(w - w^*). \end{cases}$

A second simplification linearizes system (5) in the neighborhood of (w^*, L^*) to derive

$$\begin{cases} \dot{L} = F_1(L, w) \cong aL + bw \\ \dot{w} = F_2(L, w) \cong cL + dw, \end{cases}$$

where the coefficients are the appropriate partial derivatives.

The local behavior of the system[6] is determined from the nature of the eigenvalues of the matrix of coefficients, namely the roots of $\lambda^2 + \sigma\lambda + \Delta = 0$, where $\sigma = -(a + d)$ and $\Delta = \det\begin{bmatrix} a & b \\ c & d \end{bmatrix}$. It is well known that the equilibrium will be locally stable if the roots are negative (or have negative real parts). The restrictions on h, $f(\cdot)$, and $g(\cdot)$, together with the requirement that w^* and L^* be positive and r^* non-negative, guarantee that this condition is satisfied here. At issue in the Hicks–Hollander "exception" is whether the approach to equilibrium is smooth or oscillatory, a question that can be answered by determining whether the roots are real or imaginary. If real, the approach is smooth; if imaginary, it is oscillatory.[7] Here, we need consider only two cases.

Case I: Roots Real, Distinct, and Negative

A necessary and sufficient condition for real and distinct roots is $d^2 + 4bc > 0$, or

$$(6) \qquad [(1 - h)(1 + r^*) + w^* g'(0)]^2 + 4L^* g'(0)(1 - h)f''(L^*) > 0.$$

Consider $[(1 - h)(1 + r^*) - w^* g'(0)]^2 > 0$. A sufficient condition for real, distinct roots will be

$$[(1 - h)(1 + r^*) + w^* g'(0)]^2 + 4L^* g'(0)(1 - h)f''(L^*)$$
$$\geq [(1 - h)(1 + r^*) - w^* g'(0)]^2,$$

which simplifies to

$$(7) \qquad [L^*/f'(L^*)]f''(L^*) \geq -1.$$

Case II: Roots Complex Conjugate with Negative Real Parts

A necessary and sufficient condition for complex conjugate roots is $d^2 + 4bc < 0$. The condition is analogous to Case I, but

$$[(1 - h)(1 + r^*) + w^* g'(0)]^2 + 4L^* g'(0)(1 - h)f''(L^*)$$
$$< [(1 - h)(1 + r^*) - w^* g'(0)]^2$$

is not even sufficient. Hence, we cannot give a condition analogous to (7).

While the necessary and sufficient condition (6) can be simplified, it has no apparent economic significance. The sufficient condition (7), on the other hand, is a condition on the elasticity of the marginal product curve; it is, in fact, the Hicks–Hollander condition for non-oscillation.[8] But it is only sufficient; hence, as we have seen, its converse does not necessarily result in oscillation.

It is, then, correct to say that if the elasticity of the marginal product curve equals or exceeds 1, the approach to equilibrium will be smooth; but it is not the case that for the approach to be smooth the elasticity must be greater than 1.

References

Andronov, A.A., A.A. Vitt, and S.E. Khaikin, *Theory of Oscillators*, F. Immirzi, trans. (Oxford: Pergamon Press, 1966).

Hicks, John, and Samuel Hollander, "Mr. Ricardo and the Moderns," *Quarterly Journal of Economics* XCI (Aug. 1977), 351–69.

Hicks, John, "The Ricardian System: A Comment," *Oxford Economic Papers*, N.S. XXXI (March 1979), 133–34.

Pasinetti, Luigi, 'A Mathematical Formulation of the Ricardian System," *Review of Economic Studies*, XXVII (Feb. 1960), 78–98.

——, *Lectures on the Theory of Production* (New York: Columbia University Press, 1977).

Ricardo, David, *On the Principles of Political Economy and Taxation, The Works and Correspondence of David Ricardo*, Piero Sraffa, ed., Volume I (Cambridge: Cambridge University Press, 1951).

Samuelson, Paul A. *Foundations of Economic Analysis* (New York: Atheneum, 1965).

Notes

*The author thanks, without implicating, Bill Bishopp and Peter Dooley for comments that greatly improved this paper, and Alfredo Medio for help with earlier work from which this developed.

1. Hicks and Hollander also investigated the consequences of introducing fixed capital. This paper does not address that part of their argument.

2. Ricardo [1951], p. 94: "When ... by the encouragement which high wages give to the increase of the population, the number of labourers is increased, wages again fall to their natural price, *and indeed from a re-action sometimes fall below it*" [emphasis added]. I thank Peter Dooley for bringing to my attention the relevant part of this passage.

3. A referee for the *Quarterly Journal of Economics* questioned whether the literary and diagrammatic treatment used in the Hicks–Hollander paper could be adequately represented mathematically. That a mathematical structure underlay the Hicks–Hollander paper has been confirmed by Hicks [1979, p. 133].

4. P^* is a parameter which Pasinetti assumes to be equal to zero. Following Hicks and Hollander, it is here assumed to be non-negative.

5. An unstable and trivial equilibrium occurs at $L = 0$.

6. If $F_1(\cdot)$ and $F_2(\cdot)$ are, in fact, linear, then the results on the linear version will describe the global behavior of the system as well. Beyond suggesting that the maximum annual rate of population growth (the maximum value of $g(\cdot)$ in our terms) is about 0.028 [Ricardo, 1951, p. 98], Ricardo himself gave us no guidance on the forms to assign to these functions.

7. If the time path of the wage is oscillatory, the possibility arises that the system exhibits Samuelson's "stability of the second kind," oscillating around the equilibrium but never converging on it [Samuelson, 1965, p. 262]. There exists, however, a theorem due to Bendixson, commonly known as the "negative criterion of Bendixson," that applies here and rules out such behavior (see, for example, Andronov *et al.* [1966], p. 305).

8. The Hicks–Hollander condition, quoted earlier, is that "the elasticity of the marginal product curve must be greater than 1," where elasticity, they say, is "measured in the Marshallian manner, with ... the marginal product ... being treated as if it were the independent variable" [1977], p. 356]. Applying this definition, and including the conventional negative sign, we get $e = -f'(L)/Lf''(L) > 1$, which becomes condition (7).

76

Lowe, Dobb and Hicks[†]

J. Halevi

Introduction

John Hicks coined the term "traverse" in his book *Capital and Growth* to describe the process of transition from one equilibrium growth path to another. A structural approach to this transition raises the question of whether the several sectors of the whole economy behave in a synchronic or a-synchronic manner.

This question was raised and discussed more than a decade before the publication of Hicks' work in two remarkable articles written by Adolph Lowe. These articles were themselves the continuation of theoretical and empirical research conducted by the author at the University of Kiel in Germany in the 1920s. More recently, the ideas contained in those writings were brought together in a fully fledged theory of discontinuous growth in a book which Lowe titled *"The Path of Economic Growth."*

The basic structure of Lowe's approach is to represent the economy in terms of reproduction conditions, which is a marked departure from the theory of factor proportions. In his early writings and in the first part of the book, Lowe sets out a stationary model and asks what must happen for such an economy to absorb a sudden increase in the labour force. This question represents the simplest formulation of the traverse problem, which will be discussed in the next section.

Lowe's 1955 monograph was of crucial importance for Dobb's theory of planned growth for underdeveloped countries, today known as the Dobb–Sen model (Dobb, 1960, Sen, 1960). Yet, the way in which Dobb used Lowe's model raises the issue of the links between choice of techniques and structural proportions. This matter is discussed in the third section of this paper where it will be argued that intersectoral relations condition the very choice of techniques. Because of the similarities between the Dobb and Hicks models with respect to reproduction conditions, the latter will also be analysed in that section.

*

[†]Source: *Eastern Economic Journal*, Vol. 10 (2), April–June 1984, pp. 157–67.

Change of Coefficients and Structural Proportions

Lowe's 1955 paper presented a model based on strict circularity and flexible specificity of production. The strict circularity condition is necessary in order to account for the intersectoral input–output relations of the system, which determine the way in which the economy reproduces itself. In this context Lowe identifies the machine tool sector as that branch of the economy which can reproduce itself as well as produce machines for different uses. Hence in addition to themselves machine tools produce capital goods which can only be installed in the consumption goods sector. Flexible specificity arises from the dual utilisation of machine tools and from the single use of the machine designed for the consumption sector. To anticipate a point which will be made in the next section, the above mentioned type of specificity is required in order to keep the picture of economic activity as a circular process; i.e. if every capital good were specific the only sequence possible would be linear, with no structural feedback.

The basic model starts from the assumption that the system is in a stationary state and it can be formalized as follows. Let K_m, K_I, K_z be the capital equipment in the machine tool, investment and consumption good sectors, respectively. The stocks K_m and K_1 are physically homogeneous and K_z, which is the result of the output generated by K_1, is heterogeneous, vis-à-vis the rest of the capital stock since it can produce only items of consumption. Each sector is vertically integrated, i.e., it produces its own raw materials. Moreover, the output of each sector consists of only one type of commodity, so that, for instance, the consumption good can be represented as corn, and the investment good as tractors, while machine tools constitute the equipment necessary to produce tractors as well as the means of production which are needed to reproduce those machine tools themselves.

Let α β γ be the output coefficients of the capital stock in each sector, u the uniform rate of depreciation, M, I, Z the respective outputs and a, b, c the labour coefficients for each unit of output in the respective sectors. Under stationary conditions we have:

(1) $\quad M = \alpha K_m = u(K_m + K_I)$

(2) $\quad I = \beta K_T = uK_z$

(3) $\quad Z = \gamma K_z = z(\alpha M + bI + cZ) = (\gamma/u)\, I$

The per capita rate of consumption is z defined in Sraffian terms, i.e., as being above subsistence.

The same structural relations would hold in the case of a uniformly growing economy, provided we add the increments in K_m, K_I and K_z to eqs. (1) and (2). Given the coefficients of production, if the economy experiences growth the rate of per capita consumption z will be lower than in eq. (3). Hence the state of the economy described by eqs (1), (2) and (3) corresponds exactly to what the late Joan Robinson termed a state of bliss; in this situation there is no longer any objective need for capital accumulation. (A similar line of thought is inherent in Keynes's recommendation that capital goods be made so abundant that the marginal efficiency of capital is reduced to zero, which leads to the disappearance of a rate of return on accumulated wealth.)

From eqs. (1) and (2) it is inferred that:

(4) $\dfrac{M}{I} = q = \dfrac{u\alpha}{\beta(d-u)}$ implying: $\dfrac{dq}{d\alpha} < 0; \dfrac{dq}{d\beta} < 0$

(5) $Z\dfrac{(1-cz)}{(z)} = aM + bI$

Equation (5) formed the basis for Dobb's analysis of the choice of techniques in a planned developing economy. It states that employment in the investment industries is determined by the surplus in the consumption sector, divided by the per capita rate of consumption z. A lower z, however, does not increase aM+bI *ipso facto*, but rather creates the conditions for such an expansion because a smaller proportion of machine tools has to be allocated for the production of equipment-producing means of consumption.

The expression for the rate of per capita consumption now taken as the dependent variable, reads:

(6) $z = \dfrac{x}{aq+b+cx}$; where: $\gamma/u = x$

In Lowe's tightly integrated structural framework z is always a dependent variable, whereas it is a parameter for Dobb. Hence, while Dobb used Lowe's model as the starting point of his analysis, the change in the assumption about z led Dobb to modify implicitly Lowe's basic approach.

From equation (6) it follows that z is positively related to changes in the production coefficients and negatively related to changes in labour coefficients. Yet if, for instance, there is a fall in labour coefficients, only the increase in z will prevent the problem of effective demand for consumption and then capital goods from making its appearance, but it will not prevent the emergence of unemployment. Equipment is fully utilised in a technical sense and the increase in the rate of per capita consumption assures that no shortage of demand for consumers' goods exists, which in turn guarantees no deficit in the demand for capital goods. Nevertheless, there is unemployment. The problem of the traverse begins here with the question of how to absorb the unemployed.

Clearly, the preceding question is of a social rather than strictly economic nature. The system, as such, is in equilibrium in the goods market and therefore there are no economic forces at work to alter the investment process. It should be stressed that an economy of this kind is not capitalistic since all the productivity increment (fall in labour coefficients) goes into higher wages. The model of the economy is closer to that of a cooperative-Kibbutz in which collective labour works side by side with hired wage labour, but it is the former that enjoys most of the fruits of technological advances.

The assumption of a Kibbutz type of cooperative economy provides a useful basis for the study of the traverse under stationary conditions. It is possible to postulate that, as equipment wears out, its replacement will display lower coefficients but unchanged output coefficients. The process is carried out until all equipment is recast, after which every unit of replacement equipment has the same labour coefficient as the corresponding machinery going out of use. If, for simplicity, we assume labour co-efficients to change only in the two investment goods sectors, the size of the labour force in the consumption goods industry is unaffected. From equation (3) we see that the amount of labour discharged when recasting ends is:

(7) $U = I b - b^* + q(a - a^*)$; where U is unemployment,
        where a^* and b^* are the new coefficients

Once recasting is completed and the system settles at the new co-efficients a^* and b^*, unemployment is equivalent to an exogenous one-time increase in the supply of labour to an otherwise fully employed system.

The main obstacle to the absorption of unemployment lies in the division of the labour force between cooperative members and hired workers since it is from within the latter group that unemployment arises. From a structural point of view the terminal equilibrium conditions for the traverse process are, however, already known. The proportions between the sectors, after absorption is completed, remain exactly the same in all the three equilibrium positions. This is not difficult to verify; given the output coefficients, the ratios M/I and I/Z must be the same in all three cases (see equations (1) and (2)). The traverse process consists therefore in raising the capital stock K_m producing machine tools to the new equilibrium determined by the percentage increase in the employable labour force; i.e. by U/E. Having reached its new required level K^*_m, the machine tool sector will devote all its net output to building up the capital stock in the intermediate sector. As the latter sector's equipment attains K^*_I, it will set in motion the process by which machinery in the consumption goods sector will be lifted to K^*_z. Once all the three sectors have come to the terminal position of full employment and zero rate of accumulation, the rate of per capita consumption z will equal the rate prevailing when recasting was completed. (See equations (6) and (7).)

The obstacles arise from the fact that, in so far as the community is divided into cooperative members, who therefore own the means of production and make decisions about them, and wage labour, it may not be convenient for owners to undergo the hardship of expanding the stock of capital in order to absorb redundant workers. To raise K_m to K^*_m it is necessary to withhold a part of all of replacement equipment going to K_I. The new level of the capital stock in the machine tool sector will be:

$$(8) \qquad K^*_m = M\{1 + \frac{1}{\alpha}[1-u+\delta(a-u)]\}; \qquad \text{where } \delta \text{ is the coefficient of nonreplacement of capital stock } K_I.$$

As a consequence, the stock of equipment K_I shrinks by δu, causing a transfer of labour from the intermediate to the machine tool sector.[3] Likewise, the stock of capital installed in the consumption goods sector will decline in the wake of the shrinkage of its source of equipment. It follows that the supply of consumption goods will also decline while the economy is set on a path of expansion for both capital and employment.

If we assume that the construction period of every unit of equipment is one time unit, then the increase in employment will take place ahead of the recovery in the output of consumption goods, which causes a fall in z relative to its level at the end of the recasting phase. Indeed, during the whole transition period z will remain below that level. Moreover, any significant fall over time of the labour coefficients increases the pressure on the machine tool sector if surplus labour is to be re-employed.

Two cases can be identified out. The first relates to the possibility of raising K_m to K^*_m in just one period by withholding replacement of K_I altogether. This means that the coefficient in equation (8) is equal to one. The second case arises when K^*_m cannot be attained in the single period even when $\delta = 1$. Strictly speaking, the possibility remains of mobilizing part of the equipment which comprises the stock K_I (which is homogeneous with K_m), to bring K_m to its new required level. Yet this option implies a decline in replacement equipment flowing to the consumption sector, which will cause a drastic and sudden contraction of consumption goods output.

In all the cases considered above those who control the means of production face the option of either going through a period of reduced consumption in order to expand the stock of machinery necessary to absorb the unemployed, or foregoing a part of their current consumption by diverting it in exchange for "unskilled" services to the unemployed.[1]

In the above framework redundant labour cannot be reabsorbed via a fall in wages. Equipment and labour remain in a strict relation of complementarity even when labour coefficients change. This change is brought about by the installation of new machinery as the old is worn out, so that the economy gradually moves from one degree of complementarity to another but cannot move back and forth without continually restructuring its equipment. If wages were to remain unchanged by the end of the recasting period, the unemployment caused by the fall in labour coefficients would become worsened as a result of the lack of effective demand for consumption goods. This proposition would be true *a fortiori* if unemployment had led to a fall in wages.

*

Dobb and Hicks

Maurice Dobb made use of Lowe's stationary model not to analyse the process of traverse but to discuss the question of the choice of techniques under planned development. His main objective was to argue against the theory of factor proportions. This was done by simply postulating that the wage rate will not fall to zero even with an unlimited supply of labour; more specifically, the minimum subsistence wage in industry cannot be the same as in the agricultural sector.[2] Moreover, if the supply of consumption goods is inelastic because of the limited production capacity of the industrial sector, the rate of per capita consumption of the industrial workers, (i.e. what we called z) will in fact become a parameter. From equation (5) we see that if Z and z are given the only way to expand M and I is to choose a technique of production which lowers the labour coefficients a and b.

The three sector division is used by Dobb to discuss the case in which all investment effort is put into the self expansion of the machine tools sector, which is a process that implies a gradual absorption of K_I by K_m (they are homogeneous so that K_I can be shifted to the machine tool sector). Given the limited supply of consumption goods the expansion of investment cannot take place except in the above mentioned way. For z to remain constant under conditions of a given flow of consumption goods Z, the shift in employment must occur only within the investment sector; that is, it would occur through the absorption of workers and equipment in the I sector by the M sector, since any withdrawal of labour from the consumption goods sector will reduce the flow of output. The subdivision of the investment sector into two branches therefore becomes necessary in order to account for the distribution of the labour force changes.

Dobb's analysis rests on the assumption that capital goods last forever; the circularity of production is thus broken since the relation between the output of capital goods and replacement requirements disappears. If circularity is maintained, the rate of per capita consumption z again becomes dependent variable. Any shift in the composition of capital stock away from K_I and toward K_m will reduce the rate at which I flows into Z, negatively affecting the rate of per capita consumption. If Dobb's hypothesis about K_I being progressively drawn into K_m were to be applied under conditions of circularity, the outcome would be to halt replacement investment in the consumption sector, with a consequent shrinkage in K_z and an inevitable fall in Z.

We have thus arrived at exactly the same conclusion as the previous section, in which a change in the labour coefficients generated surplus labour, requiring intersectoral shifts with temporarily lower real wages in order to reabsorb redundant labour. The difference consists in the degree of development of the economy under consideration. In the previous case the starting point was already "a state of bliss," whereas now the constraint on productive capacity is a major obstacle to the attainment. Within a framework of circular production, the problem which predominates is the maximum length of time during which a fall in the supply of consumption goods is compatible with the diversion of investment toward the machine tool sector. It follows that the dynamics of structural proportions determines the type of technique in use since these occur only through changes in the composition of investment.

We have seen that Dobb used the basic elements of Lowe's scheme to build a model in which accumulation is based on a technique of production which does not increase employment in a degree which affects the rate of per capita consumption of the employed population. This treatment capital goods as having limits an infinite lifetime and flexible form the structural analysis to considering only the composition of the labour force, which greatly reduces the importance of intersectoral proportions with respect to the choice of techniques. However, Dobb's effort does correspond to an objective economic problem, that of guiding accumulation in countries which cannot "afford" it because of their limited productive capacity.[3]

In chapter 16 of *Capital and Growth*, John Hicks presents a model which, like Dobb's, assumes equipment of infinite life but, unlike Dobb's, makes the growth rate depend exclusively on the growth rate of population. The economy achieves a quasi state of bliss. Accumulation has to provide the whole labour force with the means of production necessary to maintain full employment. The problem of the traverse thus arises whenever there is a change in the growth rate of the labour force, since the output of machinery must be just enough to absorb the additional workers.

If, to use an expression employed by Hicks, the "Principle of Variation" is assumed to be the central tenet in economics, the question of the traverse would not even arise, nor would the problem of intersectoral proportions. As Hicks wrote in 1932: "The marginal productivity theory assumes that a change in the relative prices of the factors will always be followed by some change in the quantities of the factors employed, that is to say, it assumes that technical methods are freely available. For if that is not the case, it will be impossible to reorganize a business effectively with one unit less of one factor but with the same quantity of the others" (Hicks, 1932, p. 80). Fixed coefficients of production highlight the fact that the economy is stuck with a given set of equipment geared to definite uses, so that changes can take place only through gross investment. Thus, when Hicks cast his argument in terms of a two sector fixed coefficients model, (explicitly acknowledging that when it comes to the utilization of equipment fixity prevails over flexibility) it marks an important change in assumptions used to analyze the economic activity.

In relation to Lowe's system, Hicks's procedure can be assessed, as far as reproduction is concerned, on lines similar to those followed in the discussion of Dobb's approach. The assumption that equipment is of infinite durability is even less legitimate than in Dobb's case. In the latter there is a specifically defined historical circumstance in countries in which growth cannot be facilitated by lowering the already meager consumption standards. This explains Dobb's penchant for a model in which higher accumulation is compatible with a technique of production which is not based on still lower rates of consumption. In contrast, Hicks excludes any

historical specificity from his model. The mission of reproduction is therefore particularly serious.

Marx defined reproduction in the following terms: "The conditions of
production are also those of reproduction. No society can go on producing,
in other words, no society can reproduce, unless it constantly reconverts a
part of its products into means of production, or elements of fresh
products. (...) Hence a definition portion of each year's product belongs to
the domain of production. Destined for productive consumption from the
very first, this portion exists, for the most part, in the shape of articles
totally unfitted for individual consumption." (Marx, 1977, vol. 1, p. 531).

The implications of the absence of circular reproduction emerge in a
strikingly clear manner when Hicks's assumption of equipment of infinite
durability is applied to Lowe's model under conditions of zero growth. The
capital stock in the two investment sectors would be zero in this case, the
only equipment in operation being that installed in the consumption goods
sector. Such equipment is absolutely specific in the model, which means
that the system is totally incapable of responding to an exogenous increase
in the supply of labour. No machinery could be used for the expansion of
capital stock, since there would not be any equipment technically fitted to
perform a process of reproduction. By the same token the economy would
not possess any means to account for technical change (in the previous
section technical change was caused by replacement equipment embodying
lower labour coefficients).

Strictly speaking this problem does not arise in Hicks's framework
because his model is based on one homogeneous capital good which can be
allocated to either the capital or the consumption goods sector. Hence with
infinite durability of equipment it is always possible to switch part of the
latter back to the production of capital goods. However, in this way
structural constraints are virtually eliminated. The only serious obstacle to
an adjustment process comes from so large an increase in the influx of
labour that a backward switch to the production of capital goods would
require a fall in the rate of per capita consumption below subsistence.

The above considerations help put Hicks's model and the shortcomings
of his treatment of the traverse into perspective. For Hicks, transition to a
higher or lower rate of growth and equilibrium is dependent on the workforce–machine ratios of the two sectors. Given a change in the rate of population increase, full utilization and full employment are maintained and the
growth rate of capital stock converges towards the new growth rate (determined by the increase or decrease in the rate of growth of population).
Hence, at the beginning of each period the proportion of total equipment
allocated to each sector must be such that the total capital stock employs
the total labour force, even if the latter has increased, more slowly or more
quickly than capital equipment relative to the previous period. We can,
therefore, write:

(9) $\quad [N_k V_t + N_z(1-v_t)](1+r) = [N_k v_{t-1} + N_z(1-v_{t-1})](1+g); r \neq g$

Where N_k and N_z are the number of workers per machine in the capital and consumption goods sectors respectively; v is the share of capital stock in the capital goods sector over total capital stock; r and g are the growth rate of capital equipment and of population.

Equation (9) states the condition necessary to maintain full employment where the unknown is v_t, i.e. the new distribution of equipment between the two sectors. It is clear that a solution for (9) requires that $N_k \neq N_z$ since:

$$(10) \quad v_t = v_{t-1} + \frac{N_z (1 + q)}{N_k - N_z(1 + r)} - \frac{N_z}{N_k - N_z}$$

From equation (10) it follows that successive changes in r will cause it to converge to g as long as $N_k - N_z > 0$, i.e. as long as the machinery in the capital goods sector employs more workers than that of the consumption goods sector. This result is known as the "capital intensity theorem" on which the smoothness of Hicks's adjustment mechanism depends.

This result is essentially non-economic because it makes the entire investment process a passive by-product of the technological specifications of the model. Moreover, the most plausible case, specifically, that an already fully employed economy with no spare capacity cannot absorb an increment to the labour force in excess of that compatible with the growth rate of equipment, can only be dealt with within the very special case of uniform worker–machine ratios. In fact, from equation (9) it follows that if $N_k = N_z$, the equation can be satisfied only for $r = g$, which means that the model economy cannot cope smoothly with a divergence between the rate of growth of capital stock and labour. This situation should be considered as an important, if not general case, though, it is paradoxically brought to light only when the labour–machine ratios are uniform in Hicks's framework.

The following observations can therefore be made: By eliminating reproduction (a) Hicks's model obliterates the constraints arising from the technical composition of capital. (b) At the same time it gets bogged down in a series of special cases arising from the relative labour–machine ratios in the two sectors. The latter is the most interesting case because it implies that the economy cannot adjust immediately although it does not preclude adjustment in the future.

The formidable assumption of one physically homogenous machine able to produce everything, with different labour coefficients according to the sector in which it is put to work, lies at the heart of the ambiguities of Hicks's construction. Is it possible to build a model in which the mechanism of adjustment does not depend on whether the worker–machine ratio is greater, smaller or equal to that of the other sector? If the answer is affirmative, then the dynamics of investment is free from technological determinism, while the amount of investment is conditioned by the structural composition of equipment prevailing at any one time. Lowe's model supplies the answer to this problem although he did not specifically tackle the Hicksian formulation of the traverse.

In Lowe's model it is absolutely legitimate to assume that M, the output of machine tools, has only one type of labour–machine coefficient. In point of fact, M is physically homogeneous and is either used to reproduce itself and/or produce I, the equipment going to form the capital stock in the consumption goods sector. Hence it is legitimate to conclude that each of the identical machines will employ a given crew; likewise each unit of I, physically different from M, will employ a given crew, numerically different from the crew operating M. Since the integral of past M, net of wear and tear, represents the stocks $(K_m + K_I)$ and since the integral of past net I is the stock K_z, it follows that the argument holds true also for $(K_m + K_I = K_k)$ and for K_z.

This means that in Lowe's framework an equation like (9) in the Hicksian case, is necessarily an inequality (except when $r = g$) independently of whether the crew operating K_k is equal or unequal to the crew operating K_z.[4] A difference in the labour–machine ratios is not relevant to the system's structural response to an exogenous variation in the growth rate of the labour force in a two sector model. As a consequence, if growth of the labour force declines, unused capacity is bound to appear; in this case the employment capacity of equipment is greater than the total available labour force. Conversely, an increase in the growth rate will make unemployment unavoidable since the employment capacity of machines falls short of the available workforce. The same argument can be applied to technical progress because, as we have seen in the section discussing the basic stationary model, technical progress of a labour saving type can be reduced to an exogenous increase in the labour force.

The transition to a new equilibrium depends exclusively on the institutional characteristics of the system. In the case of a fall in the growth rate of the labour force, excess capacity can lead to a further fall in investment and employment if the economy is a capitalist demand determined economy. In a socialist system, by contrast, the central policy issue would be how to distribute the amount of unused capacity with the objective of avoiding a situation of capital dearth in a subsequent period, a situation which can arise from the concentration of unused capacity exclusively in the machine tools sector (Halevi, 1981).

Concluding Remarks

The strong point of Professor Lowe's model lies in the elimination of technological determinism in the process of transition from one phase to the next. This is achieved with remarkable simplicity by assuming two capital goods sectors with a homogeneous stock and a consumption goods sector with a totally specific stock of machines. The specificity of capital in the latter sector gives rise to a structural lag which can be extended to take into account different production periods between that required for machine tools and that required for building the machine going to the consumption goods sector. Clearly such a distinction is impossible in a two sector model in which equipment flows from a single department of production.

A legitimate question can now be raised as to whether the model presented in Hicks's "Capital and Time", in which each process has an absolutely specific capital good, supersedes Adolph Lowe's work. In "Capital and Growth", successful completion of the traverse process depends on the very special case of the worker–machine ratio in the capital goods sector being greater than that prevailing in the consumption goods sector, i.e. it rests on fulfilment of the so-called capital intensity theorem. In "Capital and Time", the traverse problem is analyzed on the basis of the special case of the "simple profile". The simple profile consists of splitting up the process of production into two periods: one in which labour is used to build up equipment and one in which labour is used with that equipment to produce a finished good. Economic activity is therefore seen as a one way avenue moving from inputs (labour) to final demand. Capital equipment becomes associated with working capital; it is, so to speak, a stage in the production of the finished consumption good.

Hicks's elimination of circularity overlooks the need for a special machine producing sector. An implicit critique of this omission is provided by Lowe. "One need only to consider an increase in the aggregate demand for coal, that is growth, in a system in which all real capital is fully utilized. Then we see at once that the critical bottleneck 'in the hierarchy of production' arises in the machine tool stage and that only after capacity has been increased there, can the output of ore-steel-extractive machinery and finally coal be increased" (Lowe, 1976, p. 34n).

Notes

1. The ample documentation about this fact ranges from Myrdal's famous *Asian Drama* to the ILO report on poverty and landlessness (Myrdal, 1968, and ILO, 1977). A cogent critique of the factors proportions approach was developed by Kaldor (1975).

2. Michael Kalecki argued against Dobb on the grounds that the model becomes irrelevant if labour productivity rises at a given rate as a result of technical progress. But the Dobb–Sen model is aimed precisely at those cases where the limited productive capacity also limits the rate of technical progress. Another criticism by Kalecki is however closer to the type of argument we developed along Lowe's lines. Kalecki points out that to raise the growth rate through an increase in the capital–output ratio the share of accumulation over total output must rise more than the capital–output ratio. From the angle of Lowe's model this raises the question of whether the composition of investment can be changed to meet the above condition. See Kalecki (1972, ch. 10).

3. If $(a\alpha)^* < (b\beta)^*$ then the shrinkage in K_l will lead partly to a transfer of labour to operate K_m and partly to an additional increase in unemployment. Since however K_m and K_l are formed by the same type of machines it is necessary to assume that $a\alpha = b\beta$, $(a\alpha)^* = (b\beta)^*$.

4. Equation (9) in the Hicksian case can be rewritten for Lowe's model in the following way: Since $K_k = K_m + K_l$ we write $K_m/K_k = V^*$ and $N_m = N_l = N_k$ (workers per unit of capital stock in the two investment sectors and N_z, workers per unit of capital equipment K_z in the consumption goods sector). Hence:

(a) (a) $$\{K_k[N_kV_t + N_k(1-v_t)] + N_zK_z\}(1+r) = (1+g)\{(K_k[N_kV_{t-1} + N_k(1-V_{t-1})]$$
$$+ N_zK_z\}$$

The left hand side of equ (a) represents the way in which the labour force has to be distributed after capital stock has grown by r. The coefficient v_t is the unknown and it is entirely a matter within the capital goods sectors. The right hand side of equ (a) represents the growth of the labour measured in terms of employment capacity of capital stock reckoned at the beginning of the period. Full employment equilibrium means that the equality between the two sides is maintained. In both sides K_m and K_z in the quantities at the beginning of the period at the end of which capital would have grown by r and labour by g. Now it is easy to see that it is not possible to satisfy eq. (a) except when r = g. Equation (a) reduces to:

(b) (b) $(N_k K_k + N_z K_z) (1+r) = (1+g) (N_k N_k + N_z K_z)$

Which is satisfied only when r = g independently of whether $N_k \gtrless N_z$.
* all V's should be read as small v's.

5. Elsewhere I tried to argue that in a socialist setting central planning is a necessary but not sufficient condition for adjustment (Halevi, 1981).

References

Dobb, M. (1960) *An Essay on Economic Growth and Planning*, Routledge and Kegan Paul, London.

Halevi, J. (1981) "The Composition of Investment under Conditions of Non Uniform Changes", in *Banca Nazionale del Lavoro Quarterly Review*, June.

Hicks, J.R. (1932) "Marginal Productivity and the Principle of Variation", in *Economica*, February.

Hicks, J.R. (1975) *Capital and Growth*, Oxford University Press, Oxford.

Hicks, J.R. (1972) *Capital and Time*, Clarendon, Oxford.

ILO (1977) *Poverty and Landlessness in Rural Asia*, Geneva.

Kaldor, N. (1975) "What is Wrong with Economic Theory?" in *Quarterly Journal of Economics*, August.

Kalecki, M. (1972) *Selected Essays on the Economic Growth of the Socialist and the Mixed Economy*, Cambridge, U.P., Cambridge U.K.

Lowe, A. (1952) "A Structural Model of Production", in *Social Research*, Vol. 19.

Lowe, A. (1955) "Structural Analysis of Real Capital Formation" in *Capital Formation and Economic Growth*, ed. by M. Abramovitz, Princeton University Press, Princeton.

Lowe, A. (1976) *The Path of Economic Growth*, Cambridge U.P., Cambridge U.K.

Marx, K. (1974) *Capital*, Vol. I. Progress Publishers, Moscow.

Myrdal, G. (1968) *Asian Drama*, Pantheon, New York.

Sen, A.K. (1960) *Choice of Techniques*, Basil Blackwell, Oxford.

Towards a Dynamic Analysis of the "Traverse"

M. Amendola

The "Traverse" and Analysis of the Innovation Process

Adolph Lowe's extensive study of the "traverse", has remained rather isolated from the mainstream of economic literature (1976). Much of the same fate has befallen John Hicks's highly controversial "Neo-Austrian theory" which purports to be a helpful new way of dealing with fixed capital in the analysis of the transition from one steady-growth path to another (1970, 1973).

The analysis of the "traverse", even in the sketchy and limited way pursued up to now, is one of the most genuine pieces of dynamic analysis produced so far; in particular, it has provided the most adequate theoretical framework for treating the process of innovation, which is the process through which technical progress reveals its truly dynamic nature. Modern growth theory, and the comparative dynamic analysis derived from it, has not proved capable of dealing properly with the phenomenon of changing technology (conceived of as the shift of a given production function) as a basis for comparing alternative equilibrium positions. That is why Hicks and Lowe, each in his own way and quite independently from the other, have followed alternative routes in their respective analysis of the "traverse", with the objective of shedding light on the way in which technical progress actually works its way through the economy.[1]

Similarity of interests and perspective, and dissimilarity of basic assumptions and proposed models, are an instructive framework in which problems and solutions can be compared and contrasted. A comparison between the two contributions, certainly the most important in the field, will single out the relevant issues (i.e. what is really meant by technical progress; how should fixed capital be dealt with in a dynamic context; how should the process of production be represented) while also focusing [on] methodological and analytical problems. From this perspective, the two models appear as logically successive steps along the path to a better understanding of the process of change of the economy.

Moving from an orthodox sectoral framework, Lowe fixes attention on time sequence rather than on the horizontal structure of production. Not

†Source: *Eastern Economic Journal*, Vol. 10, April–June 1984, pp. 203–10.

yet freed from the traditional approach, his representation of technical progress and the underlying process of production does not permit analysis of the transition process which takes place in time.

Hicks achieves a complete break with the traditional theoretical apparatus, thus going the whole way in the direction anticipated by Lowe. Sequential analysis of a process of change requires a process of production conceived as a sequence in real time: this is exactly what Neo-Austrian theory does. In this new approach, the relevant moments of a transition phase are not obscured by circular relations in production, so that the way is open for an analysis of the process of innovation.

The impossibility of carrying out a genuinely dynamic analysis within the analytical framework represented by the traditional theory of production, and the need for a radical change of perspective which extends to the very definition of the process of production, emerges from the comparison between Lowe and Hicks which is developed in the following pages.

The "Traverse" in Sectoral Models

A necessarily brief overview of the way technical progress and the process of innovation have been treated within the context of the analysis of the "traverse" will help us to get to the point. The "traverse" is the problem of the change from a particular configuration of the productive capacity of the economy to another. In some models, it is a change in the growth rate which requires a readjustment of existing capacity; in others it is technical progress which brings out, and at the same time is prompted by, a transformation of productive capacity to reflect a newly dominant technology. Productive capacity is the expression of a given technology which is identified with a given stock of fixed and/or circulating-capital goods which is combined with labour in certain proportions (technical coefficients).

Readjustment or transformation[2] of existing capacity is most easily carried out in models in which goods can be used either as consumption or as capital goods, so that a fall in consumption automatically means and increase in whatever capital goods are required to assure the transition.[3]

Hicks introduces heterogeneity between consumption goods and capital goods in his two-sector (corn, tractors) model of "traverse" in "Capital and Growth" (1965, Chapter XVI). For example, tractors and labour produce tractors and, when used in different proportions, also corn, and can move freely from one sector to the other. However, owing to the hypothesis of heterogeneity, changes in consumption no longer mean immediate opposite changes in the number of tractors, and hence are no longer able to automatically assure the "traverse". Transition from one steady-growth rate to a higher (or a lower) one can be realized only through transfers of labour and tractors between the corn sector and the tractor sector, so as to modify their relative weight in accordance with the new growth rate.[4] Readjustment of productive capacity through horizontal transfers between sectors, on the other hand, is treated as a stability problem, and the focus is on the condition required (a higher capital intensity in the consumption-good sector, in the case considered) to assure the convergence to the new steady-growth path, maintaining full employment of both capital and labour.

Technical change within a similar two-sector model is introduced by Spaventa in the form of a simple reduction of the technical coefficients: both the consumption and the (circulating) capital good do not change their physical identity in the passage from one technique to the other (1973). Formulated in this way technical progress comes to the same thing as a change in the growth rate, and the "traverse" reduces to a readjustment of the relative size of the two sectors to be realized through horizontal transfers under the same convergence condition underlined by Hicks.

To sum up: heterogeneity between consumption and capital goods implies that if the quantity of a capital good is insufficient for the requirements of a new situation, that it cannot be increased by simply "squeezing" consumption; this gives rise to a process of transition which requires transfers between the different sectors. The assumption that the inputs remain physically unchanged allows treatment of the transition as a stability problem, even in the presence of technical progress. Thus the differentiation between goods points to the process which productive capacity must undergo in order to change its configuration, but the representation of technical progress as a mere reduction of inputs cancels the need for analysis of such a process and reduces everything to a problem of convergence conditions.

The Change in Perspective in Lowe's Model

Lowe takes a further step by differentiating not only between consumption and capital goods but also between capital goods themselves. This step permits him to shift the focus of analysis to the process through which the productive capacity of the economy is actually adjusted.[5] His investigation centers on the "formation, application and liquidation of real capital", that real capital which locks the economy into a particular technique, because "if we want to change the employment capacity of the existing stock of fixed capital, we have to change its physical form" (Lowe, 1976, p. 10). By shifting focus from the new equilibrium of productive capacity to what happens on the way to it requires a sequential analysis, not in the sense of "depicting successive but separate levels of capital formed and labour trained", but in the sense of "offering insight into the intervening processes during which new capital is being formed and labour is being trained" (p. 10). This is compatible involving the process of transformation of productive capacity in *real time*.

For this purpose Lowe assumes an economy divided into three aggregate sectors, a consumer-good sector, say II, and two capital-good sectors: Ib, which produces the capital goods used as inputs in sector II, and Ia, and which produces the capital goods used as inputs both in sector Ib and in sector Ia itself. There are therefore two different kinds of capital goods (machines): those required to reproduce themselves and to produce the machines that will be used in sector II, and the latter, required to produce the consumption goods. It follows that only machines of the first kind can be transferred between the two capital-good sectors Ia and Ib, but not between the capital and consumption-good sectors, as in the traditional two-sector models.

The implications of this analytical framework go beyond the simple addition of a further sector to the model. Differentiation between the capital goods, in fact, introduces a new dimension into the process of production, establishing a sequence (Ia Ib II) according to which fixed capital in sector Ia must be increased before any increase can be obtained in the production of consumption goods. Thus the transition, that is, the re-shaping of productive capacity, can no longer be accomplished by simply readjusting the relative weight of the different sectors through mere horizontal transfers between them. Thus the sectors lose their character of simple compartments in the economy and become instead different phases in a sequential process of production articulated, what emerges is a vertical transfer of resources between different phases, to be carried out in time. The stability approach is no longer able to encompass the full sequence of adjustment of the various sectors one at a time; the timing of the events matters, and intertemporal complementarity calls for a sequential analysis of the process. Thus the model brings to light the strict relationship between the sectoral representation of the economy and the hypothesis of transferability, and the loss of analytical relevance of such a representation as the capital goods become more and more specialized and hence not transferable.

While Lowe's model implies a sequence, it also retains circularity within the capital-good sectors, where the equipment considered is technically suited to reproduce itself as well as to produce the equipment required as inputs to the consumption good sector. The capacity of physical self-reproduction, according to Lowe is, in fact, the only way to stop the infinite technical regress with which we would otherwise get involved. Another sector is needed to produce the machines used as inputs in sector Ia, and then another one, and so on ... (pp. 29–30). Circularity, however, makes the differentiation between the capital goods vanish; so we are back to the orthodox sectoral representation in which the adjustment can be realized through horizontal transfers, namely between sectors Ib and Ia.

Both sequentially (unilateral dependence over time) and circularity (mutual interdependence) are thus present side by side in the model; and it is just this hybrid character, we shall see, that while disclosing the real dynamic problems involved in a process of transition between techniques, will not permit their proper treatment.

The Neo-Austrian Approach

In Hicks' Neo-Austrian model, capital goods become *internal* to each process of production and labour is envisioned as a stream of freely transferable inputs which become converted into a stream of final outputs (consumption goods). Production is fully integrated vertically: the capital good used in each process is produced within it, and the process must be taken as a whole over time. The sectors disappear and real, irreversible time emerges as the fundamental dimension of the process of production. Thus, the time articulation of the different phases (the "time profile") becomes the distinctive feature.

With the help of this analytical framework Hicks turns to the same problem considered by Lowe; the analysis of the path along which an economy adjusts itself to an external disturbance, specifically a change in the technique.[6] Given the strong intertemporal complementarity which characterizes the process of production, this sort of study clearly lends itself to sequential analysis. It is, in fact, with the help of sequential analysis that Hicks seeks to build a bridge between equilibrium economics and an economics which must be securely *in time*, like the analysis of the "traverse".

Hicks envisions the process of production as extending over a sequence of periods (weeks) integrating different successive phases lasting one or more years[7]: "The one week relations ... determine the course of the model in week T, when everything that has happened before week T is taken as given. Having determined the course in week T, we can then proceed to week T+1, applying similar relations, but with the performance of week T forming part of the past. And so on, and so on. The path of the economy, over any number of successive weeks, can thus be determined" (1973, p. 63). In particular, the output and the employment, at week T, depend entirely on the processes that have been started in the past, and on the techniques that are used in those processes.

The basic element of the sequence is the rate of new process starts, which is endogenized and made dependent on the rate of starts in the past. This is obtained assuming that all output which is not consumed is invested (i.e. under the "Full Performance" hypothesis activity is limited only by savings) and that consumption out of profits (i.e. the take-out which cannot be used to start new processes) is constant in absolute terms (Q-hypothesis) (1973, Chapter V). Since the rate of starts is made endogenous, the model is sequential and can be used to describe the "traverse" from one steady-growth path to another in the case of a technological innovation and under the alternative constraints of a fixed wage rate and of full employment (1973, Chapter VIII, (X). In brief: technical progress brings about an increase in profits, all surplus profits — given the Full Performance and the Q-hypothesis — are saved and invested, hence there is an increase in the rate of starts and, in a first moment, increased activity in the construction phase. Thus the path of output and employment is determined and the "traverse" is traced out.[6]

Circular Relations in Production and the Process of Acquisition of a New Technology

It has been seen that, in models with a horizontal sectoral structure of production, the "traverse" is accomplished through a reallocation of capital goods and labour between different sectors. Innovation uses the same inputs as the old technique although in different proportions. Technical progress, therefore, does not imply the appearance of new (different) capital goods or require a transformation of productive capacity but takes the form of a reduction of technical coefficients. Issues of capital formation and capital liquidation — to recall Lowe's words — are not in the foreground.

If technical progress consists of a simple reduction of technical coefficients, it can be analysed by comparing equilibria; each exhibits a productive structure already completely adjusted to the newly dominating technology. The process of transition, in the sense of "what happens on the way", fades away, and the "traverse" can be treated as a stability problem, identifying the conditions for convergence to a new equilibrium.

The traditional representation of technical progress, and the analysis of the "traverse" which is based on it, portrays a sequence of technological states which differ from one another with respect to the quantity of capital and labour and their combination, but, to use again Lowe's words, "is not able to offer an insight into the intervening processes during which new capital is being formed and labour is being trained". This has been clearly recognized by Spaventa, who treats technical progress as a simple reduction in inputs in his standard two-sector model, but cautions that "the real problems, however, still lie ahead. What happens if the two techniques employ fixed capital and if the machines appropriate to each of them are physically different? If this is the case, the stocks left over from technique 2 are not only quantitatively, but also qualitatively inappropriate to the technique 1. These, and not the ones we have so far considered, are the true problems of transition" (Spaventa, p. 183).

Thus everything comes down to what is meant by technical progress. If the relevant aspect of this phenomenon is the process in which the productive capacity of the economy is transformed so as to acquire a different specification, and 2) the transformation of productive capacity requires the liquidation of old equipment and the building of new and different capital goods, then the problem cannot properly be dealt with in models having a horizontal sectoral structure; i.e. "if the Method of Sectoral Disintegration is adopted ... the time taken to make the machine is liable to be forgotten" (Hicks, 1973, p. 5).

But *the time taken to make the machine* — machines being the concrete expression of productive capacity — is the relevant moment of the process of acquisition of innovation; it is exactly the analysis of this moment which is lost in Lowe's model, in consequence of the hypothesis of circularity between sectors Ia and Ib. Sequential analysis is thus excluded at the most needed point. Circularity, in fact, implies that Lowe's "liberation of existing capacity, is in the first phase of the "traverse" merely involves "a shift in the physical aggregate that the two equipment-good sectors produce, in the direction of less secondary and more primary equipment". Thus, "the capacity that is located in sector Ib is freed in part from its original task of replacing and expanding capacity in sector II. This liberated capacity is now to be used to expand sector Ia" (Lowe, pp. 110–111).

When a change in the technique is considered, however, the capacity liberated is to be used to produce not only *more* but *different* capital equipment, which not only expands sector Ia but changes the way it works. As in the case of a change in the growth rate — where the stock of capital is quantitatively inappropriate to the new situation, but no problem of change in its physical identity is involved — there is again a simple transfer of machines from one sector to the other which starts the transition in Lowe's model. There is reliance on the assumption, common to all standard sectoral models, that *old* machines can be used to produce the *new* ones. "Any improved equipment must be initially produced with the help of preexisting, that is unimproved, equipment goods ... Only when, in this manner, old ways have succeeded in making improved primary or secondary equipment, will the application of such novel equipment reduce average unit costs of output" (p. 238). Circularity can thus be retained in [the] presence of technical progress, and the reshaping of productive capacity realized through transfers of machines between sectors Ib and Ia.

Old ways of producing new equipment, however, clearly means that no change in the process of production takes place in the relevant moment of the embodiment of the new technology; that is, in the machine-making phase. This is why simple expansion of sector Ia can be identified as technical progress. Yet, the assumption that the old machines, and old ways, can be used to produce the new equipment conceives of the process through which productive capacity acquires a different specification in the easiest way: it cancels it.

Capital in a Dynamic Context

Although useful for the understanding of the working of the economy, circular relations in production are an obstacle in the analysis of the process of innovation. A model which hypothesizes a horizontal sectoral structure implies that capital goods exist in their own right and can take part in different processes of production. In Hicks' view, when innovation is considered, "it is undesirable that these goods should be physically specified, since there is no way of establishing a physical relation between the capital goods that are required in the one technique and those that are required in the other" (Hicks, 1970, p. 193). If we want to maintain this relation, if we want the capital goods to go on serving as a link between two different technological states assuming that old machines can produce the new ones, the process of acquiring the new technology to the simple and instantaneous shifting of existing equipment to a different task and/or to a different compartment of the economy.

In Hicks' view "The only relation that can be established (between the old and the new technique) runs in terms of costs and of capacity to produce final output; and this is precisely what is preserved in an Austrian theory" (ibid.). In other words, capital goods must be dealt with in a different way, and this, in turn, requires a different way of conceiving the process of production. In the Neo-Austrian full vertical integration model, fixed capital goods are implied, but they are regarded as intermediate products; they become the particular expression of each given kind of process, and cannot exist outside it. Only labour, uncommitted unspecified labour, will be present at the moment one technique gives way to another: this conception requires a completely new start of the process of production for each innovation, and analysis of the phase during which the process itself acquires its new profile, building its own specific equipment in its own original way.

While this is as far as Hicks goes, it is possible to envision farther reaching developments. In a thoroughly dynamic context "technique" cannot be reduced to a mere combination of physical inputs petrified in a given piece of equipment, but must be seen as a time articulated sequence of phases in which the *machine*, in the traditional sense, is only one aspect (and in some cases not even a significant aspect). This calls for a reconstruction from a much wider perspective. Further, the question of how to deal in this new framework, with the concept of capital and the respective roles of capital and labour in the process of innovation, opens a whole new field of analysis. All that is still virgin land which has become opened to exploration by the breakthrough which Adolph Lowe and John Hicks have made in the traditional body of theory.

References

Amendola, Mario, "Modelle neo-austriaco e transizione fra equilibri dinamice." Note *Economiche*, November, 1972.
Hicks, J.R., *Capital and Time*, Clarendon Press, Oxford, 1973. "A Neo-Austrian Growth Theory", *Economic Journal*, June, 1970.
Hicks, J.R. *Economic Perspectives*, Clarendon Press, Oxford.
Lowe, A. *The Path of Economic Growth*, Cambridge University Press, Cambridge, 1976.
Solow, R. "The Interest Rate and Transition Between Techniques", *Socialism, Capitalism and Economic Growth: Essays Presented to Maurice Dobb*, ed. C.H. Feinstein, Cambridge, 1967.
Spaventa, L. "Notes on Problems of Transition Between Techniques", *Models of Economic Growth*, eds. J. Mirrlees, N.H. Stern, Macmillan, London, 1973.

Notes

1. Lowe's book, "The Path of Economic Growth", in effect, takes up the problem of the "traverse" in general, and not only the case of a transition between techniques to which on the contrary Hicks devotes the whole of his analysis. It is just this case, however, which appears to be the most interesting for its implications in terms of dynamic analysis.

2. The two terms can be used indifferently in most of the models where, as we shall see, changes in the growth rate and technological innovations are treated in the same way.

3. This is the case in Solow's circulating-capital-goods model proposed for the analysis of transition between two equally profitable techniques at the switch-point of a wage-interest frontier, in "The Interest Rate and Transition Between Techniques", *Socialism, Capitalism and Economic Growth: Essays Presented to Maurice Dobb*, ed. C.H. Feinstein, Cambridge 1967.

4. A higher (lower) steady-growth rate requires in fact a greater (smaller) relative size of the capital-good sector.

5. This is in fact quite different from a stability analysis. As Hicks points out, "even if we

were assured (as we may not be) that the model has a tendency to converge to a new equilibrium, it remains a matter of importance what happens on the way", *Capital and Time*, p. 11.

6. "The problem with which we shall be concerned ... is the determination of the path of our economy when it is not in a steady-state. Such a path must have a definite time-reference, for out of steady-state one point is not like any other. In particular it must have a beginning ... One would like to assume that this initial state (taken as given) is itself ... the result of a transition which is still incomplete; but a state of that sort we do not yet understand. So it seems inevitable that we would begin from what we do understand, that we should begin with an economy which is in a steady-state is subjected to some kind of disturbance", "1973", p. 81. Lowe, on the other hand, writes "Our task consists in examining the initial impact of the technological change on a preexisting, dynamic equilibrium, and in elaborating the structural and motorial conditions for the establishment of a new dynamic equilibrium after the innovation has been absorbed", (1976, p. 249).

7. Hicks considers in particular the simple case of two phases: a construction phase, during which the machine embodying a given technique is built, and a utilization phase, during which the machine is used for the production of the consumption good.

8. The relation between the construction phase and the utilization phase, which determines the time-profile of the process of production in the simple case proposed by Hicks is of paramount importance, in this context. It is, in fact, what happens during the construction phase, and the time required by the latter before the utilization of the new machines can begin, which makes it possible to sort out the relevant phenomena of a process of transition. In particular, the highly controversial issue of technological unemployment is dealt with in a systematic way, and a proof of Ricardo's "machinery effect" (the introduction of machinery has an adverse effect on employment in the short run) is the outcome of a particular kind of innovation. For an extension of the "machinery effect" to all cases of technical progress in processes of production with a more general time-profile, see M. Amendola, (1972).

78

Causation, Social Science and Sir John Hicks*†

J.T. Addison, J. Burton and T.S. Torrance

I. Introduction

Typically, the work of an economist or other social scientist makes much use of the notions of causation (or causality) and cause. Rarely however are these concepts subjected to a sustained analysis of their meaning in the context of the social sciences as opposed to the natural sciences. An exception to this comparative neglect is provided by Professor Sir John Hicks' recent text, *Causality in Economics* (1979). In this work, Hicks first discusses the development of ideas of causality since the sixteenth century with especial reference to the movement from what he calls 'Old Causality' (causation regarded as stemming from the decisions of an agent) to the 'New Causality' (causation viewed as part of the pattern of inexorable lawfulness). Secondly, Hicks attempts to relate the modern conception of causation to the social sciences and, in particular, to investigate what such a conception implies for traditional philosophical problems concerning the place of man and of purposive action within the universe (e.g., the free will versus determinism problem).

The present paper, while inspired in its origin by Hicks, is not an attempt to review or provide a commentary on *Causality in Economics* as a whole. Rather it seeks to explore in further detail the matter of the precise nature of causation in the socio-economic sphere. It should also be noted at the outset that a great deal of Hicks' own treatment is concerned not so much with a philosophical enquiry into the essence of causation as with particular problems (both empirical and theoretical) that arise within the discipline of economics and which make use of the notion of causation. Our concern here is not to probe these specific problems nor to evaluate Hicks' treatment of them, interesting though they undoubtedly are in their own right; rather, we seek to explain the nature of causation itself as it functions within social reality.

Modern philosophers are accustomed to explaining the concept of causality in terms of the notions of *necessity* and *sufficiency* (e.g., Hart and Honoré, 1959; Nagel, 1968). These concepts have moreover been much utilised in discussions of causality in economics, as for example in the

†Source: *Oxford Economic Papers*, Vol. 36 (1), March 1984, pp. 1–11.

debate on the causation of inflation.[1] We have no quarrel with this contemporary philosophical treatment as a broad approach, but one of our
main intentions nevertheless is to investigate whether these notions of
necessity and sufficiency can indeed be employed with complete philosophical propriety when the field of enquiry consists of human and societal
phenomena rather than purely physical phenomena.

II. Some Basic Propositions about Causality Statements

To begin with, we hold that any discussion of the nature of causation
(whether of social or physical processes) should start by making the distinction between the causation of a particular single phenomenon individuated
by unique spatial and temporal parameters, and the causation of any particular instance of a given *kind* of event. We shall refer to the former as
'singular causation' and to the latter as 'general causation'. Failure to note
this basic distinction greatly muddies an investigation into what can
properly be considered to constitute the 'cause' of something. To take but
one example from contemporary economics: part of the confusion in the
discussion over the causation of inflation would seem to reflect the fact that
some commentators are concerned with explaining singular events of
causation while others perceive it to be a general event. Thus there is some
tendency for cost-push analysts to be concerned with singular inflationary
events such as the British wage explosion of the late 1960s (Williamson
and Wood, 1976). There is a contrasting tendency for 'monetarists' to
concentrate upon the causation of inflation as a general event: a perspective implicit in Friedman's (1966, p. 18) famous dictum that 'inflation
is always and everywhere a monetary phenomenon'. The debate between
these two schools of thought concerning the causation of inflation is often
conducted as if both groups were dealing with the same type of inflationary
event, but this may not be the case. A clearer recognition of the distinction
between inflation as a singular and general event would help clarify
discussion of the causes of inflation.

In the case of singular causation, we have a dated effect (phenomenon)
occurring at a particular spatial location or set of locations (e.g., the foreign
exchange market does function at a single location but events occur in the
market as a result of buying/selling pressures emanating from various
financial centres). Invariably, we shall find that such an event will have
been 'produced' or 'brought about' (we shall examine these philosophically
perplexing notions further on in the paper) by a set of prior events and
conditions. We then say that this *set* was itself sufficient, in some sense of
this term, for the occurrence of the effect in question, while each member
of this set was necessary — again, in some sense of the term — for its
occurrence. What is causally sufficient, therefore, for a single phenomenon
is a set of antecedent events and circumstances, while what is necessary for
the same phenomenon is that each and every member of the set occur. (At
times it may of course be appropriate to consider the relationships between
the members of each set, although this procedure is arguably more relevant

to certain areas of the physical sciences.) This immediately means that what is sufficient and what is necessary for an event are things belonging to fundamentally different categories: a whole set is sufficient, while each element or member of that set is what is necessary.

On the face of it, what has just been outlined appears to apply equally to social and physical phenomena. If we seek 'the causes' of an event (of whatever sort) in historical time, what we attempt to do is to find which of the events and conditions which antedated it in time were such that if they had *not* occurred the phenomenon itself would not have occurred. Each such antecedent event can thus be said to have been necessary for the phenomenon, while the set or whole cluster of these necessary conditions would have constituted what was at the time in question sufficient to produce the phenomenon. (For the moment, it should be remembered, we are leaving aside the matter of whether the words 'sufficient' and 'necessary' have precisely the same connotation when applied in the context of social as well as physical science.) Finally, in the context of singular causation, we should observe that there appears nothing objectionable in principle in holding that among the necessary factors for a phenomenon we can count absences of events or forces as well as events or forces that actually existed. An absence of something can be a necessary condition for a singular event if it was the case that if what was absent had occurred on the occasion under examination the phenomenon itself would *not* have occurred.

If we turn our attention to the causation of general events (i.e., all the particular instances of some one kind of event), we find that we have to pay heed to the problems raised by the plurality of causes. By this we mean the empirical fact that different instances of the same kind of event may be brought about by sufficient sets of factors which contain different sorts of members. To give an abstract illustration: factors $a_1 b_1 c_1 d_1$ (i.e., instances of factors of kind *ABCD*) were sufficient to cause p_1 (an instance of phenomenon of kind *P*), while factors $a_2 e_1 f_1 g_1$ and $h_1 i_1 j_1 k_1$ were sufficient to cause p_2 and p_3 respectively. From this theoretical example, it should be clear that the instances of no single type of factor (e.g., *B*) can correctly be described as either sufficient or necessary for instances of phenomenon *P*. Factor b_1 was a necessary condition for p_1, but to say this does not by itself imply that the prior occurrence of some instance of *B* is a necessary condition for the occurrence of any instance of *P*. Following the helpful terminology developed by Mackie (1965), *B* is an example of an INUS condition of *P*. *B*, in other words, is a certain type of factor, and while an instance of *B* is always *insufficient* on its own to produce an instance of *P*, such an instance of *B* could be a *necessary* part of some set of conditions which, while being *unnecessary*, would nevertheless be *sufficient* (if it should occur) to bring about an instance of *P*.

As yet, the terminology of INUS conditions has not filtered into general usage in economics and other social sciences. However, its introduction would be of value in clarifying the discussion of causation. Consider, for example, the protracted debate on the role of investment in economic growth. It has long been recognised that investment has 'something' to do with growth. But clearly it is not a sufficient condition for growth. This, investment of capital in wasteful projects does not produce growth; rather, it results in the squandering of resources, not their more efficient use. Equally clearly, physical capital accumulation is not a necessary condition for economic growth, since growth can occur in its absence. Accordingly, investment is neither a necessary nor a sufficient condition for growth. Is it therefore not a cause of growth? We would argue that it clarifies matters to perceive of investment as an INUS condition for economic growth. It is insufficient on its own but could be a necessary element of a set of conditions (including, for example, a social coordination mechanism that promotes the allocation of capital resources to their most productive uses) which, while being unnecessary, appear to be sufficient (according to the available evidence) to bring about economic growth.

When discussing what causal statements mean it is obviously important to appreciate the distinction between singular and general causation (and the closely associated distinction between an actual historical event or phenomenon and the general type of which it is an instance). Failure to do so raises the danger of manufacturing a whole range of meaningless problems and pseudo-paradoxes. For example, we may start to wonder how it can be possible for a factor both to be and yet not to be a necessary condition of an event.

Before we start to consider what differentiates causality in the natural and the social sciences, we need to raise the (epistemological) question of what entitles us to characterise a sequence of events as a causal rather than a coincidental sequence. To answer this, as Hicks emphasises in his first chapter, what is required is a theory about how the events we are studying are ordered. This point, which incidentally was first brought to philosophical prominence by the philosopher David Hume in 1738, is that causal (of whatever kind) and coincidental connections can be distinguished only on the basis of a tested theory as to the specific principles of order that hold within a particular domain of events. By 'tested' here we do not of course mean 'conclusively established', but rather that we have some reason, based on past experience, for thinking that events in reality may be connected together in the way hypothesised. It does not follow from this that a causal connection always reflects precisely a statable principle or order or 'law' (e.g., we may be justified in saying that at a particular time the set of factors $a_1 b_1 c_1 d_1$ caused event e_1, without committing ourselves to a formal principle that instances of $ABCD$ are always followed by an instance of E, even though this may well be true); what a causal connection does reflect is some body of formal principles or 'laws' from which in conjunction with the fact of the occurrence of, say, $a_1 b_1 c_1 d_1$ we could infer the occurrence of e_1. The main point here, however, is that judgements of causation imply the existence of some fairly well articulated theory of how the events under study are related together. If this were not the case, causality and coincidence could not be separated in our knowledge.

III. On Social and Physical Causation

A good point to begin an examination of the nature of human and social causation is to recognise that a considerable degree of incompleteness or openness affects our knowledge of causal connections, even at the best of times. Take singular causation: the sufficient condition of an (historical) event is the set of all factors, including absences, which are necessary for it. But, the question is, given the entire state of the universe as it existed before the occurrence of the event in question, how can we be *sure* that from all possible factors and absences we are selecting those, and only those, that are causally relevant for the occurrence of the event we are investigating. The answer, of course, is that we cannot be sure but that our theory or hypothesis represents our best attempt to date to inform ourselves as to what is indeed relevant and what is indeed irrelevant (for our purposes) in the state of the universe which antedated the event in question. Now, it is a fortunate and contingent fact about the universe that the antecedent factors immediately causally relevant can, in most cases, be isolated from the 'background' of the universe itself; and that also, in most cases, such relevant factors are normally fairly small in number (e.g., the different variables that are involved in the functional laws of physics are rarely enormous in quantity, even though the law itself may be complex and difficult). If it were not for this fact about the make-up of the universe, science would be virtually impossible: if thousands and thousands of factors, each of a different kind, were operative to produce a phenomenon, it would in pratice be impossible to adjust or correct a theory in the process of testing it.

Now although the conditions necessary for an event are usually small in number and isolable from the universe at large, this is true to a far greater extent in the physical sciences than in the social sciences. And this, in our view, constitutes a most significant point of difference between the physical and social sciences, and it raises questions for the methodology of the latter that are clearly not so pertinent for the former.

With very many physical events, the causal antecedents are small in number and, typically, once found should enable one to produce an explanation of the specific quantifications of the key properties of the event under examination. Thus, for example, given a mass of a particular shape and weight resting on some surface, we, knowing that it has been struck by a second body of a certain mass and velocity, should be able to account not just for the first body's movement, but the first body's movement up to a precisely measured amount. In the social sciences, on the other hand, it is usual to find single events being influenced by a large number of distant factors, and these themselves falling into a large number of kinds. A complete list of the causes of events like, say, World War I, the Islamic revolution in Iran of 1979, and the Hungarian hyper-inflation of 1945/46, would be unobtainable in practice and even if it were not the specific quantified features of the 'explananda-events' could not be accounted for in the sense that from the causes we could show why they had the exact features they did, rather than some other features.

Some writers — most notably Hayek (1967) — have fastened on to the large and often indefinite number of causal factors antedating human and social phenomena in comparison with the small and countable number of factors responsible for individual physical phenomena, and have diagnosed this difference to be the major distinction between the social and physical sciences. According to Hayek, social phenomena are *essentially* 'complex' whereas many or most physical phenomena are 'simple'. ('Simple' in this context does not mean, of course, 'easy to understand' but 'involves no more than a few kinds of causal variables in explanations'.) Hayek's point is that while we can obtain 'explanation of detail' with simple phenomena, we have to content ourselves with 'explanation of the principle' when we are concerned with complex phenomena. On this view, the sheer number and variety of the factors (and, presumably, also absences of factors) affecting social phenomena make it possible for the social scientist to seek only the main or most powerfully operative causative factors at work prior to the occurrence of the phenomenon being researched. By doing this, the social scientist would be able to give a qualitative account of why this particular single event should have emerged at the time it did rather than another, but would not be able to explain or account for the *specific quantified details* of the phenomenon itself.

This point is fundamental: it is not simply a matter of inadequate data acquisition. Hayek's point concerning the social sciences is strictly *epistemological*: it concerns facts about our knowledge and *ways of knowing*, and argues that in practice the knowledge we human investigators can obtain in the social sphere is always going to be markedly inferior in precision and extent to that which we can obtain in the physical sciences. We accept this view. However, what is of interest to follow up is to understand *why* our knowledge of social causation should be subject to these limitations of scope. What *precisely* is it about causal connections in the social sphere that makes them differ in the way we, in agreement with Hayek, have outlined from causal connections in the physical sphere?

In perhaps his most famous piece of analytical reasoning, the Scottish philosopher David Hume (1738) argued that a causal relation could be separated into three parts: the temporal priority of the cause (or causes) to the effect; the immediate or mediate spatial and temporal contiguity of the cause (or causes) to the effect; and the fact that any one sequence of such events was an instance of a general connection of events of the same kind and which had been observed to hold regularly in the past. This analysis, as philosophical commentators on Hume have long argued, is not the whole answer. For one thing — the traditional 'problem of induction' — just because a sequence has held in the past does not mean that it will hold in the future (a problem Hume himself recognised and correctly characterised as incapable of solution); and for another the causal connection in the physical realm seems to involve a sort of 'necessity' the analysis of which is not touched upon by the Humean definition. By 'necessity' in this context we mean, very roughly, that when we say for example, 'heating metal block z at time t caused it to expand to extent f', we are not merely saying that the expansion followed on the heels of the heating but that, in some way, the heating *produced* the expansion or *made* the expansion happen. Physical causality, then, appears to be something more than a regular contingent conjunction of events: while we may not be able to give anything like a satisfactory account of the substance of 'causal necessity' (a task that has successfully defied philosophers since the time of Hume) that it is present few would seek to deny.

When we turn to causation in the human and societal sphere, it is apparent that the element of necessity, which attaches itself to 'causal links', in the purely physical arena, is lacking. What are called the 'causes' of human behaviour turn out, on closer inspection, to be the grounds or reasons for which an agent initiates an action. Of course, we do talk about 'compelling grounds' or 'coercion' when referring to an individual's activities, but what is meant in these cases is not that the agent literally *could* not do other than what he was compelled to do, but that the coercion took the form of convincing the agent that unpalatable consequences would ensue if he acted differently from the way he was bidden. Even if subjected to coercion by an armed gangster, the agent threatened does not (literally) *have* to act in the way ordered: he would only do so because the alternative to not doing so, death or disablement, is, usually at least, more unattractive. The 'coercee' has choice but chooses to avoid the expected consequences of non-compliance with the threat of the 'coercer'.

Causality in human beings operates through the mind of an agent, and though 'force' as conceived by the political theorist undeniably exists, this concept does not have the same meaning as when employed in a description of physical causation. Human beings, unlike purely physical processes, are telic; that is, they pursue ends and purposes, and can and do conceive of the notion of adopting a means to an end. Furthermore, human agents can endow objects and circumstances with meaning or significance (e.g., a coin is not just a flat piece of metal, it is also a socially meaningful entity — this social meaning stemming from its role within economies co-ordinated by monetary exchange) and, frequently, how an object is construed to have meaning makes it a reason (or cause) for a certain type of action. And it is precisely because anything at all can be, or can become, a cause of behaviour if significance is bestowed on it that the causal factors which bring about a social event are typically so numerous and are of so many varied kinds, in comparison with the causes of a physical event.

IV. Sir John Hicks on Social and Physical Causality: An Evaluation

The foregoing discussion of social causation leads us toward an evaluation of Hicks' recent work as it appertains to our more general discussion. In his *Causality in Economics*, Hicks draws the distinction between Old Causality and New Causality:[2] the former is construed as happenings which occur as a result of purposive intent, while the latter is taken as purposeless events determined by inexorable laws of nature. Although at the time of the scientific revolution in the fifteenth and sixteenth centuries, when the study of nature was struggling to emerge from the confines of medieval metaphysics, investigators gave up attempting to discern the purpose or ends pursued by inanimate objects and processes in favour of the notion of the operation of physical law, this is not to say that one conception of causality was replaced by another. Rather, what happened was that attempts to perceive purpose and meaning were abandoned in the physical arena, and kept just to those areas inhabited by conscious life. In other words, the scientific revolution did not involve the wholesale surrender of one type of causality ('Old Causality') and its replacement by another ('New Causality'). Rather, it involved using concepts of causality that were deemed appropriate given the nature of the subject-matter. It would thus be as absurd and philosophically improper to disregard the purposes and meanings present in the social sphere as it would be to read purposes and meanings into the inanimate and non-sentient sphere.

These matters concerning types of causality are closely intertwined with questions concerning the problem of 'determinism', namely the doctrine that every event in the whole universe is uniquely shaped down to the last detail by physical laws. Determinism is in direct conflict with the view that human beings can make genuine decisions and choices and, within the limits laid down by physical and social barriers, have freedom of will in initiating their behaviour. Hicks at one point makes the (to us extraordinary) claim that: 'The struggle between free will and determinism, which was such a burning issue in the latter days of the Old Causality, is still of relevance to economics. But in economics we find a solution.'[3] The contention that economics is able to show us a way of achieving an answer to the age-old issues of determinism and free will is an exceedingly bold one: we cannot agree however that Hicks does anything to justify the assertion. The argument he offers runs as follows:

'There is no reason, when looking forward, to doubt that we are free, as we feel ourselves to be, to choose one course of action rather than another. But no decision made now can affect what *has happened* in the past. Decisions were made in the past, but *now* they are past events. They cannot be affected by what is decided now, so there can be no free will about them — now. So, with respect to the past, one can be fully determinist.'[4]

Do these words live up to the high claim made for them?

In our view, Hicks' argument is unsuccessful. If what he is saying here is that past events, because they occur in the past, are beyond change then this is of course an unexceptional but wholly uncontroversial statement. What lies in the past, whatever it may be, has occurred and that fact is indeed final and irreversible. But Hicks is surely claiming something different. We understand him to be saying that looking back at actions in the past we are able to explain in detail why they occurred rather than did not occur: but in looking forward into the future no precise prediction of action is possible because we cannot ascertain now how people will decide their future courses of action. Hicks seems to be inconsistent at this point. If we indeed have free will as regards the present and future, then it cannot be the case that (to quote) 'with respect to the past, one can be fully deter-minist'. (By 'determinist', we assume Hicks means that past actions can be explained in precisely the same sort of detailed way that classical physics can explain past physical interactions.) If we hold to a free will position for the present and future, then surely we cannot at the same time claim that it is possible to explain past action down to the last detail. In other words, to be 'fully determinist' about human actions in the past requires us to be determinist about actions in the present and future. Hicks, therefore, despite his assertions to the contrary, does not show us a way of throwing light on the vexed question of free will versus determination. That this turns out to be so is perhaps less than surprising for this very issue is amongst the most intractable of all philosophical problems.

Ultimately, how one construes the nature of causality in the human and social spheres does stem from one's view on the crucial philosophical issue of free will. For if everything that occurs in society, including purposive behaviour, consciousness and the ability to bestow meaning, is brought about in the final analysis by physical forces alone, then it would indeed be difficult to maintain that in substance social causality was anything other than a species of physical causality. On the other hand, we can hold that human beings are free agents: this does not mean that we are bound to explain what purposiveness or consciousness *is* (nobody as yet has been able to do this satisfactorily) but simply that we regard these phenomena of society as being non-reducible to the purely physical. And on the free will stance, of course, the nature of social causality must have inherent differ-ences from that found in physical reality. In this case, it is surely not at all unsurprising that the problems encountered in the process of social enquiry should in part be of a kind unique to that sort of study.

To claim that agents are free, human behaviour is purposive and genuine choices and decisions can be initiated, is not to say that human beings should be viewed as entities abstracted from a physical and social environment. To be consistent with the view that determinism is false, all we need hold is that human behaviour and thought are not fashioned down to the last detail by factors and processes that are governed wholly by the operation of physical law. It is thus in tune with the free will position if we look upon human agents as being to a large extent, perhaps even mostly, the creatures of their situation: but while the physical and social setting may well be the largest single factor shaping human conduct and inter-action, creativity, novel thought and genuinely deliberative action are also to be found.

In keeping with an anti-determinist approach to a social causality, the modern philosopher Karl Popper (1957) bases his well known refutation of the view that long term social prediction can be achieved (what he calls 'historicism') on the fact that human society is strongly influenced by advances in theoretical science. He argues that since the creative effort of formulating a new theory cannot *in principle* be predicted from even the most perfect knowledge of antecedent factors the future course of society itself cannot be predicted.

In view of the nature of human agency that we have laid out here is, as we think, correct, the methodological implications for the social sciences are far-reaching. Particularly, we will have to abandon the idea that a 'Newtonian revolution' has yet to be won in this area: such an idea would be a mere chimera if it is indeed the case that the material studied by the social sciences was inherently different in its causal connections from that studied by, say, classical mechanics. Indeed, when today the study of physical reality has, (for its own special reasons) largely jettisoned the framework of universal determinism, there would seem something atavistic and even absurd in social scientists striving to adopt the notion as an ultimate hypothesis as to the intrinsic nature of causal connections in society.

V. One Final Reflection

Finally, a concluding remark on Hicks: although in *Causality in Economics* Hicks sets out to expound a philosophical thesis, what he actually produces is a discussion of a series of conundrums in theoretical economics. It seems to us that while Hicks may himself consider that the underlying reasons for these problems are philosophical in character, he in fact nowhere explicitly articulates the fundamental features of these philosophical issues. We argue in this paper, however, that it is a basic mistake even to regard the failure of the social sciences, including economics, to measure up to the quantitative exactness and explanatory and predictive precision of physics *as a problem.* Our claim, at the root, is simply that in the social sciences we are dealing with phenomena that belong to a different category of existence from that of the phenomena studied by the physical sciences.

References

Addison, J.T., Burton, J. and Torrance, T.S. (1980), "On the Causation of Inflation", *Manchester School*, Vol. 48, No. 2, pp. 140–156.

Friedman, M. (1966), "What Price Guideposts?" in Schultz, G.P. and Aliber, R.Z. (eds), *Guidelines, Informal Controls and the Market Place*, Chicago, Ill.: University of Chicago Press, pp. 17–39.

Hart, H.L.A. and Honoré, A.M. (1959), *Causation in the Law*, Oxford: The Clarendon Press.

Hayek, F.A. (1967), *Studies in Philosophy, Politics and Economics*, London: Routledge and Kegan Paul.

Hicks, J.R. (1979), *Causality in Economics*, London: Blackwell.

Hume, D. (1738), *A Treatise on Human Nature.* (The most accessible modern edition is Selby-Bigge, L.A. (ed.) (1978), *A Treatise on Human Nature*, Oxford: Oxford University Press.)

Mackie, J.L. (1965), 'Causes and Conditions", *American Philosophical Quarterly*, Vol. 2, No. 4, pp. 245–264.

Nagel, E. (1968) (2nd ed.), *The Structure of Science*, London: Routledge and Kegan Paul.

Popper, K.R. (1957), *The Poverty of Historicism*, London: Routledge and Kegan Paul.

Williamson, J. and Wood, G.E. (1976), "The British Inflation: Indigenous or Imported?", *American Economic Review*, Vol. 66, No. 4, pp. 520–531.

Notes

*We are much indebted to Professor David Pearce for his helpful comments on an earlier draft of this paper. The usual disclaimers apply.

1. For an example of the use and abuse of the notions of necessity and sufficiency in this particular debate, see Addison, Burton and Torrance (1980).
2. Hicks, *op. cit.*, p. 6ff.
3. Hicks, *op. cit.*, p. 9.
4. Hicks, *op. cit.*, p. 11.

A Note on Hicks's 'Contemporaneous Causality'[†]

V. Termini*

In *Causality in Economics* Hicks (1979) proposes a distinction between three categories of temporal causality: 'static', 'contemporaneous' and 'sequential' causality. In this note I wish to comment on the concept of 'contemporaneous causality'; in particular I shall try to show that the examples of 'contemporaneous causality' chosen by Hicks from the literature properly belong instead to his category of 'static causality'. I shall argue that the only temporal distinction which may be drawn following Hicks's own definitions separates causal atemporal schemes from causal temporal ones, i.e. contemporaneous causality disappears from the picture.

Furthermore, I shall try to show that Hicks's distinction between 'contemporaneous' and 'sequential' causality (i.e. the existence of lags between the cause and the effects) may hide a pitfall which is not made explicit by Hicks to his readers.

Hicks's propositions concentrate on temporal structures as the basis of causal relations in theoretical models. This is because the central task, as he sees it, is to define causal relations according to whether they express *static causality* (in which the analytical scheme is out of time); *contemporaneous causality* (in which 'cause and effect relate to the same time period'); or *sequential causality* (in which 'cause precedes effect') (Hicks, 1979, p. 26).

The reasons for rejecting 'Hume's principle that cause necessarily precedes effects' (Hicks, 1979, p. 26) are not questioned here. The separation of the concept of causality from that of temporal sequentiality may also be found in the writings of other economists. Simon, for instance, insisted that, if A causes B and it also precedes it in time, the *asymmetry* of the relation linking A and B is the relevant feature which defines the causal relation, not the temporal sequence by itself (Simon, 1953, p. 51.) Feigl, from a different perspective, describing the 'domains' of causal laws, distinguished the sequential domains from the simultaneous domain of these laws (Feigl, 1953).

Our concern here is with Hicks's distinction between the three categories of causality and the problems that arise when Hicks's concept of contemporaneous causality is applied to theoretical models.

[†]Source: *Cambridge Journal of Economics*, Vol. 8 (1), March 1984, pp. 87–92.

The basic feature which distinguishes static causality from contemporaneous causality is that the latter has a temporal reference absent from the former. 'Static causality', Hicks explains, 'may indeed be regarded as a limiting case of contemporaneous causality in which the period, during which the cause operates and takes effect, has been stretched out to become indefinite'; in static causality 'both the cause and the effect are permanencies'. 'However', he adds, 'when we proceed to this limit there is a change of character'. There is *no uncertainty* to distinguish past from future values of the variables because, as Hicks further explains, 'in the static models time is not taken seriously. *Past and future are the same*; they remain the same as far forward and as far back as we care to look' (Hicks, 1979, p. 62).[1]

Uncertainty, it thus emerges, is the distinctive feature of temporal causality. In contemporaneous and sequential causality, uncertainty about future events is the only feature, according to Hicks, which forces us to recognise that the future is qualitatively different from the past (and therefore that both contemporaneous and sequential causality are framed in time).

These two categories, of course, are themselves further distinguished by the fact that in sequential causality the cause precedes the effect. In the present paper this distinction is of only secondary importance.

One of Hicks's examples of static causality is taken from Adam Smith: 'the relative cheapness of water transport is a *cause* of the relative wealth of some places that have good water communications.' Hicks maintains, 'Thus, in terms of our analysis, Adam Smith is comparing what was in his time with *what would have been if*, other things being equal, the relative cost of land and water carriage had been different' (p. 45). 'The model itself', Hicks stresses 'must be unchanging' and 'the method belongs in comparative *statics*' (p. 57). As an example of contemporaneous causality Hicks points to the theoretical scheme of the *General Theory*. In the multiplier there is a cause (investment) and its effect (income), and their relation is contemporaneous, according to Hicks, because 'income is a flow over a period' and 'investment is a flow over the same period'.

There are, however, two critical points:

(i) For Hicks the multiplier is an example of contemporaneous causality, because it explains 'what income would have been in that period if investment had been different over the same period, *ceteris paribus*' (Hicks, 1979, pp. 74–75)[2]. But this example is not formally different from Hicks's description of Adam Smith's static analysis, i.e. 'comparing what was in his time with what would have been if, other things being equal, the relative cost of land and water carriage had been different' (Hicks, 1979, p. 45). However, Hicks explained in that example that Smith's 'model must be unchanging', so that 'the method belongs in comparative *statics*' (p. 57): 'both the cause and the effect are *permanencies*'.

(ii) The unit of time is irrelevant for the analytical purpose of any theory which focuses on the causal structure of a process and which tries to identify the forces determining the process according to the causal relations which the theory specifies. This is because such a causal structure is independent of time; it only implies a set of general relations of a qualitative character. The process can therefore be analytically squeezed at will and the causes can be assumed to work out their effects *instantaneously*, in exactly the same way they may be stretched *ad infinitum*, provided that the *logical priorities* are respected. In the former case we have Keynes's 'instantaneous' multiplier and the simultaneous occurrence of investment and saving; in the latter we have Smith's 'permanencies'. It is this very feature of Keynes's method and analytical aim in the *General Theory* (i.e. that of 'studying *the forces* which determine the scale of output') which entitles us to classify it instead within Hicks's category of static causality. This point is more fully argued in a previous article (Termini, 1981, para. 5) and only the main line of reasoning is recounted here.

The analytical feature of the *General Theory* enables Keynes to leave out of his analysis of the multiplier any temporal process, and to neglect the time lags and the disequilibrium positions which are required by the adjustment mechanisms of the variables. Keynes writes: 'the logical theory of the multiplier holds good continuously, without time lag, at all moments of time' (Keynes, 1936, p. 122). Because this causality is framed within a logical scheme, logical precedence does not entail any chronological precedence; any temporal reference is absent from these laws.

Keynes further stresses that 'the *General Theory* has evolved into primarily a study of the forces which determine the scale of output' (Keynes, 1936, pp. VI–VII). It should be clear, but has to be emphasised, that to single out the determinants of a process of change does not imply the study of the dynamics of the changing process itself. Of course, if we leave the field of analysis where causal laws may be generally inferred to explain the relations which govern the economic structure and instead set out to study the *actual* development of these relations in time, one can no longer relate I_0 at time t_0 with Y_1 at time t_1 (according to an *a priori* given parametric relation). Keynes himself supplies us with several examples of uncertain outcomes in the *General Theory*, when he considers the alternative paths which may prevail if he follows, *in time*, the *actual* development of his logical relations.

The multiplier thus emerges as the logical expedient which enabled Keynes to maintain his causal chain (in particular the causality from Investment to Saving flows) irrespective of the temporal relations that may have existed in the analysis.

These atemporal features of the multiplier have been underlined by Hicks previously (1976, p. 140. See also Davidson, 1978, pp. 372–378). These features, contrary to later claims, now seem essentially to be without question features of static analysis, according to Hicks's own classification.

The second example of contemporaneous causality given by Hicks is the marginal efficiency of capital. Here, Hicks again underlines the temporal dimension of this relation and thereby separates it from the static concept of the marginal productivity of capital. Hicks states, 'the marginal efficiency of capital is forward looking', and he stresses 'ignorance of the future is essential to it'. Hicks also points out, however, that the marginal efficiency of capital has to remain unchanged through time and the only possible way to assume this, he specifies, is to assume that '*expectations remain unchanged*, over a period, provided that *within the period* expectations are correct. What was expected in January to happen in June does happen in June, what was expected to happen in September does happen in September' (p. 82). This assumption is required, according to Hicks, if one is not prepared to follow Keynes's own solution to the problem, namely 'to confine attention to Fixed Capital Investment, the incentive for which depended on expectations on the further future'.[3] Hicks specifies: 'if we refuse to accept Keynes's line of escape, what can we do?' And he answers: 'As for the expectations of the further future, nothing is to have happened within the year which changes them. So nothing is to have happened within the year which has been unexpected' (p. 83). Again, as before, *uncertainty has thus to be explicitly ruled out* or, as I could rephrase it, the variables have to be considered in their *ex post* registered values. What then is left of the analytical feature by which Hicks has distinguished the atemporal static framework of the first category (i.e. static causality) from the temporal non-static one (i.e. contemporaneous causality)? Do the causal relations of Keynes's multiplier and marginal efficiency of capital lack a temporal reference and, if so, does it follow that they properly belong within the 'static' models?

*

Hicks himself supplies a peculiar answer to these questions. In order to maintain his earlier distinction between *static* and *contemporaneous* causal concepts he stretched the definition of equilibrium which he had stated in static terms so that it could be equally applied to 'non-static' models. Thus, if, as in the static case, the model is in equilibrium when 'it is unchanging over time' (e.g. in the example from Adam Smith), in the second model this is said to be in equilibrium 'when expectations are realized' (see pp. 45–46 for the static definition of equilibrium, pp. 82–83 for the temporal definition). By introducing this elaboration, it appears that temporal coordinates can be maintained in the scheme of the *General Theory*, and attention focused on the requirement that all flows of real variables, in particular investment and income, refer to the same time periods.

It is interesting to note that a similar definition of equilibrium is used by Lindahl in defining Keynes's theory, in his reformulation of 'Keynes's model' in 1954. 'Keynes's constructions refer to equilibrium positions', Lindahl writes, 'provided that *the concept of equilibrium can be applied to correctly anticipated processes*'.[4] It will be appreciated, however, that Lindahl does *not* interpret the scheme of the *General Theory* in causal terms in his 1954 model. Lindahl described it as 'an equilibrium with *simultaneous interdependence* of the various magnitudes' (1954, pp. 25, 20–23). Coherently enough, he then drew a complete picture of both the method and the results of Keynes's scheme in terms of an atemporal simultaneous interdependent system. But this is not the case, of course, according to Hicks's interpretation, for he repeatedly warned against the picturing of simultaneity in Keynes's approach (see Hicks, 1976).

By assuming that expectations are realised, we immediately recognise that Hicks is assuming, in an alternative way, that *uncertainty has no effect on these relations.*[5] Therefore, until meaningful alternative examples are found to fit contemporaneous causality, the category is, it seems, empty. It follows, provided a basic distinction is drawn between analyses which are causally framed and analyses which are framed according to inter-dependent and simultaneous equilibria (on the relevance of which I totally agree with Hicks), that the only temporal distinction which may be further drawn separates causal atemporal models from causal temporal ones, i.e. contemporaneous causality disappears from the picture.

*

Furthermore, the second distinction introduced by Hicks between con-temporaneous and sequential causality within temporal structures, i.e. the existence of lags between the cause and the effect, may hide a pitfall which is not made explicit by Hicks to his readers. There is no doubt that 'sequential causality' implies lags. But the reverse condition does not hold. We can find many examples in the literature where a 'temporally' lagged structure is based upon a set of *ceteris paribus* conditions which effectively exclude uncertainty from models. Lags may be devices to describe mechan-isms that are implied by static causal models.[6] Indeed, what *conceptual* considerations could enable us to distinguish a model where $C_t = f(Y_t)$ from a model where $C_t = f(Y_{t-n})$ (i.e. a model where the cause brings about its effects after a time lag) *if* all the parameters and functions are the same as in the previous model?

The pitfall lies in the fact that the first scheme may account for a set of causal relations which are *logically* framed, out of time. In this case, to extend these relations merely mechanically by means of a lagged structure necessarily implies a change of character. The same kind of problems are involved as in the direct use in quantitative terms of the logical relations of a static model. It may be added that this represents a translation which Keynes was very worried about and strongly opposed to (see Keynes, 1939).[7]

Let us explore the argument by means of an example. Within the field of causal relations considered by Hicks, we find several models which turn the *logical* relations identified by Keynes in the *General Theory* into lagged structural relations. The variables are dated in order to follow the sequence of their values. We may recognise, however, that these models set out a step by step development of the process precisely because they assume a mechanical notion of time. They show us that the different phases of the multiple increase of income determined by a given increase of investment are merely an expository expedient of static analysis which has nothing to do with time.

Indeed, if we follow the different phases of the income generation through time, we necessarily encounter disequilibrium points of the variables. We are then faced with the choice of ignoring them or dealing with them. In the first case, the analysis corresponds to a logical scheme which is atemporally framed, and *the same* final values of variables in equi-librium, are reached for all variables. In the second case, it is important to acknowledge that one can no longer relate I_0 at time t_0 with $Y = Y_n$ at time

t_n according to parameters that are *quantitatively given a priori*: during the process, expectations may be unfulfilled, the functions changed, decisions altered.[8]

It is possible to show, therefore, that these kinds of lagged models have nothing necessarily to do with a framework where uncertainty dominates economic relations, which Hicks has described as a temporal model. It follows, if we wish to consider these lagged models in a separate category — as I think we should — that we may need to introduce an *ad hoc* subcategory of *'mechanical time'* sequentiality which belongs within Hicks's static causality. Such a subcategory should help to distinguish these apparently temporal relations from the 'truly' temporal ones, i.e. from those relations where the future is different from the past, as Joan Robinson would say, or where there is uncertainty, as Hicks's classification suggests.

Bibliography

Chick, V. 1982. *Macroeconomics after Keynes*, Oxford, Philip Allan
Davidson, P. 1978. *Money and the Real World*, London, Macmillan
Davidson, P. 1982. *International Money and the Real World*, London, Macmillan
Feigl, H. 1953. Note on Causality, in Feigl and Brodbeck (eds), *Readings in the Philosophy of Science*, New York
Hayek, F. 1935. *Prices and Production*, London, Routledge and Kegan Paul
Hayek, F. 1941. *The Pure Theory of Capital*, London, Routledge and Kegan Paul (1976)
Hicks, J. 1965. *Capital and Growth*, Oxford, Oxford University Press
Hicks, J. 1976. Some questions of time in economics, in Tang, A., Westfield, F. and Worley, J. (eds), *Evolution, Welfare and Time in Economics*, Heath, Lexington Books
Hicks, J. 1979. *Causality in Economics*, Oxford, Basil Blackwell
Kahn, R. 1931. The relation of home investment to unemployment, *Economic Journal*, June
Keynes, J.M. 1936. *The General Theory of Employment, Interest and Money*, London, Macmillan
Keynes, J.M. 1939. Professor Tinbergen's method, *Economic Journal*, September
Keynes, J.M. 1971-. *Collected Writings*, vols XIV, XXII, XXIX, London, Macmillan
Kregel, J. 1976. Economic methodology in the face of uncertainty: the modelling methods of Keynes and the post-keynesians, *Economic Journal*, June
Lindahl, E. 1939. *Studies in the Theory of Money and Capital*, London, A.M. Kelley
Lindahl, E. 1954. On Keynes' economic system, *Economic Record*, May–November
Minsky, H. 1957. Monetary systems and accelerator models, *American Economic Review*, December
Minsky, H. 1975. *John Maynard Keynes*, New York, Columbia University Press
Robinson, J. 1964. *Essays in the Theory of Economic Growth*, London, Macmillan
Simon, H. 1953. Causal Ordering and Identifiability, in Hood, W. and Coopmans, T. (eds), *Studies in Econometric Method*, New York, Cowles Commission, Monograph 14
Termini, V. 1981. Logical, mechanical and historical time in economics, *Economic Notes* by Monte dei Paschi di Siena, no. 3
Thomas, B. 1936. *Monetary Policy and Crises*, London, Routledge and Sons Ltd

Notes

*I should like to thank an anonymous referee and the editors of the *CJE* for their helpful comments, and R. McDowell for advice in editing a previous draft of this paper.

1. Hicks compares this change of character to the change between the short period and the long period of Marshall. Insofar as 'the short period effects are in time, they relate to what happens in a period'. 'Long period effects, on the contrary, are not in that way in time, for the long period has no clear beginning and no clear end'. Hicks has stressed these features of static models on several occasions (see, for example, Hicks, 1965, Ch. 1).

2. Considering the consumption function in more detail, Hicks notices that the model assumes that planned savings and realised savings are the same (pp. 77–78). This means that 'expectations, within the period, are correct' (p. 82).

3. This solution is recalled by Kregel (1976, p. 213 ff.), and by Chick (1982), among others.

4. Lindahl writes: 'If consumers plan to spend a certain fraction of their income during the period, but the income is determined only after the consumers' purchases are finished, the only possibility of avoiding the distinction between the expected income which is the result of the carrying through of the plans ... is to make them equal, i.e. implicitly to assume that individuals correctly anticipate their income' (1954, p. 29). See also Hicks (1976) and also Pasinetti (1974); this is further discussed in Termini (1981, para. 5). The fact that the equilibrium concept is used differently in different places has been stressed recently by Davidson (1982, pp. 61–62).

5. By ignoring 'uncertainty' in Keynes's scheme, Hicks is led to classify the *General Theory* among those models which according to Thomas's accurate classification may be called 'quasi-static'. They 'cover the situation where future changes are accurately foreseen and people dispose of their resources in the light of the perfect foresight'. This, it should be noticed, corresponds to the stream of intertemporal equilibrium theories (where complete future markets or perfect foresights actually prevent the analysis from considering past, present, and future in different terms) and which, started by Hayek (1928), was followed by Lindahl (1929) and more recently by Arrow-Debreu and Benassy, among others.

6. I am referring here to Keynesian aggregate cyclical models and neo-Keynesian models of growth among those which fit Hicks's general definition of causality. In intertemporal equilibrium models and models of temporary equilibrium which do not fit Hicks's definition of causality, we can find the examples of lagged structures which do not deal with time and uncertainty.

7. This point has been argued in paras 3 and 4 of my 1981 article.

8. For instance, it is often implied that a given ratio of consumption to income is a fixed constant at any point of time. Of course, this excludes by definition the possibility of interpreting in the same theory situations where the changing behaviour of economic units has to be explained. In such cases, changes of the parameters and functions during the process of the generation of income should themselves be the object of explanation, and the parameters cannot be assumed to be unchanging. The typical example of a situation which cannot be studied in terms of fixed parameters and functions is the cyclical path of the economy.

80

The Ascent of High Theory: A View from the Foothills[†]

D. Collard*

1

The extended metaphor which I shall employ in this essay is suggested to me by Hicks's own language. I remember first falling under the spell of his style when I chose the *Trade Cycle*, published some four or five years earlier, as a school prize. The style of that book, as of so many of his others, is exploratory rather than (overtly) didactic and even the beginner felt himself to be taken into Hicks's confidence. It was Hicks and I together (he somehow made it appear) who deliberately chose too high a value for the investment coefficient, thereby discovering floors and ceilings. He had already hinted that to follow the usual route would be a mistake. Yet for a while we did so: 'we have a river to cross; while we are thinking about building a bridge on the stretch in front of us, we note that our neighbours have already built a bridge somewhere upstream; it seems only sensible to make a detour in order to use it'. Now, in Chapter 7, we were stuck with too high an accelerator: 'at first sight this alternative looks quite ridiculous; one's first reaction is to reject it out of hand ... but suppose there is some constraint which prevents any fluctuations from passing outside certain limits ...'. And the Hicksian theory of the cycle was ready.

Chapter 12 of *Capital and Time* has the same sort of feel about it; 'from the point now reached, several roads open out, several of which look like being worth exploring. I shall do no more than take a few steps on some of them'. So (to give widely differing examples) do Hicks's search for the lag, in 'The Hayek story', his analogy between regional and international inequality in *World Economics*, and his assessment of the production function in *Capital and Growth*. This business of treating the reader as confidant is, of course, an expository trick: but it is more than a trick, it is part of the art of persuasion, for the reader is implicated in what has come to pass. Often, in Hicks, there are choices to be made, alternative paths to be considered, alternatives which are discussed with the reader. He delights in keeping his secrets back until, given enough clues, we may stumble upon

†Source: *Oxford Economic Papers*, Vol. 36, Supplement November 1984, pp. 1–12.

them for ourselves. Sometimes even Hicks finds the trick difficult to perform: 'I must confess', he writes in his 'Turnpike' essay (*Essays* iii. 20) 'that when I reached this point in my thinking I was very puzzled, ... is there another way out? ... There is another way out, and (knowing the answer) it has been hard to write out the foregoing without revealing it'. (The secret in question here was the long-run tendency to constant cost under no joint supply.)

2

We have not yet reached our central metaphor. Indeed my remarks so far may even have obscured it, portraying Hicks as an enchanter and, even, a tease. Yet there are already hints of the next main strand in the metaphor, that of journeys and explorations. They have been great journeys and Hicks the traveller, guide, and chronicler has allowed the rest of us to travel with him. Images of journey and exploration abound: only a few need be recalled here:

the present volume is the first systematic exploration of the territory which Slutsky opened up (*Value and Capital*, p. 19).

we are within sight of a unifying principle for the whole of economics ... but this is running ahead. Before we can explore these long avenues much preparation is needed (ibid., p. 24).

major questions lie ahead ... I shall do more than peer a little into these further regions. (*Capital and Growth*, p. 279).

it will be a narrow passage, but one must hope that there will be a way through (*Critical Essays*, p. 173).

we are emerging from our mathematical tunnel: we are coming out into economic daylight (*Capital and Growth*, p. 235).

There are many similar images. I have so far held back those which give too obvious a clue to the main metaphor. Some are explicit. Thus when discussing the Simplex method (*Essays* iii. 19) Hicks remarks: 'if one was trying to climb a mountain (without valleys or saddles), the shortest way of getting to the top would be ... straight up, from wherever one happened to be'. And in seeking an analogy for Ricardo's theory of rent (*Essays* iii. 13): 'If a mountaineer starts at sea level and finishes the day at the top of his mountain, he must on the whole have been climbing; but it is, of course, not excluded that he had to get over a smaller range on the way, and was descending for a while as he came down from it'. Then, to clinch the matter, there is the whole gamut of terms used in the analysis itself. Starting with the utility analysis of *Value and Capital* and proceeding through *Capital and Growth* to *Capital and Time*, we come across surfaces, slopes, frontiers, balanced growth paths, full employment paths, dismal paths, ups, downs, peaks, traverses, profiles, and perspectives. We frequently deliberate about the route, assess the state of the terrain, and consider the view from the point so far reached. And, almost always, our eye is on the territory ahead.

We now have our metaphor and can set it to work. Hicks is explorer, mountaineer, and guide — hence the title of this paper. The mountain, or range of mountains, which he explores is the subject-matter of economics. It is a strange mountain, subject to avalanches, storms, mists, and other dramatic changes in weather conditions. On each expedition we discover fresh facts about the mountain and we absorb them into our mountaincraft; some of the old facts have to be discarded as they are no longer true. The mountaineer has to make sense of the facts, to discover how his information fits together. He (or she) has to find routes and guide others along them. Where necessary he must climb sheer rock, devising specialist tools for the purpose. But often a shoulder or ridge route will be available and enable us to make easy progress. Occasionally we reach a summit and get a glimpse of other tops and valleys; for much of the time we are not sure whether the clump of rocks ahead is on a summit (most walkers will be familiar with the 'law of the receding summit' which applies to largely convex hills).

Hicks could be read, it is true, at the fireside, not as guide but as reporter or teller of traveller's tales. This is much easier, much less demanding, much more comfortable. But it is also less rewarding and less useful to those planning expeditions of their own.

3

It is never wise to venture out totally unequipped, even with so sure a guide as Hicks. Yet, surprisingly, a stout pair of boots, and waterproofs to cope with the odd shower, will very often do. There are easy and sunny slopes even in, say, *Capital and Growth* and most fit ramblers are able to cope with *A Theory of Economics History* or *Causality in Economics* if they are careful to keep their wits about them. There are safe, outlying hills suitable for the middle-aged and elderly, but visibility is always in danger of being curtailed, so a map and compass should normally be carried. Once we come to the ascent of High Theory itself this rudimentary gear will no longer do: ice-axe, nylon rope, and survival kit must be included.

Our guide's attitude to the use of artificial climbing aids on difficult rock is a sceptical one. He is not interested in technical accomplishments for their own sake when there are simpler ways up or where progress may be made by avoiding an overhang altogether. Very occasionally pitons, etriers, and the like have to be used. Hicks is certainly capable of using them but has come to regard such activities as something of a side show and to view them (almost) with disdain. In 'Formation of an Economist' he refers to the younger generation of American economists who (in the post-War period) 'with far more skill in mathematics than mine, were sharpening the analysis which I had merely roughed out. But I am afraid I disappointed them; and have continued to disappoint them. Their achievements have been great but they are not in my line.' It may be true, as he writes in 'IS–LM: an explanation', that he had to learn matrix algebra in the fifteen years between the *Trade Cycle* and *Capital Growth*, but the tool-kit used in *Value and Capital* was already a sophisticated one by then contemporary standards.

Hicks has put up an impressive number of 'firsts' on 'severe' or 'very severe' faces using techniques that have proved useful to several subsequent expeditions. Let us consider some of these.

(i) The elasticity of substitution was devised and refined for production functions in the *Theory of Wages* and for utility functions in the Hicks–Allen paper and has become an indispensable part of everyone's equipment. A pioneer from a rather different expedition, Mrs Robinson, was employing the same device at more or less the same time.

(ii) The next 'first', the Slutsky equation, had already been scaled, unobserved, by an obscure Russian climber in 1915 and was soon to be absorbed into the standard curriculum of the training schools. It is interesting that Hicks still prefers the elasticity version of the formula. These two tools, the elasticity of substitution and the Slutsky equation were, for Hicks, the keys not only to the theory of demand but also to the theory of general equilibrium.

(iii) Which brings us to the Hicksian week. Our analogy serves us quite well in the case of the Hicksian week. For, although the general outlines of the whole expedition are reasonably clear, the thing has to be done in stages. At each stage we hold counsel (Hicks's Monday) and decide where to aim for next — another top or, in the case of really major expeditions, another camp. Then the plan works itself out (with given expectations) during the following 'week'. On Monday week we have a further consultation ... and so on. It does not really happen quite like this but the temporary equilibrium established each Monday is not too bad an approximation. If the mountain is at all interesting, or if it offers any surprises — which it usually does — a complete and detailed plan is impossible. Something like the Temporary Equilibrium seems to be essential to any interesting dynamics.

(iv) Another major first ascent permitted the integration of monetary and value theory ('A Suggestion for Simplifying the Theory of Money'): from the new ridge one was able to gain fresh and stimulating views of peaks only previously seen from their separate valleys. Others had glimpsed the view but had failed to make sense of it. The work appeared to have a great deal to do with the theory of portfolio selection but, as Hicks was later to argue, portfolio selection was only part of the story: (it is) 'an area in which we may try our wings, before we venture (if we dare to venture) upon the more difficult and exciting parts of the territory' ('Portfolio Selection'). Those exciting parts are about uncertainty and have still to be understood; shafts of light from 'rational expectations' can never fully illuminate them. Hence his abiding interest in liquidity and fundamental uncertainty.

(v) IS–LM (1937) is the Hicksian device best known to students of macro-economics. It was a sharp tool, subsequently honed in the *Trade Cycle* and in a 1957 paper, 'The "Classics" Again' (*Critical Essays* 8). But Hicks has made it abundantly clear that it was a tool only to be used in training exercises, not on real expeditions.

This catalogue of tools invented by or, at least improved by, Hicks could be greatly extended. Rather than extend the list let us look at references to Hicks, and to Hicksian devices, in two recent textbooks on micro-economics. Deaton and Muellbauer (1980)[1] refer to *Value and Capital* for Hicksian aggregation (the composite commodity theorem), for Hicksian compensated demand functions, and for technical work on the relationship between demand and cost functions; he is a 'pioneer of duality'. They refer to *Revision* for compensating and equivalent variation and to *Value and Capital* again for definitions of substitutes and complements. Layard and Walters (1978)[2] refer to the Hicksian version of the Kaldor–Hicks criterion for an increase in economic efficiency, to the Hicksian formula for the elasticity of the derived demand for labour, to Hicks on substitutes and complements and to the Hicks–Slutsky decomposition of price change. Hicks is alive and well in the training manuals.

4

So far we have noticed Hicks the instructor, inventor of tools and pioneer of some very tricky rock-climbs. Now we shall spend some time with Hicks the mountain guide. In the ascent of high theory it is important to devise useful rules for making progress. On the long haul it is always easier to find a steadily rising path up a shoulder or along a ridge than to proceed by a series of scrambles: it is easier to find a stationary (or rather a progressively stationary) state, a 'turnpike'. If the mountain was well charted, unchanging and clearly visible, such paths would be obvious and we would take a little trouble to get ourselves on to them. But, given his experience of the mountain, Hicks is reluctant to advise a steady path. It is true that much of *Capital and Growth* and even of *Capital and Time* is devoted to working out steady-state growth paths but in the first he is expounding (and making his own) the then current state of growth theory and in the second he is putting his new 'Austrian' theory through its paces. His first love is still a true dynamics. Notice that any complete path, charted for the whole expedition and rigidly adhered to, is subject to the same sort of criticism as the steady state path. The whole thing is known *ab initio* so there can be no surprises; there is perfect foresight. At any one time we are, in practice, unlikely to be able to plan far ahead.

We must not expect that the whole of this large territory will come into sight at once. I believe that the route we shall pursue is such that it will bring most (if not all) in the end into sight (*Capital and Growth*, p. 76).

The far future is vastly uncertain: it is the near future for which we are always really planning. For the determination of these first steps (even if we are to consider them as an approach to the Turnpike) consideration of the properties of the Turnpike is not much guide (*Capital and Growth*, p. 237).

I am very sceptical of the importance of such 'steady state' theory. The real world (perhaps fortunately) is not, and never is, in a steady state; it has adventures which are much more interesting (*Essays*, iii. 8).

And, even if there are steady paths, something is bound to happen to make us change our plan — a detour to catch a magnificent view, a shortage of rations, a storm, or whatever. While, for some stretches, we would expect to regain a steady path, 'there must always be a problem of traverse', ('IS–LM: an Explanation'). So, parts of *Capital and Growth* and much of *Capital and Time* were devoted to analysing the traverse, under alternative assumptions.

Is it possible (or how is it possible) for the economy to get into the new equilibrium, which is appropriate to the new conditions? We do not greatly diminish the generality of our study of disequilibrium if we regard it in this way, as a Traverse from one path to another (*Capital and Growth*, p. 184).

The whole of Part 2 of *Capital and Time* is devoted to the traverse. 'We should begin with an economy which is in a steady state, and should proceed to trace out the path which will be followed when the steady state is subjected to some kind of disturbance: ... such a path must have a finite time-reference' (p. 81). Two sorts of path are analysed closely, a full employment path, and a fixwage path. The disturbance is technical change and the traverse takes a long time to bring us back to the new steady path. Even then the device is a simplification. For in real life a fresh disturbance will occur while the traverse is working itself out so even the new steady path will no longer be appropriate. Having completed his traverse for the 'simple profile', Hicks sees various ways ahead.

From the point now reached, several roads open out, several of which look like being worth exploring. I shall do no more than take a few steps on some of them (p. 135).

A particularly interesting road is opened up once technical change is super-imposed upon a (pessimistic) Malthusian Dismal path; since it is 'only to be used as a reference path, we need not worry about its end — in a Malthusian Apocalypse' (*Capital and Time*, p. 148). The mountaineering analogy, rough though it is, brings out very well that our inability to plan depends upon uncertainty, its nature and degree. It also warns us not to overdo our healthy mistrust of steady states or (their equivalent) perfect foresight; for there are very few mountains that fail to offer some sort of steady path at least part of the way up; we know roughly the direction in which we want to go and have some idea of when (with luck) we shall get there. To allow more uncertainty than Hicks does takes us dangerously near to an inch by inch scramble over the scree, avoiding any sort of path whatsoever.

5

So far I have avoided the question of what constitutes 'progress'. It must have something to do with gaining height and moving in the right direction. But it has also to do with views and perspectives. Writing on what he regarded as Keynes's odd methodology Hicks remarks that 'we shall be able to walk around these disturbing considerations, surveying them from several points of view and making up our minds about them' (*Value and Capital*, p. 4). On the central massif of capital theory he writes: 'it is as if one were making pictures of a building; though it is the same building, it looks quite different from different angles. As I now realise I have been walking around my subject, taking different views of it' (*Capital and Time*, preface). On the early sections of *Value and Capital* he recalls 'taking step after step along a road which seemed pre-ordained as soon as one had taken the first step ... The vistas that opened up were in their way exciting' (*Perspectives*, pp. v, vi). In a review of Scitovsky he remarked that 'it is no criticism of the guide who has helped us over the brow of the hill that he has not yet also led us into the more fertile country which lies ahead' (*Essays*, iii, 11). Thus, for Hicks, the view is not merely a luxury, it is of use, for the task is to understand the whole of the mountain range, not just to climb single peaks.

General equilibrium theory offers, *par excellence*, the possibility, but only the possibility, of perspective. It cannot yield up its perspectives as long as it remains a barren system of formal questions. The guide has to explain how everything hangs together; the nature of the watersheds, the stream courses in wet and dry conditions, the relationship between forestry and animal husbandry, the location of old mineral workings, the stability of the glacier and so on. Hicks laboured in monetary and wage theory (and even in the building industry) before attempting his general equilibrium synopsis. He knew the terrain and was able to make sense of it.

Height is a *sine qua non*, for without it there can be no progress and no improvements in the view. Though it has to do with progress it is not, however, the only measure of progress and Hicks, like all good explorers, takes with him scientific instruments of measurement, some of his own devising. One of them (consumers' surplus) makes use of area and is a measure of gain; it is very useful in deciding whether or not small movements on the surface are worth the costs. It comes in (at least) four subtly different varieties following the much simpler prototype used by Marshall and is closely related to the notion of compensation. Progress clearly has to do with movement in the right direction as well as height and effort, with utility as well as costs.

The analogue of income must be efficient progress along the surface, just as the analogue of capital must be the underlying rock itself. To the beginner the best known of Hicks's practical discussions on measuring income was *The Social Framework*, first published in 1942 and still very widely used (I can testify) in the late 1950s. The appearance of a fourth edition in 1972 and collaborative Japanese and Indian versions in 1974 and 1983 indicate that others have found it useful more recently. The *Value and Capital* discussion of income definition is, of course, standard and was referred to, for example, in the *Meade Report* of 1978. It is matched, on the mountain, by a distinction between progress and sustainable progress. The question of income measurement, particularly its relationship to the theory of index numbers and to the utility–cost duality has long fascinated Hicks. His particular contribution has been theoretical rigour tempered by practical acceptance that rough-and-ready statistical artefacts have to be used. The statistician has to use the cost measure so, argues Hicks, we must see what there is to be said for it (a great deal if we use the opportunity cost rather than the real cost version). Back on the mountain the statistician measures height or distance to chart our progress, but his calculations are unable to reveal how much 'better off' we are at different stages of the expedition or *a fortiori* as between different expeditions: 'the statistical measure of Real Income which we are examining is throughout a simple price-weighted index number of Σ pq type. Our problem is not one of the kind of measure to use, for we have no choice about that: it is a problem of the meaning which we can give to the measures which we have to employ' (*Essays* i, 7).

I have suggested the analogue of mass, for capital. But 'capital' is so all pervasive and so central to Hicks's writings that it cannot be confined within a section simply on measurement. It deserves a discussion of its own. Capital features in the title of three of Hicks's major books and has a (fully justified) reputation for being difficult terrain. One of the controversies surrounding capital (the famous Cambridge controversy) is now an old controversy and not one in which Hicks played a major part; though *Capital and Growth* did contain a discussion of reswitching. On the question of measurement it has been clear, from Walras on, that backward-looking measures (based on historical cost but allowing for depreciation) and forward-looking measures (based on expected receipts) would give the same values in equilibrium. But they do not do so in practice and some sort of compromise becomes inevitable (*Essays*, iii. 9). Another (related) controversial issue is which (if any) concept of capital best fits into the production function. The answer seems to be that if it is not to fit merely tautologically then the backward (or cost) notion is the more relevant. However, this 'backward'-looking idea of capital leads us very strongly in a direction which Hicks was not ready to follow until a revival of his interest in 'Austrian' theory, leading up to *Capital and Time*.

It is here that if our metaphor is to continue to hold at all we shall have to move from the Hicksian week into history. Strictly, it dictates that we move into geological time, but this would be unfortunate. Although a Hicksian week may be a long time in economics (as it was once said to be in politics), it is surely not aeons long? The reason for moving into history is that present capital stock is a mixture of processes based on past impulses for change. Some processes will be new, some not. There are, as it were, a number of geological layers of capital stock. At the surface we are dependent on all of them even though only one or two strata push their way through. In this way, Hicks's theorizing about capital and his theorizing about history come together.

Perhaps it is not entirely surprising that our metaphor begins to crumble in the face of capital theory which provides a severe test of any sort of economic reasoning. Now that it is crumbling it is as well to refer to its other defects of which there are at least two: its ambivalence and its unresponsiveness. It is ambivalent because it seems unable to make up its mind whether it is about progress in economics or economic progress; this is not serious. It is unresponsive (unable to be moved, like rock) because, on the whole, the mountain is totally unaffected by what the climber does. True, there can be avalanches, brought on by noise and human movement and we may cut steps in the ice. But our behaviour makes little difference and this is certainly a defect. For the Hicksian expeditions have had some effect on economics, if not upon economies; the mountain *has* responded.

6

It is clear from the essay on *Industrialism* that the Hicksian impulse which works its way through must (compared with the surface phenomena which we usually analyse) have originated in 'geological' time. At its simplest the impulse comes very close to being the industrial revolution itself. Unless disturbed by further impulses the system eventually converges to a new steady state — Hicks is very sympathetic to classical analysis of the steady state. This approach is a development subsequent to, but not inconsistent with, *A Theory of Economic History*, where, in a flexprice system, the merchant was absolutely essential to economic progress. The impulse ties up economic history not only with the Austrian theory of capital, in which time is of the essence, but also with the Ricardian analysis of machinery. For the various phases in the traverse may be seen to correspond with the temporal sequence in Ricardo's *Principles* where machinery may cause initial unemployment but is sure to generate more employment eventually. If capital theory is the central massif of economics Hicks has approached it from every direction. The impulse is an heroic attempt to bring these approaches together at a high level of generality; with Hicks, economic history is not to be confined to the foothills.

These references to Ricardo and to the Austrians reflect a continuing interest in the notebooks of earlier explorers. Among economists, interest in the history of their subject is, I think, at two levels. At one level (a perfectly respectable level) is the history of economic thought as a specialist area of study, with its textbooks, readings, and so on. At another level the great economic theorist often has some feel for what his predecessors have done. He had read the travelogues, diaries, accounts, and maps of earlier explorers and has absorbed their lessons. When Hicks comes across a difficult ascent or sees a new view it is as though he asks what Ricardo, or Mill or Wicksell or Hawtrey (to give examples) would have made of it. How would they have tackled it? Similarly he asks of their own problems: what were they trying to do; where did they go wrong, was there a better route? There is a sense in which Hicks *works with* some of his illustrious predecessors.

Hicks has never written a systematic treatise on the history of economics, but it is a recurring theme in his work, and there are set pieces in *Collected Essays* iii. The first group of economists to be considered is the one with which Hicks was working at the LSE — Robbins, Hayek, Allen, Sayers, Kaldor, Lerner, Bowley, and Ursula Webb (later Mrs, then Lady, Hicks). Of these Hayek casts the longest shadow. 'The Hayek Story' (*Critical Essays*, pp. 13) combines Hicks's confidential style (already referred to) with his desire to relate others' theories to his own. 'There was some inner mystery to which we failed to penetrate ... something central that was missing'. The key has to be a lag of some sort but 'where is the lag to be found; ... what ... was Hayek's lag?' It turned out to be an (unacceptable) consumption lag, so Hayek's theory could not be about fluctuations, it must be about growth. The fascination with Hayek has been a long and special one. In general the other economists at the LSE had profound technical influences but were essentially taking part in the same theoretical expedition under the encouragement of Robbins.

The second group of economists consists of those whose ascents had a direct effect upon Hicks's early work. Marshall was one of the most remote of these and his routes (old-fashioned though they may be) almost invariably earn respect. Pareto had made brilliant use of contour maps but had lost his way, having been distracted by ideology. Wicksell had, it is true, concentrated on the process of change and had a profound effect on Hicksian monetary theory but was (for Hicks's taste) too much concerned with movement from one steady path to another. Pigou had devised a new measure of progress (an 'income' measure) which Hicks christens the new plutology. He sees the similarities between the *Wealth of Nations* and *Wealth and Welfare* and claims 'a line of descent, from Pigou through (his) own *Theory of Wages* to a great deal of modern growth theory' (*Essays*, 11, 1). Of the other British economists outside of the LSE group the most important direct influences seem to have been Hawtrey, Robertson, and Keynes. Hicks's repeated favourable references to Robertson (e.g. *Essays*, ii. 10) will be perplexing to some; they were earned not just by friendship but by a consistent emphasis on the dynamic aspects of theory. In *Essays* (ii. 31) Hicks mentions, among the other influences upon him, Myrdal, Taussig, Viner, Mises, Schumpeter, Ohlin, and Lindahl. But the greatest though, of course, indirect influence on his greatest book, *Value and Capital*, came from Walras; not on money but certainly on the structure of general equilibrium systems and even (perhaps surprisingly) on capital.

The third group consists simply of the Classics — mainly Ricardo and Mill. I have already noticed how Ricardo's 'machinery' model fits in with Hicks's view of the world, 'It is instructive to think of each invention as setting up what might be called an "impulse" — which, if it were not succeeded by other impulses, would peter out. Ricardo's theory is a theory of the working of the industrial impulse' (*Essays*, iii, 3). Ricardo gets high marks because although his theory is a static one it is rigorously carried through, and attempts to analyse the process of growth in a series of static pictures. Mill, too, gets high marks for his analysis of 'International Trade' and the 'Influence of Consumption on Production' in *Unsettled Questions* and of money and growth in *Principles*. But again, his method was static. So the classics are important because they chose the big questions, the important questions; unlike the catallactists (who had other defects) they are of little help in method.

Finally, there is Keynes, who made a spectacularly successful dash for the summit while Hicks was busy preparing himself for the big haul; indeed he was constructing some of the same climbing aids. There is general agreement I think, that in the weather conditions then prevailing, the Keynesian route was a good one, brilliantly established. But, although well-worn, it is not a safe route in all conditions. Hicks has therefore taken great pains, as one familiar with it, to assess when it may be used without danger and to compare it with other routes. Sometimes the attractions of the short dash may be harmful to the long-run success of the expedition (*The Crisis in Keynesian Economics*).

7

Early in *Value and Capital* Hicks distinguished between the study of theory and the study of institutions (via history). 'It is only when both these tasks are accomplished that economics begins to near the end of its journey' (*Value and Capital*, p. 7). On this journey Hicks is an excellent guide and protects us (even if he teases us a little) from the greatest dangers. 'The trap is in fact not one that it was at all easy to suspect; it would therefore seem that it needs to have a signpost upon it, lest others fall into it also' (*Essays*, iii. 20). Hicks is that very rare guide who not only knows his mountain craft but is enthusiastic and imaginative. He offers no 'ism'. Because he is so accomplished a theoretician, it is not always appreciated how deeply sceptical he is about so many of the features of mainstream economics; econometrics (for Hicks econometricians are econometrists), theory for the sake of theory, positivism, and the scientific status of the subject. Circumstances change. A theory appropriate to one set of circumstances will not be appropriate to another (indeed, in *Critical Essays* Hicks notes that surges in monetary theory are generated by monetary crises); our theories must be devised to explain current and recent facts. 'There is, there can be, no economic theory which will do for us everything we want all the time' (*Essays*, iii. 1). It is not so much that we make progress; merely that different things engage our attention. Even the discarded theories that litter our route may be pressed into service once again. How important it is, then, to be in the hands of a first-class guide with an open and receptive mind; one who is 'too Open to be an Austrian; for I am an Open

Marshallian, and Ricardian and Keynesian, perhaps even Lausannian, as well' (*Essays*, iii. 9). In this sense we should all try to be Hicksian.

Works by Hicks cited in the text

The Theory of Wages (Macmillan, 1932).
'A Suggestion for Simplifying the Theory of Money', *Economica* (1935). Reprinted in *Collected Essays*, vol. ii.
Value and Capital (Clarendon Press, 1939).
The Social Framework; An Introduction to Economics (Clarendon Press, 1942).
A Contribution to the Theory of the Trade Cycle (Clarendon Press, 1950).
A Revision of Demand Theory (Clarendon Press, 1956).
Essays in World Economics (Clarendon Press, 1959).
Capital and Growth (Clarendon Press, 1965).
Critical Essays in Monetary Theory (Clarendon Press, 1967), including 'The Hayek Story' and 'The Pure Theory of Portfolio Selection' (Clarendon Press, 1967).
A Theory of Economic History (Clarendon Press, 1969).
Capital and Time (Clarendon Press, 1973).
'Industrialism', *International Affairs* (1974).
The Crisis in Keynesian Economics (Blackwell, 1974).
Economic Perspectives (Clarendon Press, 1977).
Causality in Economics (Blackwell, 1979).
Wealth and Welfare; Collected Essays on Economic Theory i (Blackwell, 1981).
Money, Interest and Wages: Collected Essays on Economic Theory, ii (Blackwell, 1982).
Classics and Moderns: Collected Essays on Economic Theory, iii (Blackwell, 1983).

Notes

*I am grateful to Walter Eltis, Dieter Helm and Amartya Sen for comments on an earlier draft.
1. A. Deaton and J. Muellbauer. *Economics and Consumer Behaviour*, (CUP, 1980).
2. P.R.G. Layard and A.A. Walters, *Microeconomic Theory* (McGraw-Hill, 1978).

81

Mr Hicks and the Classics*†

R.M. Solow

I am grateful to everyone who has come here today to do honour to John Hicks. My gratitude is, however, tempered by the realization that you are all thinking to yourselves how nice it is that you are sitting down there while I am standing up here. You are right. This is indeed a terrifying experience. The realization came too late that giving the first Hicks Lecture with John Hicks sitting here is a little like contracting to give a talk on how to paint water lilies, and then suddenly remembering that Claude Monet will be in the audience.

I promised myself at the very beginning that I would not take this lecture as the occasion for an hour-long encomium on John Hicks. In fact, as you will see, I intend to dissent mildly but firmly from some of Sir John's mature reflections. I shall speak up in defence of one of his targets, a young man whom I shall call J.R. (The J.R. I have in mind is not named Ewing.)

But before I come to that, I have to take account of the fact that there are many economists here who are much younger than I, to whom John Hicks is merely a Presence, a Great Name, a Past Master. I come from precisely the generation of economists to whom, in their student days, *Value and Capital* was more than a breath of fresh air. It was the very air itself. It was what made economic theory seem at last to be a subject with depth and rigour. I had my first course in economics as a freshman at Harvard College in 1940. I can still remember the outside of the three textbooks we read, all written by pillars of the profession. But I can no longer remember the inside of any of them. They were dull; they were anecdotal. There did not seem to be any bony structure underneath the flesh. I remember being bored and unhappy. Between 1942 and 1945 I found other things to do; and in 1945 Wassily Leontief gave us *Value and Capital* to read. All of a sudden economics seemed to be a subject worth studying for its own sake, for its intrinsic intellectual interest, and not merely because the 1930s were still a living memory. *Value and Capital*, the *General Theory*, and Paul Samuelson's *Foundations of Economic Analysis*, were the books that formed the way my friends and I thought about economics. I hate to say this, but I think most of you in this room would be better off if you had had the same experience.

†Source: *Oxford Economic Papers*, Vol. 36, Supplement, November 1984, pp. 13–25.

With the publication of *Value and Capital* in 1939 John Hicks had already written three works, two articles and a book, whose influence can clearly be seen even today, almost fifty years later, in the daily practice of economics. The two articles were, of course, 'A Suggestion for Simplifying the Theory of Money' in 1935 and 'Mr Keynes and the Classics' published in 1937 but written for an Econometric Society conference that took place in September 1936, here in Oxford. (Can you imagine writing a paper in September 1936 and seeing it in print in *Econometrica* in April 1937?) In fact, it is that one, the origin, as everyone knows, of the IS–LM model, that gave me both the title and the subject of this lecture. When I speak of J.R., I mean the author of that article.

Let me get one thing out of the way at once. I am not at all concerned with the question as to whether the IS–LM model fairly represents Keynes, in whole or even in part. No more do I care on this occasion who were the classics and what they thought. I take the firm view that what we loosely call 'Keynesian economics' is a collective product. The analogies I have in mind are Newtonian mechanics and the Darwinian theory of evolution. You ask of a piece of evolutionary biology whether it is right, or useful, or interesting, not whether it copies or contradicts a passage of *The Origin of Species*. To a large extent the IS–LM model for almost fifty years has *been* Keynesian economics, though only a part of Keynesian economics it is fair to say. More recently the IS–LM model has come under attack. One of those who have criticized it is the personage I shall refer to as Sir John. On the whole, I propose to take J.R.'s side.

A Methodological Standpoint

It suits my argument to start with some general — even methodological — considerations that seem to me very important, and not only in this particular context. They have to do with one's attitude toward economic theory itself. James Tobin once described the IS–LM apparatus as 'the trained intuition of many of us'. That seems exactly right to me. You will have to speak for yourself. If I pick up the morning paper and read that the US Congress may soon pass a package of tax and expenditure measures intended to reduce the Federal deficit by $180 billion over the next three years, I know that my mind naturally draws IS and LM curves and shifts them. The same thing happens whenever I try to interpret routine macro-economic events in an underemployed economy. It goes without saying that some questions force you well beyond the scope of the IS–LM apparatus right away. Almost any serious question will do that if you push its ramifications far enough. Tobin only described this two-equation model as the basis for our trained intuition, not as the complete system of the world.

Why was it precisely J.R.'s paper that wormed its way into our imaginations and our intuitions? At that very same meeting of the Econometric Society in Oxford in September 1936, there were three papers that tried to extract a model from the *General Theory*, not just one. Roy Harrod's was published before J.R.'s, in the January issue of *Econometrica*, and James Meade's appeared shortly afterward in the detailed Report of the Oxford meeting. It is not too far-fetched to say that the same basic equations could be detected in all three versions. At some celestial level of abstraction, they could be described as identical products. But it was the IS–LM model that established itself as our trained intuition. What — since I have mentioned Darwin — was the source of its survival value?

If economics were really a science — in the aggressive sense — as most modern ecnomists think it is, then there would be little or nothing to choose among alternative models so long as one way or another they contain the same equations, and thus have the same implications. Either there would be nothing to choose, or else we would choose on fundamentally trivial grounds. But suppose economics is not a complete science in that sense, and maybe even has very little prospect of becoming one. Suppose all it can do is help us to organize our necessarily incomplete perceptions about the economy, to see connections the untutored eye would miss, to tell plausible stories with the help of a few central principles. Suppose, in other words, that economics is 'a discipline, not a science'. Those are Sir John's words, actually, although he used them to express a different, but only slightly different, thought. In that case what we want a piece of economic theory to do is precisely to train our intuition, to give us a handle on the facts in the inelegant American phrase.

IS–LM survived because it proved to be a marvellously simple and useful way to organize and process some of the main macroeconomic facts. I think J.R. saw it that way too. 'We have invented a little apparatus' he says, and proceeds to 'give it a little run on its own'. That is the spirit in which I want to consider it, and to defend it.

I hope no one will fall into the error of thinking that this low-key view of the nature of economics is a licence for loose thinking. Logical rigour is exactly as important in this scheme of things as it is in the more self-consciously scientific one. The difference is not in the standards of model-building but in the scope and ambitions of model-building. Nor should I have to explain — but I will — that a framework like IS–LM is a container whose contents can evolve. There is always research to be done to refine our understanding of the basic components and the forces that shift them. The answer to old questions changes as economic and social institutions evolve; and new questions appear, partly for the same reason and partly as the counterpart of historical accidents. It is certainly possible — and here the analogy with Newton and Darwin breaks down — that historical change may cause Keynesian or Hicksian economics or the IS–LM model to become obsolete, no longer fit training for our intuitions. My argument is only that it has not happened yet.

When Sir John came to reconsider J.R.'s handiwork some five years ago, he was not entirely hostile to it. But he did suggest that the original construction had some pretty fundamental problems to get over; and the reader comes away with the feeling that Sir John is at best mildly optimistic that the repairs can be done and not especially regretful if they can not. Others, especially Axel Leijonhufvud, who never had much sympathy with

IS–LM — as Sir John may once in his youth have done — have made some of the same criticisms and added others. (I am leaving out of the picture those whose main source of dissatisfaction with J.R.'s little apparatus is that it is not about Chapter 12 of the *General Theory.* My answer to them is: No, it's not.) I want to discuss four of those zones of weakness that have attracted unfriendly fire: the fix-price assumption, the treatment of expectations, the stock-flow problem, and — in order to meet Leijonhufvud head on — the 'informational' presumptions. It seems to me that there are interconnections among all of them.

Prices and Wages

J.R. was explicitly assuming the IS and LM curves to refer to a unit period within which the nominal wage could be taken as fixed. That does not mean that he believed the nominal wage to be a constant of nature. Hardly anyone could have believed that in 1936. In fact he remarks that most economists of the time had 'a pretty fair idea of what the relation between money wages and employment actually was'. It does mean that J.R. thought it would be a mistake to rely on endogenous wage movements within the period (a year, say) to govern the level of employment. It is not so clear what he was assuming about the price level for goods. Forty-odd years later, Sir John seems to take it for granted that J.R. was assuming that to be fixed too, and goes on to verify that the appropriate version of Walras's Law holds even if the interest rate is the only flexible price in the model. The reason he gives for this presumption — that nominal output is used as an index of real output and employment — is not convincing to me. It would be enough for that purpose if real output were an increasing function of nominal output; proportionality is not necessary.

By itself there does not appear to be much at stake here. For the 'many of us' whose trained intuition is represented by IS–LM, I think the common presumption has been that the price level should or could be taken to be equal to (or more or less proportional to) the marginal cost of output, and therefore rising (relative to the wage) as output and employment rise, at least to the extent that there are short-run diminishing returns to labour. One of the uses of this presumption is that it reinforces the tendency of the LM curve to be relatively flat at low levels of output, when marginal cost is likely to be flat, and to be very steep at high levels of output, when marginal cost is likely to be steep. But the story can equally well be told as if the price level were given too, so that firms as well as workers are 'off their supply curves'. The stylized facts suggest that a more complicated story is needed than either of these.

Obviously this is not a suitable way to model an inflationary economy. (It is curious that the deflation of wages and prices in the 1930s did not leave much of an impression on J.R., or on other theorists of the time. Maybe the explanation is that the deflation was over by 1936 and was regarded as an episode, not as the harbinger of a 'deflationary economy'.) The apparatus is clearly designed to deal with an economy in which *either* the wage and price levels undergo only fairly small and fairly irregular movements *or* there is more substantial, sustained, presumably anticipated, inflation but its behavioural consequences can be taken into account simply by modifying the underlying expenditure and asset-preference functions. When the macro-economic problem is dominated by partial adjustment to inflation and its aggregative and distributional consequences, IS–LM is not the right model, or is only a part of the right model.

Let me get back to the major issue: J.R.'s assumption that the money wage is given for the market period to which IS–LM applies. At an intermediate date — I am thinking of 'The Classics Again', written in 1957 — someone I suppose I could call Professor H. remarked that the IS–LM diagram had 'laid excessive weight on the assumption of fixed money wages'. Well, that is a complicated question. There is one point about inflation: where it is relevant we must either modify IS–LM or supplement it or worse. I do not think that consideration is really decisive. The degree of wage flexibility one needs to allow for will also depend on the time one is allowing for adjustment, on the 'length of the run'. I have already accepted Sir John's estimate that we are talking about a year (by which I mean not a month and not a decade). Barring rapid inflation, I doubt that it violates common observation to suggest that in fact wage rates do not respond very flexibly to economic events on a time-scale less than a year. Most collective-bargaining contracts last for a year or more. Even where trade unions are not much of a factor, there are obvious reasons why employers should not try to alter wage rates frequently in response to every moderate change in the economic environment.

Then there is a deeper point. For many purposes it is convenient to carry on this sort of discussion in nominal terms. It is the nominal wage that forms the object of explicit or implicit bargaining. But economic agents, we like to believe, react to real wages and real costs. Whatever the case with nominal wages, there is ample evidence that real wages have no strong endogenous pattern in modern industrial economies. (Some econometricians find real wage rates to be pro-cyclical; some find them to be anti-cyclical. All find the correlation to be small. A reasonable person would stand with my first statement.) One has to be careful about the LM-curve in this story, but that ought not to be too complicated either for the Central Bank or the economist–observer. Once again, labour-market adjustments do not seem to undermine the IS–LM story.

Professor H. in 1957 backtracked a little after his first negative remark about wage-rigidity. He judged that endogenous wage movements might be important at very low and at very high levels of employment, but that in between there might well be a zone where the assumptions of given wage rates — even given nominal wage rates — might be entirely reasonable. J.R. could live with that.

The truth is, I fear, that the profession's disdain for the fix-wage assumption is much less respectable in origin. We have a sort of prior disposition to think that prices equate supply and demand. To say that a price does not do so under ordinary circumstances is seen as too crude, like eating peas with a knife. The accepted putdown is that the assumption of wage-rigidity is *ad hoc*. Perhaps it is, but if the *hoc* it is *ad* is the economy we live in, then there must be worse sins. In that kind of world, the assumption of flexible market-clearing does not even have the merit of being *ad hoc*. If the function of macroeconomic theory is to train our intuitions, J.R.'s path seems like the right one. It will certainly not do for the intuition to react like a society dowager: if that is the sort of economy we have, let us not invite it to tea.

There is an intellectually respectable way out. In all of this discussion the tendency is to personify the wage: *it* moves or *it* does not. But in fact wages are set; they do not just happen. Sir John, in his commentary, is rightly insistent that IS–LM is an equilibrium conception. The trained intuition writes: Supply = Demand. That is an excessively narrow notion of equilibrium. What we really mean by equilibrium in the labour market is a set of wage and employment conventions that no party to the transaction feels impelled to take direct action to change. Price-mediated market-clearing is one concept of equilibrium, but only one and an extreme one at that. As soon as we begin to consider other equilibrium concepts having to do with contracts, bargaining, conventions about eligible strategies, arbitration schemes and all that, the range of possibilities is tremendously enlarged. It is not at all unlikely that convincing stories can be found that will make excellent equilibrium sense of a labour market that converts real shocks (at least) into magnified and sustained fluctuations in output and employment. Primitive examples already exist. J.R. could not have been expected to think in these terms. It is entertaining to see how the modern theory of implicit contracts instinctively starts by finding its way unerringly to those assumptions that make a contract economy just like a spot-market economy. We will outgrow that. Meanwhile I suggest that we practise thinking of the IS curve not as a locus along which 'the goods market clears' but as a locus along which the 'wage–employment bargain is an equilibrium given a goods–market outcome that is an equilibrium given the wage–employment bargain'. Practice makes perfect.

Expectations

I turn now briefly to expectations. J.R. had almost nothing to say about expectations. (One remark he did make in passing is a blockbuster, but I will come to that later.) Presumably he took it for granted that in a short-run model the state of expectations could safely be treated as exogenous. Sir John, of course, is much more sensitive to this set of issues.

There is a minor problem and a major problem. The minor problem is the investment component of effective demand. J.R. wrote the demand for investment as a function for the level of output and the interest rate. Every teacher of macroeconomics has had to squirm a bit and explain to students more or less apologetically that this is altogether too simple. 'The interest rate' has to do duty for a whole complex of credit conditions and other determinants of the cost of capital. And investment decisions, being necessarily forward-looking, cannot be reduced to a mere reflex of current output. Expected sales or expected profitability over the lifetime of durable equipment is what we really want. The teacher then goes on to suggest that current output may be a fair indicator of the current state of business expectations, and anyway we will take up more detailed theories of investment next week. For a static model, this may be the best we can do. Sir John says much the same thing.

There is an intermediate step one can take that gives the intuition something to hang on to, without completely overloading the static model. Introduce a separate variable to be thought of as 'expected output', some sort of one-dimensional surrogate for future sales prospects. The demand for investment goods can be written as a function of 'expected output' *and* current output, as well as the interest rate. (I suppose the existing stock of capital goods belongs in there too, because otherwise the partial derivative of investment with respect to current output might have to be negative. One comes close this way to a form of the capital–stock adjustment principle.) Then there is a family of IS curves indexed by the state of expectations (relative to the current stock of capital). That seems reasonable, and simple enough to be useful. To take the next step and endogenize the formation of expectations, at least partially, is probably an inevitable ambition. It will take us well beyond IS–LM and into models that are essentially sequential. One simply has to admit that J.R.'s little biplane will not fly that high. It has not yet been shown that any machine we can build will fly that high, but there is always an Icarus waiting to try.

I call that a minor problem about expectations. The major problem posed by Sir John has to do with the LM curve. J.R. has smuggled a stock into what is otherwise a flow model, and not just any old stock, but a stock of money. If the model is an equilibrium construction with a unit period about a year in length, then the intersection of IS and LM must be describing a situation in which the flows of income and expenditure are in equilibrium during the year, so that at most intended inventory accumulation takes place. But the LM curve represents a stock relation, something that must hold, if it holds at all, at a point in time. The natural counterpart to flow equilibrium throughout the period is stock equilibrium at every instant during this period. Expectations, then, at least the expectations that bear on asset demands, must be confirmed throughout the period. That, says Sir John, is a peculiar foundation on which to build a theory that turns on liquidity preference. The very existence of a demand for money as liquid asset presupposes that expectations may be unfulfilled. The expectations in question cannot be point expectations, because we have just seen that point expectations must be confirmed during the period. Then, in a passage that I confess I do not understand, Sir John rejects the option of formalizing the relevant expectations as ordinary probabilistic expectations. He settles, tentatively and uncomfortably, for the very special notion that those expectations relevant to asset demands take the form of a simple range. They are therefore confirmed if observed values fall within the anticipated range. But the instant-by-instant confirmation of such expectations does not eliminate all uncertainty, so the basis for liquidity preference remains.

I think, or at least I think I think, that there are several different mysteries getting in one another's way here. One is the difficulty we always seem to have in integrating stocks and flows. A second is the difficulty we always have in fitting money into equilibrium models. A third is the difficulty that some of us always have in handling stochastic equilibria — the difficulty, namely, that the usual probabilistic formulation seems to make too small a concession, i.e. no concession at all, to 'truc' uncertainty. Perhaps this last is what Sir John meant in the passage I said a moment ago I did not understand. If we are willing to accept the now standard sort of stationary expectational equilibrium, I do not see why it is not applicable here. I sympathize with anyone who is not willing to accept it, but I have no constructive help to offer. Anyway, none of these difficulties is peculiar to IS–LM. The only one I want to say more about is the first, the general problem of stocks and flows.

Stocks and Flows

The broad issue of integrating stocks and flows merges seamlessly into even broader questions about the strategy of macroeconomic modelling. One extreme approach is to make the unit period vanishingly short, to treat time as continuous in other words. The flow relations determine true rates of flow at an instant. The flow equations have the stocks, measured at the same instant, as parameters. Some of the flows thus determined are rates of change — time derivatives — of the stocks that appear in the model. 'Integration' is the *mot juste* for this sort of model. Stock–flow questions are submerged in existence theorems for solutions of differential equations. There are some circumstances in which this is the right way to proceed: when the focus of attention is on long-run equilibrium, the mutual adjustment of stocks to one another in a stationary or steady state. For instance, the work that Alan Blinder and I did some years ago had explicitly this orientation. We made use of a travelling IS–LM system as the instantaneous part of a model whose real object was to study stock equilibrium. The question was precisely whether these stock equilibrium considerations necessarily upset the intuitions fostered by IS–LM. The substantive analysis has since been much improved by others. But the integration of stocks and flows did not seem problematical in that setting.

Sir John would not be happy to stop here, and neither should I. The Blinder–Solow device is not merely technical. It enforces a commitment with economic content: that the IS–LM mechanism works itself out instantaneously, with the economy being at every instant at the intersection of continuously shifting IS and LM curves. This may be suitable for long-run analysis, but it will not do for someone who cares about the short run, and therefore about the IS–LM outcome itself. Then the interplay between short run and long run, between stocks and flows, becomes complicated, and choices have to be made. The early chapters of *Capital and Growth* contain a careful study of this problem. There Sir John points out that one reasonable definition of flow equilibrium entails that if stock disequilibrium rules at the beginning of the short period it will rule throughout the short period. Of course it is also possible that initial stock equilibrium will be upset by the flow developments within the period. There would be something awkward and implausible about a theory which had stock equilibrium being restored, with a jerk, 'between' periods. But if stock equilibrium is allowed to persist for several periods, the basic data that underlie successive short-period solutions begin to crumble. Some economists may be willing to make strong asumptions about expectations — one or another version of rational expectations, for example, but no doubt other devices would do — to bridge this gap. I have the impression that neither J.R. nor Sir John is among them, and neither am I.

I want only to make a pragmatic point that bears on the usefulness of IS–LM. I think it is unnecessary to make an issue of principle out of stocks-and-flows. All modelling runs into trouble when it has to cope with two or more processes that work themselves out at drastically different speeds, a fast process and a slow process, say. When Bach manages it in a suite for unaccompanied cello, it seems like a miracle. Even on the mechanical level, the representation of such systems is messy; and my experience is that on the conceptual level as well the synchronization of short-run and long-run processes is naggingly obscure. One makeshift that economists — and others — sometimes employ is to alternate. One lets the fast process converge while the variables of the slow process stand still at their initial values. (This is exactly Keynes's procedure, of course; ignore capital accumulation even though net investment is non-zero.) Then one stops the fast process for a moment and lets the slow process take a step, just one step, driven by the outcome of the fast process. Now the slow process is frozen again in its new state and the fast process is allowed to converge once more. And so on. I do not want to make this sound easy. The substantive question is the nature of the interaction of the two processes. This is where expectations come in. That part of the problem has economic content. The timing and meshing is often just a matter of making do with whatever analytical techniques are at hand. Tobin has given an excellent example of the pragmatic approach in *Asset Accumulation and Economic Activity*. Apart from the proliferation of assets, his model is very much like IS–LM. Growth theory should ideally be carried on this way too. What I have been describing is very much like what Sir John calls traverse. That is the easiest part of skiiing, but the hardest part of economics.

I would not want to be misunderstood as meaning that stock–flow problems are easy or unimportant or merely matters of finding some catch-as-catch-can technique. It is genuinely hard to analyse interacting fast and slow processes intelligibly; and it can be very hard for the monetary authorities, say, to manage an economy with interacting fast and slow processes. They will have to worry, for instance, whether exploiting the short-run real effects of monetary injection will damage their capacity to control slower price-level effects. That is a fact of life, not of modelling. My point is that the modelling problem is substantive, not philosophical.

'Information' and All That

Finally, I want to take a few minutes to defend IS–LM against a quite different antagonist, Axel Leijonhufvud. My original plan was to keep to the dialogue between J.R. and Sir John, a sort of family affair. My reason for widening the net is mainly that doing so gives me an opportunity to make one or two general points in defence of the modelling tradition in which IS–LM is at home, and against a contemporary tendency to shift the emphasis from market failure to 'information' failure.

I do not want to give the impression that I am hostile to all of Leijonhufvud's thoughts on this subject, root and branch. On the contrary, I think some of the ideas expressed in 'The Wicksell Connection' and in 'What Was the Matter with IS–LM?' are quite wholesome, and would probably have met with J.R.'s approval. Let me give an example, so it will be clear that I am not merely being polite. Leijonhufvud argues emphatically that it is both wrong and unhistorical to lay all the blame for prolonged unemployment on wage rigidity, real or nominal. All that talk about Saving and Investment must have been somehow relevant to macroeconomics. Leijonhufvud maintains that the key to — I do not know if he would settle for 'another key to' — the theory of economic fluctuations is a failure of the interest-rate mechanism. Suppose that the typical macroeconomic shock is a change in the perceived profitability of future investment. A smoothly functioning market economy would adapt to that contingency by shifting resources to the production of, and shifting expenditure flows to the purchase of, consumer goods. When it does not do so, there is trouble. In 'The Wicksell Connection' Leijonhufvud describes — rather sketchily — his own favourite way of analyzing that sort of problem, but there is no need to discuss it now.

J.R. would probably have been glad to agree about the importance of the interest-mechanism. Professor H., in 'The Classics Again', is quite explicit on that score: '...There are conditions in which the price-mechanism will not work — more specifically ... there are conditions in which the interest-mechanism will not work'. In 1936, J.R. put a lot of emphasis on the liquidity-trap case, when the long term interest rate has reached its practical floor. Twenty years later, Professor H. was at pains to go further. There are other possible malfunctions in the interest–investment mechanism. Today, of course, we are all aware that a developed system of financial intermediaries undermines the independence of the IS and LM curves and makes the whole analysis more complicated. This part of Leijonhufvud's argument has a lot to recommend it. Especially recast in terms of the broader equilibrium concept I was urging earlier, I think it has a place in anybody's trained intuition.

The more characteristic aspect of Leijonhufvud's argument against IS–LM is what I find unacceptable. It traces the difference between IS–LM and other (monetarist or 'new classical') models to different assumptions about the diffusion of knowledge, about 'who knows what'. I find emphasis misleading.

Leijonhufvud begins by setting up a benchmark that he calls 'full-information macroeconomics'. It need not correspond to complete certainty, but 'in a full-information state, agents have learned all that can (profitably) be learned about their environment and about each other's behaviour'. In effect, this benchmark state is a kind of (more or less Walrasian) growth equilibrium. The real point is that there are no un-exploited opportunities for *ex ante* mutually advantageous trades. That being so, macroeconomic malfunctions — at least those that do not, like price rigidities, suggest that the economy is kept from efficiency by *force majeure* — can usually be traced to some 'information failure', something that keeps agents from knowing about mutually advantageous adjustments they could make. Alternative macroeconomic models, therefore, are most fruitfully distinguished by their informational assumptions. The trouble with IS–LM is that it has nothing to say about — and in fact hides — the process by which the diffusion of information moves a malfunctioning economy back toward full-information equilibrium. This process inevitably involves shifts in both IS and LM, and that is the main reason why they are inferior tools, undependable guides to the intuition.

My response — I say mine because I do not know how this argument would have struck J.R. — is that the emphasis on information is seriously misleading. ('Co-ordination' is another matter entirely.) It suggests that there is something knowable that, if known, would forestall macroeconomic malfunction. I suppose it would follow that macroeconomic policy could usefully be restricted to the production and dissemination of the missing information. The trouble with this line of argument, I think, is that it funda-mentally overworks the concept of 'information'. One could equally say that the Second World War was an example of information failure: if Hitler had known what was going to happen, he would never have invaded Russia, perhaps not even Poland. If Caesar had known what was going to happen, he would not have crossed the Rubicon, or would he?

The point is not merely that the information in question is complex and ill-formed, nor even that it would have to include information about the behaviour of others, including things they do not know about themselves. My objection is deeper. This opaqueness of economic events is not a misadventure of the economic system; it is an intrinsic characteristic of a decentralized market economy, dependent on market signals — prices and quantities — for the direction of individual behaviour.

There is an enlightening difference of approach to be pointed out here. Modern monetarists like to start with a purely nominal disturbance — the famous helicopter drop of money — as the archetypical shock to the eco-nomy. I think that is because the purely nominal shock is the one instance where the claim might plausibly be made that if only everyone knew what was going on the economy could go to its new equilibrium — a pro-portional increase in all nominal prices, with no real change at all — with little or no disturbance. Leijonhufvud is rightly scornful. His choice for the archetypical shock is the one I mentioned earlier: an unforeseen shift in the expected profitability of future investment. But that should alert him to the pointlessness of describing ignorance about the consequences as an infor-mation failure. No one could *possibly* know what the new equilibrium would look like after the discovery of electricity. It is a bit like describing an airplane crash as a gravitational failure.

To the extent that the economy tends to return to its equilibrium path after being shocked away from it, the diffusion of information, in the ordinary sense, does not seem to describe and control the process. To my eye, it is much more nearly a matter of the resolution of intrinsic uncertainty, the unwinding of explicit and implicit contracts, and the frictions of imperfect markets. Besides, here and now, in the fifth year of a deep recession (one that the trained intuition finds it perfectly natural to analyse in the IS–LM framework) after only the early stages of recovery and with a long way to go to reach the trend, one is not much impressed by the speed and power of the economy's automatic return to growth equilibrium.

Conclusion

I have been so busy defending J.R.'s construction against slings and arrows that I may have given the impression of mere piety. That is not what I intend. In passing, I have mentioned two developments that do seem to surpass the capacity of so simple a model to comprehend: one is the behaviour of a strongly inflationary economy and the other is the operation of a system of financial intermediaries that tends to link IS and LM together. For reasons of time and space I have not even mentioned a third: the predominance of open-economy forces in many circumstances. (By the way, now I want to mention J.R.'s startling remark on expectations referred to earlier: 'There may be other conditions when expectations are tinder, when a slight inflationary tendency lights them up very easily.' In 1936, remember.)

There is yet another problem with IS–LM that I must acknowledge. Just because the apparatus is so simple, it lends itself to the arithmetization of macroeconomic theory. There is a tendency for even generally subtle people to treat it not merely as a guide to the intuition but as a substitute for intuition, and for more extended and deeper theory. That is undoubtedly a bad thing; and it may be for that reason that Sir John has taken such a jaundiced view.

It would be terribly subversive of macroeconomic theory if a two-equation model could sum up most of what we need to know. There is no serious danger of that. Nevertheless it is remarkable that a simple system like IS–LM has served us so long and so well. There are other examples: Mendel's Laws, the elasticity of demand, the Blackwood Convention, the wheel. The story speaks well both for J.R.'s inspiration, and also for the view of macroeconomic theory not as a branch of physics but as a sort of Blue Guide that points out right directions, rough distances, and excellent places to stop, study the landscape, and enjoy the view.

When I was a small child, probably about the time the *Theory of Wages* was being written, I read a little vignette that has stuck in my memory ever since. A woman against whom Philip of Macedon had given his verdict after drinking more than he ought, declared forthwith : 'I appeal against the decision.' 'To *whom* do you appeal?' thundered the King. 'I appeal from King Philip drunk to King Philip sober' was the reply, and the King, seeing the point, reversed himself. I cannot imagine Sir John in any state other than sober, but nevertheless I appeal to him to look with more kindness on this offering from his youthful servant J.R. and from J.R.'s ageing emissary.

Note

*The first annual Hicks Lecture, delivered in Oxford on 3 May 1984.

Hicks on Time and Money†

A. Leijonhufvud

Modern macroeconomic theory has been shaped to an extraordinary degree by Keynes and by Hicks. My assignment was to discuss them both, but I have found it too large for a paper. I will confine my discussion of Hicks' role to two related themes: Time and Money.

Even within these boundaries, the following attempt at an interpretation cannot be definitive.[1] Among the several reasons for this, one is germane: I know that I shall learn more from Sir John Hicks in the future. But I cannot know exactly what I shall learn next time I sit down to read or re-read him. Hence today's assessment cannot be my 'optimal' or final one. Rather than commit myself fully, I should retain a measure of 'flexibility'.[2]

In certain types of situations, it is rational to commit oneself fully or contingently. In others, where the future contingencies cannot be enumerated or their nature anticipated, one should retain flexibility. One difference between neo-classical and Keynesian theory is that the former tends to exclude, whereas the latter must include, situations of the second sort.[3] The younger Hicks is remembered for his contributions to neo-classical economics; over the years the elder Hicks has become more insistently Keynesian in this particular sense.

Time and Equilibrium

'Every economist is familiar with the accomplishments of Hicks the Younger, whether he has read him or not. That brilliant young man was supremely successful — by reformulating utility theory, by simplifying monetary theory, by interpreting Keynes and the Classics, and by reviving general equilibrium theory — in constructing the moulds into which 40 years of subsequent theoretical developments were to be cast'.[4] It is helpful to try to see the young Hicks in historical context.

What went on at the London School in the early thirties appears in retrospect almost as important as what was going on in Cambridge. At LSE, the world of Anglo-American economics was being won over from

---

†Source: *Oxford Economic Papers*, N.S., Vol. 36 Supplement, November 1984, pp. 26–46.

the traditions of Ricardo and Marshall to modern neo-classical economics — or, in the terms of Hicks the Elder, from 'plutology' to 'catallactics'. If Cambridge was sufficient unto its British self, Lionel Robbins's London School encouraged the study of the Austrian and Lausanne schools, of the Americans and the Swedes. ('We were such "good Europeans" in London that it was Cambridge that seemed "foreign".')[5] Robbins brought Hayek to London and assembled a stable of superbly talented junior people: R.G.D. Allen, Marian Bowley, John Hicks and Ursula Webb-Hicks, Nicholas Kaldor, Abba Lerner, Vera Smith-Lutz, Richard Sayers, and G.L.S. Shackle. Most importantly, Robbins wrote the programmatic tract that, highly controversial in its time, has long since permeated the teaching of economics to the point where its main message has become a platitude (thus depriving its author of the Nobel Prize?). His *Nature and Significance of Economic Science* argued the 'scarcity' definition of economics, a definition that fundamentally changed both the scope and the content of Marshall's subject. Robbins made rational means–ends calculation the core of economics.

It was the younger Hicks that demonstrated how this Robbins programme could be realized. The Hicks–Allen 'Reconsideration' recast demand theory in terms of rational decision theory. Hicks' simplification of monetary theory drew Money into the orbit of marginalist calculation. 'Taking step after step along a road which seemed pre-ordained as soon as one had taken the first step' in a few years time led to the 'static' parts (chs. I–VIII) of *Value and Capital*.[6] These were the parts of Hicks' early work that, together with 'Keynes and the Classics', were to have such a profound and pervasive influence on how economics was to be taught in the United States in the era when American economics was becoming strongly predominant. Perhaps it is more accurate to say that these parts of Hicks' work were selected by the generation of American economists led by Paul Samuelson that were re-erecting the structure of economic theory using constrained optimization building blocks.

Pure decision theory, formalized as optimization subject to constraints, is essentially timeless. The choice among the foreseen outcomes of alternative actions[7] is a purely logical calculus that does not involve time in any essential way. Thus was created a durable tension between neo-Walrasian microtheory and Keynesian macrotheory that, decades later, was to culminate in crisis.

This could hardly have been foreseen. As Robert Clower has remarked,[8]

... it was only natural for economists generally to proceed on the presumption that general equilibrium theory had no inherent limitations ... That any even moderately 'general' economic model should [be incapable of representing Keynesian processes] ... would hardly occur naturally to any but a very perverse mind. That the elaborate Neo-Walrasian model set out in Hicks' *Value and Capital* might fail [in this respect] would have seemed correspondingly incredible to any sensible person at the outset of the Neo-Walrasian Revolution.

The younger Hicks knew that Time was a problem. We find him wrestling with it in almost all the parts of his early work that did *not* become a part of the American neo-classical canon. It was to become even more of a preoccupation — an unfashionable preoccupation — for Hicks the Elder.

From the first, it seems, Hicks saw it as a supreme theoretical challenge, deserving the most sustained effort, to find a mode of process analysis that would retain a role for equilibrium constructions without denying (or trivializing) change. In the early going, this amounted to finding a workable way between Walras and Pareto, on the one hand, and Knight and Hayek on the other.[9] Thirty or forty years later, the opposed alternatives — Arrow–Debreu *v.* Shackle or Lachmann — are clearer and also further apart. In the Arrow–Debreu construction, the rational choice of each agent is defined over all dimensions of commodity–time–contingency space; the result is that all decisions are made once and for all at the origin of time. To obtain a model in which decisions are made in temporal sequence, agents must be ignorant of some of the information that is necessary in order to calculate all optimal allocations at the beginning of time. Thus Shackle poses the issue with uncompromising force: '... the theoretician is confronted with a stark choice. He can reject rationality or time.'[10]

The American Neo-Walrasians, from Paul Samuelson to Robert Lucas, have not seen this choice as at all difficult. In general, they have simply gone whole hog for Rationality, letting Time and Change be trampled underfoot in the philosophical muck as unfit food for economic thought. If forced (somehow) to choose, it is possible that Hicks the Younger might also have opted for rational allocation theory; Hicks the Elder almost certainly would opt for economic history. In actuality, Hicks fought fifty years to maintain a conceptual middle ground.

The issue may have come into focus at LSE precisely because all of the neo-classical schools were to some extent cultivated in the circle around Robbins and Hayek. Marshall had been aware of the problem[11] and had devised a method that at least partly evaded it. Hayek had worked on the construction of an equilibrium process 'in time' and had found himself forced back onto 'perfect foresight' assumptions.[12] Robbins had drawn the conclusion that 'The main postulate of the theory of dynamics is the fact that we are not certain regarding future scarcities'.[13]

As matters stood around 1930, the static toolbox of economic theory was strictly applicable to stationary, perfect foresight processes. It was not at all clear that economic theory provided any foundation for the disciplined analysis of monetary questions or business cycles. Hicks's earliest work dramatized the predicament. In particular, his remarkable 1933 paper on 'Equilibrium and the Cycle'[14] drove home a point made by Knight: that in a perfect foresight equilibrium process, people would not demand cash-balances. This spelt trouble for the most sophisticated cycle theory available at the time. What became of Hayek's notion of 'neutral money' as a criterion for maintaining macroeconomic equilibrium, if in equilibrium there could be no place for money, 'neutral' or otherwise?

The Swedish followers of Wicksell had run into similar quandaries and it was from Myrdal and Lindahl that Hicks got help with the next step.[15] The next step had to be a method of describing economic processes that (a) was not confined to just 'perfect foresight' processes, and (b) still did not force the abandonment of the entire apparatus of inherited static theory. Lindahl's temporary equilibrium method[16]

> reduced the process of change to a sequence of single periods, such that, in the interior of each, change could be neglected ... Everything is just the same as with the 'static' kind of process analysis ... save for one thing: that expectations are explicitly introduced as independent variables in the determination of the single-period equilibrium.

Thus, when the *General Theory* appeared, Hicks had been working along these lines for some time. His first reaction gave pride of place to Keynes's use of a similar device: a short-run equilibrium adapting to independently specified long-term expectations.[17] But the kinship was not all that close. Keynes had applied the 'methods of expectations' to a Marshallian short period. Marshall had invented a kind of analysis ('with some slight dynamic flavouring'[18]) which definitely was 'in time' but that left the line between statics and dynamics unclear. In *Value and Capital*, Hicks developed an alternative line of attack.

The attack starts with the famous definition of 'Economic Dynamics' as those parts of economic theory 'where every quantity must be dated'.[19] This was an important step. The Marshallians, for example, had not taken it.

By itself, the dating of goods only adds dimensions to the commodity space considered in 'timeless' statics. Studies in efficient intertemporal resource allocation following Fisher and Hicks have improved our understanding of capital, growth, and interest theory immensely. But the course of this development became quite similar to what happened to British classical theory, about which Hicks observed: 'The more precise capital theory became, the more static it became; the study of equilibrium conditions only resulted in the study of stationary states.'[20] We have to substitute 'steady' for 'stationary', of course, but otherwise the conclusion holds. It is presumably for this reason that Hicks no longer favours his old static–dynamic distinction but prefers to talk of analysis that is 'out of time' or 'in time'.[21]

Dating brings in future time, but it does not necessarily help in bringing in the passage of time. If the usual (stochastically) perfect knowledge assumptions are made, the end result will be the Arrow–Debreu contingency market model in which all decisions are made at the origin of time. There is no business left to transact at later dates. Money and liquidity can be forced into such a structure only by obvious artifice.

The present-day practice at this juncture is for the theorist to retire behind a smoke screen while intoning some incantation about transactions costs. Hicks, in 1939, did a bit better. What must be done is to weaken the informational assumptions of the model so as to make agents postpone at least *some* decisions 'until they know better'.[22] Hicks discussed several types of uncertainty and decided, I think correctly, that agents' uncertainty about their own intentions was the most fundamental[23]

... in particular, they know that they cannot foretell at all exactly what quantities they will themselves desire to buy or sell at a future period ... and this it is, in the end, which limits the extent to which forward trading can be carried on in practice.

This argument is the bridge by which Hicks made his escape from steady-state capital theory into temporary equilibrium theory. In the temporary equilibrium theory of *Value and Capital*, time is divided into a sequence of 'weeks'. Planned demands and supplies for the week depend on current prices and expected future prices. Current prices are determined on 'Monday' and rule unchanged for the rest of the week. On 'Sunday' (we may imagine), the parameters of the equilibrium system are updated: changes in stocks are accounted for and price-expectations revised. The system is then ready for another Monday morning.

In this story, all markets cleared each Monday. Hicks understood perfectly that this assumption by itself did not preclude periods of sub-normal activity in the system. The defence of the assumption that he suggested is exactly the one so strenuously insisted upon by Lucas, Barro *et alia* almost forty years later. In Hicksian terms, if price-expectations are inelastic, a fall in current prices will induce intertemporal substitution: supplies will be shifted from this week into next.[24] Market-clearing, however, was equilibrium in a 'limited sense'; in the more fundamental sense of 'Equilibrium over Time', Hicks emphasized, the economic system was 'usually out of equilibrium'.[25]

This temporary equilibrium method is thus clearly distinct both from Keynes's short-run equilibrium, on the one hand, and from the new classical equilibrium method of more recent years. It avoids some of the problems of the alternatives and deserves further exploration, therefore,[26] although of course, it has problems of its own. But, while Hicks has resumed the struggle for a systematic 'in time' analysis later — and on more difficult ground even[27] — he chose to abandon the Temporary Equilibrium approach.

Why? The Elder Hicks has given his retrospective reasons. There were problems *within* the 'week' and *between* 'weeks':[28]

Much too much had to happen on that 'Monday'! And ... I was really at a loss how to deal with the further problem of how to string my 'weeks' and my 'Mondays' together.

Getting from one 'week' to the next required both a theory of capital accumulation and a theory of the revision of expectations. The first problem by itself was forbidding at the time; only the later development of modern growth theory made it manageable. Forty years have not brought us much advance on the second problem.[29]

In his retrospective evaluation, Hicks does not point to the problems that the temporary equilibrium method would have to overcome in order to provide a 'continuation' theory; instead, he focuses on how the method dealt with events 'within the week':[30]

...I tried to go further [than to work with *given* expectations], to allow for the effects of current transactions on expectations; supposing that these effects could (somehow) be contemporaneous with the transactions themselves ... That however was nonsense ... It does deliberate violence to the *order* in which the real world (in *any* real world) events occur.

It was this device, this indefensible trick, which ruined the 'dynamic' theory of *Value and Capital*. It was this that led it back in a static, and so in a neo-classical, direction.

What an extraordinarily harsh judgement this is! Why? Because in obliterating the *sequence* in which things happen, the model comes to ignore the structure of markets. It matters, for instance, whether people commit themselves on quantities and discover their mistakes through price-change 'surprises' or set their prices and see their errors revealed in the behaviour of quantities.[31] It matters, in Hicks's terms, whether the markets in the system are mostly of the *flex-price* or the *fix-price* variety. In this century, 'the unorganized flexprice market, the old type, is on the way out ... modern markets are predominantly of the fixprice type ...'[32] In Hicks's view, this historical transformation is of major macroeconomic significance. The change in the predominant market form is a change in the way that impulses are propagated through the system. The harsh language becomes understandable — for, of course, Hicks sees the 'indefensible trick' still being practised all over!

IS–LM

The younger Hicks may have had somewhat different reasons for abandoning his temporary equilibrium method. One of them surely was that Keynes had come up with an alternative method of short-period analysis. It was a rough-and-ready sort of short-period method and Hicks the Younger would have realized it better than anybody else how rough it was. But it seemed to be adequate to Keynes' purposes and Hicks agreed that Keynes' purposes were the supremely important ones.

Soon after his original review, Hicks returned to the *General Theory* and wrote 'Mr Keynes and the "Classics": A Suggested Interpretation'. The IS–LM apparatus of this immensely influential paper was not a Walrasian (or Paretian) construction but a hybrid. Keynes' macrotheory was built with Marshallian microcomponents. But the modelling idea was, as Hicks has himself explained,[33] borrowed from *Value and Capital*, where he had worked out a two-dimensional representation of the equilibrium for a Walrasian system of three markets.

The IS–LM model summarized numerous features of the *General Theory* with admirable economy and it was to serve in the deduction of numerous Keynesian comparative statics propositions that Keynes had not thought of. The model became the backbone of instruction in macroeconomics for forty years. Nonetheless, something was just a bit askew with it. In later years, Hicks has several times come back to reassess it and the uses to which it has been put. In brief, (a) he has remained fairly content with it as a synopsis of Keynes' theory;[34] (b) he has become less satisfied with it as a way of portraying the 'classics' and hence as a tool for isolating Keynes' contribution by IS–LM comparisons;[35] and (c) he has grown somewhat sceptical about it as a general purpose framework for macro-economic analysis.[36] His several commentaries on IS–LM all focus on the problem of time.

From the early fifties to the mid-sixties, Hicks did not participate much in ongoing developments in economic theory.[37] When he returned to theoretical work full time, he was eager to learn what had been accomplished in growth theory but found himself out of sympathy with the directions taken in macroeconomics and monetary theory. The trouble was that these directions had been set by Hicks the Younger — in those parts of his work that the American economists had chosen to cultivate. Hicks' first dismaying confrontation with his own brain-children — now fully grown and so independent! — came, it appears, in 1957 when he was asked to review Patinkin's first edition. Patinkin's work had been systematically and rigorously built on the basis of the Hicks–Allen 'Reconsideration', the paper 'simplifying' monetary theory, 'Keynes and the Classics', and the first eight chapters of *Value and Capital* (together with some closely related works by Oscar Lange).[38] But the theoretical structure that Patinkin had erected on these foundations, Hicks thought, threatened to emasculate Keynesian economics.[39] Never a whole-hearted Keynesian, Hicks was nonetheless too much of a Keynesian to stand idly by under the circumstances.

Patinkin's basic model was a Walrasian general equilibrium model, built up from choice-theoretical individual experiments, via aggregation, to equilibrium market experiments. It allowed no Marshallian distinctions between short-run and long-run equilibria. It was either in 'the' equilibrium or not in the equilibrium at all. Patinkin used the Hicksian technique for portraying the equilibrium of an aggregative version of the system as the intersection of two reduced forms in interest/income space. It 'looked' exactly like IS–LM — except that this version would not allow for unemployment.[40]

Hicks set out to show that 'classical' and Keynesian theory 'do not overlap all the way' — that all the Keynesian furore had not been pointless. His point of departure was the right one:[41]

> The crucial point, as I now feel quite clear, on which the individuality of the Keynes theory depends, is the implication ... that there are conditions in which the interest-mechanism will not work.

In the original Patinkin review, Hicks tried to show this in two ways. His first argument, however, amounted to a reassertion of the liquidity trap explanation of unemployment and Patinkin had only to repeat his demonstration of how, with flexible wages, the Pigou effect would restore full employment. Within the IS–LM context, the explanation of unemployment is thus thrown back unto the 'rigid wages' postulate.[42] Hicks's second and surviving argument attempted to clarify the relationship between Keynes and the 'classics' by showing how the parameters of the IS–LM model depend on the *length of period* assumed. The extent to which wages are variable, Hicks pointed out, will depend not only on the magnitude of excess demand (or supply) of labour but also on the length of time allowed for adjustment. Over a sufficiently long period, the IS-schedule should then be infinitely elastic (at the 'natural rate' of interest), while the speculative component disappears from money demand so that the LM-schedule becomes quite inelastic. With a shorter period, the 'classical' dichotomy fails, and the shorter the period the more 'Keynesian' the picture: IS becomes very inelastic and LM exceedingly elastic in the very short run.[43]

This defense of Keynes (if such it was) could only focus attention on Keynes's own treatment of time, however. Hicks's reservations on this score (as well as those of other 'critical readers') went back all the way to the thirties: '... but we have agreed to suspend our doubts because of the power of the analysis which Keynes constructed on this (perhaps) shaky foundation.'[44] It could not be left at that indefinitely. In his 1974 effort to address *The Crisis in Keynesian Economics*, Hicks left the matter to one side and simply made no use of IS–LM at all. But in *The Crisis*, he advanced the theory of liquidity as flexibility as one of the needed cures for the ailing Keynesian tradition. In contrast to how it emerges in static portfolio theory,[45]

> ... liquidity is not a property of a single choice; it is a matter of sequence of choices, a related sequence. It is concerned with the passage from the known to the unknown with the knowledge that if we wait we can have more knowledge. So it is not sufficient, in liquidity theory, to make a single dichotomy between the known and the unknown. There is a further category, of things which are unknown now, but will become known in time.

This, clearly, lends urgency to the question of how time is to be treated in Keynesian models. Immediately afterward, therefore, Hicks turned to re-examine the compromises of Keynes's method and found them, on close inspections, less and less satisfactory:[46]

> Keynes' theory has one leg which is *in* time, but another which is not. It is a hybrid. I am not blaming him for this; he was looking for a theory which would be effective, and he found it ... but what a muddle he made for his successors!

In brief, the 'leg in time' is LM, the 'leg in equilibrium' is IS. (Clearly, this 'straddle', as Hicks called it, was a position that had to become uncomfortable with the passage of time!) Hicks's own temporary equilibrium method[47]

> also was divided; there was a part that was *in* time and a part that was

not. But we did not divide in the same place. While Keynes had relegated the whole theory of production and prices to equilibrium economics, I tried to keep production *in* time, just leaving *prices* to be determined in an equilibrium manner.

Production will not be equilibrated in a 'week'. Hicks's 1983 'IS–LM: An explanation' carries the argument forward:[48]

> If one is to make sense of the IS–LM model while paying proper attention to time, one must, I think, insist on two things: (1) that the period in question is a relatively long period, a 'year' rather than a 'week'; and (2) that, because the behaviour of the economy over that 'year' is to be determined by propensities and such-like data, it must be assumed to be, in an appropriate sense, *in equilibrium.*

Product markets are in *flow* equilibrium throughout the 'year'; production plans are being carried through without disappointment or surprise; this, in Hicks's view, is how we must interpret the IS-curve. What about the LM-curve? It is a *stock*-relation and, by itself, could apply simply to a point in time. But to be consistent with the IS-construction, Hicks points out, a more restrictive equilibrium condition should be applied, namely, maintenance of stock equilibrium throughout the 'year'. Expectations and realizations must be consistent within the period. But at this point of his 1983 argument, we are suddenly back facing the dilemma of that 1933 paper: 'Disequilibrium is the Disappointment of Expectations' — and in equilibrium processes there is no place for money! The 'Equilibrium method, applied to liquidity over a period, will not do'.[49]

Within the IS–LM construction itself, therefore, we find this tension between Equilibrium and Change which I see as a *Leitmotiv* through five decades of Hicks's work: Hicks is 'quite prepared to believe that there are cases' where we are 'entitled to overlook' the potential inconsistency between the ways that the IS and the LM have been constructed. But he clearly no longer regards it as a robust tool for the analysis of almost all macroeconomic questions.[50]

IS–LM served us well for so long (didn't it?). How could we not have run into obvious problems with it, if it teeters on the brink of conceptual inconsistency? IS–LM exercises produce the right answers (most of us will agree) to a large number of standard macroquestions. Yet, it produces the wrong conclusions (some of us insist) on some issues. Hicks leaves us with a general scepticism about the method which does not help us much in determining what uses are safe and what uses are not.

In an attempt to find out 'What was the Matter with IS–LM?', I came to a conclusion very similar to Hicks' judgement on the temporal equilibrium method: as with all equilibrium constructions, IS–LM ignores the *sequence* of events *within the period.* The result can be nonsense:[51]

> IS–LM, handled as if it were a static construction ... produced a

nonsensical conclusion to the *Keynes and the classics* debate: namely, that Keynes had revolutionized economic theory by advancing the platitude that wages too high for full employment and rigid downwards imply persistent unemployment. It failed to capture essential elements of Keynes's theory: namely, that the typical shock is a shift in investors' expectations and that it is the failure of intertemporal prices to respond appropriately to this change in perceived intertemporal opportunities that prevents rational adaptation to the shock. The same 'as if static' method produced the conclusion that *liquidity preference versus loanable funds* was not a meaningful issue; that it does not matter whether the system is or is not potentially capable of adjusting intertemporal prices appropriately in response to changes in intertemporal opportunities.[52]

Ignoring sequencing becomes a source of trouble in particular in connection with *comparative statics* uses of the IS–LM model — i.e. the uses that are the stuff which macrotexts have been made of for several decades, but which Hicks did not consider in reassessing the model.

Consider, for illustrative purposes, the analysis of an increase in the supply of money in the common textbook context where the money supply is simply an exogenously fixed *M*. Full adjustment to this parametric disturbance requires a proportional rise in all money prices with no effect on output, employment or other real magnitudes. In an IS–LM diagram with money income on the horizontal axis, *both* schedules have shifted the same distance rightwards. In a Lucas model, if *M* is observable, the system goes to this position immediately. In a Friedman model (of, say, ten years ago), on the other hand, nominal income responds strongly in relatively short order, but part of this is an increase in real output and employment and full adjustment to the neutral equilibrium takes 'longer'. In a Keynesian model (of 20 years ago?), finally, the 'short-run' reactions are that the interest rate falls, velocity declines, investment and employment increase a bit, while the price-level stays about the same.

All three possibilities can be demonstrated with the same basic model. How, then, do they differ? To Friedman, the Phillips-curve is vertical only over the 'long run', not already in the 'short run' as in Lucas. In Friedman's short run, the monetary disturbance has output effects because the people temporarily miscalculate real wages. To the Keynesians, the (approximately) proportional increase in nominal income occurs only over the 'long run', not already in the 'short run' as in Friedman. In the Keynesian short run, the monetary disturbance has only weak effects on nominal income now because people fail to anticipate the effect that it must have on nominal aggregate demand sooner or later; hence the short run effects on income occur only in so far as some firms are induced by a fall in the interest rate to increase their investment even though their expectations of future nominal aggregate demand have not improved.[53]

So, Lucas's people are assumed to know something that Friedman people do not, and Friedman people something that Keynesian people do not.[54] The temporal order of decisions matters when information is incomplete, when people have to react to situations they did not foresee and when they learn from realizations they did not anticipate. Such learning can be slow or fast or, in some cases, unnecessary.

Note how these knowledge or learning assumptions are reflected in the mechanics of manipulating the IS–LM diagram. In the Keynesian exercise, LM shifts right, IS stays put, and the short-run effects depend on the elasticities of the two reduced forms. In the Friedman case, IS also shifts, although perhaps *not quite* all the way; the elasticities then are practically irrelevant. In the Lucas case, both reduced forms shift in parallel fashion. The IS–LM modelling strategy would seem to presuppose that we have to deal with a Keynesian world of slow learners. Otherwise it does not seem to make sense to adopt the two-stage procedure of, first, deriving the two reduced forms and, second, getting the answers by shifting one and keeping the other constant. The use of IS–LM as if it were a comparative static apparatus involves the lag-assumption that one schedule shifts before the other and that there will be a well-defined 'short-run' solution halfway in the equilibrating process. This sequencing or lag structure rests on assumptions of incomplete information on the part of various agents in the model.[55]

This conclusion we have derived from an illustrative case where monetarist assumptions are made about the supply of money. There is, however, also another possible interpretation of Keynesian IS–LM analysis which we will come to later.

Money and history

In the most exciting chapter of his *Critical Essays in Monetary Theory*, Hicks sought to structure two centuries of monetary writings in a simple, striking, and informative way. His 'Monetary Theory and History — An Attempt at Perspective' was critical of ahistorical monetary theorizing and insisted on the necessity of doing monetary theory in historical and institutional context. It also suggested that the history of monetary controversy could be understood as a running battle between two traditions, a 'metallic money' tradition and a 'credit money' tradition.

The 'metallic money' theorists, in Hicks's schema, focused on equilibrium propositions in their theorizing, dealt analytically with money 'as if' it were a commodity, and strove to reduce monetary policy to obedience to some 'mechanical rule'. Credit theorists, on the other hand, saw money as part of the overall system of debits and credits that extends beyond the banking system to encompass the entire economy; credit expansions and contractions were central to their conception of the subject and so obliged them to try their luck at disequilibrium analyses; always aware that credit rests on confidence; finally, writers in this tradition saw monetary policy as an exercise in judgement of contemporary conditions. Hicks named Ricardo the patron saint of the 'metallic' tradition and gave Thornton the same status in the 'credit' school of thought. He saw the Currency School and, later, Hayek, Pigou, Rueff, and Friedman as Ricardo's followers and put the Banking School, Bagehot, Wicksell, Hawtrey, Robertson, and Keynes in line of descent from Thornton.

In insisting on the close link between monetary theory and history, Hicks thought above all of the evolution of credit markets and financial institutions: 'In a world of banks and insurance companies, money markets and stock exchanges, money is quite a different thing from what it was before these institutions came into being.'[56] The metallic money theorists (including the modern monetarists) seemed determined to ignore this historical development. Consequently, Hicks's analysis suggested, time had put an ever-increasing distance between their theory and reality.[57]

The 1967 'Perspective' helps one understand what Hicks regards as the important themes running through his own contributions to monetary theory.[58] Consider, once again, what aspects of the work of Hicks the Younger came to be influential and what aspects ignored. For decades, all graduate students have learned that the modern choice-theoretical money demand function stems from his 1935 'Simplifying' paper. Most will know that Hicks already had the demand for money depending on wealth, on anticipated yields on alternative placements, and on the cost of asset transactions. Some may recall that his analysis was anything but reassuring on the stability of the function in terms of these arguments. Few (I am guessing) will remember that, in Hicks's hands, the theory immediately suggested the beginnings of a theory of financial structure, of the composition of balance sheets and of intermediation. Balance sheet equilibria, he noted,[59]

[are] determined by subjective factors like anticipations, instead of objective factors like prices, [which] means that this purely theoretical study of money can never hope to reach results so tangible and precise as those which value theory in its more limited field can hope to attain. If I am right, the whole problem of applying monetary theory is largely one of deducing changes in anticipations from the changes in the objective data which call them forth. Obviously, this is not an easy task, and, above all, it is not one which can be performed in mechanical fashion.

In our textbooks, Hicks's paper is remembered for a money demand function with which any latter-day monetarist could be comfortable. But, clearly, he was in the Credit tradition from the beginning!

Moreover, it is the neglected themes of Hicks the Younger that the Elder has taken up and carried forward. The first step beyond his 1935 position, came three decades later with the sketch in *Capital and Growth* [1965] of a simple financial system, consisting of a bank, household savers, and firms:[60]

Savers can hold their assets in bank money, or in securities (loans or equities) of the producing firms; ... Firms have real assets, and they may have bank money; they have debts to the bank, and to the savers. The bank has debts owing to it from the firms; it owed debts (bank money) to the firms and to the savers.

The 'Two Triads' of 1967 introduced the classification of assets into running assets, reserve assets, and investment assets; the specific assets that served these functions would differ between the balance sheets of households, of firms, and of banks; for each type of transactor, the three classes of assets could be matched up with Keynes's Transactions, Precautionary, and Speculative motives; in Hicks's treatment, however, these three were no longer just motives for holding money but for preferring balance sheets of a certain structure. In 'Monetary Experience and the Theory of Money' [1977], the financial structure of Keynes's world was envisaged as three concentric sectors: (1) a banking 'core' with monetary liabilities and financial securities as assets; (2) a financial 'mantle' owing financial securities and holding industrial securities; and (3) an outer 'industry' owning the industrial securities and holding the (hard crust of?) the economy's productive assets (and some financial assets and money). In the 1982 'Foundations of Monetary Theory', Hicks added to this 'monocentric' credit economy model, some analysis also of a 'polycentric' world of multiple central banks (and flexible exchange rates).

What do we get out of this 'Credit' approach that a monetarist supply and demand for 'money' apparatus would not provide with less trouble? Hicks, of course, uses his financial structure model routinely in the analysis of a broad range of questions. In my view, however, the significant advantage of his approach is that it gives a better picture of the financial and monetary consequences of 'real causes': a rise in the anticipated yields on real capital will change the configuration of balance sheets desired by the business, household, and banking sectors; the financing of investment will in part be intermediated by the banks; consequently, an increase in income due to a rise in marginal efficiency of capital will normally be associated not only with a rise in velocity but also with an *endogenous* increase in the money supply.

Hicks's insistence on linking monetary theory to monetary history has been echoed in recent years by rational expectations theorists who insist that we must link short-run monetary theory to *monetary regimes*. These modern writers, however, have come to their preoccupation with the conditional nature of monetary theory from an entirely different angle. Their concern has been to keep track, not of slowly evolving financial institutions and markets, but of rapidly changing nominal (price level) expectations. A 'monetary regime' may be defined as a system of expectations that governs the behaviour of the public and is sustained by the consistent behaviour of the monetary authorities.[61] Since the short-run effects of particular policy-actions, for example, depend upon the expectations of the public, it follows that we need a different short-run macromodel for each monetary regime. A regime change occurs when the behaviour rules followed by the monetary authorities change. This 'regime approach' directs our attention to the history of monetary standards, viewed as methods for controlling the level of nominal prices, and to the system of nominal expectations that would (rationally) go with each such method.

Historically, we find two basic but contrasting conceptions of how price level control can be accomplished. I have labelled them the 'quantity principle' and the 'convertibility principle', respectively. Briefly (and perhaps a bit too simply) we may say that the quantity principle dictates that the government should control the 'quantity of money' while the private sector sets the price level; the convertibility principle, in contrast, dictates that the government set the nominal price of some 'standard commodity' while the private sector determines the quantity of money.[62] The logically tidiest version of the first would be a fiat standard with flexible exchange rates, and of the second a commodity standard with 'hard money' still in circulation. Price expectations on the fiat standard are almost entirely a matter of beliefs about what the government might choose to do; price expectations on the commodity standard (conditional on the belief that the standard will be adhered to!) are almost entirely a matter of forecasting 'real' business developments.

The two contrasting systems give the extremes on a more or less continuous spectrum of monetary regimes. The last fifty-odd years have taken us from a position rather close to the commodity standard end (in 1929) all the way to the extreme fiat standard end (after 1971). We could proceed to classify macrotheories according to the segment of the regime-spectrum over which they might claim validity.

This classification of theories according to control-regime differs from the Hicksian schema of metallic money theories *v.* credit theories and may be a useful complement to it. This may be seen, for instance, by considering how the American monetarists fit into Hicks's schema. In a metallic money world, money is a produced commodity and thus not neutral; the price level is determined (in the long run) by the cost of producing the metal; the money stock is endogenous and not subject to policy control; the 'mechanical' policy rule is to maintain the metallic standard. The 'mechanical' rule of the monetarists is to fix the growth rate of some '*M*'; it is predicated on the beliefs that '*M*' is neutral and controllable (and 'more or less' independent of endogenous real factors); the object is to control nominal income in the short run and the price level over the longer run; fixed exchange rates are readily sacrificed to this end. When Hicks includes both Ricardo and Friedman in the same 'metallic' tradition these points of contrast are obscured (even as the contrasts between Ricardo and Friedman, on the one hand, and Thornton and the Radcliffe Report, on the other, are brought into focus). Similarly, Hicks has come to prefer Wicksell's 'pure credit' model (of an economy without 'hard money') as his vehicle for explaining the central theoretical message of the 'credit tradition'.[63] But to a monetarist audience, for instance, the main lesson of Wicksell's cumulative process is simply that, on a fiat standard, interest targeting of monetary policy produces *nominal* instability. A model of a system where convertibility anchors the price level — and, therefore, anchors rational price expectations as well — does a better job of fitting credit as a *real* magnitude into monetary theory. It is easier, in such a model, to show both how banking policy can influence investment and employment via the price and volume of 'real' credit and how real income movements can influence the supply of nominal money via the demand for 'real' credit.

Keynesian theory, to take a case in point, seems suited to regimes that behave as if monetary policy were constrained by the requirements of external if not also internal convertibility. The real quantity of money varies endogenously over the cycle in such regimes, nominal price level expectations should be inelastic, and the *numéraire* component of prices correspondingly sticky. This brings us back to IS–LM. Clearly, the old text-book repertory of IS LM exercises will pass muster much better if interpreted as applying to an economy which retains some significant vestiges of convertible money systems. (An open economy with fixed exchange rates will do, for instance, as long as we are not thinking of the dominant reserve currency country). But the textbook should not have specified '*M*' as a given parameter, controlled by the central bank.[64] Under convertibility, the monetary authorities do not have the powers to regulate nominal income assumed by Friedman or by Lucas. The Keynesian picture (of LM shifting, IS staying put) of relatively modest effectiveness of monetary policy, transmitted via the price and volume of credit, is nearer to the mark.

Keynesian theory should do fairly well, I have argued elsewhere,[65] as long as the monetary system still resembles the kind of system which Keynes strove for as a monetary reformer. Its lack of attention to inflationary expectations was on the whole appropriate to the Bretton Woods world. When the last vestiges of Bretton Woods were swept away, its neglect of inflationary expectations became a critical flaw. We should not have been so surprised!

Conclusion

In some quarters, Hicks is routinely blamed for the paths we have taken from his path-breaking early contributions. Those who do so blame him have not studied him very closely. 'One of the best reasons for studying the elder Hicks, in fact, is precisely that he is less a prisoner of the younger Hicks's constructions than are most of us.'[66] Among the lessons that Hicks the Elder would impress on us, I have tried to bring out two:[67]

> One must assume that the people in one's models do not know what is going to happen, and know that they do not know just what is going to happen. As in history!

Monetary theory, especially, has to be developed 'in time [with] future becoming present, and present becoming past, as time goes on'.[68] And 'it belongs to monetary history in a way that economic theory does not always belong to economic history'.[69]

Critical Assessments 85

References

Coddington, A. (1983), *Keynesian Economics: The Search for First Principles*, London: Allen & Unwin.

Clower, R.W. (1975), 'Reflections on the Keynesian Perplex', *Zeitschrift für National-ökonomie*.

Clower, R.W. and Leijonhufvud, A. (1975), 'The Coordination of Economic Activities: A Keynesian Perspective', *American Economic Review*, May.

Fitoussi, J.-P. (ed.) (1983), *Modern Macroeconomic Theory*, Oxford: Blackwell.

Grandmont, J.M. (1975), 'Temporary General Equilibrium Theory', *Econometrica*.

Hart, A.G. (1942), 'Risk, Uncertainty, and the Unprofitability of Compounding Probabilities', in O. Lange *et al.*, *Studies in Mathematical Economics and Econometrics*, Chicago. Reprinted in W. Fellner and B.F. Haley (eds), (1951), *Readings in the Theory of Income Distribution*, Philadelphia: Blakeston.

Hayek, F.A. von (1928), 'Das intertemporale Gleichgewichtssystem', *Weltwirtschaftliches Archiv*.

Hayer, F.A. von (ed.) (1933), *Beiträge zur Geldtheorie*.

Heiner, R. (1983). 'The Origin of Predictable Behavior', *American Economic Review*, September.

Hicks, J.R. and Allen, R.G.D. (1934), 'A Reconsideration of the Theory of Value: Parts I and II', *Economica N.S.*

Hicks, J.R. (1939), *Value and Capital*, Oxford: Oxford University Press.

Hicks, J.R. (1956), 'Methods of Dynamic Analysis', in *25 Economic Essays in Honour of Erik Lindahl*, ed. by the eds of *Ekonomisk Tidskrift*, Stockholm.

Hicks, J.R. (1957), 'A Rehabilitation of "Classical" Economics?' *Economic Journal*, June.

Hicks, Sir John (1965), *Capital and Growth*, Oxford: Oxford University Press.

Hicks, Sir John (1967), *Critical Essays in Monetary Theory*, Oxford: Oxford University Press.

Hicks, Sir John (1974), *The Crisis in Keynesian Economics*, Oxford: Blackwell.

Hicks, Sir John (1977), *Economic Perspectives: Further Essays on Money and Growth*, Oxford: Oxford University Press.

Hicks, Sir John (1979a), *Causality in Economics*, Oxford: Blackwell.

Hicks, Sir John (1979b), 'The Formation of an Economist', *Banca Nazionale del Lavoro Quarterly Review*, September.

Hicks, Sir John (1979c), 'On Coddington's Interpretation: A Reply', *Journal of Economic Literature*, September.

Hicks, Sir John (1981), *Wealth and Welfare: Collected Essays on Economic Theory*, I, Oxford: Blackwell.

Hicks, Sir John (1982), *Money, Interest and Wages: Collected Essays on Economic Theory*, II, Oxford: Blackwell.

Hicks, Sir John (1983), *Classics and Moderns: Collected Essays on Economic Theory*, III, Oxford: Blackwell.

Lange, O. [1942], 'Say's Law: A Restatement and Criticism', in O. Lange *et al.*, *Studies in Mathematical Economics and Econometrics*, Chicago: University of Chicago Press.

Lange, O. [1944], *Price Flexibility and Full Employment*, Chicago: Cowles Commission.

Leijonhufvud, A. (1968), *On Keynesian and the Economics of Keynes*, New York: Oxford University Press.

Leijonhuvud, A. (1979), 'Review of *Economic Perspectives by* Sir John Hicks', *Journal of Economic Literature*, June, pp. 525–27.

Leijonhufvud, A. (1981), *Information and Coordination: Essays in Macroeconomic Theory*, New York: Oxford University Press.

Leijonhufvud, A. (1982), 'Rational Expectations and Monetary Institutions', paper presented at the International Economic Association Conference on *Monetary Theory and Monetary Institutions*, Florence, Italy, September.

Leijonhufvud, A. (1983a), 'What Would Keynes Have Thought of Rational Expectations?' in G.D.N. Worswick and J.S. Trevithick (eds), *Keynes and the Modern World*, Cambridge: Cambridge University Press.

Leijonhufvud, A. (1983b), 'What Was the Matter with IS–LM?' in Jean-Paul Fitoussi (ed.), *Modern Macroeconomic Theory: An Overview*, Oxford: Blackwell.

Marshall, A. (1928), *Principles of Economics* 8 edn. London: Macmillan.

Myrdal, G. (1933), 'Geldtheoretisches Gleichgewicht', in F.A. Hayek (ed.), (1933).

Patinkin, D. (1948), 'Price Flexibility and Full Employment', *American Economic Review*, September.

Patinkin, D. (1956), *Money, Interest, and Prices*, Evanston, Ill.:Row, Peterson & Co.

Patinkin, D. (1959), 'Keynesian Ecnomics Rehabilitated: A Rejoinder to Professor Hicks', *Economic Journal*, September.

Robbins, L. (1932), *An Essay on the Nature and Significance of Economic Science*, London: Macmillan.

Shackle, G.L.S. (1967), *The Years of High Theory: Invention and Tradition in Economic Thought, 1926–1939*, Cambridge: Cambridge University Press.

Shackle, G.L.S. (1972), *Epistemics and Economics: A Critique of Economic Doctrines*, Cambridge: Cambridge University Press.

Notes

1. I have made one previous attempt. My 'Monetary Theory in Hicksian Perspective' was written in 1968 but not published until 1981, at which time I was still reasonably content with the paper. Once it was in print my understanding of some of the issues began to change — as I shall explain below.

2. Cf. Hicks, *The Crisis in Keynesian Economics*, ch. 2, and the antecedent Hart (1942).

3. In stressing this particular distinction between neo-classical and Keynesian theory over others, I am following G.L.S. Shackle more than my own earlier work. Cf. esp. Shackle (1972).

4. Quoting my own (1979) review of Hicks' *Economic Perspectives* (1977).

5. Cf. the 'Commentary' to *The Theory of Wages*, (1963), p. 306. 'Plutology' and 'catal-lactics' are discussed in Hicks, 'Revolutions in Economics', in Spiro Latsis (ed.), (1976) reprinted in Hicks, *Classics and Moderns* (1983).

6. *Economic Perspectives*, pp. v–vi.

7. The foreseen consequences may of course be probability distributions of outcomes. This does not alter the problem.

8. Cf. Clower (1975), p. 134.

9. Cf. Hicks, 'The Formation of an Economist', (1979*b*, p. 199), now reprinted in id. (1983).

10. Cf. Shackle (1972), Preface.

11. Hicks, *Capital and Growth*, pp. 47–8 quotes Marshall (1928), p. 379, n. 1: 'A theoretically perfect long period ... will be found to involve the supposition of a stationary state of industry, in which the requirements of a future age can be anticipated an indefinite time beforehand ... and it is to this cause more than to any other that we must attribute that simplicity and sharpness of outline, from which the economic doctrines in fashion in the first half of this century derived some of their seductive charm, as well as most of whatever tendency that may have had to lead to false practical conclusions.' Of course, the second half of the 20th Century takes a generally more permissive attitude to 'seductive charms' than this most eminent Victorian among economists. Shackle's aptly titled chapter 'Marshall's Accom-modation of Time', in id. (1972), gives a sample of other remarks of Marshall's indicating his preoccupation with the issue.

12. Cf. Hayek (1928).

13. Robbins (1932), p. 79.

14. 'Gleichgewicht und Konjunktur', *Zeitschrift für Nationalökonomie*, iv (1933). This remarkably modern, historically important paper was finally translated and published in *Economic Enquiry* (Nov. 1980), thanks to its then editor, Robert Clower. It is now reprinted in Hicks (1982).

15. G. Myrdal, 'Geldtheoretisches Gleichgewicht', in F.A. Hayek (ed.). *Beiträge zur Geldtheorie* (1933), was reviewed by Hicks in *Economica*, (Nov. 1934). The review is reprinted in Hicks (1982). G.L.S. Shackle, also a member of the Robbins circle, testifies to the great influence and importance of Myrdal's contribution in his (1967), Chapters 9 and 10. Of

Lindahl's temporary equilibrium concept, Hicks first learned through personal acquaintance. He has discussed temporary equilibrium methods repeatedly, e.g., in *Value and Capital*, esp. chs. IX–X and XX–XXII, in 'Methods of Dynamic Analysis' (1956) now reprinted in Hicks (1982), and in *Capital and Growth*, ch. VI.

16. Hicks (1965), p. 60.

17. Hicks' 1936 *Economic Journal* review is reprinted in *Money, Interest and Wages* as 'The General Theory: A First Impression'.

18. Surely, Hicks was thinking of Marshall when (*Value and Capital*, pp. 115–16) he declined to follow 'the usual course of economists in the past ... and give(s) one's static theory some slight dynamic flavouring, (so that) it can be made to look much more directly applicable to the real world ... But it will still be quite incompetent to deal properly with capital and interest, or trade fluctuations, or even money ...'

19. *Value and Capital*, p. 115.

20. *Capital and Growth*, p. 47.

21. Cf. esp. his 'Time in Economics', as reprinted in (1982), e.g. p. 291: '(Steady State economics) ... has encouraged economists to waste their time upon constructions that are often of great intellectual complexity but which are so much out of time, and out of history, as to be practically futile and indeed misleading. It has many bad marks to be set against it.'

22. It is for this reason that I have proposed changing the Hicksian definition of dynamics to 'those parts of economic theory where *decisions* must be dated'. Cf. Leijonhufvud (1983*b*).

23. *Value and Capital*, p. 137. Of course, this way out of the predicament ultimately requires us to formulate a theory of the behaviour of agents who *know* that they are likely to 'foresee their own wants incorrectly' (p. 134). *This* problem Hicks did not tackle in 1939. It is in his *Crisis in Keynesian Economics*, Chapter II, thirty-five years later, that we find it addressed. Decision-making by agents who know that they will know better later (but don't know, even probabalistically, what it is they will learn) will not fit naturally into the usual constrained optimization apparatus. For a comprehensive attack on the problem, cf. Ron Heiner (1983).

24. Cf. *Value and Capital*, p. 131: 'There is a sense in which current supplies and current demands are always equated in competitive conditions. Stocks may indeed be left in the shops unsold; but they are unsold because people prefer to take the chance of being able to sell them at a future date rather than cut prices in order to sell them now. The tendency for the current price to fall leads to a shift in supply from present to future. An excess of supply over demand which means more than this is only possible if the price falls to zero, or if the commodity is monopolized, or if the price is conventionally fixed.'

25. *Value and Capital*, loc. cit.

26. It took more than 30 years for the profession to catch on to what Hicks had been up to in 1939. Grandmont's survey (1975) shows how the crisis of Keynesianism, which was in part a crisis of Keynes' method, had produced a more profound appreciation of the difficulties that the temporary equilibrium approach had been designed to address.

27. The 'Traverse' problem which Hicks set himself in chapter XVI of *Capital and Growth* and analysed at length in *Capital and Time* adds a forbidding burden of capital theory to the difficulties discussed in the text.

28. Cf. 'Time in Economics', in Hicks (1982), p. 290. In 1956, ('Methods of Dynamic Analysis'), Hicks distinguished between the problems of *single-period theory* and those of *continuation theory*. Cf. the reprint in (1982).

29. A 'Robertson lag' in income is yet another possible bridge from 'week' to 'week'. In Leijonhufvud (1968), I tried to get to the *General Theory* by this route: I had a first period in which sales declined because sellers had inelastic price expectations and thus did not cut prices fast enough; in the next week, demand was then 'income-constrained' with consequent Keynesian multiplier-effects, etc. I thought at the time that I had, in effect, got over from *Value and Capital* to the *General Theory* in fairly good order and it puzzled me why Hicks had not tried this route. But Hicks had defined his temporary equilibrium in such a way as to preclude unintended shortfalls in sales. See his comments below on the 'indefensible trick'.

30. *Economic Perspectives*, p. vii. The sentence in quotes is from *Capital and Growth*, ch. VI, where the matter is also discussed. Compare also Clower (1975) and Clower and Leijonhufvud (1975).

31. 'Methods of Dynamic Analysis', section iv.

32. *Economic Perspectives*, p. xi. Cf. also *Capital and Growth*, Chapter VII. *Money, Interest and Wages*, pp. 226–35, 296–99, 320–4.

33. Cf. 'IS–LM: An Explanation', in Fitoussi (ed.) (1983) and also included in Hicks (1982).

34. Cf. e.g. *The Crisis in Keynesian Economics*, p. 6, and 'Recollections and Documents' in *Economic Perspectives*, this paper also records Keynes' detailed and favourable reaction to the IS–LM representation of his theory.

35. C. *Critical Essays in Monetary Theory*, p. vii: 'But as a diagnosis of the "revolution", [IS–LM] is very unsatisfactory. It is not a bad representation of Keynes; but it does not get his predecessors (the "Classics" as he called them) at all right.'

36. Cf. e.g., 'Time in Economics', in Hicks (1982), pp. 289–90: 'All the same, I must say that the diagram is now much less popular with me than I think it still is with many other people. It reduces the *General Theory* to equilibrium economics; it is not really *in* time. That, of course, is why it has done so well'.

37. Approximately, from *A Contribution to the Theory of the Trade Cycle* (1950) to *Capital and Growth* (1965). Or, perhaps, for the duration of his tenure as Drummond Professor (1952–65). For his preoccupations during this period, cf. 'The Formation of an Economist', p. 202.

38. O. Lange (1942) and (1944).

39. The book, he said, was written not 'to elucidate the "Keynesian Revolution", but to deny that it is a revolution at all'. Cf. Hicks (1957). This judgement was not fair to Patinkin as Hicks has acknowledged. Cf. id. (1979c), n. 5.

40. Patinkin understood, of course, that this model would produce unemployment only if one imposed the restriction of rigid (and too high) wages. He was also quite clear on the fact that Keynes had assumed neither rigid wages nor a liquidity trap. (Patinkin (1948) had in any case demonstrated already that a liquidity trap would not by itself lead to unemployment in this type of model). Consequently, he chose to deal with Keynesian unemployment informally, discussing the unemployment dynamics of the system 'off the curves' of his formal model. Cf. Patinkin (1956, Chapter 13).

41. Cf., 'The "Classics" Again' as reprinted in Hicks (1967), p. 143. My reasons for judging this to be the right point of departure are spelt out at great length in 'The Wicksell Connection' in Leijonhufvud (1981).

42. Cf. Hicks (1957), Patinkin (1959).

43. Alan Coddington (1983) discusses this Hicksian analysis in somewhat more detail, pp. 68–73.

44. Cf. *Capital and Growth*, p. 65. The particular difficulty ('... now lulled to sleep by long familiarity') mentioned in this context was that '[Keynes theory] works with a *period* which is taken to be one of equilibrium ... and which is nonetheless identified with the Marshallian "short period", in which capital equipment ... remains unchanged. The second seems to require that the period should not be too long, but the first that it should not be too short; ... It is not easy to see that there can be any length of time that will adequately satisfy both of these requirements'. (pp. 64–65). One notes that this observation would seem to threaten the legitimacy of Hicks' accordion playing with the period in his 'The "Classics" Again'.

45. *Crisis in Keynesian Economics*, pp. 38–9.

46. 'Time in Economics', in Hicks (1982), pp. 288–9.

47. *Ibid.*, p. 290.

48. 'IS–LM: An Explanation', in Fitoussi (1983), p. 57.

49. *Causality in Economics*, p. 85.

50. Cf. 'IS–LM: An Explanation', pp. 60–2. The brief summary in the text fails, I am afraid, to do justice to the subtlety of Hicks' argument. The reader who would appraise it should consult also his *Causality in Economics*, ch. VI and VII.

51. Leijonhufvud (1983b), p. 86. But the IS–LM interpretation of Keynes still has backers who feel that the algebra cannot but lead us right. Paul Samuelson (who has, of course, advocated the sticky wages view as preserving the essentials of Keynes' theory) sees preoccupation with the model's conceptual foundations as revealing some sort of anti-mathematical obscurantism. See his Keynes centennial article in *The Economist*, 25 June, 1983.

52. The equivalence of the liquidity preference and loanable fund approaches to interest determination was argued by Hicks the Younger in his 1936 review of Keynes and in *Value and Capital*, ch. XII. There the argument was made in Temporary Equilibrium context but it has been carried over to IS–LM by others. The argument is, I think, misleading — except possibly in the context of rational expectations models; if the general equilibrium consequences of some parameter change are 'rationally anticipated', all markets would 'open' with the new equilibrium prices already 'posted'. For such a conceptual experiment, it indeed does not make sense to ask which excess demand was responsible for the change in which price. One must (to make sense) consider instances where, once price-setters have posted prices based on their best forecasts, actual trading produces excess demands and supplies thus revealing the 'errors' in the forecasts. The issue of the liquidity preference versus loanable funds squabble is how this error-activated feedback control of price works in the case of the interest rate — specifically, whether the interest rate is '*governed*' by the excess demand for money or by the excess supply for securities. To discriminate between the two hypotheses, one must then consider states of the economy which do *not* have ED for money and ES of securites (or vice versa) at the same time. In a Keynes Model, a 'decline in MEC' produces an example, namely, a state with an ES of commodities and a corresponding ED for securities while — at this stage of the *sequence* — the ED for money is still zero. If the loanable funds hypothesis is true, it is possible that the intertemporal prices mechanism will take care of the intertemporal coordination problem (without a recession); if the liquidity preference hypothesis is true, it is inconceivable.

53. For a more careful and detailed discussion, cf. Leijonhufvud, (1983*b*), pp. 69–70, 76–80.

54. This sounds suspiciously like an IQ ranking for Lucasian, Friedmanian and Keynesian economists. This Keynesian didn't mean it that way!

55. Cf. Leijonhufvud (1983*b*), p. 87.

56. Cf. *Critical Essays*, p. 158.

57. I have made a previous attempt at getting Hicks' 'Attempt at Perspective' into perspective — and pretty much failed. Cf. Leijonhufvud (1981), ch. 8. My review shows how influenced I then was by Friedman and Schwartz, Brunner and Meltzer, and particularly by their work on United States monetary history since 1929. (In 1968, American monetarists had hardly begun thinking about small, open, fixed-exchange-rate economies yet). This made me critical, for instance, of Hicks' insistence on the 'inherent instability of credit'. The piece also shows my great fascination for Hicks' daring attempt to put 200 years of tangled controversies in order; for various reasons, the way I saw it, several important writers just would not fit neatly into Hicks' scheme — but I failed completely to suggest a scheme that would do better.

58. The main line of Hicks' work in monetary theory runs as follows: 'A Suggestion for Simplifying the Theory of Money' (1935); ch. XXIII, 'Keynes After Growth Theory' in *Capital and Growth* (1965); the three chapters on 'The Two Triads' in *Critical Essays* (1967); the chapter on 'Money, Interest and Liquidity' in *The Crisis* (1974); the 60-odd-page-long *Perspectives* collection (1977); and 'The Foundation of Monetary Theory' in *Money, Interest and Wages* (1982).

59. Quoted from reprint in *Critical Essays*, pp. 75–76.

60. *Capital and Growth*, pp. 284–5.

61. I have used this rather informal definition repeatedly. Cf. e.g. Leijonhufvud (1983*a*).

62. Cf. Leijonhufvud (1982) and (1983*a*) for rather more careful explanations.

63. Cf. Monetary Experience and the Theory of Money', pp. 61–73, and 'Foundations of Monetary Theory', pp. 237, 264 ff.

64. On which Hicks can rightly say: '... I may allow myself to point out that it was already observed in 'Mr Keynes and the Classics' that we do not need to suppose that the curve is drawn up on the assumption of a given stock of money. It is sufficient to suppose that there is (as I said) "a given monetary system — that up to a point, but only up to a point, monetary authorities will prefer to create new money rather than allow interest rates to rise. Such a generalized (LM) curve will then slope upwards only gradually — the elasticity of the curve depending on the elasticity of the monetary system ...".' Cf. *Money, Interest and Wages*, p. 328.

65. Cf. Leijonhufvud (1983*a*).

66. Leijonhufvud (1979), p. 526.

67. *Economic Perspectives*, p. vii.
68. Ibid.
69. 'Monetary Theory and History', in Hicks (1967), p. 156. But this too is an old Hicksian theme. One finds it in his 1943 review of Charles Rist's *History of Money and Credit Theory*. Cf. Hicks (1982), pp. 132ff.

83

Maintaining Capital Intact*†

M. Scott

'To intrude upon a controversy being waged by such paladins as Professor Pigou and Professor Hayek seems an act bold even unto rashness; but the question of maintaining capital intact just cannot be left where they left it last summer. The present note will have justified itself if it serves to provoke them to another round' (Hicks (1942)).

Alas, it never did, although the contribution made to the subject by the third paladin himself was of no mean order, as we shall see. The present intruder believes, all the same, that there is still something more to be said. Sir John Hicks showed that each side could justly claim some right, although he mainly came down on Hayek's side.[1] My conclusion, obtained by following up clues provided by Sir John himself, is that, while Hayek's arguments were sound, so were Pigou's, and that from the reconciliation of the two one can learn something which is still not yet generally accepted.

Pigou's great book *The Economics of Welfare* was first published in 1920, and the fourth edition appeared in 1932, almost ten years before the interchange in *Economica* in 1941 to which the above quotation refers. The book opens with a discussion of the meaning of 'economic welfare', and then moves on quickly to the meaning of the 'national dividend', which now (and even by 1932) would more generally be called the national income This is a key concept for the book, which analyses how this or that policy or institution affects its size (in real terms) and distribution. Its definition was therefore of importance to Pigou, and, following Marshall, he made it the flow of goods and services produced in a given period net of the amounts required to maintain capital intact. But what does *that* mean? This is the subject of a separate chapter in the book, and also of the later controversy.

Before launching into it, let us note that the *purpose* for which the definition was required was to arrive at a meaning of real national income. It was not required for a definition of capital stock for use in a production function, nor for a definition of wealth. These are interesting in themselves, and are matters on which Sir John has shed much light.[2] The purpose was not even to enable the income of an individual person or firm to be defined, as was pointed out by Sir John in his intervention. That, as we shall see, was a very important point.

---

†Source: *Oxford Economic Papers*, N.S., Supplement November 1984, Vol. 36, pp. 59–73.

Pigou's ideas on the subject changed over the years, and I shall confine myself to what seems to have been their final form.[3] He starts with the proposition that, if the quantity of every unit in the nation's capital stock is unchanged over a period, then the total capital stock has been exactly maintained even though its money value may have risen or fallen.[4] In his book he had already argued that changes in the money value of the stock due to changes in the general level of prices should not count as changes in the real capital stock for this purpose.[5] Both there and in his later *Economic Journal* article[6] he had argued that changes in the value due to changes in rates of interest, which would alter the present discounted values of future receipts, should not count either. He also excluded changes in value due to changes in the quantity of labour working in conjunction with the capital stock, as well as changes due to shifts in taste, or to competition from new equipment. 'In fact we may, I think, say quite generally, that all contractions in the money value of any parts of the capital stock that remain physically unaltered are irrelevant to the national dividend; and that their occurrence is perfectly compatible with the maintenance of capital intact' (Pigou (1946), p. 45).

Turning now to changes in the quantity, or physical characteristics, of goods in the stock, Pigou excluded all changes of an extraordinary nature (by 'act of God or the King's enemies' as he put it), but included accidental changes due to, for example, fire, which would be a 'normal' risk to be expected.[7] He then needed to specify some way of adding up the positive and negative changes so as to be able to say whether or not the total stock had been maintained. His preferred method was most clearly set out in the 1941 *Economica* article with the help of an arithmetical example. To paraphrase this, at the risk of some loss of clarity, let us suppose that one unit of good A has become worn out or scrapped on account of obsolescence in the relevant period. Let us ask how many units of good B are required to replace it. By his original proposition, had another unit of A been available, that would have sufficed to replace it. By an extension of that proposition, as many units of good B are required as are expected to yield the same income as one unit of A.

Pigou's method rests, as can be seen, on distinguishing sharply between changes in price and quantity. It only declines in quantity (including any sorts of physical deterioration, but excluding those caused by extraordinary factors) which have to be made good by replacement by new capital whose value is the same, the valuation being made at the time when the deterioration takes place.[8] The national income in any period is then the sum of consumption and gross investment minus that part of gross investment required to maintain capital intact.

Let us now turn to Hayek. Shortly after Pigou's article in the *Economic Journal* appeared, in June 1935, Hayek published an article in *Economica* (August 1935) entitled 'The Maintenance of Capital'. This was long (35 pages) and complex. It examined the evolution of Pigou's treatment in *The Economics of Welfare*, and also included references to his most recent article, just published. It was addressed to the same problem as Pigou's, namely, the relation between changes in the stock of capital and income.

However, the argument was more in terms of the income of individuals — whether persons or firms — than of national income. Much attention was given to obsolescence and to uncertainty and changes in expectations. It concluded, amongst other things, that 'the stock of capital required to keep income from any moment onwards constant cannot in any sense be defined as a constant magnitude' (op. cit., p. 269).

Subsequently, in 1941, Hayek published *The Pure Theory of Capital*, in which he said much the same things. Pigou reacted to all this by his article in *Economica* in 1941, in which he undoubtedly misinterpreted some of Hayek's argument (as Sir John pointed out in 1942). Hayek replied in the same issue by a simple example.[9] Pigou had argued that real capital, and so real income, would be maintained as long as capital goods were physically maintained. Consider, then, two[10] businessmen who simultaneously each buy 'equipment of different kinds but of the same cost and the same potential physical duration, say ten years. X expects to be able to use his machine continuously throughout the period of its physical "life". Y, who produces some fashion article, knows that at the end of one year his machine will have not more than its scrap value.' According to Pigou, since the physical deterioration of both machines is the same, X and Y should make the same deductions from their gross receipts in the first year to get their net profits (ignoring all other costs). Hence, equal gross profits will imply net profits. Yet if X deducts one-tenth of the cost of the machine and saves it, his capital at the end of the year will clearly have been maintained, whereas Y will retain only one tenth of his capital (ignoring the scrap value) if he does the same. 'I find it difficult to conceive that this procedure could have any practical value or any theoretical significance', concludes Hayek, and stresses that foreseeable obsolescence *must* be taken into account. The problem arises when some obsolescence is not foreseen and, in an uncertain world, this is bound to happen. Changes in expectations will then lead to windfall losses and gains and resulting changes in capital value. To calculate income one should not subtract such losses or add such gains in any period. It is the difficulty of separating these from the foreseeable ones that Hayek regards as making it practically impossible to arrive at a definition of the maintenance of capital that can be used in defining income.

In the spring following this exchange between Pigou and Hayek, Sir John Hicks published his 'further suggestion', whose beginning we have quoted. The views he expressed there were reaffirmed over thirty years later in *Capital and Time*, (1973) (see the note to ch. XIII). After describing Pigou's suggested method, he added, 'This principle of Professor Pigou's stands up very well to most sorts of criticism, but it has (I think) been torpedoed by Professor Hayek ... Professor Hayek, on the other hand, having demolished the rival construction, fails (in my view) to provide anything solid to put in its place.' Hayek had clung to the definition of income which Hicks himself had described and analysed with such lucidity in *Value and Capital* (1939, ch. XIV) that that has become the standard reference on the subject. The idea of income as the maximum rate of consumption which the recipient can enjoy and expect to continue to enjoy indefinitely is widely termed 'Hicksian income'. In *Value and Capital*

Hicks had, all the same, criticized this concept, along with those of saving, depreciation, and investment, as not being 'suitable tools for any analysis which aims at logical precision. There is far too much equivocation in their meaning, equivocation which cannot be removed by the most painstaking effort. At bottom, they are not logical categories at all; they are rough approximations, used by the businessman to steer himself through the bewildering changes of situation which confront him. For this purpose, strict logical categories are not what is needed; something rougher is actually better' (op. cit., p. 171). Nevertheless, he also took the view that 'calculations of social income ... play ... an important part in social statistics, and in welfare economics' (p. 180). In his *Economica* article he stressed the importance of knowing the purpose for which a definition was required in any controversy about definitions. His purpose was the same as Pigou's, namely, the measurement of net social income, and for this purpose he was prepared, apparently, to abandon the *Value and Capital* 'Hicksian income', the 'constant income stream' income, in order to get something suitable.

His suggestion was as follows. Net income in any year is consumption plus gross investment minus depreciation of the original stock of capital, where depreciation is 'The difference between the total value of the goods comprising that original stock as it is at the end of the year (C_1) and the value (C_0') *which would have been put upon the initial stock at the beginning of the year if the events of the year had been correctly foreseen, including among those events the capital value C_1 at the end of the year*' (emphasis as in the original).

At first sight this definition encounters Hayek's objection that it requires the separation of changes in the value of capital due to foreseen events from those due to unforeseen ones (windfalls). However, Hicks suggested that the procedure should not be to attempt to value C_0' which would necessitate such a separation, but rather to attempt to value $C_0' - C_1$, depreciation, by 'distinguishing, of the various experiences which the initial capital goods will have had during the year, which sorts will cause a divergence between C_0' and C_1. These are the things which will cause true depreciation. By applying the rule to each case as it comes up we ought to be able to discover them'. He then mentions wear and tear in the course of production and obsolescence of the kind described in Hayek's example as being true depreciation on this test. On the other hand, he apparently thought that most obsolescence would be excluded by the test, since most of it was due to imperfect foresight. Thus if C_1 was lower than C_0 (the actual market value of the original stock at the beginning of the year, given the expectations then held) because of unforeseen obsolescence during the year, it would *not* be lower than C_0' for that reason.

Hicks thought that this definition of income would give the same results as Hayek's in all cases where both could be employed. It would also *generally* be the same as Pigou's, but there would be exceptional cases (of the kind described in Hayek's example) when they would differ. However, he clearly thought that these differences were likely to be unimportant for Pigou's purpose. Indeed, so far as obsolescence due to changes in tastes were concerned, this could not strictly be allowed in making welfare comparisons, since one had to assume that tastes were unchanged for comparisons to be possible at all.

So far as I know, Pigou never stated whether this suggested compromise satisfied him, and nor has Hayek. In my own view, which I attempt to justify below, it was the right attempt, but did not quite go far enough. Putting myself in Hayek's place I would deny that most obsolescence can be excluded on the grounds that it is due to imperfect foresight.[11] While it is probably true that businessmen cannot predict at all accurately how fast any particular piece of equipment is going to become obsolete, the law of large numbers must come to the rescue when one considers the whole capital stock. Provisions for depreciation ought, for such a large number of heterogeneous items, to correspond reasonably well to actual depreciation in value (abstracting from inflation, as did our three paladins). In that case, while the correction made to C_0 to arrive at C_0' may sometimes reduce it, because unforeseen obsolescence has occurred, it may equally sometimes increase it, because obsolescence has been slower than expected. Now there are many (including possibly Hayek)[12] who take the view that obsolescence is the most important cause of the depreciation of capital, and I do not think it is obsolescence due to changes in tastes which they have in mind, but rather that due to a variety of other causes such as innovations, shifts in demand as income increases, and the erosion of quasi-rents as product wages rise. If that is so, the apparent gap between Hayek's and Pigou's methods becomes very large indeed. All the same, I believe the gap can be closed, and the clue as to how this may be done is the fact pointed out by Sir John himself: whereas Pigou was concerned with net social income, Hayek's examples and arguments referred essentially to individual businesses.

To make further progress it is essential to define the concepts of *invest-ment* and *maintenance* expenditures more explicitly. Only when this is done can one obtain a clear idea of *depreciation*, and relate all three concepts to 'Hicksian income' — which I regard as the best available income concept, despite Sir John's own criticisms above.

I have suggested elsewhere that investment expenditures are best regarded as all the costs of changing economic arrangements.[13] This is a wide definition, which in practice may have to be narrowed. It includes all the usual expenditures on buildings and other construction, machinery, equipment, and vehicles, and increases in stocks of goods and work in progress. It also should include such things as research and development expenditures, and some managerial, and marketing costs and some of the costs of financial intermediations. Although it is not a good description for some of these expenditures, let me call their sum gross *material* investment, to distinguish them from *human* investment, which consists of some expenditures on education and health and the training and movement of workers. In what follows I shall largely neglect human investment, although it is undoubtedly important. This is done just to simplify and shorten the exposition.

How can we distinguish between investment expenditures and maintenance expenditures? It may seem, at first sight, pedantic to point out that the latter, as well as the former, are expenditures incurred to change economic arrangements. Painting a house or oiling and greasing a machine change the house or the machine. Ploughing or sowing change the fields. It would generally be agreed that these should be treated as current costs of production, not investment, but why?

One criterion suggested in the United Nations *System of National Accounts* (1968), para. 6.56, p. 100 and para. 6.102, p. 110, is that all expenditures whose benefits last for longer than a year, the period of account, should be regarded as part of gross investment, whereas other expenditures (such as for ploughing and sowing), should be regarded as current. Unfortunately, this is arbitrary and is not in practice followed. Painting and repairs to buildings last for much longer than a year, but are nevertheless treated as current maintenance costs. Nor is this a trivial matter. Were they to be regarded as gross investment, the latter would be increased very substantially.

Another criterion to be found in systems of national accounts is that of improvement *versus* restoration. Expenditures which restore the physical condition of assets are treated as maintenance, whereas improvements are, at least in principle, included in gross investment.[14] This seems to be the best way of defining the distinction, but it has far-reaching implications which have not been generally realized. This definition at once reminds one of Pigou's starting-point for defining the maintenance of the capital stock. Both definitions are concerned with maintaining the number and physical characteristics of assets unchanged.

Strictly speaking, however, *individual* assets are not and cannot always be kept physically unchanged. In order to make this idea more precise, let us first consider a case in which assets would be kept physically unchanged in a simple sense *in aggregate*. In a static economy, with balanced stocks of all assets, the stock of each type of asset would be kept unchanged. Individual members of the stock (e.g. individual taxis, cows, or houses) would be subject to ageing or decay. However, the whole fleet of taxis, herd of cows, or housing estate would not, since periodic expenditures would be undertaken to repair damage, replace worn-out parts, or replace whole units by new ones. All these expenditures should be classified as *maintenance*, and treated just like any other current cost of production. In such a case we could say that *required maintenance*, no more and no less, was being undertaken, and this expenditure would be a (near enough) constant flow.

For the owner of an *individual* asset, however, some of the actual expenditures to maintain his asset would inevitably be lumpy. In order to estimate his income, he would need to set up a fund to which he would contribute at a constant rate, and out of which he would meet the necessary expenditures, the balance in the fund earning interest (or paying it, when the balance was negative). The correct deduction to be made from his current receipts on account of maintenance would then be his constant rate of contribution to the fund, and not the actual repair and replacement expenditures. If such funds were set up for each and every asset in our static economy, we would find that the rate of the aggregate contributions to them would equal the rate of the aggregate actual expenditures.

Consider now a closed economy in which required maintenance expenditure is undertaken, no more and no less, there being zero gross investment, so that no expenditures to *improve* assets in aggregate, or increase their number, are being made, merely expenditures to keep them unchanged in aggregate. Let us also posit a constant labour force, and no changes through 'acts of God or the King's enemies'. Then this static economy would be capable of producing a constant real flow of consumption goods and services for as long as these conditions persist. That flow is then the static economy's income in the Hicksian sense.

We are now in a position to introduce *depreciation*. It is clear that, in the economy just described, depreciation must be zero. Since gross investment is zero, and income is total consumption, and also equals total consumption plus gross investment minus depreciation, the latter must be zero. This may surprise some, and I shall be accused of changing accepted terminology. I have been able to perform my trick, it will be said, only because I have regarded wear and tear as being covered by maintenance, rather than by depreciation. Replacing junked taxis or dead cows would usually be regarded as part of gross investment, and so these replacement expenditures would have to be covered by depreciation, even in a static economy.

This objection has some force, in as much as it is correct to say that *some lumpy* replacement expenditures are conventionally included in gross investment. Nevertheless, I think the objection cannot be sustained. First, as a matter of principle rather than practice, I must ask the objectors how they propose to distinguish gross investment and maintenance expenditures? We have already seen that the durability of the benefits from the expenditure is an inadequate criterion, and I believe lumpiness is too. Are taxi replacements more lumpy than building repairs and redecoration? What is the critical 'lump' and how is it determined? I do not see how these questions can be answered satisfactorily at a theoretical level. Secondly, as a matter of practice, I believe that the criterion already suggested (i.e. whether the expenditure restores, or improves, and the extent to which it does each) agrees well enough with those generally used and which are discussed below. Admittedly *some* expenditures, which I should classify as maintenance, in practice are included in gross investment (e.g. for replacing taxis), but this helps to offset an opposite error, since there are many expenditures which are treated as current yet ought to be included in gross material investment (research and development, etc. listed above) and recorded maintenance expenditures often improve, rather than merely maintain, assets,[15] that is, if they were to be matched by a notional fund, the contributions to that fund would have to grow.

Let us now attempt to move on from a static to a growing economy. If depreciation is zero in the former, can it also be zero in the latter? In my view, and taking the *whole* of a closed economy, the answer is yes, but, I hasten to add, there *is* depreciation then for individual businesses within the economy. The reason why it is zero for the whole economy is that such depreciation is cancelled out by an equal and opposite amount of *appreciation*.

A growing economy is changing, and so investment is being undertaken. Some assets which would have to be maintained in a static economy, and which it would then pay to maintain, will now be neglected and perhaps scrapped. Maintaining them will no longer be worthwhile, since they are becoming obsolete. It is worth noting that it is often the direction of causation — from obsolescence to physical decay. Buildings, for example, can be maintained indefinitely, but many are allowed to deteriorate and are finally pulled down because they have become obsolete, and the land on which they stand can be better used. In these circumstances, what one might call ordinary maintenance expenditures will fall short of required maintenance, and some of gross investment will merely compensate for the loss of income caused by this shortfall. The question is how much, and how it can be determined.

It is important to note that, in ordinary circumstances, one would not expect that very much gross investment would be needed. The reason for this is that the loss of income due to the failure to maintain is likely to be small, *precisely because of the obsolescence that has occurred.* If some asset were, for example, fully maintained until its quasi-rent fell to zero, through competition with newer assets, and/or as a result of rising product wages, or possibly land rents, then scrapping it would involve no loss of income at all. Failure fully to maintain it during the latter part of its life is also not likely to lose much income, since its quasi-rent will then be small and one can trust the asset-owner to undertake maintenance which *is* worthwhile, and so does appreciably affect earning power. It seems probable that only a minor part of gross investment would thus have to be deducted to bring maintenance up to the required level, and that the problem of estimating how much is not an important one, since not much is involved. Furthermore, I believe that the opposite error of including as current expenditure what should be classed as gross material investment is likely to more than offset the required deduction.

The upshot of all this is, then, that conventionally defined *gross* material investment is more likely to understate than overstate true *net* material investment for the whole of a closed economy. Instead of deducting something (depreciation) from gross material investment to get net material investment, one should probably add something. Reverting to the Hicksian definition of income, the constant income flow, an economy with a static labour force could transfer all the resources engaged in producing the flow of goods and services conventionally labelled gross investment into consumption goods and services production, and expect to be able to continue to consume probably rather more than the resulting total existing consumption plus the value of gross investment indefinitely.[16] Since the transfer would probably still leave a surplus over required maintenance, total sustainable consumption, and so Hicksian income, would probably be rather higher.

So far, if I have carried the reader with me, Pigou is vindicated. But what about Hayek? He, too, can be vindicated. In a completely static economy there are no relative price changes and no obsolescence. In a growing economy, both occur. Excluding changes in the number of workers, or in human capital (as I have thus far and shall continue to do, for simplicity), all real improvements, and so all increases in real income, are due to material investment. But the *division* of that increase in income amongst different people is determined by changes in relative prices. Because relative prices are changing, some gain and some lose. An *individual's* income cannot be estimated without allowing for present and prospective relative price changes. If, on balance, these are adverse, the individual will have to deduct depreciation from his current receipts to get his net income. If they are favourable, however, he must add appreciation. An example may help to clarify all this.

A business owns assets which it maintains in a physically unchanged state, so that required maintenance, no more and no less, is being undertaken. It employs a constant labour force. The consumer price index in the economy is constant, as are interest rates. The value added in the business (the sum of gross profits and wages, net of maintenance expenditures) is constant in money terms, but, because of investment elsewhere in the economy, wages are rising. If the business continues like this, its gross profits will dwindle away to nothing, and it will then have to close down to avoid making losses. Clearly, then, the proprietor's income from the business is less than its current gross profits. Some of its gross profits must be set aside as depreciation, and invested so as to offset the loss of income which is occurring as a result of the rise in wage rates. Depreciation can, indeed, be defined so as to equal the investment required so that this loss should be just offset. I have distinguished it from maintenance, in that the loss is *due to a relative price change* instead of being due to a physical change of some kind in the assets concerned.

From the point of view of the businessman, this distinction is immaterial. Whether his assets are physically deteriorating, or whether they are becoming obsolete as relative prices change adversely, really makes no difference. In either event there is some expenditure he needs to undertake in order to offset these changes, and it is only after subtracting the cost of this expenditure that he can regard the remainder of his gross profit as Hicksian income or net profit, which could all be consumed indefinitely. Indeed, for the individual businessman the distinction between depreciation and maintenance has been made on different lines. 'Maintenance' has consisted of all those expenditures which are sufficiently small, frequent and regular that one can, without too much distortion, estimate one's income by subtracting the *actual* expenditures instead of by setting up a fund and subtracting contributions to it. It is much simpler to do the former than the latter. 'Depreciation' has been concerned with expenditures which are too large and irregular to be treated in this way, and where a fund has had to be set up if estimates of income are not to be badly distorted. 'Depreciation' then consists of contributions to the fund, and gross investment consists of those expenditures which are *not* subtracted from revenues in estimating income. The distinctions between depreciation, maintenance, and gross investment have thus rested on simple practical grounds of convenience and approximation, and this is why criteria such as the iength of the accounting period and the lumpiness of the expenditure have been used which seem quite arbitrary from a conceptual point of view.

So much for the practical businessman, but what of the practical social accountant? As we have seen, there are two important distinctions to be drawn: between gross investment and maintenance expenditures, and between depreciation and maintenance. We have suggested that the first distinction should rest on whether the expenditures improve or merely restore, but we have also admitted that this is not a precise distinction. To achieve precision, we suggested setting up a fund for each and every asset, so that gross investment would then consist of all expenditures which changed assets (or, more generally, changed economic arrangements) without distinguishing improvements from restorations. Required maintenance would then be the sum of contributions to these funds. Unfortunately, this theoretically satisfactory solution is quite impractical, since it would enormously increase gross investment and the deduction for required maintenance. Ploughing and sowing change assets, as do painting and repairing, oiling and greasing, and a vast amount of other expenditure besides. In practice, therefore, we must fall back on the same criteria as the businessman: we avoid setting up funds and include as many actual maintenance expenditures as possible with other current costs of production. The larger the group of assets in our aggregate, and the longer our period of account, the more closely will such actual expenditures approximate to the notional contributions to our notional funds. It is the closeness of this approximation at which we must aim in deciding how to treat this or that item.

If we can cover all, or nearly all, physical deterioration *in so far as it results in a loss of income for society* by actual maintenance expenditures, then we can stick to our definition of depreciation as loss of value due to current or expected relative price changes, and appreciation as the corresponding gain in value. It is then the case that, whereas maintenance expenditures offset a loss which would otherwise occur both to the individual and to society, depreciation is a loss to the individual but *not* a loss to society. Since we have defined it as being due to relative price changes, for every loser there must be a gainer, and so appreciation *should* be equal and opposite to depreciation.[17]

In the example given above, it is clear that the workers in the business are gaining exactly what the owners of the business are losing. The value added by the business is being redistributed from profits to wages. Workers could, therefore, consume more than their current wages and expect to be able to consume as much indefinitely (ignoring death, that is!). The extra amount is appreciation, and, if we could estimate depreciation and appreciation on a consistent basis and sum them for the whole of a closed economy, they would cancel out. In practice, we cannot hope for consistency, since expectations and rates of discount will differ for different individuals. Some future transfer of income which costs A £X and benefits B by the same amount, and whose present value ought to be the same for each, will not in general be given the same value by each. Indeed, conservative accounting principles teach A to reckon in the cost, so that a suitable depreciation provision is made, but also teach B to ignore the benefit until it is actually realized. Hence it is very likely that individual businesses will exaggerate depreciation provisions (although inflation is a powerful factor working in the opposite direction). In economies growing like those of Western countries since the Second World War, these errors are, however, as nothing to the errors in the accounts of workers, whose incomes as conventionally stated ignore a really vast amount of appreciation.

There is, then, much to justify Hayek's doubts about the practicality of income measurement for the individual, as well as Hicks's warnings in *Value and Capital*, where, *inter alia*, he drew attention to the inconsistencies of different people's expectations mentioned above (Hicks (1939), pp. 177–8). The difficulty of estimating individual incomes does not, all the same, translate into equal difficulty in estimating national income, since there is much cancelling of appreciation and depreciation when we sum the incomes of all individuals, and this greatly reduces the errors and uncertainties of measurement.

To summarize, let us consider the definition of net social income as consumption plus gross investment less expenditure required to maintain capital intact (which I call required maintenance). I have tried to justify the following propositions.

(1) The definition assumes that the resources used to produce net investment (i.e. gross investment less required maintenance) could be converted to produce an equivalent value of consumption. Alternatively, net investment should be measured as this equivalent value. This equivalence is needed to make the total equal to Hicksian income.

(2) Gross investment expenditures are aimed at improving, while maintaining expenditures are aimed at restoring, economic arrangements.

(3) We can avoid making this imprecise distinction between improvement and restoration by imagining a fund set up for each and every asset, into which contributions are made at a rate which would remain constant in a static economy, and out of which actual maintenance expenditures are paid. Required maintenance is then the sum of these contributions, and all actual expenditures which change assets are included in gross investment.

(4) Such a procedure would result in enormous rates of gross investment, since even expenditures such as ploughing and sowing, let alone painting, repairing, oiling, and greasing, can be regarded as changing assets. In practice, therefore, we treat actual maintenance expenditures so far as possible as current costs instead of including them in gross investment. The approximation involved becomes better as one lengthens the period of account, or as one aggregates more and more assets together. Actual maintenance expenditures then correspond more and more closely to the notional contributions to the fund mentioned in (3).

(5) In fact, it seems likely that, with two exceptions mentioned below, actual maintenance expenditures included in current costs fall not far short of required maintenance. This is because actual maintenance expenditures counter physical deterioration where it matters — the assets which are scrapped or allowed to crumble away are mostly those which are worthless. One class of physical deterioration which is certainly large for particular

countries, and perhaps for the world as a whole, is the extraction and destruction of fossil fuels. Another which may be large is the damage done to the environment by a variety of human activities: deforestation, over-grazing, over-fishing, pollution, etc.

(6) Some expenditures which improve economic arrangements (such as research and development expenditures, etc.) are included in current costs and not in gross investment, and this, for may countries, probably outweighs the shortfall mentioned in (5). It therefore seems likely (apart from the two exceptions mentioned) that gross investment as convention-ally measured *under*states, rather than *over*states, true net social invest-ment.

(7) The above all refers to expenditures which change material assets physically. Net social investment should include improvements in human assets. Neither material nor human investment should include changes in the value of assets due to changes in the general level of prices, or to changes in interest rates, or to changes in expectations (windfalls).

(8) Nor should social investment for the whole of a closed economy include changes in the value of assets due to current or expected relative price changes, and this covers nearly all obsolescence. For an individual (or for an open economy) such changes must be taken into account when income is estimated. Adverse expected price changes will result in depre-ciation of his assets and will lower his income. Favourable expected price changes will result in appreciation and will raise his income. If all asset owners held identical expectations and used identical discount rates, and if all assets, human as well as material, were covered, the sum of depreciation and appreciation in a closed economy would be zero.

The above glosses over some difficulties, including some raised by the protagonists in this discussion,[18] and so there is still more to be said.[19] But if I have succeeded in advancing matters from where they stood more than forty years ago, I shall be satisfied.

References

Conference on Research in Income and Wealth (1951), *Studies in Income and Wealth*, XIV, National Bureau of Economic Research, New York.

Conference on Research in Income and Wealth (1957), *Problems of Capital Formation, Studies in Income and Wealth*, XIX, National Bureau of Economic Research, New York, Princeton University Press, Princeton.

Hayek, F.A. (1935), 'The Maintenance of Capital', *Economica*, NS ii, August.

Hayek, F.A. (1941), 'Maintaining Capital Intact: a Reply', *Economica*, NS viii, August.

Hicks, Sir John (1939), *Value and Capital*, Oxford (1st edn., 2nd edn. in 1946).

Hicks, Sir John (1942), 'Maintaining Capital Intact: A Further Suggestion', *Economica*, NS ix, May.

Hicks, Sir John (1965), *Capital and Growth*, Oxford.

Hicks, Sir John (1969), 'Measurement of Capital — in Practice', paper given to a meeting of the International Statistical Institute and published in its Bulletin, xliii, and republished in *Wealth and Welfare, Collected Essays on Economic Theory*, i (Oxford, 1981).

Hicks, Sir John (1971), *The Social Framework*, 4th edn, Oxford.

Hicks, Sir John (1974), 'Capital Controversies: Ancient and Modern', *American Economic Review*, lxiv, May.

Lutz, F.A. and Hague, D.C. (eds) (1961), *The Theory of Capital*, London.
Maurice, R. (ed.), (1968), *National Accounts Statistics Sources and Methods*, HMSO. London.
Pigou, A.C. (1932) and (1946), *The Economics of Welfare*, 4th edn, London.
Pigou, A.C. (1935), 'Net Income and Capital Depletion', *Economic Journal*, xlv, June.
Pigou, A.C. (1941), 'Maintaining Capital Intact', *Economica* NS viii, August.
Ruggles, R. and Ruggles, N.D. (1956), *National Income Accounts and Income Analysis*, 2nd edn, New York.
Scott, M.F. (1976), Investment and Growth, *Oxford Economic Papers*, NS xxviii, November.
United Nations (1968), *A System of National Accounts*, Studies in Methods, Series F, no. 2, Rev. 3, Department of Economic and Social Affairs, Statistical Office of the United Nations, New York.

Notes

*The author is grateful to John Fleming and Geoffrey Harcourt for their comments which led to considerable improvements. They are not responsible for any remaining errors.

1. Hicks (1974), p. 315 n. 14.
2. See, for example, Hicks in Lutz and Hague (1961), and also Hicks (1965), (1969), and (1973) on the former, and Hicks (1969), (1971) (as well as earlier editions), and (1974) on the latter.
3. See Pigou (1935), (1941), and (1946). The last is a reprint of the fourth edition of *The Economics of Welfare* (1932), to which Pigou added a prefatory note in 1938 drawing attention to his 1935 *Economic Journal* article. This leaves his 1941 *Economica* article as his last published statement of the subject.
4. Pigou (1941).
5. Pigou (1946), part 1, ch. iv, p. 44.
6. Pigou (1935), p. 236.
7. Pigou also excluded, in his 1935 *Economic Journal* article (p. 238) 'physical changes which, while leaving the element as productive as ever, bring nearer the day of sudden and violent breakdown'. The most obvious example of such changes is the ageing of persons or domestic animals. I believe that in wishing to exclude *these* physical changes he was mistaken (see also n. 18 below).
8. Pigou admitted that there was some imprecision in reckoning the relative valuations of A and B in his example due to the length of the period chosen. This can, however, be avoided in theory, if not in practice, by measuring income over infinitesimally short periods. One then requires to multiply the rates of change of quantities in the stock by their values at a point in time. In his 1941 *Economica* article he did not refer to 'values' but to income yield. He did, however, refer to values in *The Economics of Welfare* (1946), p. 47.
9. In fact, Hayek had already provided an essentially similar example and argument in his 1935 *Economica* article (see pp. 257–8).
10. Hayek, in fact, considered a third businessman undertaking a risky investment, but it is sufficient for our purposes to consider only two.
11. See Hayek (1935), pp. 257–60.
12. See Hayek (1935), pp. 257, 259. '... it is obsolescence, rather than wear and tear which is the cause of mortality — homicide to make room for a new favourite, rather than natural death'. Barna in Lutz and Hague (1961), p. 85. See also Kuznets in Conference on Research in Income and Wealth (1951), p. 65.
13. Scott (1976).
14. See, for example, Maurice (1968), pp. 361–2.
15. See Barna in Lutz and Hague (1961), pp. 90–1.
16. This assumes that £X of gross investment could be transformed into £X of consumption. For a variety of reasons, precise equality is not to be expected, even if both are measured at factor cost. However, for simplicity this point is glossed over. Strictly speaking, investment should be measured by its equivalent amount of consumption if we want the sum of

consumption and net investment to equal Hicksian income.

17. Some writers, including Kuznets (in Conference on Research in Income and Wealth (1951), p. 66, but he appears to have modified his stance in Conference on Research in Income and Wealth (1957), pp. 277–9) and Ruggles and Ruggles (1956), p. 114, have questioned the view that obsolescence, which leads to the depreciation of individual assets, results in a loss of income for society as a whole. Their views do not seem to have gained general acceptance, perhaps because they failed to draw attention to the appreciation of some assets which accompanies, and offsets, the depreciation of others.

18. This footnote is confined to three difficult cases which they mentioned. First, Hayek's fashion machinery. The strict answer is that given by Hicks, namely, that real income comparisons must assume no changes in tastes. Nevertheless, as a practical matter the best solution may be to treat the loss in value as if it were a physical deterioration. I rather doubt that this is the thin end of a big wedge. Christopher Gilbert has pointed out that this treatment could also be justified by regarding the demand for changing fashion goods as an unchanging taste for being in fashion. Shifts in demand resulting from income growth do not lead to the same result, be it noted. Secondly, Pigou's case of equipment which, although it approaches nearer to the point of physical collapse, remains as currently productive as ever, my example being the ageing of humans or domestic animals. This *is* a physical change which *does* reduce the assets' present value. I think it needs to be offset by other investment if capital is to be maintained. Hicksian income will otherwise be overstated. Thirdly, Hicks' example in his 1942 article of an asset which remains physically unchanged and which is unused during the period for which we are estimating income. Hicks pointed out that the asset should appreciate in value over this period (given the usual assumptions of no change in general prices, or in expectations or interest rates), and so this appreciation should be included in income. It is not possible to do justice to this in a brief space. I believe the conclusion is correct, and that it would in principle be covered by a careful application of the definitions of Hicksian income along the lines of Scott (1976).

19. I hope to say a bit more in a forthcoming book.

84

The Living Standard*†

A. Sen

1. Introduction

In an illuminating analysis of 'the scope and status of welfare economics', Sir John Hicks (1975) makes the apparently puzzling remark: '*The Economics of Welfare* is *The Wealth of Nations* in a new guise' (p. 223). In explaining the connection between Pigou and Adam Smith, Hicks shows that Pigou was 'taking over' much of 'the *classical* theory of production and distribution' and 'turning' it into 'the economics of welfare'.

There is, in fact, a remarkable similarity even in the motivations behind Smith's and Pigou's works and their respective views of the nature of political economy and economics. Adam Smith (1776) starts his inquiry by referring to what will determine whether 'the nation will be better or worse supplied with all the necessaries and conveniences for which it has occasion' (vol. 1, p. 1). Pigou (1952) begins by arguing that 'the social enthusiasm which revolts from the sordidness of mean streets and joylessness of withered lives' is, in fact, 'the beginning of economic science' (p. 5). The central place is given to the determination of the standard of living is a part of their common view of the nature of the subject.

This paper is concerned with investigating the *concept* of the living standard. The topic falls within 'welfare economics' in a broad sense, but it is a somewhat specialized problem within that subject. In fact, in recent years, there has been a tendency for attention to move a little away from this specialized problem because of greater concern with the analysis of overall social welfare, systematized in the notions of 'social welfare functions' (see Bergson (1938), Samuelson (1947), Arrow (1951)). But the original problem of living standard comparison remains interesting and important — and one of much general interest.[1]

I begin with making two preliminary points about the concept of the standard of living. First, in so far as the living standard is a notion of welfare, it belongs to one aspect of it, not unconnected with what Pigou called 'economic welfare'. Pigou (1952) defined 'economic welfare' as 'that part of social welfare that can be brought directly or indirectly into relation with the measuring-rod of money' (p. 11). Sir John Hicks (1975) notes that

---

†Source: *Economic Papers*, NS., Supplement November 1984, Vol. 36, pp. 74–90.

'the distinctions which' Pigou 'draws, on this basis, are unquestionably interesting', but goes on to say, 'yet the concept of Economic Welfare, on which Pigou in fact based [the distinctions], or thought he was basing them, has nevertheless been very generally rejected' (p. 219). Hicks has clarified, in this essay and elsewhere (see Hicks (1940), (1958), (1959), (1981)), the main issues involved — including Pigou's rationale and the critic's reasoning. He does not provide an overall judgement, but in his own economic analysis, Hicks opts for the 'decision to treat the Social Product as primary, and to banish "economic welfare"' (Hicks (1975), pp. 230, 230–1).

The distinction between welfare and economic welfare is indeed problematic. But the approach is also, as Hicks says, 'unquestionably interesting'. The function that the distinction serves in Pigou's analysis can indeed be met in many exercises by the concept of the 'social product'. Nevertheless, there are other problems — notably those concerned with individual welfare and individual standard of living — in which a distinction closer to Pigou's own (between economic welfare and overall welfare) may well be necessary.

Let me illustrate. I haven't seen you for many years — since I was chucked out of school in fact. I run into you one day in the West End waving at me from your chauffeur-driven Rolls-Royce, looking shockingly prosperous and well-heeled. You give me a ride, and invite me to visit you at your mansion in Chelsea. I remark that I am pleased to see what a high standard of living you are enjoying. 'Not at all', you reply. 'My standard of living is very low. I am a very unhappy man.' 'Why so?' I have to probe. 'Because', you reply, 'I write poems — damn good ones too — but nobody likes my poems, not even my wife. I am always depressed about this injustice, and also sorry that the world has such deplorable taste. I am miserable and have a very low standard of living.' By now I can see no reason to doubt that you are indeed unhappy, but I feel obliged to tell you that you don't know the meaning of 'standard of living'. So you drop me off at the next Tube station (remarking: 'My standard of living high/What a plebeian lie!', adding to the set of people who don't think much of your poetry).

I think Pigou would very likely be right in maintaining that your 'economic welfare' is high even though you are unhappy and quite possibly have a low overall welfare. That would be right not because welfare or utility or happiness can plausibly be split into distinct self-contained parts, of which 'economic welfare' happens to be one. Rather, it can be argued that 'economic welfare' is an interesting concept of its own, which relates to — but is not necessarily one separable part of — welfare or utility or happiness. A person's sense of material well-being can be a sensible subject of study, without our being able to split the sense of overall well-being into several separable bits, of which the sense of material well-being is one. A 'plural' approach to utility (see Sen (1981)) permits the coexistence of various distinct concepts of utility, which are *interdependent*, without one being a separable part of another. While I shall presently argue that living standard is best seen not as a utility concept at all (roughly speaking, it can be said that it deals with material well-being and not with the *sense* of material well-being), it *is* an 'economic concept (roughly speaking, being concerned with *material* well-being). More will be said on this presently.

The second point concerns the motivation underlying studies of standard of living. It can be part of the objectives of policy-making (for example: 'we plan to raise the standard of living fastest!'). But that need not be the only motivation. We may be primarily concerned with a cognitive question, e.g. comparing standard of living between two actual persons, or two actual nations, or the same person or nation at two actual points of time. The use of 'counter-factual', if any, may not, therefore, take the rather straightforward form it tends to take in the usual 'virtual displacement' (or marginalist) analysis (e.g. what *would have* happened if this person had a different bundle of commodities at the *same* point of time, with the *same* utility function?). In making comparisons of actual living standards, there may be no reasonable basis for assuming the same utility function — the same desires, wants, temperament, and so forth.

The distinction concerns the contrast between 'comprehensive comparisons' and 'situational comparisons', discussed in Sen (1976), (1979). Comparisons of standard of living need not be confined only to situational comparisons (e.g. 'I am better off this year than I would have been if I had last year's commodity bundle this year'). They may call for comprehensive comparisons (e.g. 'I am better off this year than I was last year'). We cannot, then, just vary the commodity bundles and keep the utility *functions* (and related correspondences) *necessarily* unchanged. If the utility-functional characteristics are indeed unchanged, then this would be a further fact, and not just a part of the standard of counterfactual exercise.

2. Alternative Approaches

There are at least three general approaches to the notion of the standard of living of a person. The first is to see the living standard as some notion of the *utility* of a person. The second is some notion of *opulence*. The third is to see the standard of living as one type of *freedom*. The former two approaches have been more explored than the third, though — to put my cards on the table — it is the third that I would argue for in this essay.[2] But I begin with utility and opulence.

The utility view of the standard of living is well presented by Pigou himself. In fact, Pigou uses 'economic welfare', 'the standard of living', 'standard of real income' and 'material prosperity' as more or less synonymous (e.g., Pigou (1952), pp. 100–1, 622–3, 758–767). Economic welfare is defined, as was already stated, as 'a part of welfare as a whole' (p. 12), and 'the elements of welfare' are seen as '*states of consciousness* and, perhaps, their relations' (p. 10, italics added).

It is fair to recognize that the notion of 'utility' has, by now, several distinct meanings. Pigou (1962) himself distinguishes between 'satisfaction' and the 'intensity of desire', referring to the latter as 'desiredness' (p. 23). As a loyal 'consciousness-utilitarian', Pigou does not dispute the claim of satisfaction to be the *authentic* version of utility or welfare, and defends the desiredness view (and the willingness-to-pay measure) *contingently* by asserting that 'it is fair to suppose that most commodities, especially those of wide consumption that are required, as articles of food and clothing are, for direct personal use, will be wanted as a means to satisfaction, and will, consequently, be desired with intensities proportional to the satisfactions they are expected to yield' (p. 24).

It would appear that the more dominant schools of utilitarianism today take a 'desire' view of utility rather than the 'satisfaction' view, and put value on the fulfilment of what is desired rather than on the amount of satisfaction it generates (see Sidgwick (1874), Ramsey (1926), Harsanyi (1976), Hare (1981), Mirrlees (1982)).[3] The battle is by no means over (see Gosling (1969), Brandt (1979), among others), and there are indeed many complex issues involved (see Sen (1981), Griffin (1982)). But this need not detain us here, since it is necesary, for our purpose, to discuss *both* the 'satisfaction' view and the 'desiredness' view of utility, and related to this, to examine the two corresponding views of the standard of living (seen in terms of utility).

The identification of the living standard with *overall* utility as such is obviously open to the problem that was discussed in the last section — the problem that had led Pigou to introduce the notion of 'economic welfare' in the first place. If the standard of living has to be seen in terms of utility, then distinctions of Pigou's type would have to be made.

The second approach — that of the living standard as *opulence* — goes back at least to Adam Smith (1776). The concern with a nation being 'better or worse supplied with all the necessaries and conveniences for which it has occasion' (vol. 1, p. 1) is a concern with the opulence of the nation. Indeed, Adam Smith thought that the two objectives of 'political economy, considered as a branch of the science of a statesman or legislator' were 'first, to provide a plentiful revenue or subsistence for the people, or more properly to enable them to provide such revenue or subsistence for themselves; and secondly, to supply the state or commonwealth with a revenue sufficient for the public services.' 'The different progress of opulence in different ages and nations has given occasion to two different systems of political economy with regard to enriching the people' (vol. 1, p. 375).

The modern literature on real income indicators and the indexing of commodity bundles[4] is the inheritor of this tradition of evaluating opulence. Since this evaluation is often done with respect to an indifference map, it is tempting to think of this approach as the utility approach in disguise. But there is an important difference even when the evaluation of real income is done in terms of an indifference map representing preference, since what is being evaluated is not utility as such (in the form either of desiredness or of satisfaction), but *the commodity basis of utility*. The two approaches will be congruent only under the special assumption of constancy of the utility *function* (not to be confused with the constancy of tastes). As was discussed in Section 1, of this paper, this is a bad assumption for measuring the standard of living (even if it is acceptable for rational choice or planning involving counterfactual comparison of alternative possibilities). The distinction will be further discussed in the next section.

The third approach — that of freedom — is not much in fashion in the literature on the standard of living, but I believe it has much promise. Freedom here is interpreted in its 'positive' sense (to be free to *do this* or *be that*) rather than in its 'negative' form (not to be interfered with).[5] In this approach what is valued is the *capability* to live well, and in the specific economic context of standard of living, it values the capabilities associated with economic matters (see Sen (1980, 1984a)).

To illustrate the contrast involved, consider the problem of food and hunger. In the capability approach a person's ability to live without hunger or malnutrition may be valued. This does not amount to valuing the possession of a given amount of food as such, except indirectly through causal links, in a contingent way (since the impact of food on nutrition varies with such factors as metabolic rates, body size, climatic conditions, sex, pregnancy, lactation, and work intensity). Nor does it involve equating the value of freedom from hunger or malnutrition with the *utility* (happiness, pleasure, or desire-fulfilment) from that achievement. More will have to be said on these contrasts presently, since some complex issues are involved (see Sections 3 and 4 below).

I should like to assert that focusing on capability as freedom in the context of judging living standard is not a new approach. Its lineage certainly goes back to classical political economy, even though it may not have been explicitly stated in this form. Freedom was very much a classical concern. In fact, even in the statement about opulence that I quoted from Adam Smith earlier in this section, Smith modifies his reference to providing 'a plentiful revenue or subsistence for the people', by the statement, 'more properly to enable them to provide such revenue or subsistence for themselves' (vol i, p. 375). In a different context (dealing in fact with the value of negative freedom), Hicks (1959) has pointed out that the classical backing for 'economic freedom' went deeper than justifying it on grounds of 'economic efficiency'. The efficiency proposition, as Hicks (1959) notes, 'was no more than a secondary support', and Hicks is certainly right to question the justification for our 'forgetting, as completely as most of us have done, the other side of the argument' dealing with the value of economic freedom as such (p. 138).

When it comes to evaluating what counts as 'necessaries', with the supply of which Adam Smith was so concerned, Smith (1776) does go explicitly into certain quite complex capabilities, e.g. the freedom to appear in public without shame (vol ii, p. 352):

A linen shirt, for example, is, strictly speaking, not a necessary of life. The Greeks and Romans lived, I suppose, very comfortably though they had no linen. But in the present times, through the greater part of Europe, a creditable day-labourer would be ashamed to appear in public without a linen shirt, the want of which would be supposed to denote that disgraceful degree of poverty which, it is presumed, nobody can well fall into without extreme bad conduct. Custom, in the same manner, had rendered leather shoes a necessary of life in England. The poorest creditable person of either sex would be ashamed to appear in public without them.

Following Smith's reasoning, I have tried to argue elsewhere (Sen (1983)) that *absolute deprivation* on the space of capabilities (e.g., whether one can appear in public without shame) may follow from *relative deprivation* on the space of commodities (e.g., whether one possesses what others do, such as linen shirts or leather shoes in Smith's example). Some of the apparent conflicts in defining poverty (e.g. the 'relative' versus the 'absolute' views) may be avoided by seeing living standard in terms of capabilities and assessing the value of commodity possession in terms of its contribution to capabilities and freedoms.

The possibility of judging advantage in terms of the extent of freedom has been also discussed by Karl Marx (1846), (1858), (1875), and John Stuart Mill (1859), (1869). The roots of the capability approach and freedom-based evaluation of the standard of living, thus, go back to Smith, Marx, and Mill, among others. The standard of living — and economic freedom in the 'positive' sense — can be seen as relating to 'positive freedom' in general in ways that are not altogether dissimilar to the relationship between 'economic welfare' and 'welfare' in general. The standard of living, on this view, reflects the 'material' aspects of freedom.[6]

3. Utility, Opulence and Material Capabilities

The exact distinction between the utility approach and the opulence approach to the standard of living is worth investigating. If the commodity bundles under the opulence approach is evaluated not in terms of preference maps but in terms of costs, then the contrast would be straightforward. One of the things we have been taught by John Hicks is the need to recognize that the 'utility' method and the 'cost' method provide two *alternative* ways of evaluating real income, and that each has distinct — and quite different — merits of its own (Hicks (1940), (1958)). And while in 'equilibrium' theory the two work *together*, in the evaluation of commodity bundles, they provide *rival* methods of assessment.[7] If opulence is evaluated by the 'cost method', then that might easily lead to measures quite different from those yielded by utility weighting. This is a straightforward contrast, once Hicks's distinction is noted.

But suppose we do use the 'utility' method to evaluate commodity bundles. Would we then get an index that is an index of utilities? Not necessarily. *Weighting by utilities* (marginal utilities, to be exact) is not the same thing as *measuring utilities*. Consider the following example. A given person has utility function $U_1(.)$ in period 1 when he enjoys commodity vector x_1 and utility function $U_2(.)$ in period 2 when he has commodity vector x_2. The ordering of the four utilities is the following, in descending order:

$$U_1(\mathbf{x}_2)$$
$$U_1(\mathbf{x}_1)$$
$$U_2(\mathbf{x}_2)$$
$$U_2(\mathbf{x}_1).$$

There is no change in 'taste', as it is usually defined in economics, as given by the indifference map, or by what is observed in market behaviour. In both periods the person prefers $\mathbf{x}_2$ to $\mathbf{x}_1$. In terms of indexing the commodity bundles — the ranking of opulence — the bundle enjoyed in the second period $\mathbf{x}_2$ is clearly better than that in the first period $\mathbf{x}_1$. But while opulence is greater in the second period, utility is higher in the first, since $U_1(\mathbf{x}_1) > U_2(\mathbf{x}_2)$. Ranking commodity bundles *according to utility* is not the same as ranking *utilities*.

Pigou seems to get into a bit of a muddle on this issue. 'Considering a single individual', says Pigou (1952), 'whose tastes are taken as fixed, we say that his dividend in period II is greater than in period I if the items that are added to it in period II are items that he *wants more* than the items that are taken away from it in period II' (p. 51). Quite right that, if by 'dividend' we mean some index of opulence. What goes wrong is the belief about 'economic welfare' being 'intimately associated' with the size of this dividend. Pigou notices some lack of intimacy when tastes change, or — in the case of national dividend — when the distribution of purchasing power changes, but the problem is present even with individual dividend and even without any change of taste whatsoever. Pigou is quite right in thinking that with constant tastes, in the case of an individual (when the issue of distribution does not arise), 'this method of definition' (in terms of willingness to pay) 'would be the natural and obvious one to adopt' and 'there would be nothing to set against the advantages of this method of definition' (p. 52). But the definition would not be that of economic welfare (or of the *utility*-view of standard of living), nor necessarily correspond to it. It would be — under the circumstances specified — quite a nice definition of *opulence* (and the commodity-index view of standard of living).

To illustrate the nature of the problem, consider a person who moves from being 'high' (and nearly manic) in state 1 to being 'low' (and quite depressive) in state 2, with an unchanged indifference map. Figure 1 reflects a part of the constant preference map (two indifference curves to be exact).

In both his 'high' and 'low' states (i.e. in both states 1 and 2), he prefers (and gets more utility from) $\mathbf{x}_2$ than from $\mathbf{x}_1$. He is clearly more *opulent* with $\mathbf{x}_2$ than with $\mathbf{x}_1$. But in state 2, when he does have $\mathbf{x}_2$, he is pretty badly off ('terrible', to be candid), compared with what he is in state 1, when he had $\mathbf{x}_1$ (and when he found his position to be 'great'). The ranking of utility is as clear as the ranking of commodity bundles, except that the two go in opposite directions.

This problem would, of course, be avoided had the real utility function (and not just the preference map and the class of its real-valued representations) remained the same. In 'counterfactual' exercises involving 'virtual displacement' *that* would be definitionally guaranteed. That coun-

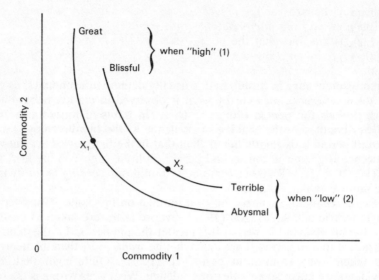

FIG. 1. A person with unchanging tastes and changing utility levels.

terfactual exercise may be perfectly sensible for a theory of planning or of rational choice, but — as was argued in Section 1 — it is quite inappropriate for comparing *actual* standards of living.

While the example chosen here deals with a purely psychological variation, to wit, between being 'high' and 'low', the utility function can vary for other reasons as well. There could be more pollution in the air, or more crime on the streets, or a touch of '1984' in our daily lives. The commodity bundle x_2 may well be invariably preferred to commodity bundle x_1, and still the person may be in a terrible way in state 2 — much worse off than in state 1. It is, of course, possible to go on inventing new '*as if* commodities' (e.g., fresh air, not-being-mugged, non-snooping) to extend the *reach* of the commodity-index view. But such 'extensions' are not easy to reconcile with the uses to which the commodity approach is put. Also, the need for 'inventing' a new commodity always remains so long as there is functional relation $U(x)$, which can vary, no matter how 'extensively' x is defined.

Which of the two approaches — utility or opulence — is a more appropriate way of seeing the standard of living? I do not know the answer to that question, but I cannot believe that either is very appropriate. In the cases under discussion, the purchased commodity bundle is better *and* utility is lower. If the utility function has changed due to purely emotional reasons (e.g., the person has lost faith in God), and not for any 'material' reason, it is not unreasonable to go with the opulence ranking in pronouncing on the living standard. It is then plausible to say that the standard of living has risen, but the person is more depressed, more unhappy, *despite* that. He may even be able to do many more things in the second period than he could in the first. But he values them less. Bad luck for him, but the badness of the luck is not due to a decline in the standard of living.

But now vary the *interpretation* of the changed utility function. It turns out, let us imagine, that the utility function $U(.)$ has dipped because of pollution in the air, thugs on the street, and snoopers peering through the window. The purchased commodity bundle may be valued higher, but the person cannot do many material things he could do in the earlier period. He cannot breathe fresh air (or avoid some lung disease); he cannot walk around freely after dark; and he cannot have privacy. It would be absurd, in this case, to say that the standard of living of this person has gone up just because the commodity bundle purchased in the second period is higher in both periods.

The message seems clear enough. Neither the utility view nor the commodity-index view will do as a *general* approach to the standard of living. The limited success of each is contingent on certain particular circumstances, which may or may not, respectively, obtain.

Before I end this section, I make two further remarks. First, the difficulties in question with the utility view can arise no matter whether we choose the 'satisfaction' interpretation or the 'desiredness' interpretation. This is easily checked by assuming conditions such that satisfaction and desiredness go together — an assumption that Pigou (1952) did in fact make (pp. 23–4). The person desires x_2 more than x_1 in each period, and would get more satisfaction from x_2 than from x_1 in either period. But he desires having utility function $U_1(.)$ with commodity bundle x_1 *more than* having utility function $U_2(.)$ with commodity bundle x_2, and he also gets more satisfaction with $U_1(x_1)$ than with $U_2(x_2)$. Everything substantial said before stands, no matter which of the two interpretations of utility we choose.

The second remark concerns the *nature of the argument* that was used to criticize universal use of either the utility view or the commodity-index view of standard of living. We referred to various things the person could or could not do under each circumstances. We invoked the person's capabilities and checked the person's particular freedoms. In the pollution–crime–1984 example, the argument against the commodity-index view rested on noting that in the second period the person could not breathe fresh air, walk around freely, or have privacy. There was, however no corresponding decline in material capabilities in the emotional-variation example (even though the capability to be happy in general was affected), and that is why, in that case, the commodity-view of standard of living seemed tentatively untarnished and certainly more relevant than the utility view. So we have, in fact, already used the capability approach to tell between the contingent appeals of the utility view and the commodity-index view. It seems natural to go on to approach the standard of living directly in terms of capabilities.

It is also worth emphasizing, to avoid ambiguity, that in focusing on particular capabilities in the two contrasting cases, we looked at those freedoms that can be seen as being associated with what Pigou calls 'material prosperity', rather than purely psychological factors. Clearly, in the emotional variation case, there is something the person is obviously not capable of achieving in the second period, to wit, to be happy. But we concentrated on a particular class of capabilities, particular types of positive freedoms, related to *material* living conditions.

The distinction between 'material' and other capabilities is not, of course, entirely clear-cut. Nor is it always very important. Its importance in the context of the analysis of the standard of living lies primarily in the fact that the standard of living figures in common usage in a form that specifically emphasizes material capabilities (e.g., being well-nourished or motorized is taken to be a part of 'the living standard' in a way that fulfilment of poetic ambitions or even being generally cheerful is not). However, even when that usage is granted, it can be asked why should it be appropriate to attach any importance at all to that distinction and regard 'the living standard' — thus conceived — to be particularly worthy of the economist's attention. At this point, a difficult issue of valuation is involved, and the answer may be similar to Pigou's motivation in being concerned specifically with economic welfare. Living standard — seen in terms of material capabilities — may be thought to be more influenceable (certainly, more *directly* influenceable) by economic policy. I should emphasize that this justification, which is not without force, is however, a strongly contingent one, and may in some contexts simply not be an adequate ground for being concerned with the material capabilities only (as reflected in the standard of living). In the present — more limited context — we are primarily concerned with *interpreting* the notion of the living standard, rather than examining how important a concept it is.

4. Functioning, Capability, and Freedom

The distinction between commodities, utility, functioning, and the capability to function, may not be altogether transparent, and call for some explanation.[9] Consider a good, e.g., bread. The utilitarian will be concerned with the fact that bread creates utility — happiness or desire-fulfilment — through its consumption. This is, of course, true. But creating utility is not the only thing that bread does. It also contributes to nutrition, among other things. In modern consumer theory in economics, the nature of the goods has been seen in terms of their 'characteristics'. Gorman (1956), Lancaster (1966) and other economists have systematically explored the view of goods as bundles of characteristics. Bread possesses nutrition-giving characteristics (calories, protein, etc.) but also other characteristics, e.g. providing stimulation, meeting social conventions, helping get-togethers.[10] A characteristic — as used in consumer theory — is a feature of a good, whereas a capability is a feature of a person in relation to goods. Having some bread gives me the capability of functioning in particular ways, e.g. being free from hunger, or living without certain nutritional deficiencies.

Four different notions need to be distinguished in this context. There is the notion of a *good* (e.g. bread); *characteristic of a good* (e.g. calories and other nutrients); that of *functioning of a person* (e.g. the person living without calorie deficiency); that of *utility* (e.g. the pleasure or desire-fulfilment from eating bread or from being well-nourished). An utility-based theory of living standard concentrates on the last item of the four — utility. Analyses of living standard in terms of opulence or 'real income' tend to concentrate on the first item — commodities. Egalitarians concerned with income distribution worry about the distribution of goods, and they too will focus on the first item. These two approaches can be refined by taking explicit note of characteristics, in line with the second item.

'Characteristics' are, of course, abstractions from goods, but they do relate ultimately to *goods* rather than to *persons.* 'Functionings' are, however, personal features; they tell us what a person is doing or achieving. 'Capability' to function reflects what a person *can* do or *can* achieve. Of course, the characteristics of goods owned by a person would *relate* to the capabilities of that person. A person achieves these capabilities through — among other things — the use of these goods. But the capabilities of persons are quite different from (though dependent on) the characteristics of goods possessed. Valuing one has *implications* on wanting the other, but valuing one is *not the same thing* as valuing the other.

If, for example, we value a person's ability to function without nutritional deficiency, we would favour arrangements in which the person has adequate food with those nutritional characteristics, but that is not the same thing as valuing the possession of a given amount of food as such. If, for example, some disease makes the person unable to achieve the capability of avoiding nutritional deficiency even with an amount of food that would suffice for others,[11] then the fact that he or she does possess that amount of food would not in any way 'neutralize' the person's inability to be well nourished. If we value the capability to function, then that is what we do value, and the possession of goods with the corresponding characteristics is only instrumentally valued and that again only to the extent that it helps in the achievement of the things that we do value (viz. capabilities).

Consider now one more example, to explain the motivation behind looking at capabilities for assessing the standard of living. Take two persons A and B. A is rather less poor than B, eats more food, and works no harder. But he is also undernourished, which B is not, since B has a smaller body size (coming from Kerala rather than Punjab, say), has a lower metabolic rate, and lives in a warmer climate. So A eats more but B is better nourished. However, it so happens that A is religious, contented with his fate, and happier than B, and has his desires more fulfilled than has B, who keeps grumbling about his lot. In the way this example has been constructed, A is doing better than B *both* in terms of commodity-index and utility (in fact, under *each* interpretation of utility: satisfaction and desire fulfilment). That is for sure, but does that imply that A has a higher standard of living? Rickety old A, chronically undernourished, riddled with avoidable morbidity, and reconciled — by the 'opium' of religion — to a lower expectation of life? It would be hard to claim, under these circumstances, that A does indeed have a higher standard of living than B. He may earn more, eat more, and may be less dissatisfied, but he does not have the capability to be well-nourished in the way B is, nor is he free from malnutrition-related diseases. Indeed, it would be hard not to say that it is B who has a higher standard of living despite *both* his unhappiness and lower income than A.

The issue of capabilities — specifically 'material' capabilities — is particularly important in judging the standard of living in people of poor countries. Are they well nourished? Are they free from avoidable morbidity? Do they live long? Can they read and write? Can they count? And so on. It is also important in dealing with poverty in rich countries (as I have tried to argue elsewhere, Sen (1983)). Can they take part in the life of the community (cf. Townsend (1979))? Can they appear in public without shame and without feeling disgraced (to go back to a question asked by Adam Smith (1776))? Can they find worthwhile jobs? Can they keep themselves warm? Can they use their school education? Can they visit friends and relations if they choose? It is a question of what the persons can do or can be, and not just a question of their earnings and opulence, nor of their being contented. Freedom is the ussue; not commodities, nor utility as such.

It is, however, worth re-emphasizing that the thesis here is not that there is no distinction between freedom — even 'positive freedom' in general — and living standard. That would be an absurd claim. It is rather that living standard can be seen as freedom (positive freedom) of particular types, related to material capabilities. It reflects a variety of freedoms of the material kind (e.g. to be able to live long, to be well-nourished, to take part in the life of the community). It does not cover all types of freedom (e.g. religious freedom). Some of the others may be very important, but not a part of the normal concept of the standard of living. Indeed, the living standard may be seen as corresponding to positive freedom in general in the way that Pigou's 'economic welfare' may be seen as corresponding to welfare as such (see Section 1 and 3 above). It is in this sense that living standard can be seen as 'economic freedom'.

It may, of course, be pointed out that the rejection of opulence or utility as the basis of assessing standard of living, does not establish the relevance of freedom as such. There is scope for ambiguity in the arguments presented. We may well value what a person *does* (or actually *achieves*) rather than what he *can do* (or *can achieve*), which is what freedom has to be concerned with. Should we not, for example, look directly at *nourishment* as such rather than the *capability to be nourished*?

There is, I believe, substance in this line of questioning, but it is not as persuasive as it may first appear. What about the ascetic who decides to fast and becomes undernourished despite his being rich and having the means of being excellently nourished? It seems rather odd to see him as deprived, with a low standard of living. He has chosen to fast; he was not forced to fast.

Capability *is* of importance. To take another example, the *capability* to visit friends and relatives may be important for standard of living. However, a person who chooses not to make use of that capability, and curls up instead with a good book, may not be sensibly seen as being deprived and having a low standard of living.

It does seem plausible to concentrate on a person's capabilities and freedoms as indicators of living standard. Variations of tastes can be accommodated more easily in a format that focuses on the capability to function in different ways rather than just on particular functionings. Also, uncertainty about our own future tastes makes us value freedom more. But on top of that some importance may be attached to the power a person has over his or her own life — that a person is not forced by circumstances to lead a specific type of life and has a genuine freedom to choose as he wants. The standard of living has much to do with what Marx described as 'replacing the domination of circumstances and chance over individuals by the domination of individuals over chance and circumstances'.[12]

5. Difficulties

I am not under any illusion that the capability approach to the standard of living would be very easy to use. It is particularly difficult to get an idea of a person's positive freedom of choice — what he or she could or could not have done or been. What we observe are the actual choices and realizations. But the case for using the capability approach is not, of course, logistic convenience, but *relevance*.

In some practical exercises with the capability approach, the logistic problems have not proved to be quite so hard as to make the effort to use existing data worthless. For example, in an exercise on checking the nature and extent of 'sex bias' in living standards in India (see Kynch and Sen (1983)), the approach has proved to be quite convenient. In fact, even the informational problems have been, if anything, eased by moving attention away from food consumption data of *particular members* of the family (almost impossible to get) to observed nutrition, morbidity, mortality, and so forth. Indeed, the move from individual *commodity consumption* to individual *functioning* would often tend to make the data problem easier, even though to identify *capability sets* fully, much harder data requirements would have to be imposed.

I end by noting three important issues that are particularly difficult to deal with. First, when there is diversity of taste, it becomes harder to surmise about capability by simply observing achievement. For extreme poverty this problem is less serious. Valuing better nourishment, less illness and longer life tend to be fairly universal, and also largely consistent with each other despite being distinct objectives. But in other cases — of greater relevance to the richer countries — the informational problems with the capability approach can be quite serious.

Second, if capabilities of different sorts have to be put together in one index, the issue of aggregation may be quite a difficult one even for a given person. There is, in addition, the problem of group aggregation. I have tried to discuss these issues elsewhere (Sen (1976), (1979), (1984a)), and the picture is far from hopeless. But I must confess that they are indeed hard problems to tackle, requiring a good deal of compromise. It is, however, worth mentioning that for many problems, an *aggregate* ranking is not needed, and for most, a *complete* aggregate ordering is quite redundant.

Third, freedom is a set (rather than just a 'point'), in the sense that it refers to various alternative bundles of things one could have done and not just to the particular bundle one did do. This makes the evaluation of 'capability sets' rather unlike that of evaluating utility or indexing commodity bundles. Often it will indeed make sense to identify the value of the set of capabilities with the worth of the 'best' element in the set, and this reduces the set-evaluation problem to a derived element-evaluation exercise. But in other contexts, the value of the 'best' element does not capture the value of freedom adequately. For example, if we remove from the feasibility set all elements other than the best one, the utility level that can be achieved with a given utility function may not be affected, but in a very real sense the person's freedom *is* reduced. In interpreting standard of living in terms of freedom (related to material capabilities), a different range of complex issues have to be faced that do not quite arise under the utility or the opulence approaches.

Nevertheless, if standard of living is best seen in terms of capabilities (as positive freedoms of particular types), then these complexities simply have to be faced. The standard of living is one of the central notions of economics. And it is one of the subjects that do interest the general public, specifically in the context of the policy. In directing attention to these questions, economists such as Adam Smith, Pigou, and Hicks have taken on issues that are complex *as well as* of deep and lasting importance.

Even if data limitations may quite often force us to make practical compromises, conceptual clarity requires that we do not smugly elevate such a compromise to a position of unquestioned significance. Hicks has explained his attitude towards welfare economics thus:

> I have been trying to show that 'welfare economics', as I would now regard it, is composed of a series of steps, steps by which we try to take more and more of the things which concern us into account. None of our 'optima' marks the top of that staircase. We must always be prepared to push one, if we can, a little further (Hicks (1981), p. xvii).

It has been argued in this paper that the capability approach to the standard of living will be a step forward — certainly conceptually and perhaps even in actual empirical application.

References

Arrow, K.J. (1951), *Social Choice and Individual Values*, New York: Wiley.
Bergson, A. (1938), 'A Reformulation of Certain Aspects of Welfare Economics', *Quarterly Journal of Economics*, 52.
Berlin, I. (1969), *Four Essays on Liberty*, Oxford: Clarendon Press.
Brandt, R. (1979), *A Theory on the Good and the Right*, Oxford: Clarendon Press.

Deaton, A. and Muellbauer, J. (1980), *Economics and Consumer Behaviour*, Cambridge University Press.

Douglas, M. and Isherwood, B. (1979), *The World of Goods*, New York: Basic Books.

Fisher, F.M. and Shell, K. (1968), 'Tastes and Quality Change in the Pure Theory of the True Cost-of-Living Index', in J.N. Wolfe, ed., *Value, Capital and Growth: Papers in Honour of Sir John Hicks*, Edinburgh University Press.

Fisher, F.M. and Shell, K. (1972), *The Economic Theory of Price Indices*, New York: Academic Press.

Gorman, W.M. (1956), 'The Demand for Related Goods', *Journal Paper J3129*, Iowa Experimental Station, Ames, Iowa.

Gosling, J.C.B. (1969), *Pleasure and Desire*, Oxford: Clarendon Press.

Graaff, J. de V. (1957), *Theoretical Welfare Economics*, Cambridge University Press.

Griffin, J. (1982), 'Modern Utilitarianism', *Revue internationale de philosophie*, 141.

Hare, R.M. (1981), *Moral Thinking*, Oxford: Clarendon Press.

Harsanyi, J. (1976), *Essays on Ethics, Social Behaviour and Scientific Explanation*, Dordrecht: Reidel.

Hicks, J.R. (1939a), *Value and Capital*, Oxford: Clarendon Press.

Hicks, J.R. (1939b), 'Foundations of Welfare Economics', *Economic Journal*, 49; reprinted in Hicks (1981).

Hicks, J.R. (1940), 'Valuation of Social Income', *Economica*, 7; reprinted in Hicks (1981).

Hicks, J.R. (1958), 'The Measurement of Real Income', *Oxford Economic Papers*, 10; reprinted in Hicks (1981).

Hicks, J.R. (1959), 'A Manifesto', in *Essays in World Economics*, Oxford: Clarendon Press; reprinted in Hicks (1981), to which the page references relate.

Hicks, J.R. (1975), 'The Scope and Status of Welfare Economics', *Oxford Economic Papers*, 27; reprinted in Hicks (1981), to which the page references relate.

Hicks, J.R. (1981), *Wealth and Welfare, Collected Essays on Economic Theory*, vol. 1, Oxford: Blackwell.

Hicks, J.R. (1983), 'A Discipline Not a Science', in his *Classics and Moderns, Collected Essays on Economic Theory*, vol. III, Oxford: Blackwell.

Kaldor, N. (1939), 'Welfare Propositions and Interpersonal Comparisons of Utility, *Economic Journal*, 49.

Kynch, J., and Sen, A.K. (1983), 'Indian Women: Well-being and Survival', *Cambridge Journal of Economics*, 7.

Lancaster, K.J. (1966), 'A New Approach to Consumer Theory', *Journal of Political Economy*, 74.

Little, I.M.D. (1950), *A Critique of Welfare Economics*, Oxford: Clarendon Press; 2nd ed., 1957.

Marx, K. (1846), *The German Ideology*, jointly with F. Engels; English translation, Moscow: Foreign Language Publishing Press, 1964.

Marx, K. (1858), *Grundrisse*; English translation, Harmondsworth: Penguin, 1973.

Marx, K. (1875), *Critique of the Gotha Program*; English translation, New York: International Publishers.

McLellan, D. (1977), ed., *Karl Marx: Selected Writings*, Oxford: Oxford University Press.

Mill, J.S. (1859), *On Liberty*; republished Harmondsworth: Penguin, 1974.

Mill, J.S. (1869), *On the Subjection of Women*; republished London: Dent, 1970.

Mirrlees, J.A. (1982), 'The Economic Uses of Utalitarianism', in Sen and Williams (1982).

Pigou, A.C. (1952), *The Economics of Welfare*, Fourth Edition, with eight new appendices, London: Macmillan.

Ramsey, F.P. (1926), 'Truth and Probability'; republished in his *Foundations: Essays in Philosophy, Logic, Mathematics and Economics*, London: Routledge, 1978.

Samuelson, P.A. (1947), *Foundations of Economic Analysis*, Cambridge, Mass.: Harvard University Press.

Scitovsky, T. (1976), *The Joyless Economy*, London: Oxford University Press.

Scrimshaw, N.S. (1977), 'Effect of Infection on Nutrient Requirements', *American Journal on Clinical Nutrition*, 30.

Sen, A.K. (1976), 'Real National Income', *Review of Economic Studies*, 43; reprinted in Sen (1982a).

Sen, A.K. (1979), 'The Welfare Basis of Real Income Comparisons', *Journal of Economic Literature*, 17; reprinted in Sen (1984 c).

Sen, A.K. (1980), 'Equality of What?' in S. McMurrin, eds., *Tanner Lectures on Human Values*, vol. I, Cambridge University Press; reprinted in Sen (1982 a).

Sen, A.K. (1981), 'Plural Utility', *Proceedings of the Aristotelian Society*, 81.

Sen, A.K. (1982 a), *Choice, Welfare and Measurement*, Oxford: Blackwell, and Cambridge, Mass.: MIT Press.

Sen, A.K. (1982 b), 'Rights and Agency', *Philosophy and Public Affairs*, 11.

Sen, A.K. (1983), 'Poor, Relatively Speaking', *Oxford Economic Papers*, 35; reprinted in Sen (1984 c).

Sen, A.K. (1984 a), *Commodities and Capabilities*, Hennipman Lecture, 1982; to be published by North-Holland, Amsterdam.

Sen, A.K. (1984 b), 'Rights and Capabilities', forthcoming in T. Honderich, ed., *Ethics and Objectivity*, Essays in Memory of John Mackie, to be published by Routledge, London.

Sen, A.K. (1984 c), *Resources, Values and Development*, Oxford: Blackwell, and Cambridge, Mass.: Harvard University Press.

Sen, A. and Williams,B., ed. (1982), *Utilitarianism and Beyond*, Cambridge: Cambridge University Press.

Sidgwick, H. (1874), *The Methods of Ethics*: 7th edn., London: Macmillan, 1907.

Smith, A. (1776), *An Inquiry into the Nature and Causes of the Wealth of Nations*. Republished, London: Home University Library.

Srinivasan, T.N. (1982), 'Hunger: Defining It. Estimating Its Global Incidence and Alleviating It', mimeographed; forthcoming in D. Gale Johnson and E. Schuh, eds., *Role of Markets in the World Food Economy*.

Sukhatme, P.V. (1977), *Nutrition and Poverty*, New Delhi: Indian Agricultural Research Institute.

Townsend, P. (1979), *Poverty in the United Kingdom*, London: Penguin.

Notes

*For many helpful comments on an earlier version, I am most grateful to David Collard, Dieter Helm, Maurice Scott, and T.N. Srinivasan.

1. See Kaldor (1939), Hicks (1940), (1958), Little (1950), Graaff (1957). See also Hicks (1983) on the various uses of economic theory.

2. I have tried to do this elsewhere in greater detail, viz., in my Hennipman Lecture (April 1982), forthcoming as a monograph, *Commodities and Capabilities*, Sen (1984 a).

3. There is a third view, quite popular among economists, that definitionally identifies the utility ranking with the binary relation of choice. As an approach it begs more questions than it answers (see Hicks (1958), Sen (1982 a)). It is also particularly unsuited for interpersonal or intertemporal comparison so essential for studies of living standards, since people do not actually face the choice of being someone else, or living at some other time.

4. The literature has been surveyed and critically examined in Sen (1979).

5. See Berlin (1969) for the contrast between 'positive' and 'negative' views of freedom in Berlin's own focus is on the 'negative' approach because of his concern with liberty as such. The nature of the contrast is further discussed in Sen (1982 b), (1984 b).

6. Note, however, that the test of whether something 'can be brought directly or indirectly into relation with the measuring-rod of money' (Pigou (1952), p. 11) may be a misleading one in examining the basis of 'material prosperity'. Many 'public goods' are not purchasable, e.g. a road or a park, but quite important for material prosperity (and presumably for economic welfare). So is the absence of crime or pollution, though none of these things are offered for sale in the market. There are many complicated issues in deciding on what counts as 'material' but it can be argued that the measuring-rod of money is not central to the idea of 'material prosperity'.

7. See also Fisher and Shell (1968), (1972) and Sen (1979).

8. See Sen (1979), pp. 12–13.

9. See also Sen (1982 a), pp. 29–31, 353–69.

10. See Scitovsky (1976), Douglas and Isherwood (1979), Deaton and Muellbauer (1980), and other explorations of different types of characteristics associated with consumption.

11. On the variability of the relation between food intake and nutritional achievements and the existence of multiple equilibria, see, among other works, Sukhatme (1977), Scrimshaw (1977), and Srinivasan (1982).

12. See Marx (1846); English translation from McLellan (1977), p. 190.

85

Predictions and Causes: A Comparison of Friedman and Hicks on Method [1][†]

D. Helm

1. Introduction

One way of presenting methodological arguments, and focusing on the issues which divide theorists, is to place the problems within the framework of broadly conflicting views. Two economists who have made important and conflicting claims about economic method are Friedman and Hicks, but the extent to which their two views differ has not been fully explored. Friedman's (1953) essay on 'The Methodology of Positive Economics',[2] with its overriding stress on economics as a predictive science, is perhaps the most famous article ever written on economic methodology. Hicks's 'Causality in Economics' (1979) represents a radically different viewpoint from Friedman's, stressing the explanatory importance of causality. Thus in comparing and contrasting these two, important issues are illustrated.

The purpose of this paper is threefold. The first intention is expositional: to outline the two approaches, and highlight the points of conflict. The second purpose is to demonstrate how confused some of the issues are, and to explore the central ones concerning the status of empirical evidence and causality. The third task is to consider what criteria, building on Hicks's work in particular, are appropriate for the appraisal of economic theories. It will be argued that neither causality nor prediction in themselves are sufficient criteria to judge between competing economic theories. To these must be added an account of how causal relations are derived from theoretical classifications, and of what is to count as an economic cause. I shall stress the importance of Hicks's claims about classification, and add my own claims concerning the content of economic causes, particularly regarding the role of human reason in causation.

The two views can be expressed as stressing on the one hand empirical testing and prediction, and on the other, causality, explanation, and classi-fication. For Friedman the science of positive economics aims to 'provide a system of generalizations that can be used to make correct predictions

[†]Source: *Oxford Economic Papers*, N.S., Vol. 36 Supplement, November 1984, pp. 118–34.

about the consequences of any change in circumstances' (p. 4). For Hicks, economics is not a science, but rather a discipline: 'economics is in time, and therefore in history, in a way that science is not', (1984*b*). These two views then are based on different conceptions of the status of economic knowledge, and hence have roots in different philosophies of science. However, although in particular Friedman has positivistic leanings which will be identified below, neither fits easily into pre-existing categories, and for two reasons. The first is that neither was familiar with the detail of the relevant philosophical literature when they wrote; the second is that the categories of the philosophy of science are neither all-encompassing, nor easily applicable to economics.

PART I: FRIEDMAN

2. Friedman's Essay in Context

The problems with interpreting Friedman's paper rest in part in its context. The paper is difficult to relate either to the debate to which it was supposed to provide a solution, or to the philosophical literature. Very little reference is made either to philosophers, or to economists who had written on methodology (with the exceptions of Lange and Marshall).[3]

Friedman's essay appeared in 1953 at the end of the debate which had raged through the 1940s, in particular in the *American Economic Review* (1946–8), on the realism of marginalist assumptions about the behaviour of firms. Hall and Hitch (1939) had shown before the war that many firms did not understand the concept of marginal cost pricing, and made the further claim that this theory was therefore not a good explanation of what firms did. Rather they argued that their evidence was consistent with an alternative explanation: full or mark-up pricing. The central problem with this kind of evidence is that it is not decisive between the two rival hypotheses, and in two senses. Firstly, as Harrod (1939) in the same issue of OEP [Oxford Economics Report] pointed out, marginalism does not require that participants consciously employ marginalist methods. Optimal decision-making does require that people do their best *ex ante*, but not necessarily that they choose the best *ex post*, where there exist search and administrative costs in a world of imperfect information. Hall and Hitch's study was not therefore sufficient to reject marginalist theories of firm's pricing behaviour. The second problem of decisiveness concerns the alternatives available and the problem of theory compatibility and commensurability. To persuade economists to drop particular theories, or assumptions embedded in certain theories, typically requires that an alternative be proposed, and no rigorous alternative of the same kind was then available. Theories must be of similar levels of generality, involve similarly defined concepts, and cover the same data set, for strict comparisons to be made.

Into this gap, created in part by the indecisiveness of the Hall and Hitch evidence, came Friedman's article. It laid out apparently clear methodological principles for a 'positive' economics. It attempted to clarify the debate by pointing to the irrelevance of the realism of assumptions, rather than taking sides directly. Friedman wrote:

> The articles on both sides of the controversy largely neglect what seems to me clearly the main issue — the conformity to experience of the implications of the marginal analysis — and concentrate on the largely irrelevant question whether businessmen do or do not in fact reach their evidence by consulting schedules, or curves, or multivariate functions showing marginal cost and marginal revenue.

3. Friedman's Inconsistent Theses

In fact the article itself advances a series of these, some of which are at best ambiguous; others are confused and, as we shall see, inconsistent. These include:

1. Positive economics can and should be separated from normative economics (pp. 3–4).
2. Positive economics 'is, or can be, an objective science, in precisely the same sense as any of the physical sciences' (p. 4).
3. Assumptions are to be chosen without regard to the correspondence between them and reality. The testing of assumptions is irrelevant. This is explicitly stated in the article, yet Friedman also tells us that they must be 'sufficiently good approximations for the purpose at hand' (p. 15).
4. The choice of assumptions is grounded in the ability to yield 'valid' predictions. 'Simplicity' and 'fruitfulness' of assumptions are relevant criteria for their choice, as well as their 'intuitive plausibility' (p. 26). 'The gains from further accuracy [of prediction] alone, which depend on the purpose in mind, must then be balanced against the costs of achieving it' (p. 17).
5. In general, the more significant the theory, the more unrealistic the assumptions (p. 14).
6. Predictions are testable by direct relation to empirical evidence which provides an independent and objective test. This can be either (a) positively by verification (strong claim); or (b) negatively by falsification.
7. The survival of predictive testing is modified by the 'frequency' of refutation with respect to alternative hypotheses (p. 9).
8. A theory is comprised of two parts: (a) a language or analytical filing-system, the theoretical categories, which can be shown to have meaningful empirical counterparts; and (b) substantive hypotheses.
9. Indeterminacy principle, according to which there exists a relationship both between the observer and the observed, and between the process of measurement and the phenomena being measured (p. 5n.).
10. 'A theory is the way we perceive "facts", and we cannot perceive "facts" without a theory' (p. 34).
11. If one hypothesis is consistent with the available evidence, then there are an infinite number which are (p. 9).

12. Empirical evidence is to be used in the construction (as well as in the testing of predictions) of hypotheses (p. 13).

13. The maximization of returns is a realist assumption, because 'unless the businessman in some way or other approximated behaviour consistent with the maximization of returns, it seems unlikely that they would remain in business for long.' Competition acts like natural selection to enforce maximization.[4]

Rather than take this set of theses as consistent, and claim it to represent a particular philosophy of science, it seems to me more appropriate to recognize that they are simply muddled and confused.[5] In particular it is not clear from propositions (3) and (4) above which are the relevant criteria of judging assumptions. Friedman adds additional criteria to predictive testing in 'fruitfulness' and 'simplicity', yet elsewhere places overriding importance of the predictive test in his (6) and (7). Elsewhere there is a confusion as to whether theories and theoretical terms can or cannot be reduced to empirical counterparts, since (8) is contradicted by (9) and (10). Finally, (11) directly undermines Friedman's 'predictive science', for if it is true, then a theory cannot be selected solely on predictive grounds.

Given this evident confusion and inconsistency in Friedman's theses, there is, contrary to much of the literature, no 'right' or unique interpretation of his methodological position. For my purposes I shall take Friedman to mean precisely what he says in the following quotation:

> Viewed as a body of substantive hypotheses, theory is to be judged by its predictive power for the class of phenomena which it is intended to 'explain'. Only factual evidence can show whether it is 'right' or 'wrong' or, better, tentatively 'accepted' or 'rejected' ... the only relevant test of the validity of the hypothesis is comparison of its predictions with experience ... Factual evidence can never 'prove' a hypothesis; it can only fail to disprove it. (pp. 8–9).

This methodology of economics crucially depends on the possibility of testing, and the independent status of empirical evidence. I shall therefore next consider what kind of a philosophy Friedman's arguments represent, placing him within the broad church of positivism. Having done that, and indicated the lines of criticism to which he is then open, I then turn to the second view, that of Hicks, to carry through those criticisms.

4. Positivist and Instrumentalist

The importance of empirical evidence and testing are central to a number of philosophies of social and natural sciences. However giving empirical evidence the central role by reducing theoretical terms to empirical meanings is unique to positivism, and in this broad sense, Friedman is a positivist. It is not merely a question of semantics in ascribing this title to him, for there are a number of well-known objections to this philosophy. Positivism involves a large subset of less well-defined beliefs deriving from and related to its emphasis on observations. Besides emphasizing observation over theory,[6] these beliefs include[7] reducing causality to temporal orderings and claiming that there is no necessary connection between cause and effect, regarding prediction rather than explanation as the goal of science, holding the analytic-synthetic distinction[8] and emphasizing verification and falsification.[9] Friedman believes in the unity of science, in the existence of a sharp distinction between theory and observation (the analytic-synthetic distinction), the possibility of reducing theoretical concepts to statements of empirical meaning, the central importance of prediction, and the timelessness of theory. In this broader sense, writers such as Wong (1973), Boland (1979), Caldwell (1982), and Boland and Frazer (1983) are not strictly correct to call Friedman an instrumentalist[10] *rather* than a positivist, since although he does claim that theories and assumptions are only instrumental to the production of predictions, Friedman is ambiguous as to whether theories themselves are true or false, whereas the instrumentalist claims that they are neither true nor false. Theory may be instrumental to the production of predictions; but there is for Friedman a relationship between the logical statements and observable reality involving their truth or falsity. Some instruments are better than others; and as we have seen above, Friedman employs a series of what Caldwell (1983) describes as conventionalist criteria. Caldwell (1982, pp. 176–7) has also pointed out that Friedman confuses the 'indirect testability hypothesis', according to which testing predictions can indirectly act as a check on the validity of assumptions, with the instrumental claim that the realism of assumptions is irrelevant.

A more charitable interpretation of Friedman, given the inconsistencies pointed out above, is that he asserts this more sophisticated view, rather than subscribing to naive instrumentalism. Furthermore, the positivist has epistemological claims to make about the status of predictions which are not equivalent to the instrumentalist view. Indeed it is on this issue that instrumentalism is incomplete.[11] It is not impossible to interpret Friedman's method as positivist on the status of empirical observations, and instrumental on assumption choice, though if the indirect testability hypothesis is what he has in mind then he is not even strictly instrumental on this. If, however, the instrumentalist were to claim that predictions are not directly testable, then the validity of assumptions on the empirical grounds of the predictions that they produce cannot be the criterion of choice. Friedman's empiricism and his commitment to predictive science is thus open to a series of objections, which stress the importance of theoretical concepts, their priority over observations, and the causal relationship between variables. At this point, let us turn to Hicks's position.

PART II: HICKS

5. Hicks's Anti-empiricism

Hicks has both in principle and in practice objected to the widespread adoption of empiricist methods in economics, from his early days as a member of the LSE group, exposed to both Robbins's and Hayek's views on the subject.[12] His objections have been grounded on two propositions. The first stems from the observation that economic theories are time-dependent. Economic institutions and behaviour alter with the passage of time, and the more characteristic problems are not static ones, but are 'problems of change, of growth and retrogression, and of fluctuation' (1979, p. xi). It is for this reason that scientific methods are less applicable to economics, since in economics everything must be dated, whereas in science Hicks claims this is not the case. At the level of observations of actual human behaviour, what might be true in one period need not be true in another, even if the motives of the agents do not themselves alter. Furthermore, dynamic theories[13] of economic behaviour need to incorporate the passage of time into processes through the relations of participants in those processes to that change. Testing is then at best limited to periods when the relevant institutions and individual behaviour remains constant, and to what is going on in those periods.

Hicks's second objection focuses on the problems of prediction, and he claims that economics can at best make only weak predictions.[14] These weak predictions are claims about what will happen if other things remain the same. Since *ceteris* is almost never *paribus*,[15] a particular set of observations can never, themselves, form the basis for testing an hypothesis. Hicks writes ((1983) pp. 371–2):

> Once it is recognised that economic theories (those which are not mere tautologies) can offer no more than weak explanations — that they are always subject to a *ceteris paribus* clause — it becomes clear that they cannot be verified (or 'falsified') by confrontation with fact. We are told that 'when theory and fact come into conflict, it is theory, not fact, that must give way'. It is very doubtful how far that dictum applies to economics. Our theories ... are not that sort of theory; but it is also true that our facts are not that sort of fact.

Thus Hicks and Friedman diverge on the central issues of methodology, the one emphasizing the predictive content of economic science, the other stressing causality and the obstacles to testing and empiricist methods. Hicks argues that given two alternative assumptions, within a theoretical system, we cannot simply refer to the evidence, and so need to look for other additional criteria. Such a problem cannot be considered without tackling the wider question of what an economic theory and explanation consists of, what are its parts, and what such a theory is for. On the broad issue as well as the narrower one, Hicks and Friedman have very different views in principle, though not always in practice. The first crucial difference comes out in Hicks's account of causality, which is not limited to temporal priority and predictive content.[16] Next that account is outlined, improvements are made to it, and further criteria of appraisal are introduced.

6. Causality

Hicksian causality is the central building-block of his non-positivistic methodology,[17] which stands in contrast to that of Friedman. There are three components to his account of causality. The first relates to weak predictions and the *ceteris paribus* clauses mentioned above, and is his distinction between strong and weak causality. The second is his counter-factual account. The third is his relation between temporal ordering and his three possibilities: static, reciprocal, and contemporaneous.

The distinction between strong and weak causality rests on the observation that in economics at least there are typically quite a number of causes operating together to produce an effect. We may consider these to make up a vector, say $(a_1, a_2, \ldots a_n)$, producing the total effect, say B. Each component of the vector is a weak cause of B; only if the vector is a one-component vector or if background conditions remain unaltered can we say that strong causality exists. The relationship between the components may be either separable or non-separable, and there is no a priori reason in economics to suppose that the former necessarily holds in any particular case. So long as it is multi-membered, prediction is also weak, since it depends on nothing happening to the other components.

The second part of the Hicksian analysis concerns counterfactuals. Hicks claims that to say that A causes B involves positing that not-A produces not-B. This Hicks asserts is a theoretical matter:

> I have insisted that the assertion 'if not-A, then not-B' is theoretical; it is derived from something which in the most general sense may be described as a theory or model (1979, p. 22).

There are considerable problems with this definition to which I shall return below. Essentially while Hicks is correct to assert that a counterfactual is required, and that it is a theoretical and not empirical matter in at least the non-experimental subjects, the definition is insufficient. In itself it says nothing about the plurality of possible counterfactuals or the content of causality, and indeed to be fair, Hicks would not claim it to be sufficient.

However, let us now add the third component of the Hicksian theory of causality. Hicks points out that time and causality need to be related carefully. In particular he notes that Hume[18] and his followers typically think of cause and effect at moments in time, and describe a temporal ordering as causality. Hicks stresses that many economic causes and effects take time; they happen in periods rather than at points or moments in time. Sequential causality is the traditional view, where one event happens after another. Hicks wants to introduce two further possibilities; that cause and effect might reciprocate each other, and that they might occur simultaneously or, as he prefers to call it, contemporaneously. Much of his book is devoted to economic examples of these in economic problems.[19]

The Hicksian theory of causality and the status of empirical claims in economics bears a strong but not complete relationship to other philosophical writings, and the tangency between what philosophers and Hicks have said on the subject proves most enlightening. The two tangencies I have in mind are firstly that between Hicks's *ceteris paribus* clauses and Mackie's INUS conditions, and secondly between Hicks's general anti-empiricism and Quine's famous critique of empiricism. I shall take each in turn.

7. Mackie and Hicks

The counterfactual definition which Hicks has proposed receives powerful support in the definition of causality put forward in John Mackie's article 'Causation and Conditionals' (1965), and his later book *The Cement of the Universe* (1975) suggested that:

> when we take A to be ... a partial cause of B, we can say that if A had not occurred, B would not; a cause is to be taken in this counterfactual sense necessary in the circumstances for B, though sometimes also sufficient in the circumstances as well, or perhaps only sufficient in the circumstance and not necessary: we have alternative counterfactual concepts of causation. But these counterfactual conditional relationships do not exhaust our concept of causation, for this concept includes also the notion of symmetry between cause and effect ... (p. xi).

Mackie's famous INUS condition for causality is

> an *insufficient* but *necessary* part of a condition which is itself *unnecessary* but *sufficient* for that result.

We can then assign A to be the cause of a dated event E if A is an INUS condition of E. As Sosa (1975), p. 4, pointed out, there is in fact very little difference between this condition and *ceteris paribus* sufficiency, excepting only in the question of unique sufficiency on a particular date.[20]

If causality were limited to the INUS condition, then this would be the end of the matter.[21] But the importance of causality arises after its counterfactual representation has been recognized, and recognized as a matter of theoretical rather than empirical epistemological status. In particular the importance of Hicks's work on causality is less the definitional second chapter of his book, but rather what he has to say about the content of causes. Hicks has considered, firstly, the way in which we arrive at causal statements, by way of the use of classifications, and secondly what the consequences of *ceteris paribus* limitations are. The former we will return to in Section 9 below, the latter concerns the extent to which weak causality limits empiricism and econometric methods. I shall next, therefore, relate Hicks's critique of predictions and testing to the more general philosophical critique of empiricism.

8. The Quine–Duhem Thesis

The Quine–Duhem thesis, concerning the relation between theory and empirical evidence, has recently received attention from economists.[22] While Hicks has stressed the weakness of predictions, the difficulties of testing, and thus the primacy of theory, philosophers have focused on the relationship between theoretical terms and empirical observations, *within* the network of logically related terms which go to make up theories. Above, we saw that Friedman held the essentially positivistic view that theories were mere filing systems, and that the terms within them could be reduced to empirical counterparts. The critique of such empiricism, of which the Quine–Duhem thesis is an important part, concentrates on this relationship.

The Quine–Duhem thesis has in fact been separately advanced by Duhem (1914) and by Quine (1953). In its latter formulation, Quine presented the thesis as the conclusion of his now classic critique of empiricism — 'Two Dogmas of Empiricism'. In that article, he was concerned to criticize the analytic–synthetic distinction and the proposition that theoretical terms could be reduced to meaningful empirical counterparts, i.e. precisely the foundations of the position which Friedman's appears to have adopted. The thesis itself is founded on two propositions. The first concerns the network of theories and beliefs[23] which we hold and their relation to experience:

> The totality of our so-called knowledge or beliefs ... is a man-made fabric which impinges on experience only along the edges. Or, to change the figure, total science is like a field of force whose boundary conditions are experience. A conflict with experience at the periphery occasions readjustments in the interior of the field ((1953), p. 42).

Thus a theoretical statement, such as that permanent consumption is a function of permanent income, to take an example from Friedman's work, involves a host of beliefs or theoretical propositions. These include, for example, the notion of consumption, the relation between different concepts of consumption, the concept of income, of permanent income, their determinants, as well as the relation between permanent income and permanent consumption. These form a nest of supporting hypotheses, which are themselves supported by deeper theoretical views about measurement and language. A conflict then between observation and theory is thus a conflict with this network of supporting beliefs. The problem then is to discover which observations relate to which parts of that network. Quine next presents his second premise, that:

> The total field is so undetermined by the boundary conditions, experience, that there is much latitude of choice as to what statements to reevaluate in the light of any single contrary experience. No particular experiences are linked with any particular statements in the interior of the field, except indirectly through considerations of equilibrium affecting the fields as a whole' (p. 43).

Thus in our example, an empirical conflict with Friedman's own permanent income hypothesis could relate to any one or more of the nest of propositions which make up the theory. A particular problem here which illustrates this relational difficulty is that permanent income and consumption are theoretical terms requiring correspondence rules with actual observations, and there is no agreed method of making this translation.[24]

Indeed Quine points out that 'it is misleading to speak of the empirical content of an individual statement' and that 'it becomes folly to seek a boundary between synthetic statements, which hold contingently on experience, and analytical statements, which hold come what may' (p. 43). Therefore Quine claims what has become known as the Quine–Duhem thesis, that:

> Any statement can be held true come what may, if we make drastic enough adjustments elsewhere in the system ... Conversely, by the same token, no statement is immune to revision (p. 43).

The claim as it stands is open to different interpretations. In particular Lakatos (1970), p. 184, has pointed out that it may either mean that targeting observations onto specific theoretical terms is impossible, or it may much more radically be taken as a denial of any empirical check on theory. In its weaker form, the thesis powerfully supports Hicks's caution on empiricism, but while he concentrates on the change in background conditions over time, Quine focuses his critique on the interconnectedness of theoretical terms. The two are thus complementary critiques of the positivist position, which Friedman at least at times expounds.[25]

We have then two views of economic method, supported by different philosophical positions on the relation between theory and evidence, and on the notion of causality. The first stresses the importance of prediction and testing, and the irrelevance of the realism of assumptions and the content of theory. The other stresses economic explanation and causal relations, and emphasizes that the understanding of behaviour is essentially theoretical, since counterfactuals are not themselves observable. But the question remains as to the choice and selection of assumptions, and in this respect there are two further components to a theory which need to be considered: first classification, and secondly the role of reasons in causality, what I shall call feasibility. Let us now look at classification and come back to feasibility later.

9. Classification

Friedman asserts that theories act as 'filing systems' and, retreating from the pure instrumentalist case, admits that there is a relationship between theories and facts. Hicks is much clearer on the implications of this relationship, arguing that when theory and fact conflict, as they often do, fact rather than theory might give way.[26] But if prediction cannot uniquely inform us, how are we to select our simplifications at this more general level; how are we to classify? The Hicksian answer is that selection depends on the problem at hand.[27] The choice of a theory depends on the sort of problem we want to solve, and that choice is at two levels: at the grand level of paradigms or research programmes,[28] and at the narrower level of particular assumptions.[29] Large theory-set changes, revolutions, occur with problem-shifts. These are not normally 'revolutions' in the violent sense, but much more natural evolutions. And Hicks claims that these Kuhnian changes are better understood as changes in classification. When two large sets of theories are appraised, say Ricardian and Keynesian, we ask what were the problems that they tried to solve, and what were the character-istics of the economies to which they referred. Common elements are checked for, to see whether, in our example, there are Ricardian traces in Keynes's writings. To ask whether one is better than another is strictly meaningless unless the problem and the time period are specified. We cannot, on the Hicksian view, compare their predictions. Economics is not that sort of science. In contrast, for example, Hicks would argue that scien-tific theories like those of Einstein and Newton can be compared at least in principle, since they are not dated.[30] Classifications are, for Hicks, problem and time-period dependent because background conditions alter, and it is only if two rival sets of theories claim to refer to the same period and answer the same questions that they are strictly commensurable. Pre-dictions are apprised only if the same *ceteris paribus* clauses apply. Unfortunately, however, the set of such cases is limited. The example of marginal and full cost pricing, discussed at the beginning of this paper, might at first glance appear to be of this type; but it runs up against the further point that these two theories do not necessarily predict different outcomes. It is the interpretations of the outcomes in this case which is at stake, not different empirical predictions. Friedman, in his confusion, admits this in his thesis about an infinite number of possible theories cover-ing the same data set, point (11) of my list on p. 124 above.

PART THREE: REASONS AND CAUSES

10. Feasibility

The last points bring us to the final methodological criterion which I shall here discuss. It relates to a distinction Hicks uses in his account of causality between what he calls the 'Old' and 'New Causality', and also to the dispute between those like Hall and Hitch on the one hand, and Friedman on the other, as to whether the reasons and motives for behaviour influence or cause particular outcomes. The central question concerns whether the purposeful or teleological nature of human behaviour implies a special and distinct social science notion of causality, including reasons as being causal in actions, and thus additionally whether they are a necessary part of human behaviour.

In what Hicks describes as the 'Old Causality' causes were considered as the action or agency of some one or more individuals whether human or supernatural. In contrast, the New Causality permitted causal explanation free from the necessity of agency (Hicks (1979), (1984*a*)). Friedman argues that reasons for an action are not necessary to theory construction. He writes that in the same way as a billiard player does not calculate the forces and resistances of a billiard ball in planning a particular shot, the inability to calculate marginal values does not invalidate marginalist theories of decision-making.[31] The confusion in Friedman concerns prediction and explanation. Because it is quite plausible that a good billiards player chooses close to optimal shots, it follows that a good predictor of his behaviour might be what he would have done if he had calculated the forces and resistances. But that in itself does not explain *how* he plays. The marginalist case is different from the billiards example in two respects. First, predictability is complicated by the possibility that both theories may predict the same outcomes. Secondly, the possibility that behaviour in the absence of marginal calculation is predictably the same as in its presence is more contentious, in the sense that it does not follow that it can be similarly *explained.* The reasoning process of managers causes certain behavioural outcomes. The way in which this happens brings together reasoning and causality.

Feasibility, whether an individual is actually capable of assumed acts, and causality thus come together. To explain an action involves positing causes. Human actions, unlike scientific observations, are partially or weakly caused by the reasons that the person has in carrying out the act.[32] Feasible actions are those of which the human mind is capable of formulating reasons for. This claim concerning the content of causality has been formally presented by Davidson (1963). He asserts that only certain types of reasons can act as causes. These he calls 'primary reasons', and defines this term as follows ((1980), p. 5):

R is a primary reason why an agent performed the action *a* under the description *d* only if R consists of a pro attitude of the agent towards actions with a certain property, and a belief of the agent that A, under the description *d*, has that property.

The inclusion of primary reasons a causal factors in explanation still leaves the substantive problem of how these might be in practice identified. A principle of charity is typically invoked, whereby the reasons an agent gives are taken to be *the* reasons for that act, unless the observer has good reason himself to think contrarily. Such a procedure is imperfect, but so are the alternatives. Now one of the restrictions placed on primary reasons is that they be feasible, and this is one of the limitations or constraints to be placed on the principle of charity. The implication of this criterion of feasibility is most clearly seen in the debate which sparked off Friedman's article, the maximization of profits, or more generally the maximization of utility. How are we to decide whether this assumption is justified? If Hicks is right, the issue is, firstly, a non-empirical one. The defenders of maximization argue that it does not matter whether people are capable of cal-

culating appropriately. These are associated with Friedman as we have
discussed above, with Becker (1976), Muth (1961), and Boland (1981).
The opponents of maximization generally argue that maximization is not
feasible. Feasibility refers both to the capacity of the brain to process information, and the quality of potential information. Simon (1955) claimed
that humans are biologically limited by the capacity of the central nervous
system, in their ability to compare alternatives, and proposed that individuals satisfice rather than maximize. Shackle (1949) has emphasized that
it is not feasible to form probability judgements under a wide variety of
uncertainty situations. Cyert and March (1963) argue that the problem of
conflicting objectives of managers and workers leads to bargaining and
trade-offs which yield non-maximizing objectives for firms.[33] Our two
views of methodology come down on different sides on this issue.
Friedman, we have seen, denies that feasibility matters. Hicks is
ambiguous, as one would expect given his problem-solving methodology,
which depends on the importance of uncertainty and the costs of
information for the problem at hand. Nevertheless, as early as 1939, he
stressed the importance of considering the limitations of human behaviour
(p. 337):

> for the understanding of the economic system we need something more,
> something which refers back, in the last resort, to the behaviour of people
> and the motives of their conduct.

He quite naturally accepts that information about probability is not always
defined, and that maximization may not always be pursued ((1983),
pp. 139, 371). But our two views represent different tasks: the one to
predict, the other to explain and thus to find causes for actions.

If feasibility counts, it is because the mental processes employed by
decision-makers affect the outcomes of their actions. In this sense, causality
and feasibility are linked. For a causal account to count as an explanation
of an act it should thus include an account of the reasons for the act.

11. Conclusion

The search for a single method of theory appraisal has proved to be unsuccessful, and methodologies which advance such principles fail. Those parts
of Friedman's article which are most positivistic in their emphasis on
prediction to the exclusion of all other criteria fail in the face of the philosophical difficulties with testing predictions outlined above. The more
reflective parts of Friedman's article deviate from this methodology, and
hence are more acceptable. It is also worth noting that Friedman rarely, if
ever, employs his procedures in his more practical work. In the theory of
the consumption function (1957), for example, he carefully devotes the
first part of the book to specifying (irrelevantly if the realism of
assumptions is irrelevant) the micro-foundations of consumer theory, and
then develops theoretical concepts without immediate empirical counterparts.[34]

But because a single principle like prediction is inadequate, it does not follow that unbridled pluralism is either permissible or desirable. Hicks's conception of causality is undoubtedly to be included as a basic explanatory criterion. But it needs to be extended to include some restrictions on the content of causes. Hicks has already carried out some of this exercise, with respect particularly to classification. I have added feasibility, and shown how that feasibility is related to causal accounts, by virtue of the causal effects of reasons on actions. Economics is, Hicks asserts, ' a discipline not a science'. As in all disciplines, however, there are limitations on what is permissible, and what is not. Feasibility, I have argued, is one such limitation.

References

Addison, J.T., Burton, J. and Torrance, T.S. (1984), 'Causation, Social Science & Sir John Hicks', *Oxford Economic Papers*, NS xxxvi (1).

Becker, G.S. (1976), *The Economic Approach to Human Behaviour*, University of Chicago Press.

Boland, L.A. (1979), 'A Critique of Friedman's Critics', *Journal of Economic Literature*, xvii, 503–22.

Boland, L.A. (1981), 'On the Futility of Criticizing the Neoclassical Maximization Hypothesis', *American Economic Review*, lxxi, 1031–6.

Caldwell, B. (1982), *Beyond Positivism*, George Allen & Unwin, London.

Caldwell, B. (1983), 'The Neoclassical Maximization Hypothesis: Comments', *American Economic Review*, lxxiii, 824–7.

Courakis, A.S. (1981), 'Monetary Targets: Conceptual Antecedents and Recent Policies in the US, UK and West Germany' in id. (ed.), *Inflation, Depression and Economic Policy in the West*, Mansell, London.

Courakis, A.S. (1984), 'The Demand for Money in South Africa', *South African Journal of Economics*, lii, 1–41.

Cross, R. (1982), 'The Duhem–Quine Thesis, Lakatos and the Appraisal of Theories in Macroeconomics', *Economic Journal*, xcii, 320–40.

Cyert, R.M. and March, J.G. (1963), *A Behavioural Theory of the Firm*, Prentice-Hall, Englewood Cliffs, NJ.

Davidson, D. (1963), 'Reasons as Causes', reprinted in id. (1980), *Essays on Actions and Events*, Oxford University Press.

Dobb, M. (1973), *Theories of Value and Distribution since Adam Smith*, Cambridge University Press.

Duhem, P. (1914), *The Aims and Structure of Physical Theory*, Rivière, Paris, translated by P. Weiner, Princeton University Press (1954).

Frazer, W.J., Jr and Boland, L.A. (1983), 'An Essay on the Foundation of Friedman's Methodology', *American Economic Review*, lxxiii, 129–44.

Friedman, M. (1953), 'The Methodology of Positive Economics', in id., *Essays in Positive Economics*, University of Chicago.

Friedman, M. (1957), *A Theory of the Consumption Function*, Princeton University Press.

Granger, C.W.J. and Newbold, P. (1977), *Forecasting Economic Time Series*, Academic Press.

Hacking, I. (1983), *Representing and Intervening*, Cambridge University Press.

Hall, R.L. and Hitch, C.J. (1939), 'Price Theory and Business Behaviour', *Oxford Economic Papers*, NS ii, 15–45.

Harrod, R. (1939), 'Price and Cost in Entrepreneur's Policy', *Oxford Economic Papers*, NS ii, 1–11.

Hayek, F. Von (1937), 'Economics and Knowledge', *Economica*, NS, iv, 33–54.

Helm, D.R. (1984), *Enforced Maximisation*. D. Phil. thesis, Oxford.

Hicks, J.R. (1939), *Value and Capital*, Oxford University Press.
Hicks, J.R. (1956), *A Revision of Demand Theory*, Oxford University Press.
Hicks, J.R. (1969), *A Theory of Economic History*, Oxford University Press.
Hicks, J.R. (1976), '" Revolutions' in Economics' in S.J. Latsis (ed.), *Method and Appraisal in Economics*, Cambridge University Press, and reprinted in Hicks (1983).
Hicks, J.R. (1979), *Causality in Economics*, Basil Blackwell, Oxford.
Hicks, J.R. (1981), *Wealth and Welfare*, Basil Blackwell, Oxford [including LSE and the Robbins Circle].
Hicks, J.R. (1982), *Money, Interest and Wages*, Basil Blackwell, Oxford [including 'Methods of Dynamic Economics'].
Hicks, J.R. (1983), *Classics and Moderns*, Basil Blackwell, Oxford [including 'A Discipline not a Science'].
Hicks, J.R. (1984a), 'The "New Causality"; an Explanation', *Oxford Economic Papers*, NS xxxvi (1).
Hicks, J.R. (1984b), 'Is Economics a Science?', *Interdisciplinary Science Review*, forthcoming.
Hoover, K. (1984), 'Comment on Boland', *American Economic Review*, forthcoming.
Hume, D. (1738), *A Treatise on Human Nature*, Modern edn., by L.A. Selby-Brigge (1978), Oxford University Press.
Kuhn, T. (1970), 'The Structure of Scientific Revolutions', *International Encyclopedia of Unified Science*, vol. ii, no. 2; 2nd enlarged edn., Chicago University Press.
Lakatos, I. (1970), 'Falsification and the Methodology of Scientific Research Programmes', in Lakatos and Musgrave (eds), *Criticism and the Growth of Knowledge*, Cambridge University Press.
Leiberstein, H. (1976), *Beyond Economic Man*, Harvard University Press.
Machlup, F. (1967), 'Theories of the Firm: Marginalist, Behavioural and Managerial', *American Economic Review*, lvii, 1–33.
Mackie, J.L. (1965), 'Causes and Conditions', *American Philosophical Quarterly*, ii (4), 245–64.
Mackie, J.L. (1975), *The Cement of the Universe*, Oxford University Press.
Muth, J.F. (1961), 'Rational Expectations and the Theory of Price Movements', *Econometrica*, xxix, 315–35.
Quine, V. (1953), 'Two Dogmas of Empiricism' in id.; *From a Logical Point of View*, Harvard University Press.
Samuelson, P.A. (1963), 'Problems of Methodology — Discussion', *American Economic Review*, P & P, liii, 231–6.
Samuelson, P.A. (1972), 'Maximum Principles in Analytical Economics', *American Economic Review*, lxii, 249–62.
Sen, A.K. (1980), 'Description as Choice', *Oxford Economic Papers*, xxxii, 353–69.
Shackle, G.L.S. (1949), *Expectations in Economics*, Cambridge University Press.
Shackle, G.L.S. (1967), *Decision, Order and Time*, Cambridge University Press.
Simon, H.A. (1955), 'A Behavioural Model of Rational Choice', *Quarterly Journal of Economics*, lxix, 99–118.
Sosa, E. (ed.) (1975), *Causation and Conditionals*, Oxford University Press.
Stroud, B. (1977), *Hume*, Routledge and Kegan Paul, London.
Tobin, J. (1970), 'Money and Income: Post Hoc Ergo Propter Hoc', *Quarterly Journal of Economics*, lxxxiv, 301–17.
Winter, S. (1964), 'Economic "natural selection" and the Theory of the Firm', *Yale Economic Essays*, iv, 225–72.
Wong, S. (1973), 'The F-Twist and the Methodology of Paul Samuelson', *American Economic Review*, lxiii 313–25.
Zellner, A. (1979), 'Causality and Econometrics', in K. Brunner and A.H. Meltzer (eds), *Three Aspects of Policy Making*, North Holland.

Notes

1. I should like to thank Amartya Sen, Jonathon Cohen, David Collard, Tony Courakis, John Vickers, and Christopher Gilbert for comments on an earlier draft. I must also gratefully acknowledge long and detailed conversations with Sir John Hicks while I have had the great privilege of being his research assistant.

2. All references to Friedman are to this 1953 article, unless otherwise stated.

3. It is hard to see what impact Hayek, who was at Chicago after the war, or Popper had on the paper. Subsequent evidence, like that provided by Frazer and Boland (1983), is based on Friedman's own memory and the relation between the arguments in the paper and others held at about that time. Simultaneity of argument does not establish connections; neither is memory entirely reliable over a thirty-year span.

4. For a critique of this assertion, see Helm (1984).

5. Boland (1979) is perhaps the most emphatic amongst those who claim Friedman to be consistent. Rather I should want to say that the critics have disagreed because individual propositions have been abstracted from context, and taken fully to represent Friedman. They have therefore been open to counter-quotation.

6. Strictly all theoretical terms have exact empirical counterparts. According to Hume's epistemological theory, what exists is limited to 'impressions' derived from sense-data. 'Ideas', and hence theoretical terms, are ultimately reducible to their empirical counterparts.

7. See Hacking (1983), pp. 41–2, on the meaning of positivism.

8. A synthetic statement refers to the world, what Hume described as matters of fact. The predicate of a synthetic proposition is attached to the subject but not contained in it. An analytic statement, by contrast, contains the predicate in its subject and refers to 'matters of reason'. The distinction is thus between claims about the world and claims which are matters of logical relation.

9. Dispute continues as to whether falsification as proposed by Popper is anti-positivist in the sense that Popper himself claimed it to be.

10. Instrumentalism is the thesis that a theory is merely an instrument for predicting observable reality, irrespective of its truth-content.

11. It is incomplete in the sense that the instrumentalist is left with no way of justifying the importance of predictions or their usefulness without a criterion of truth or falsity. In other words the consequences of the position on truth and falsity can be addressed to their own claims.

12. See for example Hicks (1956), ch. 1, 'LSE and the Robbins Circle' in (1981); 'A Discipline not a Science' in (1983); (1979); (1984a); and (1984b). Another member of the LSE group, George Shackle, has developed related points to Hicks on uncertainty, time, and predictability. See in particular his (1967).

13. Hicks uses the term 'dynamics' in a particular way. See his 'Methods of Dynamic Economics' (1956), reprinted in id. (1982), for his definitions.

14. There are few if any explicit or strong predictions in economics. Not even the 'law of demand' makes clear predictions: negatively sloped demand curves are predicted only on a joint condition concerning the income effect.

15. Friedman, p. 10, acknowledges this: 'no experiment can be completely controlled, and every experience is partially controlled'.

16. In this respect Hicks immediately parts company with what have misleadingly been called Granger 'causality tests'. Granger and Newbold (1977), p. 225, themselves acknowledge these tests to be only temporal relation tests. See Zellner (1979), pp. 10–11, for an exposition of their causality definitions. Tony Courakis has pointed out to me that Friedman, in discussing the relationship between money and income has recently been careful to dissociate himself from these 'causality test' explanations. On this see Courakis (1981), pp. 287, 345.

17. Indeed early positivists like Comte denied that causality had any meaning, discarding it as a remnant of metaphysics.

18. For a discussion of Hume's two definitions of causality, see Stroud (1977), ch. 3.

19. Temporal asymmetry is frequently stressed in defining causes, particularly in the econometric versions like that of Granger. Philosophers have, however, disagreed, arguing that this is not necessary. On this see Mackie (1975), and in the economics literature Tobin's

famous (1970) critique of the money–income relationship.

20. As Sosa defines the difference: 'the only significant difference is that if C is an INUS condition of E then C is an essential part of a condition that is *uniquely* sufficient for E on that occasion, whereas C may be *ceteris paribus* sufficient for E in circumstances where there are several sufficient conditions for E, including some that do contain C as a part.'

21. It should be noted in passing that the Granger 'causality' concept, being limited to temporal relations (see n. 16 above) is not to be confused with the Mackie or Hicks conditionals, both of the latter admitting of the possibility that causality is not unidirectional. Furthermore, counterfactuals, being theoretical assertions which cannot be observed, cannot be 'causality tested'.

22. See especially Cross (1982).

23. Quine argues not only that theories come not in isolation but in packages, or what Kuhn (1970) and Lakatos (1970) would call respectively paradigms and research programmes, but also that the theoretical terms are themselves interconnected in their meanings.

24. Friedman (1957), p. 20, himself notes that 'the magnitudes termed "permanent income" and "permanent consumption" cannot be directly observed ... They are ex ante magnitudes; empirical data is ex post', thus recognizing the further complication of expectations being unobservable.

25. The relation between the Quine–Duhem thesis and the F-Twist/S-Twist debate, following Samuelson's (1963) attempt to propose an operationalist theory, (which amounted to the claim that predictions were logically related to assumptions, such that they provided an 'indirect test'), is that Quine would want to deny that a particular prediction could be related to a particular assumption. It should also be noted that Samuelson's claim is false: because A $\Rightarrow$ B $\Rightarrow$ C, it does not follow that A $\Leftrightarrow$ B $\Leftrightarrow$ C. On this see Wong (1973) and Hoover (1984).

26. See quotation, p. 127 above.

27. Hicks writes ((1979), p. x): 'one must classify according to the kinds of problems (of real problem) to which they claim to have relevance. Many of the disputes amongst theorists can then be referred to the interests of those who construct them, in different problems.' See also Machlup (1967), p. 240, who makes a similar point.

28. Hicks would prefer not to use these terms, but rather writes of 'blinkers'. See his (1976).

29. See on assumption choice, Hicks (1939), pp. 83–4.

30. Hicks calls these theories 'static'; and essentially his claim is that whereas science is essentially static, economics is dynamic ((1979), p. 24); see also note 13 above.

31. Machlup (1967), in support of Friedman, calls this criticism 'the fallacy of misplaced concreteness'.

32. This is the point which Addison *et al.* (1984) stress in their comment on Hicks's Old or New Causality distinction. They write: 'Causality in human beings operates through the mind of an agent'. The difference between their view and my own turns on whether *the set* of reasons constitute *weak* or *strong* causes of actions. Others who have also stressed the role of reasons include Hayek (1937) and Shackle (1967).

33. Other important critiques of maximization include Leibenstein (1976) and Winter's infinite regress argument proposed in his 1964 paper.

34. In Friedman's monetary theory, another striking example of his ambivalence to the prediction criterion is to be found with regard to the unitary elasticity of the demand for money. On this see Courakis (1984).

86

Economic Growth, the Harrod Foreign Trade Multiplier and the Hicks Super-multiplier[†]

J.S.L. McCombie

1. Introduction

The post-Keynesian view of economic growth denies that the performance of the advanced countries has been seriously constrained by the growth of factor supplies. Even during the expansionary period of 1950–73 when the average annual growth of output was double that achieved over the previous eighty years, labour shortages were never a limiting factor. There was either sufficient disguised unemployment in the non-manufacturing sectors or enough immigration to satisfy the demand for labour. The rate of capital accumulation is never a long-run constraint on economic growth as investment is as much a result of the expansion of output as its cause.[1]

If growth is indeed demand rather than supply-constrained, the question naturally arises as to why some countries have performed so much better than others. Furthermore, why has it not been possible to increase the rate of growth simply by the use of traditional demand-management policies? The answers to these questions have led to a consideration of the importance of the balance of payments constraint and a revival of interest in the Harrod foreign trade multiplier.[2]

In an open economy which is not fundamentally resource-constrained, the level of income is determined by the volume of exports. Exports represent the autonomous component of demand analogous to investment in the Keynesian closed economy model. Under fixed exchange rates, or in a situation where the volume of exports and imports are relatively insensitive to price changes, it is the level of output that adjusts to ensure equilibrium in the balance of payments. If as Kaldor (1979) has noted, the average and marginal propensities to import are constant over time, investment is financed by retained profits, government expenditure is financed by taxation, and the other exogenous components of demand are ignored, then the level of income (GDP) is simply determined by the level of exports (X):[3]

[†]Source: *Applied Economics*, Vol. 17 (1), February 1985, pp. 55–72.

$$GDP = \frac{1}{m} X$$

where m is the marginal propensity to import.

A logical consequence is that the growth of output will be primarily determined by the increase in exports through the foreign trade multiplier. Moreover, the latter is often taken to be equivalent to the Hicks' super-multiplier.

It is useful to quote Kaldor's (1978, p. 146) summary of the argument.

From the point of view of any particular region,[4] the 'autonomous component of demand' is the demand emanating from *outside* the region; and the Hicks' notion of the 'super-multiplier' can be applied so as to express the doctrine of the foreign trade multiplier in a dynamic setting. So expressed, the doctrine asserts that the rate of economic development of a region is fundamentally governed by the rate of growth of its exports. For the exports, via the 'accelerator', will govern the rate of growth of industrial capacity, as well as the growth of consumption; it will also serve to adjust (again under rather severe simplifying assumptions) both the level, and the rate of growth, of imports to that of exports.

Dixon and Thirlwall (1975) have likewise invoked the super-multiplier as an explanation of the relationship between output and export growth which forms an integral part of their cumulative causation model.

The purpose of this paper is to examine and clarify the relationship between export-led growth, the Harrod foreign trade multiplier and Hicks' super-multiplier in the context of long run economic growth. It is argued that the Keynesian model which has been traditionally used to examine short run fluctuations also yields insights into the determination of the trend rate of growth. Consequently the argument will be developed in terms of the orthodox Keynesian model and the New Cambridge variant.

It will be shown that generally the workings of the Harrod foreign trade multiplier and Hicks' super-multiplier are not synonymous. It is found that due to this there is no validity to the criticism that the growth of exports cannot be an important determinant of the growth of output for those countries (such as the US) where exports form only a small fraction of *GDP*.

We conclude with a discussion of Thirlwall's 'law of economic growth' and suggest the super-multiplier as a rationale for it. We also consider the relevance of the law for analysing the post-war growth of the advanced countries.

II. Export-led Growth and the Foreign Trade Multiplier

It is useful to begin the discussion with a consideration of the simple empirical relationship between the growth of *GDP* and exports that has been often held to confirm the importance of export-led growth. The relationship is usually estimated by regression analysis using cross-country data and growth rates over a decade or more. (See, for example, Thirlwall, 1982, Table 3. Batchelor *et al.*, 1980, Table 7.4 provide a convenient summary of a number of other studies estimating this relationship.) A close fit is commonly found with a regression coefficient that is significantly less than one. Since the specification is so parsimonious, Occam's razor suggests it will be a powerful explanation of the disparate growth rates of output, *provided it can be shown to have a satisfactory theoretical rationale.*[5]

For convenience, we estimated the relationship for the advanced countries for two periods, 1955–73 and 1973–80. The year 1973 represents the turning point when the advanced countries entered a period of prolonged recession from which they have yet to recover (notwithstanding a small upturn in 1979). The regression results are reported in Table 1. It transpires that there is a close relationship for the period 1955–73 between the growth of *GDP* and the export of goods and services. This immediately raises the question of the interpretation of the equation because correlation implies nothing about the direction of causality or indeed whether it exists at all. It is perfectly possible for those factors (such as entrepreneurial dynamism) that make for a fast rate of growth of *GDP* to be likewise responsible for a rapid export growth. Furthermore, it is possible that both growth rates may be exogenously determined by the growth of factor inputs.

However, it is beyond the scope of this paper to assess the relative merits of the supply and demand oriented explanations of economic growth. We are assuming here that there has generally been no long-run supply constraint in the growth of the advanced countries. (See Cornwall, 1977 and McCombie, 1982, for a discussion of these issues.) If this is accepted then the importance of the equation is that a failure to find such a relationship between *GDP* and export growth could be taken to be a refutation of the crucial role of the balance of payments in constraining the growth of output. Indeed, the weaker correlation that is found for 1973–80 indicates that the balance of payments may not have been a binding constraint as several countries pursued deflationary policies in order to

Table 1. *The relationship between the growth of output (GDP) and that of total exports (X_{TOT})*

1973–80[a]:	$GDP = 1.549 + 0.209\ \dot{X}_{TOT}$	$\bar{R}^2 = 0.208$
	(2.78) (2.10)	
1955[b]–73:	$GDP = -0.052 = 0.600\ \dot{X}_{TOT}$	$\bar{R}^2 = 0.641$
	(4.02) (4.92)	

Note: Figures in parentheses are *t*-values. Sample consists of 15 advanced countries.
[a]Terminal date is 1979 for 3 countries.
[b]The initial year is the peak of the trade cycle and varies from 1955–57 depending upon the particular country.
Source: OECD National Accounts, 1950–79 and 1960–80.

restrict output with the supposed aim of combating inflation. In other words, the growth of *GDP* was often lower than the maximum which was made possible by the growth of exports.

If this relationship is supposed to reflect the foreign trade multiplier, then one objection, as mentioned in the introduction, is that its importance must vary considerably between the advanced countries, depending on the size of the export sector relative to *GDP*. This ratio varies from the US where it is 5% (1956) to the Netherlands, 44% (1956). Surely, the impact of an increase in exports of, for example, one percentage point will have considerably less impact in the case of the US than the Netherlands? This suggests that the relationship between *GDP* and *X̊* estimated above is wrongly specified, *providing its theoretical rationale rests solely on the foreign trade multiplier.*[6]

Severn (1967) has pursued this argument by reasoning that an allowance ought to be made in the regression for the degree of openness of the economy. He suggested that the growth of exports should be weighted by an 'openness coefficient', namely the ratio of exports to total output. The regression to be estimated now becomes:

$$G\mathring{D}P = a_1 + b_1 \left\{ \frac{X_{TOT}}{GDP} \right\} \mathring{X} \tag{2}$$

The results are reported in Table 2.

It is sufficient to note that there is now no statistically significant relationship between the two variables. However, it will be shown later that this argument is in fact erroneous if the relationship between the growth of *GDP* and exports is representing the super-multiplier.

Ideally, in order to discuss the role of the two multipliers in the context of economic growth, we should use a full-scale econometric model of the economy. Nevertheless, the main arguments can be satisfactorily demonstrated with the use of simple Keynesian models. Clearly, the theoretical rationale must be Keynesian in nature since export-led growth has no meaning under the assumptions of global monetarism.

We further accept the argument that 'money does not matter' in the sense that the money supply, broadly defined, is endogenous. By making this assumption we are presenting the strong or, no doubt some would say extreme, Keynesian interpretation of export-led growth. The differences in

Table 2. *The relationship between the growth of output (G$\mathring{D}$P) and that of total exports weighted by the 'Openness coefficient' ($\mathring{X}^*_{TOT}$)*

1973–80	$G\mathring{D}P = 1.905 + 0.526\ \mathring{X}^*_{TOT}$	$\bar{R}^2 = 0.134$
	(4.02) (1.73)	
1955–73	$G\mathring{D}P = 4.769 - 0.048\ \mathring{X}^*_{TOT}$	$\bar{R}^2 = 0.009$
	(4.69) (−0.01)	

For notes and sources, see Table 1.

the growth of the advanced countries are seen to reflect ultimately real rather than monetary forces.

The orthodox Keynesian model may be described by the following equations:

$$Y = C + I + G + X - M \tag{3.1}$$

$$C = C_o + b(Y - T) \tag{3.2}$$

$$T = tY \tag{3.3}$$

$$I = I_o \tag{3.4}$$

$$X = X_o + \gamma P \tag{3.5}$$

$$M = P\bar{M} = P\bar{M}_o + mY - \rho P \tag{3.6}$$

Y, C, I, G, X, M and T denote GDP, consumption, investment, government expenditure , exports, imports, and tax revenues. P is defined as an index of the ratio of foreign to domestic prices. $\bar{M}$ is the volume of imports.

The relationships of the model are well-known and hence need not be discussed here.

The level of income is given by:

$$Y = 1/k(X_o - P\bar{M}_o + (\gamma + \rho)P + I_o + G_o) \tag{4}$$

where

$$k = (m + (1 - b) + bt) \tag{5}$$

At this point it is worth digressing a moment to discuss the cases of fixed and flexible exchange rates. P is a policy instrument and through exchange rate adjustment the government may be able to influence to some degree the level and growth of exports and imports. Prior to the breakdown of Bretton Woods, the predominant regime was one of fixed exchange rates. In this case P is constant and hence will not affect the growth of either exports or imports. (There were, of course, the notable exceptions of the French devaluation in the late 1950s and the British devaluation of 1967.) On the other hand, it might be thought that the introduction of flexible exchange rates in the 1970s effectively destroyed the notion of export-led growth. It is often argued that under flexible exchange rates, external equilibrium can be achieved at any desired level of economic activity.

Two points arise here. Firstly, there is the problem of, for example, the translation of nominal devaluations into changes in the real exchange rate. The existence of 'real wage resistance' may mean that subsequent domestic price inflation will, after a lag, be sufficient to wipe out any initial advantage. Secondly, and more importantly for our purposes, even though there were substantial changes in the real exchange rates throughout the 1970s, these were not sufficient to achieve anything but minor changes in the relative export performances of the advanced countries. In other words, the change in total exports were mainly due to changes in X_o rather than in γP. (See Fetherstone *et al.* 1977, and Kaldor, 1977, for the empirical evidence.)

Therefore, it is plausible to assume that the growth of exports can be regarded as exogenous. Under these circumstances the growth of output is given by:

$$\Delta Y/Y = 1/k \left(a_X \frac{\Delta X}{X} + a_I \frac{\Delta I_o}{I_o} + a_G \frac{\Delta G_o}{G_o} - a_M \frac{\Delta M_o}{M_o} \right) \qquad (6)$$

where a denotes the share of the relevant variable in total output.

If the only increase in the autonomous expenditure comes from exports, the rate of growth of output is given by $\Delta Y/Y = 1/k(a_x)\Delta X/X$ which represents the impact caused by the foreign trade multiplier.

An alternative approach is to use the New Cambridge model of the economy which is similar to the orthodox Keynesian approach but with the important difference that, instead of two separate relationships for the determinants of consumption, there is only one for private expenditure (Smith, 1975).

This is given by:

$$PE = d(Y - T) - NAFA \qquad (7)$$

Private expenditure, PE, is a function of disposable income (in practice d is near unity) and the net acquisition of financial assets ($NAFA$). The latter was initially thought to be stable over time and small in relation to the level of GDP.[7] In the earliest version of the model the budget deficit ($D = G - T$) was taken to be exogenous so the rate of growth of output is given by:

$$\Delta Y/Y = 1/m(a_X\Delta X/X - a_M\Delta M_o/M_o + a_D\Delta D_o/D_o) \qquad (8)$$

since, by assumption, $\Delta NAFA = 0$

However, it is clear that, since part of the government's spending and receipts is endogenous (such as payments for unemployment benefits and tax receipts), it is unlikely that the government could be totally successful in manipulating the exogenous components to obtain the desired budget surplus or deficit. Hence, it is more plausible to make tax receipts a function of income ($T = tY$). More recent models have also made $NAFA$ a function of income (i.e. $NAFA = e(Y - T)$ although e is likely to be small). Under these circumstances

$$\Delta Y/Y = 1/(m + t + et - e)(a_X\Delta X/X - a_M\Delta M_o/M_o + a_G\Delta G_o/G_o)(9)$$

Hence the foreign trade multiplier is either $1/m$ or $1/(m + t + et - e)$. In either case it is larger than the orthodox Keynesian multiplier.

III. The Direct Impact of the Foreign Trade Multiplier

In this section we report the estimate of the increase in *GDP* induced, through the foreign trade multiplier, by an increase in the growth of exports of one percentage point per annum. In order to calculate this it is necessary to know the values of the multiplier for the various advanced countries, but unfortunately these are not always readily available. It was therefore necessary to first construct an estimate of each country's multiplier.

The multiplier used is defined as:

$$k = 1/(1 - b + bt_d + t_i + m) \tag{10}$$

where b, t_d, t_i and m are the marginal propensities to consume, to tax directly, to tax indirectly and to import.[8] Direct taxation included both social security contributions and inputed employee welfare contributions. The marginal propensities were calculated by estimating the ratios of the absolute changes in the relevant variables over the period and the data were taken from the OECD National Accounts. Since the marginal propensity to import is the propensity that varies the greatest between the countries, we also constructed an alternative estimate. The marginal propensity to import manufactures was taken to be double the average, while for raw materials and semi-processed goods the marginal propensity was taken to be equal to the average. (In practice it makes little difference as to which procedure is adopted.)

Since this approach was taken as a *pis aller*, the values of the multiplier are best regarded as orders of magnitude rather than being precise estimates. Nevertheless, the value obtained for the UK of 1.11 for the 1970s seems plausible, especially since Cuthbertson (1979) reports that the NIESR multiplier lies in the range 0.8 to 1.0, the Treasury Model gives a value of 1.1 and the CEPG's value is approximately 1.25. The value for the US of 1.37 also seems reasonable for what is virtually a closed economy.

The differences in the values of the multiplier (see Table 3, Column 4) depend primarily on differences in the marginal propensities to import. For the pre-1973 period the average value of the other leakages $(1 - b + bt_d + t_i)$, is 0.55 with eight of the countries falling within ± 0.05 of this figure. The extreme values are 0.65 for Norway and 0.47 for the US. For the period 1973–80 this stability of the marginal propensities across the countries is again observed, although the average value has fallen to 0.45.

The results of the calculations of the impact on *GDP* of a one percentage point increase in export growth is reported in Table 3, Column 5(a). It can be seen that there is a wide diversity of results across the countries. The US, although it has the largest multiplier, experiences the smallest increase in output through the foreign trade multiplier. Even Japan, often cited as the example *par excellence* in export-led growth, experiences only a small impact. In this case a one percentage point increase in total exports increases the growth of *GDP* by only 0.16 (1957) and 0.18 (1980) percentage points. Alternatively, the very open economies of Denmark, the Netherlands and Norway experienced an increase in their

Table 3. *The effect on the growth of GDP of an increase in the growth of total exports through the foreign trade multiplier and super-multiplier*

Country 1	Ratio of total exports to GDP % 2	Marginal propensity to import 3	Value of the multiplier 4	Increase in GDP due to an increase of one percentage point in export growth 5		Ratio of 5a to 5b 6
				Foreign trade multiplier 5a	Super-multiplier 5b	
1980						
Austria	39.0	0.50	0.78	0.30	0.78	38
Belgium	59.7	0.82	0.66	0.39	0.73	54
Canada	29.3	0.31	1.05	0.30	0.94	33
Denmark	33.3	0.36	0.91	0.30	0.92	33
France	22.4	0.29	1.04	0.23	0.77	30
Germany	27.0	0.41	0.88	0.23	0.66	36
Ireland	53.9	0.82	0.73	0.39	0.66	59
Italy	25.2	0.31	1.02	0.25	0.81	32
Japan	14.0	0.19	1.26	0.18	0.74	24
Netherlands	53.0	0.73	0.67	0.36	0.73	49
Norway	47.6	0.38	0.76	0.36	1.25	30
United Kingdom	28.4	0.26	1.11	0.32	1.09	29
United States	10.0	0.15	1.37	0.14	0.66	21
Mid-1950s						
Austria	25.1	0.38	0.90	0.23	0.66	34
Belgium	33.7	0.52	0.81	0.27	0.65	42
Canada	20.0	0.25	1.07	0.21	0.80	26
Denmark	33.9	0.34	1.12	0.38	0.99	38
France	14.1	0.20	1.18	0.17	0.70	24
Germany	20.1	0.24	1.06	0.21	0.84	25
Ireland	31.0	0.46	0.99	0.31	0.67	46
Italy	10.9	0.21	1.27	0.14	0.52	27
Japan	11.5	0.16	1.43	0.16	0.72	22
Netherlands	43.9	0.60	0.94	0.41	0.73	56
Norway	43.8	0.46	0.76	0.33	0.95	35
United Kingdom	21.9	0.31	1.08	0.24	0.71	33
United States	5.0	0.08	1.42	0.07	0.62	11

growth rates in the mid-1950s by over a third of a percentage point.

Over time, the impact of the foreign trade multiplier has generally increased slightly as the increase of the size of the export sector has more than offset the decline in the value of the multiplier.[9]

The variation of the importance of the impact of the foreign trade multiplier across the countries would superficially seem to confirm the criticisms noted above.

A further objection to the fundamental role of the foreign trade multiplier in determining economic growth may be seen by considering Equation 6 again. This may be written equivalently as:

$$\Delta Y/Y = 1/k\{a_X \Delta X/X + a_E \Delta E_o/E_o\} \tag{11}$$

where E_o is the sum of all other autonomous expenditures. It has been questioned as to why an increase in X should have any greater impact on the level of economic activity than an equal increase in E_o. The answer is, of course, that the growth of exports is the only element that simultaneously relaxes the balance of payments constraint. For example, the post-war history of the UK has been consumption-led expansion (1954, 1959, 1963, 1973) which resulted in an expansion of output above the trend rate of growth. This was brought to an abrupt end by the rapid increase in induced imports which led to the familiar balance of payments crises. It is therefore necessary to turn to an examination of the role of import growth in constraining growth, which leads to a consideration of the super-multiplier.

IV. Export-led Growth and the Hicks' Super-Multiplier

The direct influence of an increase in exports through the foreign trade multiplier is only one mechanism by which *GDP* will be increased. A secondary route is that, by initially relaxing the balance of payments constraint, an increase in exports will allow other autonomous expenditures to be increased until income has risen by enough to induce an increase in imports equivalent to the initial increase in exports.

We have seen, in the short run, that the absolute increase of output through the foreign trade multiplier is given by:

$$\Delta Y = \frac{1}{k} \Delta X \tag{12}$$

The increase in imports induced by the expansion of output is given by the marginal import–output ratio:

$$\Delta M = m \Delta Y \tag{13}$$

$$\Delta M = \frac{m}{k} \Delta X \tag{14}$$

Since $k > m$ the increase in imports will be less than the increase in exports and a balance of trade surplus will accrue, equal to

$$\left(\frac{k-m}{m} \right) \Delta X. \tag{15}$$

However, in the long run the super-multiplier operates increasing the level of activity until the induced level of imports equals the increase in the volume of exports.

Consequently as $\Delta M = \Delta X$, it follows that:

$$\Delta Y/Y = 1/m(a_X)\Delta X/X \tag{16}$$

$$= 1/k \left\{ a_X \frac{\Delta X}{X} + a_E \frac{\Delta E_o}{E_o} \right\} \tag{17}$$

Equations 16 and 17 represent the working of the Hicks' super-multiplier. Apart from the direct increase in output through the foreign trade multiplier $(1/k(a_x)\Delta X/X)$, the initial relaxation of the balance of payments constraint permits (rather than automatically causes) an increase in 'autonomous' expenditure given by:

$$\Delta E_o/E = k(1/m - 1/k)(a_X/a_E)\Delta X/X \tag{18}$$

If autonomous expenditure is not expanded by the amount implied by Equation 18, then the increase in output will be commensurately less and a balance of payments surplus will occur as outlined above.[10]

An idea of the magnitude of the impact of the super-multiplier may be seen again from Table 3 (Column 5(b)) where the percentage point increase in *GDP* resulting from a one percentage point increase in exports is reported. It can be seen that the increase in *GDP* is greater and shows less inter-country variation when the foreign trade multiplier operates. It is noticeable that the US and Japan now experience one of the greatest increases in *GDP* from a given increase in exports. Table 3 also reports the percentage of the increase in output resulting from the increase in exports that is attributable to the Harrod foreign trade multiplier (column 6). In the mid-1950s the percentage ranged from 11 (the US) to 56 (the Netherlands). The proportion has increased over time reflecting the increasing share of exports (and imports) in *GDP* leading to an increase in the impact of the foreign trade multiplier relative to the super-multiplier.

With these arguments in mind, we are now in a position to reconsider the relationship between the growth of *GDP* and exports, namely

$$G\mathring{D}P = a + b\mathring{X} \tag{19}$$

It is clear that its most plausible rationale is as a reduced form equation reflecting the super-multiplier rather than as a mis-specified representation of the foreign trade multiplier, as was suggested in the second section above. It is therefore erroneous to weight the growth of exports by an 'openness coefficient' in the manner suggested by Severn.

While the coefficient b is an estimate of the value of the super-multiplier, it is clear that the use of cross-country data is to a certain extent inappropriate as the value of b shows some variation between the countries.[11] (The estimate of b for 1955–73 of 0.6 compares with the average value of Table 3, Column 5(b), of 0.74.)

V. The Impact of an Increase in Autonomous Expenditure on Imports

Up to now the analysis has been in relation to the change in output that an increase in exports will induce, both directly through the foreign trade multiplier and indirectly by allowing other autonomous expenditure to increase through the initial relaxation of the balance of payment constraint. However, there is one important component of autonomous expenditure which is unaffected by the super-multiplier, namely autonomous imports. In this section, the impact of a change in the latter is examined.

The marginal (induced) import–output ratio is given by:

$$\Delta M_I / \Delta Y = m \tag{20}$$

where $M = M_I + M_o$, M_I and M_o being induced and autonomous imports, respectively.

If changes in autonomous imports are introduced together with changes in exports, the balance of payments equilibrium condition becomes.

$$\Delta M = \Delta X - \Delta M_o \tag{21}$$

or

$$\Delta M_I / M_I = (X/M_I) \Delta X / X - (M_o/M_I) \Delta M_o / M_o \tag{22}$$

Consequently, the impact of the super-multiplier on total growth becomes:

$$\Delta Y / Y = 1 / m (M_I / Y) [(X/M_I) \Delta X / X - (M_o/M_I) \Delta M_o / M_o] \tag{23}$$

$$= 1 / m [a_X \Delta X / X - a_{M_o} \Delta M_o / M_o] \tag{24}$$

It can be seen that an increase in autonomous imports acts to reduce the rate of growth of output analogously to a decline in export growth, acting directly through the foreign trade multiplier and indirectly through the balance of payments constraint.

VI. Thirlwall's Law of Economic Growth

Thirlwall (1979, 1982a, 1982b) has argued that the long-run growth of output is constrained by the balance of payments and empirical confirmation is given by the rule:

$$\Delta Y / Y_e = (1/\pi) \Delta X / X \tag{25}$$

where $\Delta Y / Y_e$ is the rate of growth of output consistent with a balance of payments equilibrium and π is the income elasticity of demand for imports. Using values for π estimated by Houthhakker and Magee (1969) and observed growth rates of exports, the equilibrium output growth may be calculated on the assumption of the 'law of one price' and that capital transfers are negligible. It is found that these values accord closely with the actual growth rates (see Table 5).

Equation 25 is not merely an identity because the close fit suggests that the above assumptions are realistic. Equation 25 is similar to 19 although π varies between countries. (This may again explain the relatively large standard error of the regression coefficient when Equation 19 is estimated using cross-country data for 1955–73, see Table 1.)

Thirlwall has argued that Equation 25 is best interpreted as representing the Harrod foreign trade multiplier when made dynamic. However, this interpretation rests on certain simplifying assumptions. Thirlwall's simple Keynesian model (1982b, pp. 5–6) yields the following solution for output:

$$Y = \frac{X - M_o + E_o}{m + s + t - a - g} \tag{26}$$

where E_o is the sum of autonomous expenditure excluding that on imports, s, t, a, g are the marginal propensities of saving, taxation, investment and government expenditure respectively.

In the special case where $s + t = a + g$ (or, in other words, all induced expenditure equals induced leakages) and there is no autonomous expenditure, Equation 26 gives the foreign trade multiplier:

$$Y = \frac{X}{m} \tag{27}$$

where $m = k$.

It follows that:

$$\Delta Y/Y = \frac{1}{m} \, a_X \Delta X/X \tag{28}$$

Consequently, in balanced growth $a_X = a_m$

$$\Delta Y/Y = \frac{1}{\pi} \Delta X/X \tag{29}$$

However, the assumptions underlying this interpretation are not innocuous, as in the first case, implausibly high values are required for the multipliers. (In the case of the UK the value would be over three.) Moreover, it is unlikely that there would be any autonomous expenditure in which case there would be a permanent balance of payments deficit.

These restrictions disappear if Equation 29 is interpreted as the super-multiplier, so that:

$$\Delta Y/Y = 1/k\{ a_X \Delta X/X + a_E \Delta E/E\} \tag{30}$$

$$= \frac{1}{m} a_X \Delta X/X \tag{31}$$

and $m \neq k$.

There is one further problem with the interpretation of the law given by Equation 31 as being a dynamic version of the traditional Harrod foreign trade multiplier. For expositional purposes, let us accept Thirlwall's assumptions.

The Keynesian import function is given by:

$$M = N'_o + mY \tag{32}$$

with equilibrium condition for balanced trade, $X = M$.

The dynamic model, Equation 29, expressed in static terms is:

$$M = M''_o y^\pi \tag{33}$$

Thirlwall derives the equivalence as follows. Assuming no change in autonomous imports Equation 32 may be expressed as:

$$\Delta M/\Delta Y = m \tag{34}$$

and:

$$(\Delta M/\Delta Y).(Y/M) = mY/M \tag{35}$$

or:

$$\pi = \frac{Y}{M} \cdot \frac{M - M'_o}{Y} \tag{36}$$

where m is given in Equation 32.

Since π is empirically greater than unity it is necessary for M'_o to be negative.[12] (If M'_o is constant and M and Y increase over time, then π will decline tending towards unity.) However, in this case Equations 32 and 33 are not consistent because if M'_o equals M''_o the level of imports given by 33 will always be negative. It is also likely that the volume of autonomous imports will increase over time and eventually become positive (which of course implies π will fall below unity).

In a later paper, Kennedy and Thirlwall (1983, p. 128) argue (omitting a footnote):

With a slight modification to the balanced trade model, however, the two models are easily reconcilable. If an autonomous term is included in

the multiplicative import function of the balanced trade model, we then
have as the long run growth rule with relative price constant:

$$y = \frac{x - m_o}{\pi^*}$$

where m_a is the growth of imports independent of the growth of income,
holding other factors constant, and π^* is the 'true' or 'pure' income elasticity of demand for imports.

m_a is $\Delta M_o / M_o$ in our notation.

Hence it is clear that M_o'' in Equation 33 is regarded as positive.[13]

If M_o' is also positive, then the Keynesian model derives the growth of
output as

$$\Delta Y/Y = \frac{\Delta X/X(X/M_1) - \Delta M_o'/M_o'(M_o'/M_1)}{\pi} \tag{38}$$

(This is the same result as the more general super-multiplier model.)

In order to avoid these inconsistencies and to reconcile the models, it is
useful to regard the import function from the Keynesian model as a short-
run relationship, while the multiplicative function represents the long-run
relationship derived from the shift of the short-run function over time as
autonomous imports and output increase.

The interpretation has the advantage that it is no longer necessary to
enforce the equivalence of the elasticity of the linear import function ($mY/
M = \eta$) and π. Consequently, it is possible for $\pi > 1$ and M_o' to be positive
(and $\eta < 1$). An increase in the growth of autonomous imports would, *ceteris paribus*, tend to increase the value of π, the long-run elasticity. This
differs from the interpretation of Kennedy and Thirlwall who prefer to
assume that the multiplicative function shifts over time.

Nevertheless, the exact relationship between the two import functions
that is chosen, the important point still remains that it is the external sector
through the multiplier that determines the long-run growth of the advanced
countries, and in the next section we assess the relevance of the law in
explaining the post-war growth of the advanced countries.

VII. Economic Growth in Open Economies

Given the assumptions underlying the super-multiplier and following
Thirlwall's analysis, we have seen that the growth of output of a particular
country, consistent with a balance of payments equilibrium, is given by the
simple rule:[14]

$$\mathring{Y}_B = \mathring{X}/\pi \tag{39}$$

or, if exports are determined by world income ($X = aY_w^\varepsilon$),

$$\hat{Y}_B = (\varepsilon \hat{Y}_w)/\pi \tag{40}$$

Table 4 reports the values of the world income elasticity of demand for the exports of the six largest countries, together with their income elasticities of demand for imports. Table 5 gives these countries' rates of growth of *GDP*, exports and the balance of payments equilibrium growth (calculated from Equation 39) for the years 1951–73 and 1973–80. The equilibrium growth of *GDP* is found to approximate the observed growth rates. (Using the standard errors of the estimates of the income elasticities by Houthakker and Magee, the difference between the equilibrium and actual growth rates are not statistically significant.) In the period 1973–80, two countries (Japan and the UK) have equilibrium growth rates significantly above their actual growth rates. This could be because demand was

Table 4. *Export and import income elasticities of the six largest advanced countries*

Country	World income elasticity of demand for exports	Domestic income elasticity of demand for imports (a)	(b)
Japan	3.55	1.23	n.a.
Italy	2.95	2.19	n.a.
West Germany	2.08	1.80	1.31
France	1.53	1.66	1.63
United States	0.99	1.51	n.a.
United Kingdom	0.86	1.66	1.82

Sources: Houthakker and Magee (1969); import elasticity (b) Panic (1976).

Table 5. *Observed and equilibrium growth rates of GDP, and growth of exports, six largest advanced countries*

Country	1951–73 Growth of (i) GDP	(ii) Exports	Equilibrium growth of GDP	1973–80 Growth of (i) GDP	(ii) Exports	Equilibrium growth of GDP
Japan	9.79	12.67	10.30	3.68	10.64	8.65
Italy	5.22	11.13	5.08	2.75	6.54	2.91
West Germany	5.64	9.88	5.48(7.54)	2.30	5.03	2.66(3.83)
France	5.11	7.59	4.57(4.65)	2.80	6.21	3.83(3.81)
United States	3.58	5.04	3.33	2.22	5.58	3.70
United Kingdom	2.91	4.27	2.61(2.35)	0.91	3.30	2.19(1.81)

Note: Equilibrium growth of GDP derived using import elasticities from Houthakker and Magee except those in parentheses which use Panic's estimates.
Sources: OECD National Accounts.

not expanded enough for fear of inflationary pressures or, as may well be the case in the UK, there was a marked increase in the propensity to import in the late 1970s.[16]

In the context of long term growth, it is readily apparent that the differing export elasticities are more important in expanding the different *GDP* growth rates than the income elasticities. For example, the countries with the fastest and the second fastest growth of *GDP*, Japan and Italy, had the lowest and highest income elasticities respectively. To put the matter another way: if the UK had Japan's income elasticity of demand for imports then the equilibrium growth rate would increase by a little over 0.5% p.a., *ceteris paribus.* If, on the other hand, the UK's exports were sufficiently competitive that her export elasticity matched even that of West Germany, the equilibrium growth rate would be double the actual equilibrium rate of 2.61% p.a.[15, 16]

This approach to economic growth is sometimes termed 'demand oriented' because of its emphasis on the role of the multiplier. Nevertheless, it places great emphasis on the importance of supply characteristics and provides no justification for the conventional Keynesian demand-management policies as applied particularly to the post-war UK economy.

The key to the long run growth of the economy is the rate of expansion of exports. This has more to do with such factors as quality, design and delivery dates than with price competitiveness (Connell, 1979). Thus attempts to increase the trend rate of growth of exports through macro-policies, such as exchange rate adjustment, are unlikely to be very successful. The problem of the poor performance of UK exports is a structural problem requiring an industrial strategy at the microeconomic level. The fallacy of past UK policy has rested in the belief that if only growth generated by fiscal policies could be maintained for long enough (albeit at the expense of a 'temporary' balance of payments deficit) there should be no reason why the growth of the UK could not match that of the other European countries. However, this myth was finally exploded with the Barber boom of 1971–73. Even an 18% devaluation could not prevent the occurrence of an untenable balance of payments deficit. An attempt to increase $\mathring{Y}_B$ by a consumption-led boom leads to an immediate increase in imports. It may be that increasing the trend rate of growth of output would eventually increase the growth of exports (through, for example, the Verdoorn effect) but such results are achievable only in the long term and would not have very much influence over a period of two or three years. It was hardly surprising that such attempts at demand management, based as they were on a theory essentially concerned with a closed economy, were bound to end in failure (Eltis, 1976).

Up to now, the analysis using the law has been based on a partial equilibrium model and neglects the interrelationships between the advanced countries. It explains how a given growth in world income (taken to be that of the combined OECD countries) and in world trade is distributed between the advanced countries, but it does not explain what determines the former. For example, the output of the advanced countries grew at about 5% p.a. during the period 1951–73 but in the subsequent decade it fell by about half. The reasons for the post-war rapid expansion of world trade prior to 1973 was based, *inter alia*, on the initial willingness of the US to run a trade deficit and to ensure sufficient international liquidity. This has been well documented and need not be repeated here (Cripps, 1978).

However, the interrelatedness of the advanced countries has had serious implications especially for the last decade. The immediate cause of the present world recession was undoubtedly due to the rise in oil prices, but the subsequent failure of the advanced countries to take sufficient measures to ensure a return to full employment must be due to an acceptance of the argument that this would inevitably lead to unacceptably high levels of inflation. The problem is that should one country disagree and try to obtain a return to full employment by reflating in isolation, then for the reasons outlined above, it would run into serious balance of payments problems. Even though there is widespread underutilization of resources throughout the western world, the multiplier effects will not be sufficient to generate a sufficient rise in world income to prevent the reflating country from running into a balance of payments deficit. This is, of course, a reflection of the $n - 1$ 'redundancy problem'. If the other countries are content with their balance of payments position and assume the level of output is unalterable, then the nth country (such as France in the early 1980s) has no degrees of freedom within which to act.

The irony is that for any individual country the only satisfactory method of increasing its growth is by improving its export performance rather than by stimulating internal demand. But for the advanced countries as a whole, such measures as competitive devaluation and the imposition of 'beggar-my-neighbour' tariffs and quotas (in an attempt to reduce the growth of imports) will be self-defeating. The most effective solution is the one, advocated long ago by Keynes himself, of co-ordinated expansionary policies simultaneous in all the advanced countries. This would act to increase output in a manner analogous to the closed economy since there would be no deterioration of any country's balance of payments. The problem is of course that such a policy is highly unlikely so long as certain governments retain faith in monetarism.

VIII. Concluding Comments

The most satisfactory basis of the export-led growth theory is the operation of the Hicks' super-multiplier. A corollary of this is that while some of the faster growing countries (most notably Japan and West Germany since the mid-1960s) may have experienced a labour supply constraint, the growth of factor inputs has never been the exogenous determinant of growth. This role belongs to the growth of exports which, by relaxing the balance of payments constraint determines the maximum growth of *GDP* even though this may not be sufficient to ensure the full utilization of the factors of production. The reason why the slower growing countries did not experience a marked acceleration in the rate of unemployment until the late 1960s was that the tertiary sector absorbed much of the labour supply even though it led to disguised unemployment.

Although the theory outlined in this paper is post-Keynesian, in the sense that it is demand-oriented, in fact it emphasizes the importance of the supply side of the economy. The efficiency with which goods destined for the foreign market are produced ultimately determines the performance of the economy as a whole.

The export-led growth is also reflected in Thirlwall's 'law of growth'. It has been shown that the law (being based on a *multiplicative* import function) cannot be easily reconciled with the foreign trade multiplier (which is based on a *linear* import function) unless a distinction is made between short and long run relationships. Nevertheless the law, in spite of, or perhaps because of, its simplicity provides many insights into the post-war growth of the advanced countries. Of course, it is unlikely that the UK could ever have matched the economic performance of Japan, but if exports had grown at 7% p.a. over the post-war period she must surely have been capable of a growth of *GDP* of between 4 and $4^{1}/_{2}$% p.a.

Acknowledgements

I am grateful to Tony Thirlwall and an anonymous referee for their helpful comments.

References

Cambridge Economic Policy Group (1981) The European Community: problems and prospects, *Cambridge Economic Policy Review*, **7**(2).
Connell, D. (1979) *The UK's performance in export markets — some evidence from international trade data*, NEDC Discussion Paper 6.
Cornwall, J. (1977) *Modern capitalism: its growth and transformation*, Martin Robertson.
Cripps, F. (1978) Causes of growth and recession in world trade, *Cambridge Economic Policy Review*, **4**, 37–43.
Cuthbertson, K. (1979) *Macroeconomic policy. The new Cambridge Keynesian and monetarist controversies*, Macmillan, London.
Dixon, R.J. and Thirlwall, A.P. (1975) A model of regional growth rate differences on Kaldorian lines, *Oxford Economic Papers* **27**, 201–14.
Eltis, W. (1976) The failure of the Keynesian conventional wisdom, *Lloyds Bank Review*, **122**, 1–17.
Fetherston, M., Moore, B. and Rhodes, J. (1977) Manufacturing export shares and cost competitiveness of advanced industrial countries, *Cambridge Economic Policy Review*, **3**, 62–70.
Godley, W. (1979) Britain's chronic recession: can anything be done? in *Slow Growth in Britain: Causes and Consequences*, (Ed.) W. Beckerman, Clarendon Press, Oxford.
Hicks, J. (1950) *The trade cycle*, Clarendon Press, Oxford.
Houthakker, H. and Magee, S. (1969) Income and price elasticities in world trade, *Review of Economics and Statistics*, **51**, 111–25.
Kaldor, N. (1977) The effect of devaluation of trade in manufactures, in Kaldor (1978).
Kaldor, N. (1978) *Further essays on applied economics*, Duckworth.
Kaldor, N. (1979) Comment, in *De-industrialisation*, (Ed.) F. Blackaby (1979), NIESR, Heinemann, London.
Kennedy, C. and Thirlwall, A.P. (1983) Import and export ratios and the dynamic Harrod trade multiplier: a reply to McGregor and Swales, *Oxford Economic Papers*, **35**, 125–9.

McCombie, J.S.L. (1982) *Post-war productivity and output growth in the advanced countries*, Doctoral Thesis, University of Cambridge.

Panic, M. (1975) Why the UK's propensity to import is high, *Lloyds Bank Review*, **115**, 1–12.

Severn, A.K. (1968) Exports and economic growth: comment, *Kyklos*, **21**, 546–8.

Smith, A.P. (1976) Demand management and the 'New School', *Applied Economics*, **8**, 193–205.

Thirlwall, A.P. (1979) The balance of payments constraint as an explanation of international growth rate differences, *Banca Nazionale Del Lavoro Quarterly Review*, **128**, 44–53.

Thirlwall, A.P. and Nureldon Hussain, M. (1982a) The balance of payments constraint, capital flows and growth rate differences between developing countries, *Oxford Economic Papers*, **34**, 498–509.

Thirlwall, A.P. (1982b) The Harrod trade multiplier and the importance of export-led growth, *Pakistan Journal of Applied Economics*, **1**, 1–21.

Thirlwall, A.P. (1983) Foreign trade elasticities in centre periphery models of growth and development, *Banca Nazianale Del Lavoro Quarterly Review*, **146**, 249–61.

Notes

1. See Cornwall (1977) for an exposition and survey of this approach.

2. Harrod's formulation of the foreign trade multiplier actually predated the Keynesian investment multiplier by three years although it was subsequently overshadowed by the latter. The revival and reassessment of the foreign trade multiplier is largely due to Kaldor (1978, 1979) and Thirlwall (1979, 1982a, 1982b).

3. These are very restrictive assumptions which we shall relax later.

4. Kaldor uses the term regions to denote different countries, groups of countries or different areas within the same country.

5. Some studies included other exogenous variables in the regression apart from export growth. These include the ratio of capital flows to *GDP* and the share of manufactured exports to total expenditure. However, the theoretical basis of these equations is often not made clear and only Thirlwall (1982) has explicitly interpreted the relationship as reflecting the (dynamic) foreign trade multiplier. We shall show later that the relationship is best regarded as a reduced form equation derived from the operation of the super-multiplier. In this case, it is not a mis-specification to exclude the growth of other variables that are often held to be important determinants of growth (such as the level of investment). This is because these variables are in their turn determined by the balance of payments constraint and the rate of growth of exports. Strictly speaking, the rate of growth of capital flows (weighted by the share of the capital flows to total foreign exchange receipts) should also be included as a regressor in addition to the growth of exports (weighted by the value of exports in total receipts). In practice, the former is so small compared to the latter that for expositional purposes we can safely ignore it.

6. This criticism is based solely on the direct impact of export growth on that of output through the foreign trade multiplier and ignores the increase in output made possible through the relaxation of the balance of payments constraint. This point will be dealt with more fully below.

7. See the Cambridge Economic Policy Group (1981, p. 9).

8. The multiplier associated with the New Cambridge Model was also calculated but as it is not clear how applicable this approach is to the other advanced countries we only report the results of the orthodox Keynesian multiplier.

9. One exception that calls for comment is the case of the Netherlands which experienced a decline in the impact of the foreign trade multiplier from the mid-1950s to 1980. This occurred because, although there was an increase in both the marginal properties to tax (both directly and indirectly) and to import, this was more than offset by a decrease in the marginal propensity to save. Indeed over the period 1973–80 the Netherlands' increase in consumption was greater than the increase in disposable income.

10. In the earliest New Cambridge model the Harrod foreign trade multiplier and the Hicks' super-multiplier were formally identical. An increase in exports would affect only the level of income and not the trade balance. In other words an increase in exports *automatically* induces an equivalent inflow of imports.

The level of income is given by:

$$Y = 1/m[X - M_o - (D + NAFA)]$$

If only exports are growing, $\Delta Y / Y = 1/m(\Delta X / X)$ but since the multiplier $k = m$, it follows that $\Delta M = \Delta X$ in the short run.

Subsequent versions of this model do not have this property since, rather more realistically, the tax revenue and the $NAFA$ are both deemed to be functions of income and $k = (m + t + et - e) > m$.

11. It would be useful to estimate this relationship or each country separately using time-series data but this is outside the scope of this paper.

12. It is difficult to give an intuitive interpretation of the concept of a negative level of imports.

13. If we wish to have initially a negative value for autonomous imports (K) but an increase in the volume of autonomous imports over time then Equation 33 should be

$$M = (e^{at} + K_o'' - 1) Y^\tau \tag{37}$$

but the simplicity of the law is lost.

14. We assume that the impact of changes in the terms of trade and net capital flows are not significant when compared with the influence of the growth of exports. Of course, this may not be such a satisfactory assumption when short-run deviation about a country's equilibrium growth rate are considered. Thirlwall (1983) has derived a more general expression for Equation 39 incorporating these effects.

15. The differences in income elasticities to import can be largely explained by the differing composition of imports and, in particular the share of manufactures imported. The income elasticity of demand for manufactures is approximately 2 for most of the advanced countries (although for the UK it is nearer 3). The income elasticities for raw materials and fuels are generally less than unity. The low aggregate import elasticity of Japan may be explained by the fact that in 1973 the share of manufactures in Japan's merchandise import bill was 33% whereas for the remaining five advanced countries the lowest was the UK with 57%.

16. The fact that the variations in income elasticity of demand are not a relatively significant factor in explaining the disparate long-term growth rates of the advanced countries and does not preclude the growth of imports being an important short-run influence on the growth of GDP. Indeed, in the case of the UK, the recent growth of imports has had a serious impact on the growth prospects of the UK. Over the period 1973–82 the growth of exports held up comparatively well, growing at 2.46% p.a., while imports grew at 1.75%. However this conceals the remarkable change that occurred in 1978. During the last four years GDP declined at $- 0.94\%$ p.a. and the de-industrialization accelerated at an alarming rate to $- 4.0\%$ p.a. A consideration of merely the aggregate growth of imports and exports does not reveal the proximate cause of this dramatic erosion of the UK's industrial base. The reason lies in the fact that the growth of finished manufactures has grown at a staggering rate of 12.23% p.a. over the period 1978–82. (Total imports grew at 2.47% p.a. over this period while exports grew at 0.31%.) Moreover, after several years of fast growth the share of finished manufactures in the total import bill rose from being insignificant in the early post-war years to 40% in 1982 (current prices). The only reason why the aggregate import did not rise faster than it did was due to the rapid fall in fuel imports (at $- 5.07\%$). The immediate cause of the destruction of British manufacturing thus seems to be the overvalued exchange rate induced by monetarist policies causing a rapid increase in relative import price competitiveness. The problem is, when oil is exhausted and, presumably, the exchange rate adjusts, whether or not the decline in manufacturing is reversible. (For a remarkably prescient account written in 1978 of the then future course of British recession, see Godley, 1979.)

87

The Evolution of Hicks' Theory of Money[1][†]

O.F. Hamouda

The object of this paper is to discuss how Hicks' growing awareness of the importance of the time element led him to conceive a monetary theory in a different manner from that of a pure economic theory and also to reconsider some of his theory of money.[2] We will focus our attention mainly on how money, time and history are linked together.

We propose to look chronologically at the development of Hicks' theory of money. We begin with how he analysed factors which determined the quantity of money to be held and how he determined the rate of interest. We then explain why he came to reject the portfolio approach to transaction balances and how he began to shape his liquidity theory. Finally, we discuss how all of this fits in with recent monetary events.

Unlike his pure economic theory which has been developed gradually over the years the essential aspects of Hicks' theory of money were delivered separately in two different time periods:

(i) In the 1930s, he, on the one hand, provided a micro-economic simplification of the theory of money in which he suggested that the techniques and principles of the theory of value be applied to money. On the other hand, he supplied a macro-economic simplification of Keynes' *General Theory*, in which he made use of Walrasian General Equilibrium analysis.[3] It should be observed that these two developments dealt with two different issues: in the former, Hicks tried to identify and explain the motive for holding money, while in the latter, he was concerned with how the rate of interest was determined.

(ii) The manner in which Hicks' early monetary work was received and extended in literature, his growing awareness of the importance of the role of the time element in dealing with monetary theory, and his concern about the relevance of monetary theory with respect to practical problems, led him, in the 1960s and onward, to reconsider part of his former work. He then *avoided* the dichotomy between the micro and macro aspects of his monetary theory. He *rejected* the equilibrium and static approaches in monetary theory. He *stressed* that a monetary theory should deal with practical and current problems. He *provided* a dynamic approach (in a

[†]Source: *Bulletin of Economic Research*, Vol. 37 (2), May 1985, pp. 131–51.

descriptive manner) to monetary analysis. He *considered* institutional, historical and economic aspects in his analysis. He *emphasized* the time element even more than before. Time intervened in various ways. First, there was a distinction made between the past and the future: on the one hand, considering the *past* meant that Hicks took into account the historical evolution of the financial system, and the past developments of economic, as well as institutional events. On the other hand, looking at the *unknown future*, he justified the notion of the uncertainty involved in planning ahead and the risk attached to undertaking decisions. Here he accepted that both the objective and subjective factors must be considered. Second, there was the question of the length of time, the conditions under which money was lent or borrowed, depended on the length of time agreed upon. Finally, there was the mere passage of time, in which the economic system underwent structural change. The economic structure and the financial system were changing in such a way that the new situation was never the same as that observed in the past. Here the monetary theory, which deals with current and practical problems, must take these changes into account. It was these considerations of the time aspect which made Hicks' theory different from his pure economic theory analysis.

1. The Dichotomy between Economic Theory and Monetary Theory

Although Hicks admitted that *The Theory of Wages* was written 'in a state of monstrous ignorance about everything monetary',[4] we cannot say that such was the case for everything else written after 1933. Soon after, he not only filled in the gap, but he also made contributions which have had a great impact on the development of monetary theory. Some of the earlier statements he made concerning monetary theory, its link with economic fluctuations and the implications of monetary policies were remarkable given the school of thought to which he belonged at that time (see *MIW* essay I). In the early 1930s, he wrote,

(i)   'Monetary theory, in the strict sense, falls outside equilibrium theory' (*ETC*, p. 528);
(ii)   'Whatever the *causa causans* of an economic crisis, it is bound to have a monetary aspect' (*ETC*, p. 529);
(iii) 'Even a system of pure *laissez-faire* would be subject to monetary disturbances' (*ETC*, p. 529).

It is clear that for Hicks, money belonged to Economic Dynamics and could not be dismissed from the analysis of cyclical fluctuations, and this reflected his position all along. From then on, his work evolved in two different directions: one was concerned with the construction of a pure theory of value influenced by the Lausanne school, from which he slowly tried to reshape into a pure theory of dynamics. In his attempts, many of the monetary complications were avoided.[5] The second was represented by another part of his work which was almost completely independent of the rest and from which he developed his monetary theory. Hicks believed that,

> Monetary theory is less abstract than most economic theory; it cannot avoid a relation to reality, which in other economic theory is sometimes missing. It belongs to monetary history, in a way that economic theory does not always belong to economic history (*CEMT*, p. 156).

Although he was cautious in his wording, we are tempted to suggest that there was a sharp division between his monetary theory and his pure economic theory. We believe that in his latest work, these two converged into a more integrated historical framework. Prior to *The Crisis in Keynesian Economics* (1974), however, these two theories were dealt with separately.

2. Hicks' Perception of the History of Monetary Theory

Hicks' own monetary theory was very much linked, on the one hand, to the development of the overall monetary theory. Particular attention was given to those economists who had influenced him. On the other hand, his theory was also associated to the development of the monetary institutions and systems which were particular to each epoch in history. To understand Hicks' position, it is important to visualize in perspective how various people taking part in these developments reacted to the specific economic problems of their time, and how they tried to provide an explanation.[6]

(a) *The Mainstream of Monetary Development*

As a response to Keynes, who treated all his predecessors as classics, Hicks tried to identify the different schools of thought. He returned to the origins of classical economics and investigated how a handful of theorists (whom he thought were the principal contributors), had dealt with the money question. According to Hicks, a distinction should be made between two major schools of thought. There were Ricardo and his followers, who believed that 'All would be well if by some device credit money could be made to behave like metallic money' (*CEMT*, p. 167). This constituted the basic principle for the *Currency School*, in which Hicks included Lord Overstone, Mises, Hayek, Pigou, Friedman and all the neo-Quantity theorists. And there were Thornton and Mill, who thought that 'credit money must be managed, even though it is difficult to manage it' (*CEMT*, p. 167). The followers of this theory, referred to as the *Banking* or *Credit School*, were Bagehot, Tooke, Hawtrey and Robertson. Hicks identified himself with the Credit School. He was Keynesian in the sense that he shared many of Keynes' ideas without, as he said, 'holding that the text of his book was divinely inspired' (*CI*, p. 993). He suggested that Keynes' ideas should be analysed together with the work of Hawtrey, Robertson and many others, and it is within these developments that Hicks' own work should be understood.

(b) *Development of the Monetary System and its Institutions*

Hicks paid tremendous attention to the various economic developments which occurred at different periods in the historical evolution of the capitalist system. He believed that every great economist who had left a mark in the field of monetary theory began his study by analysing the current economic problems of the time and tried to come up with relevant policy recommendations. To grasp the meaning of the old monetary theories, one must consider two aspects of their development: First when, why and how particular historical economic events, as related to monetary issues, have occurred, and second the state and the changes in the character of the monetary system and its institutions.

It is only when these theories are returned to their historical perspective that one can proceed to discuss or analyse their content. For instance, Hicks thought that it was the timing of their work which made the names of Ricardo, Wicksell and Keynes more distinguished than others. All three dealt with serious and urgent problems of their time. They all faced different situations. Ricardo was concerned 'with monetary reconstruction after the War with Napoleon' (*EP*, p. 45). Wicksell faced a world-wide slowdown in economic activity which took place in the last 20 years of the nineteenth century and resulted in a gradual decrease in prices during this period. Keynes was profoundly influenced by the unexpected and unprecedented world-wide depression which had a devastating effect on the mechanism of the workings of world economies. All of these events occurred in different periods, and were different in nature, but because of the seriousness of the problems, the economic debates were carried beyond the academic circle and became political. Although their work was theoretical, they were, according to Hicks, dealing with practical issues and they succeeded in getting their message across.

Hicks insisted that when one was dealing with money, one should be 'consistent with the broad facts of monetary evolution' (*CEMT*, p. 59). As changes in the nature of money took place, its function and appropriation were affected. These were based on the people's confidence in the credit and financial institutions and this was why he believed that, 'money is not a mechanism' but 'a human institution' (*CEMT*, p. 59), which belonged to a specific system and was appropriate to each period of history. It took a long time before people trusted paper money as a substitute for metallic money. Nonetheless, as time passed, the medium of exchange evolved from commodity, to metallic, to paper, and finally to money deposits. These changes simplified the use of money and considerably reduced its transportation cost. Its cost of production became almost nil as compared to the cost of extracting gold from the ground. These changes also made its issue much easier and consequently became the target of much abuse. For instance, when optimism prevailed in a well-developed economy, credit expanded beyond the limits of economic activity, often resulting in crisis. Conversely, when times were hard, credit makers were reluctant to take the first step, thus delaying recovery. While money itself evolved, there was also 'growth in the financial institutions, — ... fundamental change in the whole character of the monetary system' (*CEMT*, p. 158). As these changes took place, the entire economic system faced a new environment which in turn required a new institutional framework to guarantee its smooth functioning.

According to Hicks, after Bretton-Woods, there were many changes in the structure and institutions, of the economies, in international relations and government functions, and finally, in the political environment itself. Since the beginning of the 1970s, the world has experienced social, political and economic upheaval. Hicks felt that we were at another historical turning point which necessitated a new monetary theory. Hicks did not claim to have one, but tried to help us understand what was going on. He suggested that the old theories may be adapted to fit present day need.

3. Hicks' Early Theory of Money[7]

With respect to Hicks' early work on the monetary theory, we can say that he was dealing with two issues separately:

(i) the determinant factors of the demand for money to be held, found in his 'SSTM' and;
(ii) a determination of the interest rate which is found in the 'Wages and Interest' article and in *Value and Capital.*

(a) *What Determines the Quantity of Money to be Held*

At a microeconomic level, and under the strong influence of the Marginal Value Theory, he suggested ways of simplifying the theory of money (SSTM). One of his conclusions was that a monetary theory should be based on an analysis similar to that of the Value Theory, which was used to explain the adjustment of a private individual's income to his expenditure, and a private firm's production to its cost; all of whom try to maximize their utility and production (*CEMT*, p. 74). He suggested using a similar analysis to that of the value theory which determined the ordinary demand for goods and services.

> ... we ought to regard every individual in the community as being on a small scale, a bank. Monetary theory becomes a sort of generalization of banking theory ... a sort of generalized balance-sheet, suitable for all individuals and institutions (*CEMT*, p. 74).

In this balance-sheet would be found assets such as consumption goods (perishable and durable goods), equipment and goods in process, bank deposits, short and long-term debts, and money. The amount of money an individual would hold, would depend upon the quantity of the assets an individual possessed. What are the determining factors of how much money an individual is willing to hold? According to Hicks, this depended on one's wealth and the choice of holding non-interest-bearing money. Interest-yielding capital assets would depend on the cost of converting these assets from one form to another[8] and on the *risk* involved in making an investment. In 1934 he also [wrote]

> ... risk is present, the *particular* expectation of a riskless situation is replaced by a band of probabilities ... It is convenient to represent these probabilities to oneself, in statistical fashion, by a mean value, and some appropriate measure of dispersion (*CEMT*, p. 69).

This idea will be developed by J. Tobin.[9] Although Hicks did not write down a utility function with money incorporated into it, the hint was very clear. Along these lines, he discussed other factors influencing the money demand, and distinguished between money and other assets.

Despite all of this initial work, Hicks did not pursue these monetary developments. His favourite topic at the time was the determination of prices in a General Equilibrium model, where the rate of interest was one price among many to be determined.

(b) *What Determines the Rate of Interest*

In his 'Wages and Interest' article Hicks wrote

> ... we have to take into account, when analysing the production plan, not only current and expected rates of wages and interest, but also the current price of the product, and the expected movement of that price ... since money is now taken as a standard of value, it is the equation of demand and supply for money which is available to determine the rate of interest, p. 284.

First, the fact that the rate of interest was determined in the money market was not new, as he said, it has been known at least since Wicksell (*KTE*, p. 245). Second, despite all of the warnings about the importance of expectation, risk and uncertainty needed to integrate money into a comprehensible model from which the rate of interest can be determined, Hicks went too far in his simplifications (*VC*, pp. 142, 145–50). Hicks made use of Walras law to determine the rate of interest in a static manner (*KTE*, p. 246 and *VC*, p. 158). Furthermore, as a result of a new development generated by *The General Theory*, Hicks shifted some of his attention towards a macroeconomic analysis. He praised Keynes for bringing money out of its isolation (*KTE*, p. 238). To make Keynes' theory more accessible, Hicks suggested bringing in another kind of simplification which resulted in his famous *IS–LM* device.

The way in which the monetary theory evolved left Hicks dissatisfied. Partly in reaction to these new developments and partly because of the changes in his views concerning Economic Dynamics, he slowly moved away from the Equilibrium Theory and questioned his own simplifications.

4. Some Objections to Hicks' Early Suggestions

Since he gave insufficient attention to the time element in the development of his earlier work on monetary theory, Hicks reconsidered some of his own works and then suggested a new direction which he called the 'Foundation of Monetary Theory'. He rejected the portfolio approach to transaction balances, i.e., he shifted the emphasis to the precautionary and speculative motives for holding money, and questioned the relevance of a Walrasian approach applied to monetary analysis.

(a) *The Demand for Money*

Hicks had not constructed a precise model from which the demand for money could be calculated in a deterministic manner. He simply identified the various elements which would have affected the amount of money an individual would hold. Time was of prime importance in Hicks' analysis since he distinguished between the notion of past and future. He considered the risk factor, mentioning subjective and objective elements. He referred to the importance of the time duration involved when lending and borrowing money. Hicks analysed the demand for money from a practical point of view and did not provide a set of definite principles which allowed him to explain precisely what the demand for money would be.

However, Hicks' proposal to apply the principles from the theory of value to a monetary theory has led others, namely Patinkin, to further develop the idea. Patinkin constructed a Walrasian General Equilibrium model, in which he developed a 'marginal utility theory of money' based on 'the principle of utility maximization',[10] then provided a macro basis for his monetary theory. This reduced Hicks' initial proposition to a timeless theory, and prompted him to reconsider certain aspects of his earlier suggestions.

With regard to his earlier stand on the money demand, Hicks then accepted Keynes' M_1 and M_2 distinction, and rejected 'the portfolio approach to transaction balances' (*EP*, p. xiv). The Cambridge Quantity Theory authors[11] referred to the transaction demand for money as the 'over voluntarized' demand. Hicks considered the speculative and precautionary demand as the voluntary demand for money to hold while the transaction demand was not voluntary.[12] The transaction aspect of money was usually associated with the Fisher equation, M.V. = P.T., or with the Cambridge equation. In either case, it reflected an equilibrium situation which stressed the function of money as a medium of exchange. Hicks shifted the emphasis to the precautionary and speculative aspect of money by attributing more importance to the store of the value function of money. He also considered that the existing outstanding volume of money was a result of a disequilibrium situation due to risk, uncertainty and speculation. With these considerations, Hicks brought money back to the dynamic world where it belonged and where it was more appropriately linked with the Time Element.

Given this newly defined money demand, Hicks pursued his analysis further. First of all, he distinguished the significance of the precautionary purpose from the speculative motive, and studied each separately. Secondly, he paid more attention to the dynamic aspect of the factors affecting the changes in the money demand. He also said that 'even with respect to M_2 I now reject the simple portfolio approach because it is not sufficiently in time', adding that 'I do not mean to reject it for other purpose' (*EP*, p. xiv). Another major reconsideration of one of his earlier propositions dealt with the distinction between money and other assets; the former was considered non-interest-bearing while the opposite was believed for the latter. He believed that 'All things fit into place, once we abandon the view that money is inherently non-interest-bearing. It may be non-interest-bearing, but it may not' (*CEMT*, p. 19). Hicks extended his definition of money to encompass the relationship these changes hold with one another.

(b) *The Rate of Interest*

With regard to the determination of the rate of interest, Hicks' analysis neglected the time element. The interest rate was determined by the supply and demand for money, together with other prices in a General Equilibrium analysis. Even with the pseudo-intertemporal analysis, he did not differentiate between past and future; only the objective factors were considered while the risk factor was ignored. He assumed perfect foresight and used an equilibrium approach to analyse the monetary economy. This was on the one hand inconsistent with his idea that monetary theory 'falls outside equilibrium theory' and on the other hand it was a timeless theory.

As far as his simplification of Keynes' theory was concerned, Hicks questioned the essence of the *IS–LM* apparatus. As he said, we may be 'at liberty to regard interest and "income" as being simultaneously determined, on general-equilibrium lines', but to explain Keynes' case, 'it is no longer possible to use the general-equilibrium bridge to show that classical and Keynesian theories come to the same thing'. It was here that Hicks began to question his Walrasian influence and the consequences it implied. Although the *IS–LM* diagram considerably simplified the understanding of Keynes' economics (as well as that of the classical economists), it was misleading. Hicks himself said that this diagram 'reduces the *General Theory* to equilibrium economics, it is not really in time'. This we believe created, on an abstract level, a whole range of technical difficulties which not only changed the character of the debate but also diverted the attention from the initial question. It was the importance given to the static aspect of his device which Hicks rebuked. This change of attitude must not be seen in isolation, both should be considered in light of the overall development of his own ideas about Economic Dynamics.[13]

Even if Hicks' early attempt to provide a basis for a monetary theory was not satisfactory, nevertheless there are indications showing that he sensed from the beginning that *money*, *time* and *disequilibrium* belong together.

5. Hicks' Liquidity Theory[14]

Hicks wrote much in the 1960s and 1970s where he elaborated on the financial system and how it worked. Money would now be linked to the concept of liquidity. Hicks believed that to an investor, liquidity meant freedom. When a firm diminished its liquidity, 'it diminishes its freedom; for it exposes itself to the risk that it will have diminished, or retarded, its ability to respond to future opportunities' (*CE*, p. 94). Hence, liquidity was crucial in the decision to invest. Hicks also was convinced that, 'it is outside the financial sphere that liquidity is potentially of the greater importance' (CE, p. 95). Here he shifted the emphasis from the middle agent (i.e. the banks) to the investors.

We now outline what we think are the essentials of Hicks' liquidity theory. We begin with Hicks' 'Two Triads' essay in which he attempted to find a correspondence between the traditional functions of money and Keynes' three motives for holding money. He showed how they were related, although his interpretation of the precaution and speculative demand was slightly different from that of Keynes (see *CEMT*, p. 37). His definition of the liquidity preference also varied from Keynes' definition. While Keynes was interested in the substitution effect of money and bonds as a whole,[15] Hicks classified assets in terms of liquid, more or less liquid and illiquid forms, and considered various substitutions within the spectrum of assets. With Keynes' three motives for holding money, Hicks associated another Triad: *Running Assets, Reserve Assets* and *Investment Assets*. These three assets were either Real Assets or Financial Assets. Running Assets were held as a means of payment for everyday operations. Reserve Assets were held for precautionary measures; they had to be easily marketable, while in the meantime they were profit-yielding. Investment Assets were usually illiquid and not easily marketable. Given the various securities (i.e. bonds, bills, equities, etc.), and depending on whether they were in the hands of the (bank) *Financier*, or in the hands of (Investor) *Funds*, they were considered differently in Hicks' Triad. These same securities were viewed as Reserve Assets and Running Assets when they were in the hands of the Financier whose function was financial trading. They were Investment Assets if held by Funds who were less informed and less sensitive to marginal financial changes.

Reserve Assets were held for precautionary motives; they were the most susceptible to liquidity shifts, and constituted, for Hicks, the real demand for liquidity. Now that all terminology is explained, we can expose how the financial system functions. Hicks dealt with this in three stages. First, he dealt with short-run effects due to changes in the security market. Second, he considered the impacts of the short-run policies on long-run interest rates and on industrial investment. Third, he looked at the short and long-run policies in a depressed economy. Let us explain:

(i) The buying and selling of securities (which were counted as Financial Running Assets and Financial Reserve Assets) affected the individual prices of securities differently, which in turn affected the demand for liquidity and created a substitution effect between various assets. Hicks called this effect the *Hawtrey Effect*. This effect would take place regardless of whether the economy was moving toward a recession or a recovery situation. As these substitution effects took place, they created an excess or shortage of liquidity which was referred to as the *Liquidity Pressure* or the *Liquidity Effect*. When the Monetary Authority intervened in the market via the open market operation, it created a liquidity pressure. According to Hicks, these liquidity pressures had different effects when applied, depending on whether the economy was prosperous or in a slump. Tightening the liquidity would bring an end to the boom, while relaxing the liquidity during a slump would not guarantee that a recovery would take place.

(ii) Unlike Keynes, who

> retained some faith in the influence of the long rate of interest upon industrial investment. He did indeed believe that the changes in the long-run rate of interest could be induced by monetary policy were less than might at first be expected ... Even so, he believed that such effect as occur was of major importance' (*CEMT*, p. 54).[16]

Hicks argued that past experience revealed the long-run interest rate to be too volatile. While the monetary authority may manipulate a long-run interest rate, speculation would dampen the effect. Hicks believed that it would be difficult to control investment because of this speculation effect, and also because financial investment and industrial investment were related. With respect to the latter, he distinguished between new investment and net investment. The latter in this case was referred to as a defensive investment; it was that investment made to build up stocks and the replacement of equipment in order to be better prepared for possible future developments. These decisions, he said, reduced the uncertainty of the future (see *CEMT*, pp. 55–56). The other type of investment, which introduced a new technique or a new product, in effect would increase the uncertainty because of the unknown reaction from the market. Hicks believed that in a time of prosperity, most of the investment made would be defensive investment. However, as the need for liquidity was felt on the industry side, there would be shortage of liquidity on the financial side. Conversely, during an economic slump situation, most of the investment needed would be new investment. However, even if there was an excess liquidity in the economy, the uncertainty would be so high that Financiers would be reluctant to take the risk, and this would only delay the recovery.

(iii) As a matter of policy in a depressed economy, Hicks agreed with Keynes that, in the short-run, if a great deal of money were to be idle, any increase in the amount of the money supply by the Monetary Authority would also end up idle. In the longer run, however, Hicks argued that these piles of money could not lie indefinitely idle. Even in the long-run equilibrium 'the marginal cost of capital to industry will not be reduced to zero. It is in this sense that there can be "a floor to the interest rate"' (*CEMT*, p. 58). In the long-run, it would be possible for the financial organizers to improve upon the transferring of funds, i.e. lowering the cost of lending money, and this would be sufficient for the investment to resume. It seems that Hicks did not totally reject the idea that a monetary policy could be effective during an economic slump.[17]

As we can see, these three points are interrelated and analysed with respect to the phases of the economic cycle, and there was also a distinction made between the short- and long-run effects of monetary policy. So how do these changes in liquidity take place?

To look at a simple example, Hicks divided his economy into three sectors; a Monetary Authority, or a *Core*, issued money which was transmitted to the *Industry*[18] via the financial system or *Mantle*, which was the only intermediary between the other two sectors. In a national balance sheet, all liabilities corresponded to assets, except for the Real Assets of the Industry which appeared as 'a pure residual' (*EP*, p. 76). Hicks explained that in a closed economy, the Core would not have any liquidity problem since it had the power to increase liquidity whenever necessary. In an open economy, however, the situation would be different; its liquidity could be constrained by the flow of international liquidity. The Mantle and Industry have their own liquidity constraints within and between sectors; here again, let us not complicate the picture but be concerned only with the sectors as a whole.

Now let us assume a closed economy in which the Industry wants to expand and needs money. What would be the effect of such an expansion on the liquidity?

Hicks concluded that this would all depend on how the expansion were to be financed. If the government was to lend money to the Industry by increasing the money supply, there would be no problem of liquidity. If on the other hand, the Industry was to borrow that money from the Financial Sector, the liquidity of the Financial Sector would be diminished. If the Industry exchanged its less liquid Reserve Assets for money, the burden of the decrease in the liquidity reserves would fall on both sectors; the Financial Sector would receive less liquid assets for more liquid assets, and would therefore lose some of its liquidity potential, while the Industry, by getting rid of some of its less liquid assets, would also reduce its liquidity reserves. Finally, if the Industry was to have enough liquidity potential, when the expansion was needed, this expansion could be financed with its own resources; time would not have to be wasted in bargaining or begging for funds and leaving the Industry at the mercy of the Financiers.

When we turn to the situation of an open economy, the picture becomes more complicated in terms of the borrowing ability strategy, and in terms of the portfolio holding strategy. For instance, holding very liquid assets during an inflation period can be very costly; also, when times are difficult, borrowing gets harder.

We hope, we have given a brief and accurate account of what Hicks himself referred to as no 'more than the beginning of the theory of the liquidity' (*C.E.*, p. 100). The workings of the financial system are much more complicated than presented here, but this simple illustration is sufficient to give an idea of how money is related to investment decisions. It also illustrates how Hicks found that to control investment was difficult, and that liquidity was crucial to the business operation of a firm. It was not merely a matter of profit and loss, but a question of survival or bankruptcy. This led him to believe that it was 'wrong to think investment is governed by the rate of interest' (*CE*, p. 96) as Keynes had maintained.

So far, we have not related Hicks' monetary theory to any specific historical situation. How does all this fit into Hicks' interpretation of the economic events of the last few decades?

6. Post-war Economic Developments

Hicks described the period which elapsed from 1950 to the Dollar Crisis[19] (which he referred to as the Bretton-Woods period) as being characterized by 'moderately, but continually rising prices, with a high level of unemployment ... on a world scale'. This was followed by 'a much more rapid inflation of prices with much worse employment ... again on a world scale'. (*EP*, p. 86) This situation was of a different nature from that experienced in the time of Ricardo, Wicksell or Keynes. According to Hicks, it needed an analysis of its own. He showed how the present day's high inflation, coupled with high unemployment, could not be cured with monetary or fiscal policies. Before explaining the reasons for the ineffectiveness of these policies, let us look at his explanation of why prices and unemployment behaved in the manner he described. Some graphic illustrations maybe needed in order to help visualize this situation. Hicks borrowed Keynes' 'supply curve of output',[20] and transformed it in such a way as to handle a long-run analysis. He used the rate of inflation as p instead of the price level, and the rate of growth of a real output as q instead of the level of output. He constructed what he called the 'growth supply curve' (G.S.C.) as shown in Figure 1. The *FF* line represented the full employment barrier.

Consider Curve 1, which represents a locus of alternative situations corresponding to a combination of growth and inflation rates. At a zero growth rate, inflation is negative, but as the growth rate increases at the beginning, the productivity rises faster than the increase in price, thus making the whole curve slope downward. As soon as the factors become scarce, prices will begin to rise faster than the increase in productivity, thus making the curve slope upward at an increasing rate and eventually becoming asymptotic to the full employment barrier *FF*.

Point *M* in the diagram represents a situation of zero inflation with some unemployment, and this is referred to as the *Natural Rate of Unemployment*. Hicks believed that, for political reasons, little inflation with less unemployment was acceptable, thus he labelled point *A* as the *Political Equilibrium*.

Given the growth supply curve, we can now discuss some of the hypothetical possibilities which may arise:

(i) If there is no change in the structure of the economy and no change in its technology or in the available resources, then by applying monetary or fiscal policies, it is possible to move the economy from point *M* to *A* or vice versa.

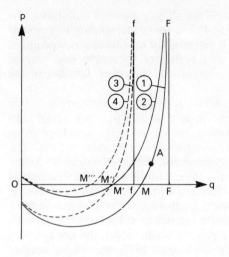

An upward movement of the
↑↑↑ G.S.C. is due to an independent
Wage-push.

A downward movement of the
↓↓↓ G.S.C. can be obtained by a
Labour Market policy.

A leftward movement of the
← G.S.C. is the result of a
← decrease in the raw material or
the primary products available.

A rightward movement of the
G.S.C. is possible when there is
growth in the productivity of
→ the supply of primary products,
→ an increase in efficiency in
production from existing
sources, or development of
new sources of supply.

Fig. 1. Growth supply curve (G.S.C.).

(ii) If, as in the previous case, there is no change in the structure, technology and resources, and if at the same time there is a wage-push independent of the economic activity, then the whole of Curve 1 will shift upward to Curve 2 and create an inflationary pressure. In the new situation, we may incur the same level of unemployment as before, but with higher inflation; or we may incur a minor decrease in inflation at the cost of a higher level of unemployment.

(iii) If there is no change in technology, and no independent wage-push, but there is a decrease in the raw material or industrial resources available, then it is the full employment barrier which shifts to the left *ff*, thus making the natural rate of unemployment higher, and the *A* situation then becomes impossible to reach, since we are now on Curve 3.

(iv) If there is no change in the technology, but there is a reduction in the resources available, and there is also an independent wage-push, then not only does the barrier shrink to the left, making the curve steeper, but there is also a shift of the growth curve upward, which shows a further deterioration of the situation.

All of these cases are illustrated by Figure 1. Let us now see whether these curves are meaningful with resepct to what Hicks believed would have happened.

During the Bretton-Woods period certain countries grew faster than others, and these rates of growth were 'in historical terms quite unusually large' (*EP*, p. 93). As the faster growing countries tried to control inflation (i.e. keep export prices down)[21] this attempt, coupled with their high productivity relative to that of the slower growing countries, made it very difficult for the slower countries to compete. This resulted in an unfavourable balance of payment for many of the slower growing countries. The situation worsened, the faster growing countries began lending to the slow countries, further strengthening their position by exporting more products than before. During a great part of the Bretton-Woods period, export prices remained steady in absolute terms. In fact, they fell relative to domestic prices, which rose.

As a whole, the high productivity which lasted for some time (in certain industries more than others) permitted most countries to enjoy a high level of employment. During the same period, the money wage also kept rising in the high productivity sectors spreading to less productive sectors. The result of all these changes made it difficult for certain countries to follow the trend. The 1967 devaluation of the Pound Sterling was the first sign of the crack. This was followed by the 'floating' of the Dollar which in theory, according to Hicks, should have eased the situation of the slower countries, making it more difficult for the fastest countries to sell all of their exports. What took place instead, was a 'very general boom' which did not last very long. At the same time as 'the harvest failure of 1972, the Oil Squeeze of 1973 and the shortage of raw industrial materials' (*EP*, p. 98) hit hard in every country, thus considerably reducing production and employment potential. The increase in prices which started in the primary sectors was passed on to the manufacturing sectors; higher money wages responding to higher food and energy prices created a further justification for the price increases, and the spiral accelerated.

In terms of Figure 1, we can now see how the real reduction in the availability of raw materials and the effect of the oil squeeze explained the shift of the full employment barrier from *FF* to *ff*, making the growth supply curve move from 1 to 3, thus increasing the natural unemployment to a higher level. During the years of high productivity, labour became accustomed to a continual increase in its money and real wage, and always pressured 'for fair wages'. A worker resisted, according to Hicks, not only 'a reduction in the purchasing power in the money wage' but also 'a reduction in the growth of that purchasing power to which he has become accustomed'.[22] Whenever these pressures were applied independently, mainly when there was no improvement in the method of production or the productivity itself of an economy, an upward shift in the growth supply curve resulted. For all of the events cited here which took place in the last few decades, there was according to Hicks, a north–west movement of the growth supply curve which resulted in a much higher level of inflation and unemployment.

> ... neither can be cured by monetary policy, or by fiscal policy. All that can be done in these ways is to get less of one by having more of the other. But both, it may well be, are already intolerable. (*EP*, p. 104)

It seems, therefore, that the conventional Keynesian policies were not the answer. What could be done to remedy this awkward situation which made most of the western governments very nervous?

Hicks believed that the answer could be found if there was a way to move the growth supply curve back to its initial position, thus extending the full employment barrier and reducing the wage pressures. In order to achieve such a move, he suggested:

(i) Applying a 'labour market policy'. He did not specify how, but we suppose that a certain agreement between the employers and the employees could be reached to ensure that any increase in the money wage would be geared to productivity and not to any other reason independent of economic considerations.

(ii) Finding 'a new source of supply' and increasing 'efficiency in production from existing sources'; this in turn would displace the full employment barrier and create more employment potential.

(iii) Changing 'the method of production of existing commodities ...' using more labour and less of the primary products of equivalent value (*EP*, p. 107). If this could be done, no doubt more employment would be created.

While the first two propositions (which are recently beginning to be shared by many other economists)[23] are actually in effect in some industries,[24] the third is of a different nature, and ahead of its time. Hicks, we believe, did not imply that we should turn back to the older methods of production but that we should try to make 'greater use of his (man's) intelligence in the production of articles of superior quality' (*EP*, p. 107). No matter what one's objections were to these suggestions, Hicks' work was commendable in that he based his theory on the description of what was actually happening at the time and came up with recommendations with respect to the current economic problems of the day. Whether these policies were acceptable or applicable is an altogether different story.

To sum up: we have first discussed the change occurring in the evolution of Hicks' theory of money. We have seen how the emphasis was shifted from the traditional transactions demand for money to the liquidity theory and the working of the financial system. We then looked at the monetary considerations in a much broader sense. We explained Hicks' theoretical and historical correlation between the rates of inflation and of growth of employment. We saw what the monetary policy and the fiscal policy could and could not do, and finally we presented Hicks' new policy recommendations which, surprisingly enough, was not dealing with monetary questions. Here we must be careful not to confuse the issues. On the one hand, there can be non-monetary causes which are responsible for the general slowdown of the economy as explained above, and which may or may not require some non-monetary policy action. On the other hand, depending whether one is dealing with a private or government level, and whether the economy is in an expanding or in a contracting situation, money considerations cannot be dismissed. The liquidity question is of prime importance to the working of any economic system. Although these issues are presented separately, they *are* interrelated.

We presented Hicks' monetary theory within a very general framework, as well as Hicks' account of the development of economic facts. It is clear that not only did Hicks master the efforts of those who initially shaped monetary theory, but he also contributed to our understanding of monetary economics. In the literature, however, his name remains very much associated with that of Keynes, and perhaps a few words about this association should be added.

7. Some Final Comments on Keynes in Hicks' Work and on the *IS–LM* Apparatus

Keynes was certainly a great source of inspiration for Hicks. In our presentation, we did not research all of the similarities and differences between Keynes' and Hicks' work. This in itself would be another topic. However, we have pointed out some important differences in the views of these authors. We mentioned that while Keynes' theory was mainly concerned with short-run analysis of a depressed economy, Hicks dealt with long-run problems in the different phases of the business cycle. We explained why Hicks did not believe that investments were governed by the interest rate. Hicks had a different view than Keynes with regards to a monetary policy impact on the long-run interest rate because of the speculation effect. Hicks introduced the cost of transferring funds in the financial system as an explanation of the floor to the interest rate. Keynes considered that money was a non-interest-bearing asset and that bonds were income yielding.[25] Hicks, on the other hand, assumed that money could be an interest-bearing asset, and dealt with the liquidity aspect in a spectrum of assets.

These are just a few observations which show that the theories of these two economists contained many differences and were not concerned with the same issues. Nonetheless, looking at the policy prescriptions of Keynes' theory as a whole, Hicks accepted that *The General Theory* was correctly designed for the circumstances. However, he reminded those who would like to keep Keynes' spirit alive that 'it does no honour to Keynes to go on applying his theory, without drastic amendment, to the very different circumstances of the time in which we are now living'.[26] Perhaps as a tribute to Keynes, Hicks himself was ready to accept the Keynesian label in 'the sense of trying to do what I (Hicks) think he (Keynes) would have tried to do, if confronted with different real problems from those with which we are now confronted' (*CI*, p. 992). As we can see, Hicks was very modest. All of these questions are hypothetical; no one can tell what Keynes would do if he were still alive, and the outcome of Hicks' theory remains, after all, Hicks' product.

Without the existence of the *IS–LM* device and the 1937 article, the course of Hicks' work probably would have evolved in a totally different manner. Hicks maintained that the *IS–LM* device corresponded to a three-way exchange reduced to a two-dimensional diagram. Although this device has become widely used in economic literature, Hicks himself became less and less satisfied with it. The *IS–LM* diagram was an equilibrium analysis which was conceived in a Walrasian manner and in which time was not taken into consideration. What bothered Hicks was:

The relation which is expressed in the *IS* curve is a flow relation, which must *refer to a period* ... But the relation expressed in the *LM* curve is, or should be, a stock relation (as Keynes so rightly insisted). It must therefore *refer to a point of time*, not to a period. (*ISLM*, pp. 150–1)

Also Hicks believed that there was no sense in bringing the liquidity preference into analysis, 'unless expectations are uncertain' (*ISLM*, p. 152). The questions which Hicks has asked himself recently are how to reconcile a flow with a stock analysis; how is it that liquidity and money, which do not belong to equilibrium theory, are mixed up with the equilibrium devices; and how is the long-run rate of interest to be considered in such a static strait-jacket? These few incompatibilities raised sufficient doubt to the usefulness of such curves. Hicks had thus moved away from his own device.

In this paper we have been more concerned with the explanation of Hicks' theory of money, and less interested in making any criticism of the method of approach. Hicks' approach to the monetary theory was very different from that of his pure theory. Except in the Temporal Equilibrium Model, where money was introduced explicitly in a general equilibrium model, everywhere else there had not been any formal or mechanical model of a monetary system. Hicks announced very early that money did not belong to the equilibrium theory, and this he maintained all along. He said the monetary theory belonged to a monetary system and its institutions, and he tried very hard to be consistent. Although some of his monetary theory was presented in a very simple form and not restricted to any particular system, there was a tremendous concern with the historical developments in terms of theory, facts, institutions and events. His monetary analysis was discussed with respect to the workings of the economy as a whole; he was mostly interested in explaining what actually happened and what would happen.

Notes

1. I would like to thank Professor R. Clower and Dr G.C. Harcourt for their encouragement and suggestions. I am also much indebted to A. Asimakopulos, E.F. Beach, V. Chick, D. Helm, A. Roncaglia, J.C.R. Rowley and the referee for their helpful comments. I am grateful to the editors of this Journal [*The Bulletin of Economic Research*] who kindly allowed me to respond to some interesting and important questions raised by the referee.

2. The essentials of Hicks' monetary work can be found in his various publications, especially in 'Equilibrium and the Trade Cycle', *Economic Inquiry* (*ETC*), November 1980; 'A Suggestion for Simplifying the Theory of Money', *Economica* (*SSTM*), February 1935, pp. 1–19; 'Mr Keynes' Theory of Employment', *Economic Journal* (*KTE*), June 1936, pp. 238–53; 'Mr Keynes and the Classics', *Econometrica*, April 1937, pp. 147–59; *Critical Essays in Monetary Theory* (*CEMT*), Oxford, 1967; *Capital and Growth*, 1965; *The Crisis in Keynesian Economics*, Oxford, 1974; *Economic Perspectives* (*EP*), 1977; *Causality in Economics* (*CE*), New York, 1979; 'On Coddington's Interpretation: A Reply', *Journal of Economic Literature* (*CI*), September 1979, pp. 989–95; '*IS–LM*: An Explanation', *The Journal of Post Keynesian Economics* (*ISLM*), 1980, pp. 139–54. *Money, Interest and Wages, Collected Essays on Economic Theory* (*MIW*), Vol. II, Harvard: H.U.P., 1982. See also my PhD Thesis 'The Treatment of Time in the Theoretical Writings of Sir John Hicks', McGill University, January 1983.

3. The main ideas behind this simplification, he said, could be found in his 'Wages and Interest: The Dynamic Problem', *Economic Journal* (*WIDP*), 1935.

4. *The Theory of Wages*, 2nd edn, 1962, p. 335.

5. In *Value and Capital*, money was introduced as a numéraire. The Temporary Equilibrium Model was constructed with the assumption of perfect competition, no uncertainty and given expectations (see Hicks' discussion, in *Capital and Growth*, pp. 69–75). Elsewhere he said that 'The use of money is closely connected with imperfect foresight, it needs to be analysed in association with the theory of Risk', in 'Equilibrium and The Trade Cycle', p. 528, op. cit. Because the Temporary Equilibrium Method failed in its dynamic objective, the whole discussion on money became inconsistent with the model as presented and should thus be viewed in that context as an independent part of the model. In *A Contribution to the Theory of the Trade Cycle*, Hicks took a different approach. He constructed a model in which the 'Emphasis on the *real* (non-monetary) character of the cycle process has of course been entirely deliberate', p. 136. *Capital and Time* was designed in the same way as far as money was concerned. In this particular work, he explicitly said 'one of my objects in writing this book' is to show that 'There has been no money in my model; yet it has plenty of adjustment difficulties. It is not true that by getting rid of money, one is automatically in "equilibrium",' p. 133. His avoidance of 'money' was deliberate. By doing so, in addition to the reason given, he considerably simplified his analysis, but again, nowhere did he deny or underestimate the importance of money and monetary repercussions in the real world.

6. This is found in his *Critical Essays* and in *Economic Perspectives*, op. cit.

7. Our analysis is only concerned with Hicks' work and in a sense neglects the fact that during the 1930s there was already available in literature an extensive analysis of the demand for money. For example, some of these discussions are found in A.W. Marget, *The Theory of Prices*, New York, I & II, 1936, 1942 and E. Eshag, *From Marshall to Keynes*, Oxford 1963. See also the writings of A.C. Pigou, H.D. Robertson, R.G. Hawtrey, J.M. Keynes, F.A. Hayek, R.F. Harrod on the related issue.

8. A further development on this line is found in Baumol's Transaction Cast Theory: W.J. Baumol, 'The Transaction Demand for Cash', *Quarterly Journal of Economics*, 1952.

9. J. Tobin, 'Liquidity Preference as Behaviour Toward Risk', *Review of Economic Studies*, 1958. See also his Nobel lecture 'Money and Finance in the Macroeconomic Process', *Journal of Money, Credit and Banking*, 1982.

10. D. Patinkin, *Money, Interest and Prices*, 2nd edn, New York, Harper & Row, 1965, p. xxv.

11. Here, Hicks is referring to Marshall, Pigou, Hawtrey and the early Robertson.

12. Ironically, he remarked that what these authors (including himself in his earlier writings), called idle money was in fact the active part of money, while concentrating on what Hicks then believed was the passive part. Looking back to those former priorities, he said, 'This, I now feel, was confusing; it has sent many of us (myself included) chasing what I now feel to be will-o'-the-wisps', and adds, 'among my own works, the latter part of my "simplification" article is liable to this stricture; so is much of the monetary section of *Value and Capital*' (*CEMT*, p. 16).

13. See O. Hamouda, 'Hicks' Economic Theory: An Overview', Working Paper, Sherbrooke University.

14. Most of Hicks' new monetary theory is found in his 'The Two Triads' in *Critical Essays*, 1967, op. cit.; *The Crisis in Keynesian Economics*, 1974; *Economic Perspectives*, 1977, op. cit.; and in *Causality in Economics*, 1979, op. cit. Although 'written quite separately, they are I believe broadly consistent with one another', *Economic Perspectives*, op. cit., p. xiv

15. This is true of Keynes' *General Theory*, 1936, but not of *A Treatise on Money*, London: Macmillan, 1930.

16. For further explanation of this point see Hicks' essay on Hawtrey in Economic Perspectives.

17. This point is related indirectly to the discussion found in his paper on 'Hawtrey', in *Economic Perspectives*, op. cit.

18. In Hicks' terminology, 'Industry' includes households.

19. Nixon's 1971 decision to suspend the dollar convertibility.

20. This is the price–employment relationship which is usually drawn as a reversed

L-shape. For example, when the economy is under less than full employment, any change in the money supply will increase employment, leaving the price level unchanged. Once full employment is reached, then its effect will be a proportional increase in the level of price. Keynes, however, allows for the increase in both price level and employment as full employment is approached. See Keynes' *General Theory*, Chapter 21, and Hicks' *Economic Perspectives*, op. cit., p. 82–3.

21. See his 'Expected Inflation', *Economic Perspectives*, 'What is Wrong with Monetarism?', *Lloyds Bank Review*, October 1975, pp. 1–13, and 'The Little that is Right with Monetarism', *Lloyds Bank Review*, July 1976, pp. 16–18.

22. 'What is Wrong with Monetarism', *Lloyds Bank Review*, op. cit., p. 5.

23. See, for instance, L.C. Thowrow, 'The Productivity Problem' in *Policies for Stagflation: Focus on Supply, Ontario Economic Council*, 1981. See also the literature on tax-related income policies (*TIPS*).

24. An example would be the automobile industry.

25. We are referring here to *The General Theory*. In the *Treatise*, Keynes makes the distinction between the various assets.

26. Hicks in S.J. Latsis, *Method and Appraisal in Economics*, Cambridge: Cambridge University Press, 1976, p. 217.

88

Hicks and the Keynesian Revolution[†]

F. Mahloudji

I. Introduction

Among leading economic theorists, Hicks occupies a most unique position. Gradually, he has dissociated himself from all major schools without either taking refuge in nihilism or promoting the establishment of a new Hicksian school: "I am too open to be an Austrian; for I am an open Marshallian, and Ricardian and Keynesian, perhaps even Lausannian, as well" (Hicks 1979a, 63).

The Hicksian "openness" is most salutary. In a profession torn by factionalism, he has performed the task of a reconciler and a bridge builder. As Lachmann has argued:

> For forty years Hicks has been the great broker of ideas who regarded it as his main task to accomplish a synthesis of the ideas of the age ... It may happen that when ... the history of economic thought in the twentieth century comes to be written the last forty years will be described as the *age of Hicks* [Lachmann, 69].

A full study of the Hicksian 'synthesis' is far beyond the scope of a single article. Here we shall limit ourselves to his appraisal of the Keynesian revolution and its impact on his thinking.

We need to say a few words on Hicks's ideas concerning the nature of revolution and progress in economics, for it is there that we find the clue to his 'synthetic' approach. In his 'Revolutions in economics' (1976a), he argues that economics, in contrast to natural sciences, is characterized by the fact that new theories do not completely overthrow or supersede the old ones. This uncomfortable and somewhat embarrassing situation, we are told, is due to the nature of the subject: 'the facts that we study are not permanent or repeatable, like the facts of natural sciences; they change incessantly, and change without repetition" (ibid. 207). To explain these facts "before it is too late, we must select, even select quite violently" (ibid. 208). Useful theories, being great simplifiers, are of limited applicability: 'They are rays of light, which illuminate a part of the target, leaving the rest

[†]Source: *History of Political Economy*, Vol. 17 (2), Summer 1985, pp. 287–307.

in the dark" (ibid.). He argues that since we cannot have a fully general, all-purpose theory which is useful for all times and places, we should select those theories that are "appropriate" to our problems and be ready to discard them as soon as they cease to be so. Unfortunately, Hicks does not offer any demarcation principle on the basis of which we can distinguish "appropriate" from "inappropriate" theories. Given his "little faith in econometrics" (1979b, 202), by "appropriateness" he must mean institutional-historical relevance, which ultimately boils down to a plea for descriptive accuracy and realistic assumptions.[1] Clearly he is not a "falsi-ficationist"; "We may be right to reject our present theories, not because they are wrong, but because they have become inappropriate" (1976a, 208).

Hicks views the emergence of new theories as resulting from rapid shifts in the concentration of attention which are in turn due either to outside factors, such as the pressure of events, or to internal factors, such as changes in intellectual preoccupations. Classifying theories according to the focus of their attention, Hicks points out that the classics and Marx looked at economic life from the standpoint of production and distribution of wealth, marginalists (or better, catallactists) reconstructed economic theory on the basis of exchange, while Keynes drew attention to the economy in the short run.

In the Hicksian framework, then, different theories, once their concerns and limitations are identified, can lead a life of peaceful coexistence. Delineating the range of their applicability has been one of his major tasks; and it is here that the nature of his 'synthesis' lies: a collection of comple-mentary, rather than conflicting, special-purpose theories, each illumin-ating, as long as it is not incompatible with institutional-historical setting, certain aspects of economic life.[2]

II. Temporary Equilibrium

Unlike the majority of his British contemporaries, Hicks was profoundly influenced by continental economists: "I was deep in Pareto, before I got much out of Marshall" (Hicks 1979b, 19). At the London School of Eco-nomics, and under the influence of Robbins, he was exposed to the works of Walras, Pareto, Wicksell, the Austrians, and especially Hayek, who came to the London School of Economics as professor in 1931.[3] Beginning from this background, Hicks developed interests that were parallel to those of Keynes — that is, the need for a short-period model of the economy where expectations are not neglected and money is bound up with uncer-tainty.

Crucial first steps were taken in 'Equilibrium and the cycle: a sug-gestion for simplifying the theory of money,' and 'Wages and interest: the dynamic problem,' papers published in the years 1933–35 (reprinted in Hicks 1982).

The first of these papers, which is the most important, explores the notion of equilibrium in connection with money and the trade cycle.

Pareto's treatment of equilibrium was found unsatisfactory, for it dealt with either static or stationary conditions. To come closer to reality, "we ought to take account of the influence of future (expected) as well as current prices on ... behavior" (1982, 31). In static conditions the future is neglected, while in a stationary state, present and future prices are equal, there being no need for the explicit treatment of expectations. Outside these conditions, however, we will have equilibrium when a "set of prices ... can be carried through without supplies and demands ever becoming unequal... and so without expectations ever being mistaken" (ibid. 32). Perfect foresight, Hicks argued, is the necessary condition for dynamic equilibrium, disequilibrium being a matter of disappointed expectations. But he was quick to point out that "Such a 'dynamic equilibrium' is obviously still far from being a description of reality ... Because of ignorance of future changes of data ... such a perfect equilibrium is never attainable. A real economy is always in disequilibrium" (1982, 32).

Dynamic or progressive equilibrium was also Hayek's construction in *Prices and production* (1931) which Hicks argued must rest on perfect foresight. Hayek had claimed that, were it not for monetary disturbances, the system would remain in equilibrium. Taking his leads from Knight's *Risk, uncertainty and profit* (1921), that money, well behaving or mis-behaving, has no place in perfect-foresight equilibrium, Hicks questioned the usefulness of Hayek's model in explaining fluctuations. For if "the future course of economic data ... were exactly foreseen, there would be no demand to hold money as money" (Hicks 1982, 34). Once rejecting monetary disturbance as the ultimate source of instability, Hicks was led to the conclusion that fluctuations are due to imperfect foresight.

This was a critical turning point in Hicks's thinking. He sought a differ-ent notion of equilibrium, one that, not crippled by the assumption of perfect knowledge, is capable of dealing with monetary economies in dis-equilibrium.

Although Hicks's first major contribution to economic theory, *The theory of wages* of 1932 (Hicks 1963) relies entirely on a timeless static-stationary scheme of analysis that "soon after its birth ... began to look like the last gasp of an *ancien regime*" (1963, 305), within a year of its appear-ance he had gone through his "own personal revolution" (ibid. 306). Major influences were Myrdal 1939, *Monetary equilibrium* (1933), from which Hicks took the idea of an economy in very short-run equilibrium where expectations, certain or uncertain, are treated as data, and Lindahl's contributions to social accounting and the *ex ante, ex post* approach from which his macroeconomic way of looking at equilibrium and the necessity of providing a linkage between short-run equilibria took shape.

'Wages, interest: the dynamic problem' of 1935 (Hicks 1982, 67–69) represents Hicks's first application of short-run equilibrium and is a "first sketch for what was to become the 'dynamic' model of *Value and Capital*" (Hicks, 319). With perfect foresight abandoned, time had to be treated in a serious way. This was done by dividing the process of change into short sections within which certain variables were treated as constants. Continu-ous change is thus converted to interval change, and the static tools of analysis are again applicable to the process of change.

The model is of an economy producing one good — bread. There are two inputs, homogeneous labor and equipment. At the beginning of every "week" there is a given stock of capital, bread, and an amount of debt owned by entrepreneurs. Monetary complications are assumed away, at first, by reckoning the wage rate and rate of interest in terms of bread. The equilibrium wage rate and interest rate are determined on "Monday" by the relative preference for current versus future consumption of rentiers, workers, and entrepreneurs, on the one hand, and current as well as expected future prices on the other. So expected future wage rates and interest rates explicitly enter into the determination of each "week's" production plan.

The model is a general equilibrium of the macroeconomy in short-run equilibrium, with price expectations playing a prominent role. It is noteworthy that Hicks reached this position without knowing what was to come from Cambridge. He first saw *The general theory* (Keynes 1936) when he was asked to review it upon publication (see Hicks 1977, 142).

In a way, Hicks's continental journey led him back to Marshall. And as he observed in *Value and capital*:

> Either we have to face up to the difficulty and allow deliberately for the fact that supplies (and ultimately demand, too) are governed by expected prices quite as much as current prices; or we have to evade the issue by concentrating on the case where these difficulties are at a minimum. The first is the method of Marshall; the second ... is the method of the Austrians [1939, 117].

However, Hicks's journey did provide him with the view of the economy as one of interdependent markets. A view that some of Marshall's followers did not always adhere to.[4] Equally important is Hicks's extreme sensitivity to the notion of time. He has always emphasized that past decisions cannot be undone and future expectations influence present conduct. A satisfactory dynamic model should show how future becomes present and present becomes past; the periods need to be linked. This aspect of his thinking owes a good deal to the Austrian treatment of production as a process that takes time and the Swedish *ex ante, ex post* distinction.

Temporary equilibrium finds its fullest statement in the dynamic part of *Value and capital.* The "week" is a period short enough that price variations within it can be neglected. Markets are open on "Monday" and trading will continue until prices that equate demands and supplies are established. During the "week" production, consumption and delivery plans will be carried out at prices established on "Monday." All prices are fully flexible, and markets converge to equilibrium quickly and smoothly. Expectations are not treated as fixed; even on "Monday," as prices change, expectations are accommodated to new information that emerges: "Every change in prices, even if it is only a tentative change in prices, carries with it an adjustment of expectations" (Hicks 1965, 66). Current price variations will induce changes in price expectations and hence in plans. It is through the alteration of plans that the equilibrium of supplies and demands is eventually established.

The economy is always in temporary equilibrium. There will be equilibrium over time if prices that are worked out for each "week" are mutually consistent, that is, if prices that come to be realized on the second "Monday" are those that were expected to rule on that day.

Hicks's interests, however, were primarily confined to the behavior of the economy in temporary equilibrium. He attempted to analyze its stability by comparing systems of prices that would rule if tastes, resources, and expectations were somewhat different. Although his stability analysis was inadequate,[5] Hicks had correctly focused attention on the role of expectations in an economy without a full array of future markets:

> As soon as we take expectations into account ... the stability of the system is seriously weakened. Special reasons may indeed give it a sufficient amount of stability to enable it to carry on ... but it is not inherently and necessarily stable. It is henceforth not at all surprising that the economic system of reality should be subject to large fluctuations, nor that these fluctuations should be so very dangerous [1939, 256].

III. Coming to Terms with Keynes

Hicks reviewed *The general theory* in 1936, and as Coddington said, "he has gone on reviewing it throughout his career" (1983, 66). Hicks's model of the economy was a full employment one, while Keynes's certainly was not. To reconcile his model with that of Keynes was a task he set for himself. As is evident from the introduction of *Value and capital*, he agreed with the message of Keynes without having full confidence in his analytical procedure. He said:

> I must confess that, as I have worked with Mr. Keynes' book, I have been amazed at the way he manages, without the use of any special apparatus, to cut through the tangle of difficulties ... and to go straight for the really important things. He succeeds in doing so just because he makes free use of his superb intuition ... in order to be able to discard the inessentials and go straight for the essentials [Hicks 1939, 4].

In his 'Mr Keynes' theory of employment' of 1936 (Hicks 1982), he argued that the power of Keynes' analysis resides in applying the concept of short-period equilibrium to a non-stationary economy. Once we bring in the "missing element — anticipations — ... equilibrium analysis can be used, not only in the remote stationary conditions to which many economists have found themselves driven back, but even in the real world ... in disequilibrium" (1982, 84). The limitation of Keynes' method of expectations, Hicks argued, is that the period under consideration must be short enough that changes in expectations within it can be neglected. The longer we make our period the more precarious the assumption of given expectations becomes,' so that there is danger, when it is applied to long periods, of the whole method petering out" (1982, 82).

The challenge that Keynes posed for Hicks was not the application of the short-period equilibrium to the economy as a whole; there he was fully at home. What was new was the possibility of unemployment within that context. Before Keynes, unemployment was studied from a business-cycle point of view. Changes in prices, output, and employment were looked upon as temporary divergences from an equilibrium norm. Hicks pointed out that "the present theory breaks away from the whole range of these ideas ... if there is no norm ... it is useless to discuss deviations from it" (1982, 85). A chief innovation of Keynes was, therefore, to study unemployment independently of business-cycle theory.

Value and capital's analysis of unemployment is also an example of the cyclical approach. Stability of temporary equilibrium is made to depend on expectations regarding the normal rates of prices, interest rate, and money wages. If there is a strong sense of normality, such expectations are inelastic and the system stable. In his first review, Hicks did not extricate himself from the elasticity approach. He said Keynesian unemployment equilibrium is stable because short-term money wage and price expectations are inelastic. And he attributed this inelasticity to existence of unemployment and general excess capacity. But this takes for granted what has to be shown.

IV. Keynes and the Classics

Transition from a cyclical to a short-period view of unemployment produced a lacuna in Keynesian (or Hicksian-Keynesian!) theory for which no satisfactory solution, to this day, has been found. In the theory of price formation which Keynes received from Marshall,

> Prices responded immediately ... to fluctuations in demand and supply. This had indeed made it quite hard to see how output and employment *could* fluctuate ... In the *General Theory* Keynes formally cut the knot by assuming ... that prices, and, of course, wages remained constant during the period ... it was necessary that there should be a proper theory of the working of a fixprice market [Hicks 1982, 129–30].

In his enormously influential 1937 article 'Mr Keynes and the Classics' (in Hicks 1982), Hicks did not possess a theory of such markets; in *Value and capital*, price adjustments were quick and smooth (see Hicks 1939, 123). In his formalization of the General Theory he simply assumed money wages are exogenously given.

Hicks's purpose in 'Mr Keynes and the Classics' was to identify the analytical core of the General Theory and compare it with classical results. To put the two systems on the same footing he sets up a short-period classical model with a given money wage in which demand for money is related to nominal income via the Cambridge equation, investment depends on interest rate, and saving depends on interest and income: $M = kI$, $I_x = C(i)$, $I_x = S(i, I)$.

Given k, nominal income is determined by the quantity of money. If money wage is too high and rigid, the price level will be too high and the given nominal income cannot buy full-employment real output. Unemployment is thus explicable within a modified classical framework. And an increase in the money supply could raise output and employment. To move from a short-period classical model to Keynes, we should allow for the fact that k is not an independent variable (it depends on the state of confidence and the interest rate) and that demand for money depends on interest rate as well as income: $M = L(I, i)$, $I_x = C(i)$, $I_x = S(i, I)$.

In the classical system a change in inducement to invest or in government spending changes the interest rate without any effect on output and employment. In the Keynesian model, however, a change in the interest rate will affect the demand for money (or k) making a different level of output and employment possible. But there is some crowding out. For the same reason, a change in the money supply is not as effective as it is in the classical model. For it also changes the interest rate and demand for money (or k). But it does somewhat change the level of activity.

By allowing for the variability of k and short-term wage rigidity, Hicks minimized the difference between Keynes and the classics and absorbed the General Theory into the existing corpus of economy theory: "Is there really any difference between them, or is the whole thing a sham fight?" (Hicks 1982, 108). His answer was that the "General Theory of Employment is Economics of Depression" (ibid. 111). Only when the interest rate has reached an irreducible minimum is there no common ground between two systems.

V. The Patinkin Challenge

Although Hicks was the first to cast the General Theory into a general equilibrium mold and as Weintraub pointed out, "the microfoundations of macroeconomic theory that Hicks identified helped to create the neo-Walrasian revolution that has survived to this day" (Weintraub, 58–59), his appraisal of the General Theory came to differ radically from the appraisals of the general equilibrium theorists.

The parting of the ways became fully visible by 1956, when Patinkin's *Money, interest and prices* (Patinkin 1965) appeared. Within Patinkin's competitive-equilibrium framework, no sense could be made of unemployment; full employment exists and is stable. In his view:

Keynesian economics is the economics of unemployment disequilibrium. It argues that as a result of interest-inelasticity, on the one hand, and distribution and expectation effects, on the other, the dynamic process ... even when aided by monetary policy ... is unlikely to converge either smoothly or rapidly to the full-employment equilibrium position [Patinkin 1965, 337–38].

In 'A rehabilitation of "classical" economics' (Hicks 1957; also in Hicks 1967), a review of Patinkin's book, Hicks again demonstrated his commitment to a short-period interpretation of Keynes:

The theory which Patinkin sets out, though it owes much to Keynes, is not Keynesian; it is a modernized version of the theory which Keynes called "classical" [1957, 278].

Hicks believed that a properly reformulated classical short-period model would give results that are identical to those of Keynes. It is true, he argued, that generally in classical teaching, from Hume to Marshall and Pigou, even in the short run, money-wage rigidity was not assumed. But the classicals should not be reproached, since

in their time it would, quite clearly, not have been true. This is not a matter on which there can be any theoretical *contradiction*; it is the kind of change in the exposition of theory which we ought to be making all the time, in response to changing facts [1957, 218].

Some classicals, such as Hume and Thornton, Hicks emphasized, did possess a short-run theory with rigid wages. For them, wage rigidity was a matter of intensity of demand for labor and the time interval under consideration. There would be wage rigidity if employment was between what he called, "Full Unemployment" and "Full Employment." Outside those limits money wages would be flexible in both directions. But if enough time is allowed, that is, if our concern is with the long period as opposed to the short period, money wages become fully flexible. The classical long-period theory is a full-equilibrium and full-employment theory where the interest rate is determined by productivity and thrift and money supply determines the price level — the dichotomy between real and monetary sides being restored.

The classicals paid far more attention to their long-period theory, fearing that

if too much weight were given to short-period effects, it would play into the hand of crude inflationists. The long-period, it would be said, is just a succession of short-periods. Why not keep the stimulus going, when the first dose is exhausted, by another dose? [Hicks 1967, 162].

Hicks, in his review of Patinkin, had overlooked the real balance effect.[6] With this in mind, and arguing in a neo-Walrasian vein, Leijonhufvud pointed out that

Hicks' failure to overturn the argument that reduces Keynes' theory to the trivial special case of classical theory where money wages are rigid seems to have been virtually the last rear-guard action of those Keynesians who have tried to maintain a place for Keynes on this lofty plane of abstraction [1969, 18].

It should be evident from our inquiry that Hicks was not concerned with placing Keynes's theory on a "lofty plane of abstraction." From the outset he was no more than a critical follower, and looked at Keynes's theory as a limited but powerful simplification. He had realized the need for an analytically tractable short-period macro theory which could account for unemployment. And in the *General theory* he found a shortcut which applied the tools of equilibrium to an economy in disequilibrium (see Hicks 1982, 86). The distinction between the short-run and long-run notions of equilibrium seemed to suffice.

VI. Limitations of Equilibrium

Hicks, in his later works, has expressed a good deal of ambivalence toward the notion of equilibrium. It is exactly at this juncture that he parts company with the neoclassicals:

'Convergence to equilibrium' has been shown to be dubious; but it also has been shown to be unimportant. Even at the best, it will take a long time; and in most applications before that time has elapsed, something else (some new exogenous shock) will surely have occurred [1975a, 336].

For this reason he does not, now, think very much of the dynamic part of *Value and capital.* By allowing expectations to be influenced by current transactions, to ensure the general equilibrium of the markets during a "week," the model did "deliberate violence to the *order* in which in the real world ... events occur" (1965, 73). So:

It was this device, this indefensible trick which ruined the 'dynamic' theory of *Value and Capital.* It was this that led it back in a static, and so in a neo-classical, direction [1977, vii].

And as far as steady-state growth models are concerned:

it is my own opinion that it has been rather a curse ... it has encouraged economists to waste their time upon constructions ... which are so much out of time, and out of history, as to be practically futile and indeed misleading [Hicks 1982, 291].

The doyen of British economic theorists has even called himself an "evolutionist"; and in his latest book, *Causality in economics* (1979c), has laid emphasis on historical, irreversible aspects of the economic process. Natural sciences, with high predictive powers, deal with isolated, stationary, and repetitive systems where the dates at which experiments are conducted is immaterial.[7] Hicks believes there are economic problems that can be discussed in static terms, and the prestige of science has led economists to place undue emphasis on these aspects of economics. But the really serious problems — those dealing with change, growth, decline, and fluctuations — cannot be adequately treated by the method of natural sciences, "for at every stage in an economic process new things are happening, things that have not happened before" (1979a, xi). The element of novelty makes economic theories that deal with change necessarily incomplete and fragmentary; the term 'dynamic' is too mechanical a label for them.

There is, however, one sense in which Hicks finds the notion of equilibrium useful, and even indispensable; that is in the study of the past. To explain the past we should use the historians' 'counterfactual' approach. To establish causation between events A and B we should be able to assert that if A had not occurred, B would not have occurred. But since not-A and not-B did not take place, we are in need of a theory if we are to explain past events. And since past events cannot be undone, we can be as deterministic as we wish without doubting that we are free when choosing between various courses of action: "determination applied to the future ... is ... cramping; but determinism, applied to the past, is ... liberating" (1979c, 11). Since theories deal with hypothetical experiences, it is convenient to construct them in an equilibrium context. To compare actual experience with the hypothetical one, it must be assumed that during the period under consideration the actual system was also in equilibrium (see Hicks 1979a, 56 and 1979c, 78–83).

It is within this highly qualified framework that Hicks defends his short-period equilibrium interpretation of Keynes,[8] an interpretation that is in marked contrast to either the neo-Walrasian or the post-Keynesian views of Keynes's message. It is much less ambitious than the former, which tries to formalize Keynes within the rigorous Arrow–Debreu–McKenzie model by taking account of "the powerful influence exerted by the future and past on present and by the large modifications that must be introduced into both value and theory and stability analysis, if the requisite futures are missing" (Arrow & Hahn 1971, 369). At the same time, it is less self-denying than the post-Keynesian view, as expressed by Joan Robinson, that

> On the plane of theory, the [Keynesian] revolution lay in the change from the conception of equilibrium to the conception of history ... Once we admit that an economy exists in time, that history goes one way, from the irrevocable past into the unknown future, the conception of equilibrium ... becomes untenable [1980, 170–72].

Hicks's approach, as clarified in 'IS–LM: an explanation' (in Hicks 1982) envisages an economy with four markets: commodities (A), labor (B), bond (C) and money (X). Taking money as the numéraire, and using Walras's law, we can write:

$$S_x = P_a D_a + P_b D_b + P_c D_c \quad \text{and} \quad D_x = P_a S_a + P_b S_b + P_c S_c$$

The system has three independent supply and demand relations, $S_a = D_a$, and so on, and three relative prices to be determined. The commodity price P_a and the money wage rate P_b are assumed to be fixed, the only flexible price in the system being P_c, the interest rate.

In fixprice markets, quantity demanded and supplied will not necessarily be equal. In these markets the actual amount sold — supply or demand, whichever is smaller — is binding and enters the above relation.

The Keynesian short period is longer than *Value and capital*'s "week"; it is a "year." Within this longer period, given the product price, producers have enough time to adjust supply to demand and production to sale, so the commodity market is in equilibrium via quantity adjustment. The labor market, however, does not have enough time to adjust through withdrawal, retirement, emigration, and so on. So it fails to clear. In the IS–LM, the two fixprices are given exogenously, "a model which is restricted by this condition can be in equilibrium, so far as *other* choices are concerned, even though there is unemployment" (Hicks 1979c, 79).

In Hicks's eyes, the treacherous side of Keynes's theory is that which is concerned with the marginal Efficiency of Capital and Liquidity Preference; these are forward-looking — "time and uncertainty are written all over [them]" (Hicks 1982, 289). They can hardly be reconciled with the assumption that expectations are correct, even if only within the "year." So Keynes's theory, Hicks concedes, is a hybrid — it has one leg in equilibrium but the other in historical time. With the IS–LM "I myself fell into the trap" (Hicks 1977, 148) — and with him the majority of the profession, one should add!

VII. Hicks's Reconstruction

In his own "long struggle to escape" from the slippery world of the IS–LM, Hicks had endeavored to reformulate the Keynesian model so as to keep it in touch with its appropriate microfoundations. Hicks's position has developed with a constant eye on historical-institutional factors that made the Keynesian revolution a success but have, at the same time, limited its domain. In Hicks's view, classical macro has its micro, and there is no reason to deny Keynesian macro its micro counterpart.[9]

Prices and the expansion process

Hicks sees the development of fixprice markets as a twentieth-century phenomenon. Earlier economists' reliance on the flexprice method, he argues, was "a reflection of this kind of industrial organization which may well have been common in the nineteenth century" (1982, 234). Marshall's firms were price takers rather than price makers. The price-making initiative came from stock-carrying merchants who played the role of the Walrasian 'auctioneer.' The merchant, always alert to changes in demand

and supply, alters his offer price to manufacturers accordingly. In Hicks's *A theory of economic history* (1969), unorganized competitive markets owe their development to intermediaries who neither consume nor produce the goods they trade in. In these flexprice markets, actual stocks are always desired stocks.

In fixprice markets, the producer has taken over the price-setting function, eliminating the role of the intermediary: "the stocks that are held will be held by firms that are specialized, either to the selling or to the buying of the commodity in question" (Hicks 1974, 24). In these markets, stock disequilibrium is allowed for, and actions to correct that disequilibrium determine the path of the process. But Hicks does not find disequilibrium forces dependable:

> We can invent rules of their working, and calculate the behaviour of the resulting models; but such calculations are of illustrative value only. This is where 'states of mind' are of dominating importance; and states of mind cannot readily be reduced to rules [1965, 83].

As a result, in discussing short-period problems, Hicks has come to shun highly formal and deterministic models. He has, in this respect, moved closer to the post-Keynesian position.[10]

Fixprice markets owe their development to the increasing importance of economies of scale and product differentiation (see Hicks 1977, xi). The replacement of the mercantile function should be understood as an aspect of market evolution. We cannot turn to the theories of monopolistic or imperfect competition[11] for they are "shockingly *out of time*" (Hicks 1982, 299). Flexprice markets, Hicks contends, cannot be restored by legislative measures.

To determine prices in fixprice markets, Hicks has returned to the Marshallian notion of 'normal price.' Granting that manufacturing industry operates under diminishing-cost conditions, firms set their prices "so as to yield a 'reasonable' profit in a 'normal' condition of the market, but then letting the market determine what ... it will actually buy" (Hicks 1982, 310). In a seller's market stocks are run down, output is increased and delivery dates extended. In a buyer's market, stocks are accumulated and production is cut. In the former, profits are 'abnormally' high, in the latter 'abnormally' low.

'Normal pricing' cannot but work through supply and demand. Hicks's assertion that in fixprice markets prices "are *not* determined by supply and demand" (1977, xi) is not helpful and can only lead to the 'Keynesian' complete neglect of prices. 'Normal pricing' only means that there is stock and production variability and price rigidity.

To account for price rigidity, Hicks accepts the importance Okun (1975) attached to mutual benefit in long-term customer–producer relations. To maintain customers' goodwill, changes in demand will not be exploited. Prices will be kept steady unless there is a change in costs. Then the price rise can be presented in a justifiable manner.

The choice between fixprice and flexprice models is, ultimately, an empirical matter. Hicks prefers a mixed model where manufacturing is fixprice, speculative commodities and the primary sector are flexprice (see Hicks, 1979e, 994; 1982, 309–12).

Hicks's treatment of the multiplier theory, though suffering from a number of conceptual difficulties, is highly illuminating. His approach turns on the availability of essential stocks without which the process of expansion cannot get under way. When such stocks are available, in fixprice markets, actual stocks exceed desired stocks, and in flexprice markets stocks are 'abnormally' high and prices 'abnormally' low (see Hicks 1974, 25–27).

If there is an autonomous increase in investment, surplus stocks are run down in both markets. In flexprice markets, as stocks approach their 'normal' level, prices also rise toward 'normal.' In fixprice markets, prices are determined by 'normal cost.' Flexprice commodities enter into the production of fixprice goods, but since their prices were 'abnormally' low and have gradually become 'normal,' there is no change in the 'normal cost' of fixprice commodities. The process of expansion can, therefore, take place without a significant rise in prices of fixprice goods.

One difficulty with Hicks's approach is its excessive reliance on 'normal' values. They belong to the notion of long-run equilibrium in which he himself has lost faith.

Another problem is Hicks's insistence on the possibility of 'involuntary' stocks in fixprice markets. He has argued that the fixprice method is a disequilibrium method in which stock accumulation or decumulation may be 'involuntary' while the flexprice method is an equilibrium one where stock changes are always 'voluntary' (see Hicks 1982, 232–33). In either method, changes in stocks held cannot but be voluntary. Fixprice markets are characterized by large stock fluctuations and small price variations, the opposite being true of flexprice markets. The difference should hinge on the high cost, possibly in terms of customers' goodwill, of price changes in fixprice markets.

Still, the fixprice–flexprice distinction is essential to Keynesian microeconomics; for if all markets behaved along flexprice lines, persistent slack could not occur.

Wages and inflation

In a Keynesian world "the wage level is rigid, so that it would have been unaffected if there had been a change in other variables; it would ... be approximately the same if expansionary measures were taken or if they were not. The wage level must not just be constant; it must also be firm" (Hicks 1983, 18). Keynes, Hicks believes, made this assumption because he was a monetary economist and needed to think in terms of a standard while, at the same time, his early experience with money-wage rigidity fortified his belief in its general applicability.

When the 'labor standard' cannot be relied upon, we have moved outside the Keynesian world and have to modify our theory accordingly. Hicks starts with Keynes's wage 'theorem':

When there is a general (proportional) rise in money wages ... the *normal* effect is that all prices rise in the same proportion — provided that the money supply is increased in the same proportion [Hicks 1974, 60].

The proviso of an elastic money supply makes the "wage theorem" an alternative statement of the quantity theory. As Hicks pointed out, "So long as we stick to comparative statics ... there is no essential difference; so the difference must lie in a view ... about the route which the system is supposed to take from one equilibrium to the other" (1974, 72.). The "difference," having to do with the dominance of fixprice behavior not only in product markets but also in the labor market, is sufficient to make Hicks against both the monetarist and the 'radical' Keynesian views of inflation (see Hicks 1975b; 1976d).

That the labor market functions in a special way has been a part of the Hicksian thinking since 1932, *The theory of wages.* There he distinguished between "casual" and "regular" labor markets. The former is competitive while the latter is characterized by a large degree of bilateral monopoly and thus indeterminacy of money wages. This, Hicks argued, leads to money-wage rigidity rather than volatility. The high cost of replacing experienced workers makes firms reluctant to cut wages in slack times while the high relocation cost discourages workers from pressing for higher wages in times of labor scarcity. Non-economic arguments for wage determination, such as "fair" and "just" wages, were mentioned but quickly dismissed as mere "rough-and-ready guides whereby the working of supply and demand is anticipated" (Hicks 1963, 80).

In his later works, however, Hicks has explained the behaviour of money wages by giving an economic interpretation to "fairness." As in other fixprice markets, money wages do not necessarily fall when there is unemployment and do not necessarily rise when there is labor shortage: "forces determining money wages are in large part non-competitive" (1975b, 4). In regular labor markets where both the worker and the employer "should be able to look forward to more durability in their relationship ... it is necessary for efficiency that the wage-contract should be felt, by both parties, to be *fair*" (1974, 64). Employers are reluctant to raise wages and upset differentials whenever a certain grade of labor becomes scarce; and similarly, not wishing to alienate those they intend to employ, they do not cut wages in the face of unemployment.

Hicks is wary of exact definitions of "fairness" knowing very well that "A system of wages which will satisfy all the demands of fairness that may be made upon it is quite unattainable. No system of wages, when it is called in question, will ever be found to be fair" (1974, 65). To him "fair" is any structure of wages that has been established long enough so as to enjoy the sanction of custom; for "it then becomes what is expected; and (admittedly on a low level of fairness) what is expected is fair" (ibid. 65). The tendency to rigid wage differentials cannot, however, in Hicks's view be taken for granted. It depends on the historical situation. Wars, major fluctuations, and economic policy could erode wage stickiness. He argues that as a result of the Second World War and a shift of policy from a concern with price stability to maintenance of high employment, "pressure for rising wages has become dominant" (ibid. 69). In this sense, the post-war period is not a Keynesian one.

Fixprice product and labor markets are an integral part of Hicks's analysis of inflation. In a thoroughgoing flexprice economy, there is no need to distinguish between demand-pull and cost-push inflation — the latter is a backlash from the former. When fixprice becomes prevalent, cost-push inflation could acquire a life of its own. Although Hicks fully admits that without an elastic money supply, or "accommodation," continuous inflation cannot exist, he still regards cost push as more fundamental in explaining the postwar experience and especially that of the last decades.

Hicks's analysis of the inflationary process relies on a two-sector model: "a primary sector in which prices are determined by supply and demand, and a secondary sector in which prices are cost determined" (1977, 101). An independent wage push in the secondary sector will raise costs and hence prices. The price increase may generate further wage increases and lead to a wage–price spiral. Similarly, the shock may originate from the primary sector. Crop failures, raw material shortages, or cartels raise the cost of production and lead to higher prices. Higher cost of living then creates a situation where a wage increase is regarded as fair by both employers and workers.

The labor market is viewed in terms of two sectors noted above; casual and regular. In the casual sector, labor shortages will lead to higher wages, but the way higher wages are transmitted to the regular sector is through pressure for a fair wage structure irrespective of labor scarcity. Once established wage differentials are upset, there is no easy way of developing new ones. Each group of workers feels unfairly treated when comparing their position with that of those who have recently won wage increases and presses for still higher wages. Hicks does not see the solution in either income policy or indexation. Both are fragile and perpetuate existing misallocations without creating a lasting sense of fairness.

Hicks sees the social cost of inflation as inexorably bound up with fixprice markets. In a perfectly competitive economy, the cost of fully anticipated inflation is limited to the inconvenience cost of reduced real balances. But in fixprice markets, where prices have to be made by negotiation, inflation even when expected is damaging: "It is most apparent in deteriorating of industrial relations, but it is not confined to that field ... It extends, very importantly, to many kinds of public arrangements ... so that issues which had seemed closed have to be reopened" (1974, 79). The difficulty that many social arrangements experience in adjusting to inflation is the principal reason why it should be kept at a modest level.

These considerations have prevented Hicks from adopting the "natural rate" or the "vertical long-run Phillips curve" view of inflationary equilibrium:

> One equilibrium [may be] ... regarded 'better' than another if it puts less strain on the less flexible prices, thus enabling the economy to func-

tion with smaller excesses, of demand or of supply, in the markets where prices do not equate supply and demand quickly and easily [Hicks 1977, 71].

The optimum equilibrium[12] is one that "the economy in its institutional structure, can most easily follow" (Hicks 1977, 71). It is surprising that Hicks, given his views on equilibrium and the historical-institutional aspect of markets, should still regard inflationary equilibrium as a serious construct. It would be more consistent to go all the way with Okum 1975, 381–85, and regard fully expected inflation as an impossibility.

Liquidity and the credit economy

IS–LM, as noted above, assumed that the economy is in equilibrium during the "year." On the IS side there is flow equilibrium; production plans are carried through as intended. On the LM side there is stock equilibrium which, as Hicks has shown in *Capital and Growth* (1965), must imply flow equilibrium within a period and correct expectations. So, expectations are not only given, they ought to be correct as well.

As far as the multiplier theory is concerned, the construct is satisfactory. It does, however, inflict great violence on Marginal Efficiency of Capital and Liquidity Preference. The former is "forward-looking, ignorance of the future being essential to it" (Hicks 1979c, 80), while the latter is "a matter of provision against an uncertain future [and] ... a problem of the economy *in* time" (1982, 288).

In *The crisis in keynesian economics* (1974), Keynes's theories of money and investment are treated jointly, firstly for the above reasons and secondly because Hicks finds it misleading to look at long-term interest rates as the sole link between money and investment. In re-examining the link between money and investment, Hicks has turned away from the emphasis on the speculative motive and has focused on the role of money as an asset in the balance sheet. The balance-sheet approach was an integral feature of his 1935 'simplifying' paper where it was concluded: "This analysis has at least shown the relative size of the different items on this balance sheet is governed mainly by the anticipation of the yield of investments and of risks" (Hicks 1982, 58). Modern choice-theoretic approach to portfolio selection, which stemmed from the 'simplifying' paper's application of marginal-utility analysis to the theory of money, reduces the problem to a two-way single choice: between risk and the rate of return. It leaves no room for liquidity, for "liquidity is not a problem of single choice; it is a matter of a sequence of choices, a related sequence" (Hicks 1974, 38). Liquidity is bound up with imperfect capital markets and transaction costs. If these can be neglected, portfolio-selection theory offers the optimal strategy: the investor need only maximize the expected utility of his portfolio at any given point. The passage of time is unimportant. In the real world the function of liquidity is that "it gives us time to think" (ibid. 57). For Hicks, liquidity is nothing less than freedom (1979c, p. 94).

Hicks groups assets into running, reserve, and investment, each of which could be either financial or real. Liquid assets, those whose value "at whatever date there is realization, [are] much the same" (1982, 260), usually fall under financial reserves or investments. Inducement to invest is seen to depend on the liquidity of the firm. A decrease in liquidity is undesirable, for it narrows the band of future opportunities and makes the firm dependent on its creditors.

To discuss the impact of monetary policy on investment we should not, in Hicks's view, neglect the institutional arrangement between (a) the central bank, (b) financial intermediaries, and (c) the industry. In an "auto-economy," firms hold their own liquid reserves. A successful monetary policy lowers interest rates and raises prices of reserve securities, thereby increasing liquidity and hence investment. In an 'overdraft' economy, where firms do not hold liquid reserves, their liquidity is determined directly by the credit policy of the banks or indirectly by the lending rate.

The monetary regime envisaged by the General Theory is that of an "auto-economy" where reserve assets are held in long-term bonds, short-term bonds and money offering negligible and zero returns respectively. In such a system, Hicks concedes, speculative demand for money should occupy a central role; for without idle money, open-market operations cannot change the interest rate. But the inflationary experience of the past two decades has led to a significant rise in the yields of short-term bills and the emergence of competitive banking where interest is also paid on bank deposits.

In 'Monetary experience and theory of money' (1977) Hicks called the emerging regime a "credit economy"; and especially after the collapse of the "dollar standard" the monetary system is regarded as Wicksellian rather than Keynesian: "What that means in terms of monetary theory is that Keynes, for us, is *too* monetarist. What we need ... is something which will pay *less* attention than Keynes did to the Quantity of Money" (Hicks 1982, 264). In a "credit economy" with no "hard" money, or no money that does not bear interest, it pays, in terms of gains in liquidity, to borrow funds from the banks and redeposit them simultaneously:

> It is this ... which makes the Quantity theory inapplicable to the pure credit economy. The Quantity of Money must now mean the Quantity of bank money, but a substantial part of the Quantity of bank money is now ... idle ... The link between the total Quantity of Money and that part of it which circulates is effectively snapped [1977, 63].

The development of competitive banking has been itself a response to inflation. And once we distinguish between real and nominal interest rates it is not clear that our present system is fundamentally different. Hicks's argument that it, now, pays to hold more idle funds is not convincing. Also, in returning to interest rate as a chief instrument of monetary policy, Hicks has not faced the monetarist objection to interest-rate targeting. On the whole, he regards the credit–liquidity–investment link as the most important channel of monetary management.

The competitive financial system is seen by Hicks as highly fragile —

"whatever we think about monopoly and competition, in the rest of the economic system, there are good reasons in this monetary sphere, for not being afraid of some concentration" (1982, 273). Monetary stability he points out in 'Expected inflation' is "a psychological condition, not to be achieved by ... mechanical means ... alone" (1977, 111). Hicks's objection to monetarism is that it will work only if all money is commodity money and capital markets are undeveloped.

VIII. Conclusion

Rather than giving an overview of the foregoing, I would like to emphasize the ubiquitous tension that we found in Hicks's thinking between equilibrium and historical time. Without the notion of equilibrium, economic theorizing becomes impossible, while a total neglect of time leads to a class of theories that cannot shed much light on the world as we know it. In Hicks's earlier works, time was kept at bay, but gradually it has become the dominant theme. In refusing complete surrender to either extreme, he has achieved a delicate balance that is most illuminating.

I am indebted to Professor Axel Leijonhufvud and my colleagues Jim Dietz and David Wong for their comments on an earlier draft of this article. Remaining deficiencies are certainly mine.

References

Arrow, Kenneth J., and Frank H. Hahn 1971. *General competitive analysis.* San Francisco.
Blaug, Mark 1980. *The methodology of economics: or how economists explain.* Cambridge.
Bliss, Christopher 1983. 'Two views of macroeconomics.' *Oxford Economic Papers* 35.4 (Feb.):1–12.
Coddington, Alan 1983. *Keynesian economics: the search for first principles.* London.
Eichner, Alfred S., and J.A. Kregel 1975. 'An essay on post-Keynesian theory: a new paradigm in economics.' *Journal of Economic Literature* 13.4 (Dec.): 1293–1314.
Gram, Harvey, and Vivian Walsh 1983. 'Joan Robinson's economics in retrospect.' *Journal of Economic Literature* 21.2 (June): 518–50.
Hayek, Friedrich A. 1935. *Prices and production* (1931). London.
Hicks, John R. 1933. 'Gleichgewicht und Konjunktur.' *Zeitschrift für Nationalökonomie*, no. 4. Hicks 1982, 28–41.
—— 1935a. 'Wages and interest: the dynamic problem.' *Economic Journal* 45 (179): 456–68. In Hicks 1982, 67–69.
—— 1935b. 'A suggestion for simplifying the theory of money.' *Economica* 2 (5):1–19. In Hicks 1982, 46–63.
—— 1936. 'Mr Keynes' theory of employment.' *Economic Journal* 46 (182):238–53. In Hicks 1982, 84–99.
—— 1937. 'Mr Keynes and the classics.' *Econometrica* 5.2:147–59. In Hicks 1982, 101–15.
—— 1939. *Value and capital.* Oxford.
—— 1957. 'A rehabilitation of 'classical' economics?' *Economic Journal* 67 (266):278–89.
—— 1963. *The theory of wages* (1932). London.
—— 1965. *Capital and growth.* Oxford.
—— 1967. *Critical essays in monetary theory.* Oxford.
—— 1969. *A theory of economic history.* Oxford.
—— 1974. *The crisis in Keynesian economics.* Oxford.
—— 1975a. 'Revival of political economy: the old and the new.' *Economic Record* 51(135):365–67.

—— 1975b. 'What is wrong with monetarism.' *Lloyds Bank Review* 118 (Oct.):1–13.

—— 1976a. 'Revolutions in economics.' In Spiro J. Latsis, ed., *Method and appraisal in economics* (Cambridge), 207–18.

—— 1976b. 'Time in economics.' In A.M. Tang et al., eds, *Evolution, welfare and time in economics* (Lexington, Mass.), 135–51, and in Hicks 1982, 282–300.

—— 1976c. 'Must stimulating demand stimulate inflation!' *Economic Record* 52 (140):409–22. In Hicks 1982, 301–17.

—— 1976d. 'The little that is right with monetarism.' *Lloyds Bank Review* 121 (July): 16–18.

—— 1977. *Economic perspectives: further essays on money and growth.* Oxford.

—— 1979a. 'Is interest the price of a factor of production?' In Mario J. Rizzo, ed., *Time, uncertainty and disequilibrium* (Lexington, Mass.): 51–63.

—— 1979b. 'Formation of an economist.' *Banca Nazionale del Lavoro Quarterly Review* 130 (Sept.): 195–204.

—— 1979c. *Causality in economics.* New York.

—— 1979d. Review of Weintraub 1979. *Journal of Economic Literature* 17.4:51–54.

—— 1979. 'On Coddington's interpretation: a reply.' *Journal of Economic Literature.* 17.3:989–95.

—— 1980. 'IS–LM: an explanation.' *Journal of Post Keynesian Economics* 3.2:139–54. In Hicks 1982, 318–31.

—— 1982. *Money, interest and wages: collected essays on economic theory, Vol. 2.* Cambridge, Mass.

—— 1983. 'The Keynes centenary.' *Economist.* 287(7294):17–19.

Hutchinson, T.W. 1977. *Knowledge and ignorance in economics.* Chicago.

—— 1980. *Limitations of general theories in macro economics.* London.

Keynes, John Maynard 1936. *The general theory of employment, interest and money.* New York.

Knight, Frank H. 1921. *Risk, uncertainty and profit.* New York.

Lachmann, Ludwig M. 1979. 'Comment: Austrian economics today.' In Mario J. Rizzo, ed., *Time, uncertainty and disequilibrium* (Lexington, Mass.), 64–69.

Leijonhufvud, Axel 1969. *Keynes and the classics.* London.

Myrdal, G. 1939. *Monetary equilibrium.* London. Translated from the German edition of 1933.

Okun, Arthur M. 1975. 'Inflation: its mechanics and welfare costs.' *Brookings Papers on Economic Activity* 2:351–90.

Patinkin, Don 1959. 'Keynesian economics rehabilitated: a rejoinder to Professor Hicks.' *Economic Journal* 69(275):582–87.

—— 1965. *Money, interest and prices,* 2d ed. New York.

Robinson, Joan 1969. *The theory of imperfect competition,* 2d ed. London.

—— 1980. *Collected economic papers, Vol. 5.* Cambridge, Mass.

Solow, Robert M. 1979. 'Alternative approaches to macroeconomic theory: a partial view.' *Canadian Journal of Economics* 12.3:339–54.

Tobin, James 1980. *Asset accumulation and economic activity.* Chicago.

Weintraub, E. Roy 1979. *Microfoundations: the compatibility of microeconomics and macroeconomics.* Cambridge.

*Correspondence may be addressed to the author, Dept. of Economics, California State University, Fullerton CA 92634.

Notes

1. In one of his latest works (Hicks 1979c) he points out that the work of economists and historians "is in time, in historical time, as the work of most natural scientists is not" (p. 3) and furthermore "as economics pushes on beyond 'statics,' it becomes less like science and more like history" (p. xi).

2. His methodology is somewhat akin to the methodologies of Senior, Mill, Cairnes, and Jevons, in whose writing, "verification" is not a testing of economic theories to see whether

they are true or false, but only a method of establishing the boundaries of application of theories deemed to be obviously true" (Blaug 1980, 81).

3. For an account of his theoretical development see Hicks 1979b.

4. Joan Robinson and Dennis Robertson being outstanding examples.

5. See Weintraub 1979, 57–58.

6. See Patinkin 1959. It should be noted that Pigou's real-balance effect is, after all, intended as a long-run phenomenon; see Tobin 1980, 5–9.

7. Cf. Hutchinson 1977, 15–33.

8. Cf. Bliss 1983: "Keynes' economics cannot reasonably be interpreted as the economics of general disequilibrium ... To suppose otherwise is to make the *General Theory* impossible to understand, for it is so full of equilibrium conditions" (p. 5). Also see Solow 1979.

9. See his (Hicks, 1979d) review of Weintraub 1979.

10. See the excellent discussion of Joan Robinson's ideas by Gram & Walsh 1983; also Eichner & Kregel 1975.

11. It should be noted that Joan Robinson repudiated her *The theory of imperfect competition* (1969) a long time ago on the same grounds.

12. Given his views on convergence to long-run equilibrium he has taken care to emphasize that these equilibria are for comparative purposes only, the trade-off curve says nothing about the movement from one to the other (see Hicks 1982, 301).

89

Consumer Surplus: The First Hundred Years[†]

R.B. Ekelund Jr. and R.F. Hébert

> O happiness! our being's end and aim!
> Good, pleasure, ease, content! Whate'er thy name:
> That something still which prompts the eternal sigh,
> For which we bear to live, or dare to die.
>
> ALEXANDER POPE, *An Essay on Man*

Introduction

Some economic ideas may be likened to volcanoes — they are certain to erupt periodically. The cause of an ideational 'eruption' may be 'environmental' — a reaction to recurring economic problems — or it may be a more fundamental assault on scientific definition. One such idea is the concept of consumer surplus, the Krakatoa of economic theory. Its long and spotty history has been marked by three major eruptions: the first at its inception; the second in consequence of the peak performance in cardinal-utility/demand theory; and the third in conjunction with the ordinal reconstruction of modern demand analysis.

On the one hand, the 'doctrine of maximum satisfaction' has not been and can never be made entirely 'scientific' or objective despite periodic counterclaims by some economists. On the other hand, economics makes little sense without it. Because economics deals with maximizing behavior under scarcity constraints, the *measurement* of satisfaction will always intrigue and frustrate economists. Such has been the case with the definition and measurement of consumer surplus. Diverse, often ambivalent, arguments appear in modern economic literature, as demonstrated by this sampling of recent titles: 'The ambiguity of the consumers' surplus measure of welfare change' (Foster and Neuburger 1974); 'Consumer's surplus without apology' (Willig 1976); 'The plain truth about consumer surplus' (Mishan 1977); 'The ugly truth about consumer surplus' (Foster and Neuburger 1978); and 'The three consumers surpluses' (Dixit and Weller 1979). The historical record will show, however, that debate and controversy are not new to the doctrine of consumer surplus. Past and

---

[†]Source: *History of Political Economy*, Vol. 17 (3), Fall 1985, pp. 419–54.

present intellectual turmoil on the subject merely points up a continuing fascination with the idea. Like it or not, consumer surplus theory, as cost–benefit analysis, is the bread and butter of the practising economist.

The purpose of this article is to chronicle, analyze, and evaluate the first one hundred years of debate on the matter of consumer surplus, a debate that originated upon the very invention of the idea. The present history of the subject is, by and large, a fractured one. Previous studies have tended to slight various historical aspects that greatly illuminate the received doctrine. Of those papers dealing with early debates on the subject, neither Houghton (1958) nor Button (1979) have plumbed the true measure of Bordas's early contribution (1847). By contrast, Ahmed (1966) and Dooley (1983) virtually ignore the early development of the subject in order to concentrate on Marshall and his critics. Having a broader scope and purpose, Mishan's 1960 classic survey on welfare economics devotes relatively little space to consumer surplus. Its chief value to the matter at hand is that it provides a useful bibliography on the subject prior to 1960. Currie, Murphy, and Schmitz (1971) have surveyed the field of surplus concepts in general, concentrating almost exclusively on recent applications to international trade, taxation, and other areas of economic analysis. Despite some overlap in their treatment and ours of Marshall and Hicks, the Currie et al. study omits a number of important historical contributions that weigh heavily on the origin of the doctrine and its subsequent evolution. Moreover, our focus is exclusively on *consumer* surplus, to the neglect of other forms of economic rent.

This survey concentrates on the development of the concept from its initial formulation by Jules Dupuit (1844) through its 'rehabilitation' by J.R. Hicks (1941; 1942; 1943; 1946) roughly one hundred years later. This is followed by a modest and necessarily brief review of the present state of the literature. The conclusion of this lengthy investigation is that, instead of being the albatross of economic theory, the principle of consumer surplus is a highly useful mechanism in a world where purely scientific methods fail to accurately measure what we 'know' exists.

Dupuit and His Critics

Origins of consumer surplus

The theory of consumer surplus emerged simultaneously with the discovery of marginal utility and its application to demand theory. Although Cournot (1838 [1897, 78–81]) developed an adequate measure of producer surplus his method failed to produce the same result for consumer surplus. Cournot always measured the cost of consumers by the extra expenditure of those who continue to consume at a higher price rather than that amount *plus* the loss of those who stop consuming. Furthermore, he refused to identify utility with demand, thereby denying any operational measure of psychic gain. The modern idea of consumer surplus, and the explicit conjunction of utility and demand that supports the idea, originated in the writings of Jules Dupuit. In a series of famous papers, Dupuit (1844;

1849a; 1849b; 1853) attacked the classical value-in-use/value-in-exchange dichotomy, substituting an improved theory of value in which price became the independent and simultaneous product of the forces of scarcity and marginal utility.

Dupuit (1853, 7) unraveled the water-diamond paradox in a telling example of a city receiving ample water from a stream flowing through it. Owing to its abundance, water would have no value in exchange. In the face of scarcity, however (either natural of contrived), water takes on a value that is reflected in progressively higher prices as the quantity available for all uses declines relative to the demand for it. A city under siege, for example, may have its water supply so reduced by the enemy that none of the inhabitants would be willing to give up a liter of water, even though a diamond be offered in exchange for it. From such logic, and from observation of the markets for public works with which he was involved, Dupuit developed a workable theory of demand in which the marginal utility curve for any product or service *is* the demand curve for that good. The important corollaries that follow from this fusion are that (i) the area under the demand curve must equal the total utility of the good up to that point, and (ii) when price is zero, total utility is maximized.

Figure 1 depicts the fusion of demand and marginal utility in the form of Dupuit's *courbe de consommation.* Dupuit argued that the total utility (*l'utilité absolue*) of Or″ articles is equal to the area Or″n″P under the demand curve. From this he derived *relative utility,* or what is now called consumer surplus, by subtracting total costs of production, Or″n″p″. With reference to Figure 1, consumer surplus is equal to the area of the (curvilinear) triangle, p″n″P. The remaining area r″n″N, Dupuit called "lost utility" (*utilité perdue*) in the sense that it could not be claimed by either consumers or producers for a market the size of Or″.

According to Dupuit, a change in relative utility (consumer surplus) could be calculated in the following manner. Suppose the price falls from

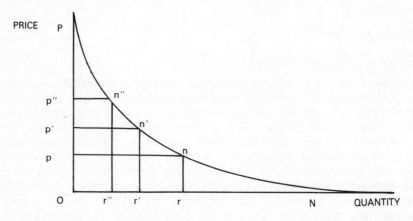

Figure 1. The demand curve as a welfare measure

p″ to p′ owing to a decrease in production costs, so that the quantity taken increases from r″ to r′. This raises absolute utility to Or′n′P. Subtracting costs of production Op′n′nr′ from this amount yields a total consumer surplus of p′Pn′. The *net gain* in consumer surplus is consequently measured by p′n′n″p″. In this way Dupuit developed a money measure of the benefit of public works and of goods in general, thereby forging the most important single tool of welfare economics. It was a significant break-through, developed in the peculiar milieu of the civil engineer forced to confront practical economic problems. But like all pioneer efforts, it was far from perfect.

Insofar as Dupuit's demand curve is a horizontal summation of indi-vidual demand curves, it presents an immediate problem. Interpersonal utility comparisons inevitably intrude on a *market* demand curve that is used to depict the utility surplus enjoyed by consumers of the product. A price may not represent the same utility to different individuals, since the price one would pay for a given quantity of a good depends not only on the utility afforded him by the good but on the income he possesses as well. In other words, the maximum price an individual is willing to pay for any unit varies with the amount of income he holds as well as with the utility the good provides. Thus we have the 'problem of the apostrophe.' If the concept under consideration is (aggregate) consumers' surplus, inter-personal utility comparisons are unavoidable; but the problem does not occur in the notion of a single individual's consumer surplus. Dupuit's discussions involved both concepts, but he put the greatest emphasis on consumers' surplus. Strictly speaking, then, differences in income distri-bution prohibit a legitimate utility summation; but as we shall see, Dupuit assumed away this problem.

A second problem in Dupuit's approach is the tacit assumption that utility is a measurable quantity. He regarded the true measure of the utility of an object as the "maximum sacrifice expressed in money that one is will-ing to make in order to procure it" (Dupuit 1849n, 177). Indeed, relative utility is defined as the difference between the maximum amount (price) the consumer would be willing to pay for each unit in his entire stock and what he must in fact pay for the entire stock. As stated above, it is the area under the demand curve above the total expenditures rectangle, and it is a *money* measure. But this measure cannot be a valid one if the marginal utility of money expenditures is allowed to change as price changes. The problem is one of distinguishing marginal utility curves on the one hand from demand curves on the other. Dupuit failed to make the distinction, with the result that his money measure, in all cases save one, tends to misstate true utility.[1]

Another objection to Dupuit's money measure of consumers' surplus arises if the demand curve does not intersect the price axis. In such a case the offer price for the first unit(s) of the commodity is infinite, and consumers' surplus is therefore unmeasurable. Dupuit (1853,26) attempted to skirt this problem by recognizing the limits to human knowledge. He observed:

when one cannot know something it is already quite a lot to know the limits of one's knowledge ... We may not know that the utility of a canal will be only 5 million, but we might know that it will not be six, and that consequently we should forgo its construction; we may not know that the utility of a bridge will be 120,000F, but we could determine periods that it will be more than 80,000F and that may be sufficient to show that it will be very beneficial.

The problems of the constancy of the marginal utility of expenditures, and all that this implies, together with the interpersonal utility comparisons associated with a *market* demand curve (although later sidestepped by Dupuit) subsequently proved troublesome in the history of consumer surplus. But this did not void Dupuit's use of the demand curve as an approximation of this surplus, nor did it render the *definition* of consumer surplus invalid. In fact, the idea persisted, and Dupuit was certainly not the last economist to proceed in such a fashion.

The Bordas offensive

Within a short time, Dupuit's attack on established notions of utility elicited a major rebuttal. Like Dupuit, Louis Bordas was an engineer of considerable economic sophistication. However, his response to Dupuit consisted mostly of a mélange of confusions on the meaning of the word utility. Bordas (1847) defended Say's theory of value, which confused utility with costs of production. Caught in a quagmire of terminology, he made some rather ill-advised statements on utility. At one point, for example, Bordas (1847, 252) stated that "current price ... depends on the intrinsic value of the monetary measure and on that of the object given in exchange." At another (1847, 258) he maintained that "the utility of ... tea is inherent to this substance and ... does not at all depend on the price at which it is sold." These statements show that Bordas had no appreciation for Dupuit's marginal utility theory or for the solution it provided to the value-in-use/value-in-exchange dichotomy.

Nevertheless, Bordas brought out important and relevant points in his assessments of Dupuit's consumers' surplus concept. These criticisms, it turns out, echoed repeatedly against the doctrine. For example, J.S. Nicholson (1893; 1894; 1903) raised them in his attack on Marshall's formulation. Bordas admitted some connection between the utility of a certain quantity of a food and the maximum sacrifice which an individual would be willing to make for it, but the point he emphasized is that the sacrifice depends on a person's income and on the price of other goods as well. As Bordas (1847, 278–79) stated:

Let us suppose that it is a matter of evaluating a kilogram of meat and that a person is asked to state the sacrifice that he is ready to make to procure it. Can this person answer categorically? Evidently not. Indeed, doesn't this sacrifice depend on the means of this person as well as the current price of other alimentary products which are capable of being substituted for the meat? ... Therefore, what theory can one establish on so variable a basis and which depends on the taste as well as the means of each consumer?

Bordas (1847, 282) pressed the argument further in reference to Dupuit's method of determining the utility and consumers' surplus of the quarry rock used in road-building:

> insofar as the rock is taxed at a progressive rate, is it necessary to sell [its substitute] brick at its original price or at a new price? The result will be quite different according to what is done.

Bordas's argument asserted that if the price of brick is not held constant, Dupuit's measure of consumer surplus is rendered inoperable, because the demand curve for rock would shift erratically under such circumstances. Moreover, Bordas implied that since the necessary assumption of 'other things equal' generally does not hold in any concrete case, Dupuit's measure of consumers' surplus is practically useless. He was within the bounds of legitimate criticism on the former point, since Dupuit failed to invoke the explicit assumption of constancy of the prices of related goods.

Bordas also cast a jaundiced eye on Dupuit's tacit interpersonal utility comparisons. In ascertaining the desirability of bridges and other public projects, Dupuit sought to compare the project's utility with its costs. The utility of the project was measured, in the case of a bridge, for example, by placing incrementally increasing tolls in a fashion that revealed the resulting use and its accompanying consumer surplus. Bordas (1847,283) objected to this calculation on the grounds that

> ... it is necessary, before applying it, to logically establish the relationship which connects the taxpayer's revenue loss to the sum of the relative utilities yielded by this approach ... This connection seems, in effect, very difficult, for the quantities to be matched or compared, although expressed in money, are altogether of a different kind.

The basis of Bordas's argument is that the marginal utility of a dollar collected from the taxpayer does not necessarily equal the marginal utility received from a dollar spent on any particular public project. In fact, Dupuit did ignore this problem, thereby leaving himself open to criticism of this sort.

The finance of public projects usually involves taxation and consequently a redistribution of income. Judgments about such redistribution require an illegitimate interpersonal welfare pronouncement. If the marginal utility of money was the same (and constant) for every individual in the economy, or alternatively, if the distribution of income were of no concern to the economist, it might be concluded that welfare is increased by a transfer, *provided* the increase in consumer surplus (in money terms) exceeds the money amount of the subsidy. Under such conditions a net increase in the money measure of utility is all that is needed. But if some such assumption is not invoked, it does not necessarily follow that welfare is increased by redistributing income from personal consumption to public projects, even if the money measure of the increase in consumer surplus is greater than the money amount of taxation required. Conceivably, such a transfer may involve a diminution in aggregate utility in spite of a net money-measure increase. This would occur if the utility decrease surrounding the tax receipts exceeded the utility increase to the consumers of the public good (i.e., the money measure of the increase in consumer surplus). Bordas (1847,284) correctly pointed out that "The whole question consists in knowing on what side the difference lies."

It is not clear whether Dupuit fully appreciated the problems posed by the distribution-of-income question, but he may have had an inkling of them, because he tried to sidestep the issue from the outset. In his first article, Dupuit (1844, 98–99) maintained that income distribution did not matter with respect to utility calculations, "because the losses and gains [from taxation and public works construction] offset each other." Further, by declaring the matter of income distribution to be the province of the state rather than political economy, Dupuit apparently thought that he had cleared a major obstacle. Bordas was not so easily satisfied, and although he failed to acknowledge that Dupuit even recognized the problem, Bordas was on the verge of unlinking demand curves from utility curves, *and* close to the discovery of a Slutsky-type income-compensation principle.

To understand Bordas's argument in detail, consider his example in which a new manufacturing process reduces the price of stockings from 6 francs to 3 francs. If the consumer has a fixed 'stocking budget,' he will be able to buy eight pairs of stockings at the new price instead of the four pairs previously purchased. But, according to Bordas (1847, 260):

> In order to consume as much as before, the individual must set aside 48 francs for the acquisition of this product, and reduce his other consumptions by 24 francs. Compared to his starting position, it is as though he had an annual gain of 24 francs, or that his income had been increased by this sum. If, instead of consuming 8 pairs of stockings, he only consumed 7 and used the 3 francs left over to buy other things whose prices have not changed, his relative gain [on stockings] would be no more than 21 francs.

In the first part of the above passage, the money expenditures on stockings do not change; consequently, the marginal utility of money expenditures is variant. Letting x represent the quantity of stockings, and M marginal utility, the mathematical expression for the price P of stockings is $P_x = M_x / m_e$. If expenditures on x remain constant when P_x falls, the marginal utility total expenditures remains constant, and the increased purchases of x lead to a decline in M_x. Ironically, Bordas's first example allowed the identification of utility and demand. This may be called Dupuit's case, since the individual's demand curve can be identified with the marginal utility curve for x, and declines in price can be associated with proportional reductions in marginal utility.

Figure 2 illustrates why the demand curve may represent a utility measure in this case. Assume that a consumer of stockings is in initial equilibrium at A. Bordas implied that the money proxy for the welfare gain is given by an amount $\Delta p \Delta q$, which is 24 francs in his example. Note that in Figure 2 this quantity of income could be removed from the consumer after the price decline, so that he or she would move to a new equilibrium at C. The same quantity of stockings (8 pairs), in other words, would be purchased (at points B and C) when the substitution effect is isolated from the income effect. In this case, and in this case only (i.e., when demand elasticity is -1 and income elasticity is 0), the marginal utility curve may be identified with the demand curve. Thus, 24 francs correctly measures the change in welfare, since the whole increase in real income is used to purchase additional stockings, and no part of the real-income increase is devoted to expenditures on other goods. Money expenditures on the good remain constant after the price decline, indicating, of course, that the demand curve is of unit elasticity. Therefore, in this special case, a money measure under the demand curve may represent consumer surplus.

However, it is in discovering the other alternative open to the consumer that Bordas exposed the principal flaw in Dupuit's (and Marshall's) consumer-surplus theory. In the latter part of the above example, the consumer buys only 7 pairs of stockings at the lower price of 3 francs. The analytics of this 'Bordas variation' are presented in Figure 3.

Initially, the consumer is in equilibrium at A'. When the price of stockings is reduced to 3 francs per pair, the budget line of the consumer shifts

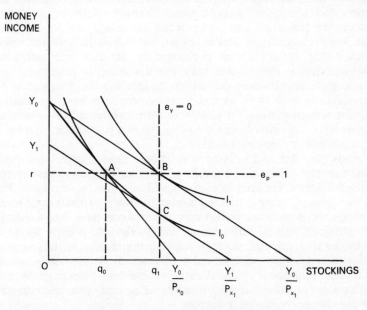

Figure 2. The Dupuit-Marshall case

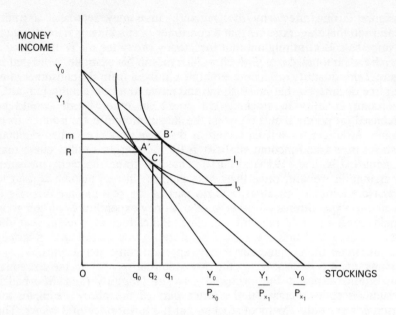

Figure 3. The Bordas variation

outward. The new point of tangency with indifference curve I_1 is at point B', *after* equilibrium is re-established and all effects have been accounted for. The new quantity taken, q_1, can be explained by both income and substitution effects in the following manner. Remove an amount of money income from the consumer equivalent to the increase in real income. The consumer would then choose combination C' of money income and stockings. Thus, owing to the decrease in price alone, the consumer purchases additional stockings in the amount $q_0 q_2$. The simultaneous price decrease/real-income increase, however, caused him to increase his purchases to q_1, and in equilibrium at B', total expenditures on stockings have declined, as shown by the reduction from $Y_0 r$ to $Y_0 m$. Alternatively, expenditures on all other goods have increased from Or to Om. Thus a part of the increase in real income is not realized by stocking gains, but by gains in other goods. Consequently, the demand curve for stockings cannot depict consumer surplus, for several reasons. In the first place, part of the increase in real income resulting from the price decline is spent on other commodities. This is a part of consumer surplus that the demand curve for stockings does not reveal. Moreover, since expenditures on other goods have increased, the marginal utility of money expenditures has decreased vis-à-vis the price decline. Given the formulation, $P_x = M_x / M_e$, the change in the marginal utility of x can no longer be assumed proportionate to the change in the price of x. The 'traditional' demand curve, where both income and substitution effects vary with price and quantity selections, cannot accurately measure the change in consumer surplus.

Although Bordas did not draw any of these implications from his discussion of income effects, it is to his credit that he suggested their existence. He did see that the entire real-income increase caused by a price decrease may not be spent entirely on additional units of the same commodity, and that the additional expenditures would disturb the demands for other goods. Had Bordas carried the argument a step further and shown that such 'income effects' may disturb the marginal utility of income or money expenditures, he would have presented the most convincing theoretical argument to date against the use of demand curves to measure consumer surplus. Although he did not adhere to a marginal utility theory of value, his discussion, as is, could at least be said to presage the theoretical concerns of Slutsky (1915) and Hicks (1934;1943;1946).[2] In any case, Bordas should be considered in the vanguard of the critics of consumers' surplus theory.

Dupuit's defense

The latent promise in Bordas's critique was unfortunately aborted by Dupuit's rejoinder (1849b), which ignored the problem of interpersonal utility comparisons and the pregnant suggestion that price changes may have 'income effects'. Dupuit took aim at easier targets: he castigated Bordas for repeating the errors of his predecessors and for adding new ones of his own invention; he denounced Bordas's multiple and ambiguous use of the term utility; and he rejected his critic's claim that utility is unmeasurable, citing Bordas's lack of proof for the assertion. With a measure of subtle irony, Dupuit enlisted Say as his ally against Bordas, reminding his fellow engineer that Say had also thought utility measurable despite its subjective and variable nature. In Dupuit's judgment, exposing the inaccuracies of Say's measure of utility was obviously one thing, whereas denying the prospect of measuring utility was quite another.

In retrospect, the one issue on which Dupuit capitulated seems less significant than those he ignored, but it nevertheless influenced later treatments of demand, especially Alfred Marshall's. In 1844 Dupuit failed to specify those 'determinants' of demand that serve to fix each individual's 'maximum sacrifice.' Bordas correctly chided Dupuit for this omission, citing the relevance of income, tastes, and the prices of related goods. Dupuit subsequently acknowledged the importance of these determinants, but cavalierly dismissed Bordas's complaint by declaring the *ceteris paribus* assumption implicit in his approach. The evidence for this is contained in Dupuit's (1849b, 184) answer to Bordas's query concerning the maximum sacrifice a consumer of meat would be willing to make (p. 202 above):

> Would this price be the same for all persons? Evidently not. Because not only does this price depend on the wealth of that person, as Mr. Bordas observes, but on his taste for meat, on his hunger, on the prices of other food products and on a *thousand other circumstances*, impossible to enumerate in complete fashion; but all these circumstances do not mean that this price does not exist for each object, each person and at each instant [emphasis supplied].

Whatever victory this provided Dupuit, it was a minor one, because he seems to have missed the flavor of Bordas's criticism, which was that Dupuit's measure of consumer surplus becomes suspect in any concrete case where the determinants of demand do in fact change.

As a whole, Dupuit's rejoinder was disappointing. Has the issue of the marginal utility of money been clarified at this early date, later theorists would have been spared considerable confusion. But Dupuit turned a deaf ear to several of Bordas's criticisms. In the end, Dupuit (1849b, 205) steadfastly affirmed his original position, declaring: "I persist in the ideas on utility that I developed in 1844; I do not wish to change the formula that I gave for the measure of utility."

Anglo-Austrian extensions and continental criticism

Although Dupuit's rejoinder was clearly not the last word on the subject, the issue of consumer surplus made little further impact on economic literature until Léon Walras called attention to Dupuit's measure in 1874. A few years before, unbeknownst to almost everyone, Fleeming Jenkin independently rediscovered Dupuit's basic measure of consumer surplus and used it to determine the incidence of various taxes. The fundamental distinction between Jenkin and Dupuit is that the former eschewed utility considerations in developing a graphical measure of consumer surplus. It cannot be said, therefore, that Jenkin improved on Dupuit's earlier performance by unlinking demand and utility curves. He never linked them in the first place, nor did he think such a linkage held much promise. Jenkin (1871, 229) noted that (Jevons' definition of) utility "admits of no practical measurement"; thus he opted for

> a numerical estimate in money of the value of any given trade, which might be approximately determined by observing the effect of a change of prices on the trade; the [demand and supply] curves could certainly not, in most cases, be determined by experiment, but statistics gathered through a few years would show approximately the steepness of each curve near the market price, ... [which] is the most important information.

Of course a purely statistical measure such as Jenkin proposed does not avoid all of the problems inherent in Dupuit's original concept. Chief among the problems it does not confront is the existence of income and substitution effects. Jenkin might have profited from the Dupuit–Bordas exchange, but he was apparently unaware of prior attempts to develop a welfare measure similar to his own. Ironically, Jenkin, like Dupuit, was a practising engineer.

A 'mature' Walras (1874, 1926 [1954,445]) considered Dupuit's doctrine fallacious, but his reasoning — except in one important respect — was unoriginal. For example, his complaints — that Dupuit neither considered the effect of the utility and price of other goods on the 'maximum sacrifice,' nor understood that the 'consumer's means' also contributed to the determination of this sacrifice — were clearly misplaced in the light of Bordas's comment and Dupuit's subsequent rejoinder.[3]

A second point made by Walras was more significant, however. In the general equilibrium framework which he pioneered, income or 'wealth' is measured in terms of a *numéraire* commodity, one of constant purchasing power. This *numéraire* is also the commodity in terms of which all other prices are expressed. Walras (1874, 1926 [1954,445]) held that "Dupuit failed to see that the maximum pecuniary sacrifice in question depends in part ... on the quantity of the wealth (measured in terms of a *numéraire* which the consumer possesses." In other words, the maximum sacrifice is determined not only by the utilities of all other goods in the consumer's array, but also by the quantity of wealth he holds in terms of the *numéraire* commodity. In the Walrasian system, however, each participant's marginal utility function for each commodity is a function of the quantity of this commodity alone. Since the *demand* curve is determined by the quantity of a consumer's wealth together with other variables (e.g., prices of related goods), Walras (1874, 1926 [1954,446]) indicated Dupuit for his "complete failure to distinguish between utility or want curves on the one hand, and demand curves on the other." At a later date, Walras (1874, 1926 [1954,486]) raised the same objection against the work of Auspitz and Lieben.[4]

Walras's intolerance masked the substantive contribution of the two Austrians. Although their graphical apparatus appears cumbersome by modern comparison, Auspitz and Lieben (1889) nevertheless clearly distinguished between the individual concept of *consumer profit* (Dupuit's money measure of relative utility) and the aggregate notion of *consumer surplus*. They also specified the explicit assumptions necessary to validate the analysis, namely: (i) constancy of the marginal utility of money; (ii) invariance of other prices; and (iii) unchanged tastes. Houghton (1958,57), for one, judged the Austrian contribution superior to Marshall's, concluding: "Many of the difficulties and confusions which gave the concept a bad name during much of the twentieth century might perhaps have been avoided if the Austrian treatment had been given a share of the close attention that was lavished on Marshall's work."

Maffeo Pantaleoni (1889) was more generous than Walras in his praise of Dupuit, even though in the end he apparently accepted Walras's fundamental criticism. The English translation of Pantaleoni's *Manuale di economia pura* contains no fewer than six references to Dupuit's pre-eminence in utility theory, including a detailed reference to the Dupuit–Bordas controversy. Nevertheless, Pantaleoni (1889 [1898,155n.]) credited Walras with the vital distinction between utility curves and demand curves and took note of a further criticism by Pareto (1896) concerning the legitimacy of the constancy-of-the-marginal-utility-of-money assumption employed by Marshall. Moreover, from Walras's correspondence (Jaffé 1965, 2:343–47) it appears that Pantaleoni accepted Walras's critique of Dupuit. Shortly after the publication of his *Manuale*, Pantaleoni wrote to Walras seeking clarification of the difference between Walras and Dupuit on the measure of consumer surplus. Walras responded at length, basing his objection, as in the *Eléments*, on the illegitimacy of identifying utility with demand in a general equilibrium world. There is no record of further correspondence on this issue, and in 1889 Pantaleoni called attention to Walras's 'contribution' without further comment.

Walras's criticisms are important for the consumer-surplus doctrine, although some of them would not have been necessary had he given Dupuit's works a more careful reading. Moreover, Walras's view of the economic system was unparalleled in his time, whereas Dupuit's frame of reference was more modest. Dupuit's theoretic objective was simply to find a standard by which public projects could be evaluated, a problem not inherently suggestive of the interdependencies of the general equilibrium system. The tools that Dupuit developed were partial-equilibrium concepts, and should be evaluated as such. Walras, after all, had very few reservations concerning the measurability of utility, yet he made no progress whatsoever in his *Eléments* toward developing a 'correct' measure of consumer surplus.

These points are not offered as apologetics for Dupuit, because Walras's criticisms were, in point of fact, fertile. But equally important for the history of economic theory is the fact that these criticisms were largely ignored by English economists before Alfred Marshall renewed the controversy late in the nineteenth century. Jevons failed to develop the doctrine even though he became aware of the Dupuit–Bordas controversy in 1879. Marshall may, in fact, have become acquainted with Dupuit through Jevons, although we find the evidence on this point unconvincing.[5]

Marshall and His Critics

The early writings, 1867–1879

Marshall gave 1867 as the year in which he began to study economics, but it is unclear when he first employed diagrams in his analysis or the extent of his debt to Dupuit, if any. By claiming Cournot, von Thünen, and Bentham as his mentors, Marshall (1890 [1961, 2:263]) implicitly denied Dupuit's influence, although Marshall's remarks on predecessors — particularly in the *Principles* — must be regarded with caution. His only reference to Dupuit's priority was curiously dropped from the fourth (1898) and subsequent editions of the *Principles*. Whitaker (1975, 2:240) and Dooley (1983,27) have corroborated Cournot's influence without comment on the deleted footnote. Marshall first read Cournot's work in 1868. He exercised a graphical measure of consumer surplus several years later. The year is uncertain because of problems in dating, but probably in the early 1870s (Whitaker, 2:281–83) Marshall set down an example of consumer surplus that bears an uncanny resemblance to the earlier preoccupation and method of Dupuit. Marshall's notebook entry, abbreviated here, is recorded in Whitaker.

[In Figure 4] when the toll equals *PM* let *OM* tolls be paid on a certain bridge. The amount levied will be greatest when *OM.MP* is greatest (i.e.,

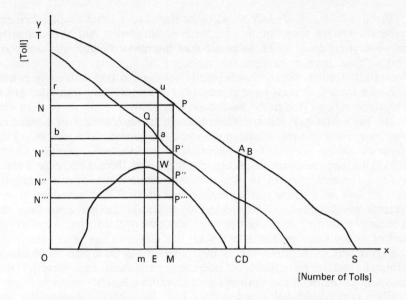

Figure 4. Marshall's early measure of consumer surplus

if a rectangular hyperbola with O_x and O_y as axes touch[es] the curve in *P*, the amount levied will be greatest when the toll equals *PM*). Let the equation to the locus of *P* be $y = f(x)$.

When *OM* carriages pass over the bridge let the damage done by each of them equal *PP'*. Let the equation to the locus of *P'* be $y = f(x) - \phi(x)$, i.e. $PP' = \phi(x)$. A toll should now be levied such as to make $Om \cdot mQ$ a maximum, i.e. *Q* should be chosen so that at *Q* the curve touches one of [the] above series of hyperbolas.

The number of people who would pay a toll *BD*, but not a toll *AC* is equal to *CD* when *CD* is very small; and the loss to those people in consequence of the tolls being greater than they will pay is *ACDB*; thus the whole loss which people who do not pay the toll *PM* undergo is equal to *PMS* [Dupuit's *utilité perdue*]. We may suppose that this loss causes to the state a loss equal in amount to *n* times it, where *n* is less than unity but dependent for its value on *OM*. Make $P'N'N''P'' = n \cdot PMS$. Then the net gain to the state resulting from a toll *PM* is *OMP″ N″*. The toll should be levied so as to make this a maximum ...

The total advantage which people gain from the bridge after deducting the tolls which they pay is *TPN* [Dupuit's relative utility], when the toll is *PM*. As before let the state gain from this an advantage *n* times its amount. Then if $(abOE) + n(Tru)$ is greater than the interest on the bridge's cost (allowing for its being perishable) the bridge ought to be built.

Perhaps Marshall should be taken at his word — that Dupuit had no influence on his formulation of consumer surplus — but the similarity between the (circa) 1872 Marshall and the 1844 Dupuit is worthy of notice. Our opinion is that the question of filiation is not historiographically settled. What is undisputed, however, is that ultimately it was Dupuit's theory of consumer surplus that found its way into Marshall's *Principles*, albeit through the back door.

By 1879 Marshall felt confident enough of his measure of consumer surplus to go into print, although the work in question, *The pure theory of domestic values*, circulated only privately. Here Marshall (Whitaker 1975, 2:213) defined consumer surplus precisely the way Dupuit had before him: as the 'economic measure' of "that which a person would be just willing to pay for any satisfaction rather than go without it." The unveiling of the concept was tentative, yet simultaneously hopeful, Marshall observing: "It is somewhat difficult to discern clearly the nature of this surplus satisfaction and of its economic measure: but when this difficulty has been overcome, the apparatus of diagrams that is here applied will be found to be easily handled, and to be capable of achieving important new results." No mention was made at this time of either Dupuit or Jenkin.

The example Marshall developed in *The pure theory of domestic values* was incorporated fully into the *Principles* eleven years later. Furthermore, Marshall had put the concept through its paces in the earlier work, investigating the effects of taxes and subsidies. In sum, the concept was highly advanced in Marshall's mind more than a decade before the *Principles* appeared. Moreover, he began to surround the analysis with protective assumptions early on, showing alertness to the pitfall of interpersonal utility comparisons. Thus in 1879 Marshall (Whitaker 1975, 2:215) cautioned that the measure of human satisfaction captured by consumer surplus

> ... is indeed a rough measure. For in this as in many other portions of economic reasoning it is necessary, as a first approximation, to treat a pleasure that is worth a shilling to one man as equivalent to a pleasure that is worth a shilling to any other man. Assumptions of this nature have indeed to be made in almost every branch of statistical science. For all social and therefore all economic statistics deal with aggregates of human feelings and affections. It is not possible to add together arithmetically any two pleasures without some more or less arbitrary mode of measuring them. Now the economic measure of the satisfaction which a man derives from any source is ... the amount of money which he will just give in order to obtain it. The economic measures ... may be used in establishing economic laws. But such laws will contain only a portion of the whole truth of the matter to which they relate. And before deductions from these laws can be used for practical purposes, allowance must be made for the fact that a satisfaction which a rich man values as a shilling is slight in comparison with one for which a poor man will be willing to pay a shilling.

The 'Principles' and its aftermath

The enormous popularity of the *Principles*, attested to by its eight editions over a thirty-year span, gave the notion of consumer surplus much more exposure than either Dupuit, Jenkin, or Auspitz and Lieben could provide. Its first statement and illustration in the *Principles*, as noted above, was transferred virtually intact from the privately circulated *Pure theory of domestic values*. Initial criticism, primarily from J.S. Nicholson (1893; 1894) and S.N. Patten (1893a; 1983b) induced Marshall to make minor emendations in the third edition (1895), duly noted by Edgeworth (1895, 67) in his review in the *Economic Journal*.

While Patten's critique has been more or less forgotten, Nicholson's has periodically echoed through the corridors of time. Particular reverberations can be detected in the subsequent criticisms of Hobson (1900), Davenport (1935), Tharakhan (1939), and Knight (1944). Nicholson (1894, 344) objected to the measurement of utility by money, observing: "Price is objective, utility is subjective. The price paid depends on one set of causes and the pleasure derived depends upon a different set." He also questioned the legitimacy of assuming the marginal utility of money to be constant. Nicholson (1894,336) wrote: "A theory of expenditure which neglects the two primary facts that incomes are limited, and that the utility of the money retained increases as it becomes smaller is in my view an unreal theory. It is only applicable to a few careless millionaires." Richard Lieben (1894) quickly refuted Nicholson's charge of unrealism, in the process reaffirming the value of Marshall's *ceteris paribus* assumption.[6] Edgeworth (1894) and Barone (1894) provided additional defenses that Marshall endorsed, but Marshall also took care to make his assumptions more explicit in the third edition of the *Principles*, which recognized Nicholson's criticisms.

A brief aside is in order here on Walras and Pareto. As we saw earlier, Walras (1874 [1926,486]) dismissed the idea of consumer surplus because "the definite integral of the demand function does not represent total utility" and therefore cannot measure consumer surplus. His criticism was blunted considerably by his refusal to acknowledge the legitimacy of a partial-equilibrium framework. Furthermore, Walras's dismissal of the doctrine was undermined by Barone's (1894) proof that a consumer surplus for one individual in isolation could be determined within a Walrasian system and that it could be reconciled with Marshall's treatment (see Dooley 1983,33). Pareto, on the other hand, had demonstrated as early as 1892 that the marginal utility of money balances will only remain theoretically constant provided the composite elasticities of demand for all the other commodities concerned are equal to 1. This constituted a much more serious threat to Marshall's constancy-of-the-marginal-utility-of money balances assumption, but Marshall took no note of it, despite his awareness of Pareto's work at the time he was preparing the third edition of the *Principles*.[7]

Simon Nelson Patten's (1893a; 1893b) critique must have been more provocative because it elicited a direct response from Marshall (1893) and was later cited by Pigou (1903,58) as inspiration for his own thoughts on consumer surplus. Patten's objection to Marshall's measure has a decidedly Austrian flavor. He readily accepted the subjective nature of utility and value, claiming, in fact, that Marshall did not go far enough in this regard: "He seeks to measure objectively and indirectly," said Patten, "what I seek to measure subjectively and directly." Specifically, Patten argued that Marshall's measure of consumer surplus *overstates* consumer welfare because it neglects the interdependence of utilities among commodity "groups," or classes of like goods. The problem Patten identified is analogous (in production space) to the 'imputation' problem that earlier occupied Menger and von Wieser, viz., if we 'remove' successive units of a single item from a commodity bundle and 'observe' the consequent loss of utility, our observations will be untrustworthy because each good in a commodity class depends for part of its utility on the other goods in the class. Adding the separate marginal utilities, therefore, produces an exaggerated sum of welfare. To quote Patten (1893a,422–23), in reference to Marshall:

> Nowhere does he try to add together the consumer's surplus of all the articles consumed by an individual to get the whole consumer's surplus ... If he did he would see an error, for the parts will not add ...[because] he estimates the surplus not from a given situation of the consumer, but from a series of situations representing different stages of supply.

For his part, Marshall (1893,619) complained that Patten misunderstood, or failed to appreciate, the significance of the *ceteris paribus* assumption, a contention in which he was later supported by Pigou (1903). Nevertheless, Patten scored some points in the skirmish, and Marshall (1890 [1961, 1:131–32]) acknowledged Patten's criticism in the third edition of the *Principles*, admitting that "when the total utilities of two commodities which contribute to the same purpose are calculated on this plan, we cannot say that the total utility of the two together is equal to the sum of the total utilities of each separately."

Like Patten, but on far less substantial ground, Henry Cunynghame (1892;1905) thought that Marshall's measure overstated true consumer surplus. Cunynghame asserted that every individual derives smaller increments of utility from each item consumed as the quantity purchased of that article *by others* increases. What this seems to suggest is that Marshall's 'normal' demand is not the appropriate concept to use in measuring consumer surplus. Marshall took no note of this in the *Principles*, but in a letter to Edgeworth of 1892, Marshall (1890 [1961, 2:809]) wrote "It is a free country. I deliberately decided that [Cunynghame's] temporary demand curves (as contrasted with normal demand curves whose shape could be shifted if need be) would not be of any practical use, and that this would encumber the reader and divert his attention from more important things."[8] Edgeworth took note of Cunynghame's argument in a later review, but failed to endorse the notion of successive demand curves as they relate to the consumer-surplus argument.

Pigou (1904; 1910) endorsed and toyed with Marshall's notion of consumer surplus in the ensuing years, supplementing in some respects the analysis found in the *Principles*. From the start, however, Pigou (1903,66) held the view that the measure is inadequate for a summation of total happiness, but is suitable for more modest applications, e.g., demonstrating how a monopolist could appropriate consumer surplus as profits through price discrimination. Indeed, Marshall never asserted any more than this. In his *Economics of Welfare*, Pigou (1920) eschewed even the partial-equilibrium notion of consumer surplus, his attention having shifted to aggregate notions of economic welfare. Most other theoreticians of the interwar period did not get past the problem of the marginal utility of money, and Marshall left the concept essentially unchanged from the third through eighth editions of his *Principles*.

The interwar years

Marshall was able to successfully defend his notion of consumer surplus against most critics because he hedged his theory all around with protective assumptions. His *ceteris paribus* mechanism included money income, the tastes and preferences of purchasers, and the prices of all other goods. Despite his awareness of the inherent difficulties of the concept, however, Marshall shared Dupuit's beliefs in the measurability of utility and the tendency of differences in income distribution to cancel out in the aggregate. Initially Marshall (1890 [1961, 1:131]) had great hope for consumer surplus as a tool of practical import. But in his later years he confessed to his nephew Claude Guillebaud (1971,6) that the concept was a major disappointment in his life because it was incapable of being quantified in a meaningful way. He reluctantly concluded that it was a theoretical rather than a practical tool in the economist's workbox.[9]

Despite its retention through eight editions of the *Principles*, theoretical interest in consumer surplus waned after the turn of the century. Perhaps this was because Marshall's two most able students, Pigou and Keynes, failed to take much interest in the idea. Minor skirmishes and/or attempts to improve the doctrine appeared during the interwar years, but without any real effect on Marshall's theory. A wartime attempt by P.G. Wright (1917) to analyze the principle of consumer surplus under different income distributions drew little or no attention. Shortly after the war, Edwin Cannan (1924) issued a broadside against the doctrine which drew prompt but uninspired rebuttal by D.H. Macgregor (1924) and by A.L. Bowley (1924). Cannan's view was probably indicative of a general feeling among economists that the doctrine had slipped beyond repair. Winch (1965,401) has aptly pinpointed the reasons for the collective disenchantment:

> Use of the Marshallian triangle when the MUM [marginal utility of money] is not constant involves measurement in money, the marginal utility of which changes in the course of measurement. While there are pitfalls in using units of measurement, money, which do not have a constant relationship to the thing being measured, utility, there must also

be objections to using any money of constant utility to measure changes in a case where the utility of money is not in fact constant.

In other words, the most serious problem with the money measure of consumer surplus goes back to the early recognition by Bordas that the presence of an 'income effect' (i.e., changing marginal utility of money), tends to misstate the losses and/or gains associated with price changes. Further progress required either a change in the demand curve to account for variability in the utility of money or alternatively a change in the definition of consumer surplus to fit the Marshallian demand curve. After a further hiatus, neoclassical economic theory made tentative advances in both directions.

Hicks and His Critics

Renascence and rehabilitation

A major theoretic development of the interwar years was the careful and systematic attempt by J.R. Hicks and R.G.D. Allen (1934) to establish a more 'objective' theory of value, which they accomplished by reintroducing concepts originated many years earlier by Edgeworth and Pareto. Hicks and Allen framed their analysis independently of rigid cardinality, proving all of the familiar properties of demand curves by using indifference curves and marginal rates of substitution, instead. In the process, they translated Marshall's marginal utility of money into "exactly definable terms," to wit:

> If the marginal utility of commodity Y is constant, the marginal rate of substitution between X and Y must depend on X only. If the quantity of X is given, the marginal rate of substitution (or the slope of the indifference curve) is given, too; the tangents to the indifference curves at all points with the same abscissa must be parallel ... and the income elasticity of demand for X must be zero.

Hicks followed this early effort with a series of papers in the 1940s reaffirming the value of consumer surplus and amending Marshall's demand curve measure to accommodate it.[10] The problem Hicks had to overcome is that Marshall's demand curve does not accurately measure consumer surplus in cases where a price change induces substantial income effects. Hicks (1941,109) faced two alternatives: either abandon the demand curve altogether in favor of indifference curves; or "adjust the ordinary demand curve so as to allow for the effects of the changes in real income." He chose the latter.

Hicks's rehabilitation of consumer surplus rests on the following assumptions: (i) that the good demanded is 'normal' with respect to changes in income; (ii) that the prices of other consumer goods remain constant during the course of measurement; and (iii) that the individual possessing a given amount of money income faces given market prices for $n - 1$ commodities to which he must confine his purchases. Given these assumptions,[11] the individual will allocate his income in a particular manner. If a new commodity is introduced with only one unit available, the individual will decide whether to purchase this nth commodity depending on its price. Hicks (1943,31) maintained that under these conditions there will be some price which serves to separate the high prices, at which the consumer will not purchase, from the low prices at which he is just on the verge of purchasing. He called this price the *marginal valuation* of the unit, recognizing that it is the same thing as Marshall's "marginal utility in terms of money."

The unit will be purchased if the actual price is less than the marginal valuation. The marginal valuations of all units can be determined *once the market price is given.* In Figure 5, for example, AV represents a marginal valuation curve corresponding to market price OH. At price OH, quantity HP will be purchased, since all units of the good less than quantity HP have marginal valuations greater than OH. Point P is found by extending a horizontal from price OH to the marginal valuation curve. A new marginal valuational curve, Av, would correspond to a lower price, Oh. In the case of a normal good (as in Figure 5), the increase in real income occasioned by the price decrease will shift the new marginal valuation curve Av to the right and above the one corresponding to the higher price OH. Other things being equal, an increase in income will raise the marginal valuation of any given quantity of the good. This is the Hicksian "income effect," which he identified with the movements from one curve to the other. By contrast, the substitution effect of a price fall consists of movements *along* the marginal valuation curves. Finally, the ordinary Marshallian demand curve can be determined by tracing the equilibrium points, e.g., the dotted

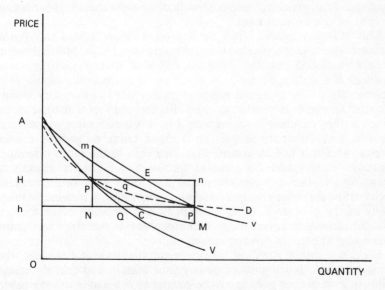

Figure 5. The Hicksian reconstruction

line APpD. It is clear that when the income effect is of little significance the Marshallian curve approaches the marginal valuation curves. But when this is not the case, Hicks provides alternative measures for consumer surplus.

Compensating and equivalent variations

When the marginal utility of money is allowed to change, or identically, when there is an income effect, the gain to the consumer from a price fall can be viewed in several ways, some of which have already been discussed in connection with the Bordas example (see Figure 3). At the core of Hicks's macro-oriented compensation principle is the development of different 'variations' as measures of consumer surplus. Hicks inquired into the amount of money income which, taken from the consumer at the new price Oh, would leave him/her no better off than he/she was at the former price OH. This amount is called a *price compensating variation*, and it is obtained (with reference to Figure 5) in the following fashion: allow the consumer to purchase HP units at price OH and, for the following unit, lower price only as far as necessary for him to purchase it. The curve HPC can be traced out by continuing in this manner. At C on this curve, the consumer is neither better nor worse off than at point P. The segment PC lies above marginal valuation curve PV, since the consumer is better off than if he/she were forced to pay OH for hC units. But segment PC is below Marshallian segment Pp because the consumer is in a worse position than if he/she were allowed to purchase *all* these units at Oh, even though the *marginal* unit can be purchased at that price. At C the consumer is in the same position as if he/she had been allowed to purchase all the units at price Oh, but he/she has been forced to part with an amount of income equal to HPCh, which is, simultaneously, the compensating variation and a measure of consumer surplus.

This Hicksian measure can be conveniently contrasted to Marshall's measure which, geometrically, is equal to the area HPph. Marshall's money measure assumed that the marginal utility of money was the same at positions P and at p, a condition which could not possibly obtain with an income effect. The marginal utility of money does in fact vary along the Marshallian curve. A positive income effect would mean that the first cent added to the consumer's income would have a higher marginal utility than the last cent. In order to get the demand curve to express consumer surplus, Marshall had to assume that each cent in the money measure of consumer surplus added a constant amount to total utility. Hicks's compensating variation assumes, more properly, that with an income effect, each cent in the money measure added a diminishing increment to the total utility of the consumer. Hicks's compensating variation takes account of this diminishing marginal utility of money and is therefore less than the area under Marshall's demand curve.

Hicks's "rehabilitation" of consumer surplus made it clear that what is being measured is amounts of money (not utility), and that the marginal utility of money does not have to be constant for the idea to have theoretic and practical value. Nevertheless, certain ambiguities in Hicks's measure were quickly identified. H.W. Robinson (1939) and A. Kozlick (1941) both argued that Hicks's measure of consumer surplus produces different results *ex ante* than it does *ex post*, a criticism later answered by Mishan (1947). A more durable criticism was made by Henderson (1941), who argued that Hicks's claim notwithstanding, the compensating variation is not the same as Marshall's consumer surplus. Henderson maintained that by Hicks's analysis, there existed four alternative expressions of consumer surplus, depending on the particular problem confronted. Hicks (1943) conceded Henderson's point and shortly thereafter expounded the notions of price (and quantity) *equivalent* variation as well as price (and quantity) *compensating* variations.

Hicks's "price equivalent variation" can be set forth in much the same terms as used to explain the compensating variation. Consider Figure 5 once again. Hicks asked the question, "What amount of money income would be required, in the absence of the price decrease, to raise the individual to the level of satisfaction attained at p?" His method requires asking the consumer, starting at p, to state the maximum price that would induce him to diminish his holdings of the commodity, *seriatim.* The price equivalent variation, area HEph, is yet another measure of consumer surplus. At point E the consumer is no worse off than at p, but he is consuming at price OH. The Hicksian equivalent variation is a larger money sum than Marshall's money measure under the demand curve because the value of money in terms of goods is different in the two situations P and p. The equivalent variation takes account of the increased level of satisfaction attained at p. In order to maintain this new level of satisfaction at price OH, the sum of money given to the consumer would have to be greater than the money amount under the Marshallian curve, since the marginal utility of money would have declined at p.

Realism and relevance

In the wake of the Hicks–Allen refinements in value theory and the Hicks–Henderson extensions of consumer surplus, Frank Knight (1944) issued a methodological broadside against the "realism and relevance" of the new theoretic developments. Of concern here are the particular arguments, on consumer surplus, which constitute a small part of Knight's broader challenge. Knight (1944,311) derogated the practical significance of the Marshallian concept, declaring it (merely) "useful in bringing out the relations between the individual demand curve and indifference curves, with which it is much confused ...[and] also useful for the pure theory of monopoly, in connection with perfectly classified monopoly price." On two occasions in the argument, Knight (1944,313n.,318n.) sided with J.S. Nicholson against Marshall, and in the end he denied any economic meaning whatsoever to the area under a demand curve. Knight further attacked the Hicks–Henderson analysis, offering in its place a more 'correct' measure of consumer surplus based on the intricate notion of a *series* of "indifference-combinations" curves for quantities of money and good X.

Knight's critique was countered by R.L. Bishop (1946), who attacked

Knight's analytics, denounced his version of consumer's surplus as "incongruous," and declared an unambiguous measure of consumer surplus to be a mere "will-o'-the-wisp." Bishop cataloged *seven* measures of consumer surplus then extant in economic literature (including Knight's), asserting (as Henderson had earlier for a smaller number of concepts) that the appropriate definition "in any one connection depends upon the purpose at hand."

Hicks (1946,68n.) ignored Knight's criticism, but recognized Bishop's refutation, apparently finding vindication therein for most of his earlier elaborations on the different measures of consumer surplus. Subsequently, Knight's critique was reconsidered, and further discredited, by Mishan (1947) and by Pfouts (1953). Mishan (1947,33) narrowed the list of 'acceptable' measures of consumer surplus from four to two (the compensating and equivalent variations)[12] and explained why no further reduction could be achieved:

> The two different measures arise simply from the fact of the diminishing marginal utility of money. It is a distinction between what the consumer would *pay* (in order to get the lower price, or in order to avoid a higher price), and what the consumer must *be paid* (to induce him to forego the lower price, or to accept a higher price). For what he would pay or pays is to be considered a *subtraction* from his money income; what he must be paid or is actually paid an *addition* to his money income ... the difference between the two situations (the difference in utility) is unequivocal, but the sum of money required to express this difference is larger for an addition to an individual's money income than for a subtraction from it.

The major American contribution of the period came not from Knight, whose concept of consumer surplus was roundly rejected, but from Harold Hotelling (1938), who drew freely from Dupuit's theoretic wellspring. Hotelling developed a line integral representation of consumer surplus consistent with Dupuit's definition and with the example from Marshall's *Principles.* His consumer surplus is a collective notion, tied to a market demand curve; but while it is an index of total utility, it does not imply that utility is measurable. Since the prospects of obtaining specific utility indicators empirically are not promising, this constitutes a distinct advantage over the Dupuit–Marshall measure. Most welfare theorists lined up behind Hicks rather than Hotelling, however, and it was the Hicksian synthesis of the welfare economics of Marshall, Pigou, and Pareto that carried the day. By 1950 the theory of consumer surplus had reached its third major plateau — the first peak having been scaled by Dupuit, the second by Marshall, and the third by Hicks.

Epilogue: The Modern Era

Mapping the theoretical terrain

Hicks's 'improvement' of the Marshallian measure was genuine in the sense that it rendered consumer surplus theoretically correct, but it was also the catalyst for a proliferation of consumer surplus measures and a new debate over the appropriateness or 'exactness' of one measure versus another. As a consequence, theoretical welfare economics in the modern period is in considerable disarray. On the one hand, the concept of consumer surplus is roundly condemned by a small group of economists, most notably Samuelson (1942; 1947), Little (1950), and Graaff (1957). On the other hand, it is favored by many microeconomists, especially those who accept the validity of partial-equilibrium analysis. Its defenders, however, are nowhere near a consensus on what constitutes the 'correct' welfare measure. The issue, as it has evolved historically, is intricate and complex.

One point of contention concerns what Marshall 'really meant' by consumer surplus. We have seen that Marshall introduced the subject by defining consumer surplus in the same fashion as Dupuit, that is, as an "all or nothing" proposition. Unfortunately, Marshall failed to distinguish this definition from two other concepts discussed in his *Principles*: (a) the area under a commodity demand curve minus expenditures on that commodity, and (b) the area under the utility curve for a good less marginal utility times the quantity consumed. After Hicks, the question arose as to whether Marshall had in mind a 'compensated' or an 'uncompensated' demand curve. Friedman (1949) defends the former interpretation, arguing that Marshall constructed his demand schedule on the assumption that the consumer's level of satisfaction was being held constant.

Whether or not Friedman's interpretation is correct, it is clear that the compensating variation has been pushed to the forefront of discussions on applied welfare economics. Nevertheless, this does not imply that all economists have jumped on the Hicksian bandwagon. In particular, Winch (1965) has rejected Hicks's rehabilitation in favor of a return to Marshall's surplus. The latter's major appeal, according to Winch, is that it is the only measure that can be taken directly from the demand curve. Moreover, its limitations, argues Winch, are no worse than the limitations of Hicks's measures. Furthermore, Marshall's measure has the specific advantage of being additive, whereas Hicks's measures are not.

Be that as it may, Foster and Neuburger (1974) caution that considerable care must be exercised to ensure the additivity of Marshall's measure once the analysis extends beyond the single-good partial-equilibrium case. It has been shown that in the case of simultaneous, multiple price changes, the Marshallian surplus is no longer uniquely defined, and that alternative evaluations of a given welfare change depend on the assumed order of price adjustments between the terminal situations being compared. This *path-dependence problem* was first recognized by Hotelling (1938) and subsequently considered by Mohring (1971), Harberger (1971), Silberberg (1972), Glaister (1974), and Turvey (1974) and in synthetic fashion by

Burns (1977). It has come to be a major obstacle to the further development of the consumer surplus concept.

Michael Burns (1973) would circumvent the path-dependency problem by assuming *a priori* that a specific simultaneous price adjustment process exists. Like Winch, he favors retention of the Marshallian measure. Mohring (1971) and Silberberg (1972) take the opposite position that Marshallian measures should be abandoned in favor of the path-independent compensating or equivalent variations. More recently, Neil Bruce (1977) has denied the operationality of such alternatives and has suggested the economic theory of index numbers as a way of making the path-dependency problem tractable. Bruce Dahlby (1977) has attempted a reconciliation of sorts by setting out the conditions under which the Marshallian measure is path-independent and those conditions under which it is not. His work falls between the efforts of Willig (1976) and Seade (1978) to identify those circumstances in which the Marshallian measure closely approximates Hicks's compensating and equivalent variations. But Hausman (1981) has pointed out certain shortcomings in Willig's approach. At bottom is the fact that Marshall's measure is based on information about uncompensated (market) demand curves whereas Hicks's measures require information on compensated demand functions. In principle it is possible to estimate the latter, but in reality the only data usually available relate to the observable market demand functions.

While the path-dependency problem has been a major recent obstacle to the further advance of the consumer surplus concept, it is only part of a broader concern for the restrictions on preferences that must be specified for some measure of consumer surplus to serve as an exact welfare indicator. This larger concern involves, in addition to the path-dependency problem, the literature on the constancy of the marginal utility of income, the cross-elasticities of demand among products, and the homotheticity of preferences. As such, it takes us beyond the narrow confines of this study.

Obviously, the battle lines are still being drawn on many aspects of consumer surplus analysis. Besides the choice between Marshall and Hicks on the 'appropriate' surplus measure, there is further indecision among the 'Hicksians' as to which of the variations provides an exact welfare indicator. Recently, Chipman and Moore (1980) have analyzed the conditions under which the compensating variation can be validly used as a generalized welfare measure, but McKenzie and Pearce (1982) insist that the equivalent variation (not the compensating variation) is the only directly observable, exact welfare indicator.

Conclusion

Despite its inherent ambiguities and difficulties, the Dupuit–Marshall concept of consumer surplus continues to offer some usefulness as a guide to practical policy issues, especially in instances where the Hicksian compensation principle is inapplicable, or the data problems insurmountable. As such it represents the economist's response to the practical imperative of approximating a measure of 'maximum satisfaction' in circumstances where a truly scientific measure is impossible.

When the concept of consumer surplus is generalized to an aggregate welfare measure, it should be noted that its usefulness and its inherent problems are no greater and no less than those involved in measuring changes in national income. Indeed, Harberger (1971), McCloskey (1982, 225–29) and others have demonstrated that changes in national income are the same as changes in aggregate consumer surplus. Estimating the bounds of a change in either requires the application of price indices. Not surprisingly, therefore, since Hicks (1942), the theory of index numbers and the theory of consumer surplus have logically merged.

Harberger and McCloskey argue that because the measure of consumer surplus is an index-number problem, it therefore does not require the usual assumption concerning the constancy of the marginal utility of income. What they do not seem to recognize is that the usual assumption regarding constancy of the marginal utility of income itself implies that some index has been chosen, at least for the individual consumer. The assumption implies that if income effects *are* significant, the Marshallian demand curve must be adjusted in order to validly register the individual's consumer surplus. In other words, it is precisely because income effects attend price change, that index numbers are customarily invoked. Yet many different measure may obtain, depending on the index chosen to measure the attendant change. Insofar as the constancy of the marginal utility of income assumption implies that a particular index has been chosen, it would appear that Harberger–McCloskey offer a distinction without a difference. Nevertheless, the inherent dependence of consumer's and consumers' surplus measures on index numbers is an indisputable fact, verified by the historical record.

In the final analysis, the history of the concept of consumer surplus reveals a theoretical proposition beset on all sides by challenges to its usefulness and desirability. It has been praised and reviled, expanded and contracted, tinkered with, rehabilitated, 'improved', and above all *used* over and over again. At the same time, its indispensability has been constantly questioned or denied. As Arvidsson (1974,286) has aptly noted, referring only to its Marshallian (not its French) roots:

> It is as though consumers' surplus not only has to carry the burden of a Victorian past but also is subjected to lingering Victorian double standards in quite the same way as the classical object of those double standards; in other words, the concept is generally used but held in low esteem by respectable people.

Much of the rejection of the concept itself stems from a desire to make economics something it is not and probably never will be: a 'pure' science akin to physics. Specifically, the attempt to 'objectivize' economics into a science via the theory of revealed preference has been largely unsuccessful. In its defense, Bergson (1975,43) has argued that the revealed-preference approach may be more accurate in cases where the subject of analysis is the *individual* household, or a collection of households with identical tastes. But when tastes differ, income redistribution occurs, or aggregate measures of consumer surplus are required, Samuelson's revealed preference measure is, for all practical purposes, computationally impossible. Thus, Bergson's (1980) recent attempt to integrate consumer surplus with the social welfare function in a general equilibrium context ignores the revealed preference approach.

The very durability of consumer surplus, not to mention its recent extension into other microeconomic areas such as option demand (Lindsay 1969; Byerlee 1971; Cichetti and Freeman 1971; Schmalensee 1972, 1975; Bohm 1975) and 'full-price' demand (Lyon 1978), belies Samuelson's (1947,195) judgment that "the concept is of [mere] historical and doctrinal interest, with a limited appeal as a purely mathematical puzzle." On the contrary, the idea invented by Dupuit over a century ago is of continuing importance and concern to economists. A doctrine possessed of such a long and interesting history, not to mention its continuous use, will not easily retire to the historical scrapheap of 'superfluous' theories, notwithstanding Samuelson's (1947,195ff.) judgment that it belongs there. Nor will it likely be cast aside as a "totally useless theoretical toy" (Little 1950,175). Despite a difficult birth, a troublesome adolescence, and an uncertain adulthood, the Dupuit–Marshall theory of consumer surplus has survived and prospered through periodic trials of criticism and doubt. Any idea which brings the premier economic aim of 'maximum satisfaction' into full focus, especially within the context of general demand theory, most assuredly has a future, however turbulent, in the annals of economic theory and practice.

We would like to acknowledge the helpful suggestions of William Stober, Denis O'Brien, Randall Holcombe, and two anonymous referees of this journal. The authors alone are responsible for any errors that remain.

Bibliography, in Chronological Order

1838. Cournot, A.A. *Researches Into the Mathematical Principles of the Theory of Wealth*, translated by N.T. Bacon. New York, 1897.

1844. Dupuit, Jules. "On the Measurement of the Utility of Public Works," translated by R.H. Barback, *International Economic Papers*, no. 2 (1952), pp. 83–110.

1847. Bordas, Louis. "De la mesure de l'utilité des travaux publics." *Annales des Ponts et Chaussées*, 2d ser., 13:249–284.

1849a. Dupuit, Jules. "On Tolls and Transport Charges," translated by E. Henderson. *International Economic Papers*, no. 11 (1962), pp. 7–31.

1849b. Dupuit, Jules. "De l'influence des péages sur l'utilité des voies de communication." *Annales des Ponts et Chaussées*. Mémoires et Documents, 2d ser., 7:170–248.

1853. Dupuit, Jules. "De l'utilité et sa mesure – de l'utilité publique." *Journal des Economistes*, 36:1–27.

1871. Jenkin, Fleeming. "On the Principles Which Regulate the Incidence of Taxes," in Musgrave, R.A., and Shoup, C.S. (eds), *Readings in the Economics of Taxation*. Homewood, Ill., 1959.

1874. [1926] Walras, Léon. *Elements of Pure Economics*, 4th ed., translated by W. Jaffé. London, 1954.

1879. [1975] Marshall, Alfred. *The Pure Theory of Domestic Values.* In Whitaker 1975, 2:181–236.

1889. Auspitz, R., and Lieben, R. *Untersuchungen über die Theorie des Preises.* Leipzig.

1889. [1898] Pantaleoni, Maffeo. *Pure Economics,* translated by T.B. Bruce. London.

1890. [1961]. Marshall, Alfred. *Principles of Economics,* 2 vols. Ninth variorum edition, ed. C.W. Guillebaud. London.

1892. Cunynghame, Henry. "Some Improvements in Simple Geometrical Methods of Treating Exchange Value, Monopoly and Rent." *Economic Journal,* 2:35–52.

1892. Fisher, Irving. *Mathematical Investigations in the Theory of Value and Prices.* New York, 1965.

1893. Nicholson, J.S. *Principles of Political Economy,* 3 vols. London.

1893a. Patten, S.N. "Cost and Utility." *Annals of the American Academy of Political and Social Science,* 3:409–428.

1893b. Patten, S.N. "Cost and Expense." *Annals of the American Academy of Political and Social Science,* 3:703–735.

1893. Marshall, Alfred. "Consumer's Surplus." *Annals of the American Academy of Political and Social Science,* 3:618–621.

1894a. Barone, Enrico. "A proposito delle indagini del Fisher." *Giornale degli Economisti,* 2d ser., 8:413–439.

1894b. Barone, Enrico. "Sulla 'consumers' rent.'" *Giornale degli Economisti,* 2d ser., 9:211–224.

1894. Edgeworth, F.Y. "Professor J.S. Nicholson on 'Consumer's Rent.'" *Economic Journal,* 4:151–158.

1894. Nicholson, J.S. "The Measurement of Utility by Money." *Economic Journal,* 4:342–347.

1894. Lieben, Richard. "On Consumer's Rent." *Economic Journal,* 4:716–719.

1895. Edgeworth, F.Y. Review of Marshall's *Principles of Economics,* 3d ed. In *Papers Relating to Political Economy,* 3:64–69. London, 1925.

1895. Sanger, C.P. "Recent Contributions to Mathematical Economics," *Economic Journal,* 5:113–128.

1896. Pareto, Vilfredo. *Cours d'économie politique.* Lausanne.

1900. Hobson, J.A. *The Economics of Distribution.* New York.

1903. Nicholson, J.S. *Elements of Political Economy.* London.

1903. Pigou, A.C. "Some Remarks on Utility." *Economic Journal,* 13:58–68.

1904. Pigou, A.C. "Monopoly and Consumers' Surplus." *Economic Journal,* 14:388–394.

1905. Cunynghame, Henry. *A Geometrical Political Economy.* Oxford.

1910. Pigou, A.C. "Producers' and Consumers' Surplus." *Economic Journal,* 20:358–370.

1915. Slutsky, E.E. "On the Theory of the Budget of the Consumer," translated by O. Ragusa. Reprinted in Stigler, G.J., and Boulding, K.E., *Readings in Price Theory.* Homewood, Ill., 1952.

1917. Wright, P.G. "Total Utility and Consumers' Surplus Under Varying Conditions of the Distribution of Income." *Quarterly Journal of Economics,* 31:307–318.

1920. Pigou, A.C. *Economics of Welfare.* London.

1924. Cannan, Edwin. "Total Utility and Consumer's Surplus." *Economica,* 4:21–26.

1924. Macgregor, D.H. "Consumer's Surplus: A Reply." *Economica,* 4:131–134.

1924. Bowley, A.L. "Does Mathematical Analysis Explain?" *Economica,* 4:135–139.

1924. Young, A.A. "Marshall on Consumers' Surplus in International Trade." *Quarterly Journal of Economics,* 39:144–150.

1925. Young, A.A. "Consumers' Surplus in International Trade: A Supplementary Note." *Quarterly Journal of Economics,* 39:498–499.

1926. Mayer, Joseph. "Consumer's Surplus." *American Economic Review,* 16:77–80.

1927. Miller, H.E. "Utility Curves, Total Utility, and Consumer's Surplus." *Quarterly Journal of Economics,* 41:292–316.

1928. Meriam, R.S. "Supply Curves and Maximum Satisfaction." *Quarterly Journal of Economics,* 42:169–198.

1928. Terborgh, G.W. "Psychic Income, Total Utility, and Consumer's Surplus." *American Economic Review,* 18:75–79.

1934. Hicks, J.R., and Allen, R.G.D. "A Reconsideration of the Theory of Value." *Econom-

ica, 1:52–76; 196–219.

1935. Davenport, H.J. *The Economics of Alfred Marshall*, Ithaca, N.Y.

1937.Kadir, A.B.A. "A Note on the Theory of Consumer's Surplus." *Indian Journal of Economics*, 18:41–44.

1939. Hicks, J.R. *Value and Capital*. London [2d ed., 1946].

1939. Robinson, H.W. "Consumer's Surplus and Taxation: Ex Ante or Ex Post?" *South African Journal of Economics*, 7:270–280.

1939. Tharakhan, K.J.M. "The Theory of Consumer's Surplus: A Defence." *Indian Journal of Economics*, 19:413–420.

1939. Gopal, M.H. "Consumer's Surplus: A Reply." *Indian Journal of Economics*, 20:161–172.

1941. Tharakhan, K.J.M. "Consumer's Surplus: A Rejoinder." *Indian Journal of Economics*, 21:307–319.

1941. Hicks, J.R. "The Rehabilitation of Consumer's Surplus." *Review of Economic Studies*, 8:108–116.

1941. Henderson, A.M. "Consumer's Surplus and the Compensating Variation." *Review of Economic Studies*, 8:117–121.

1941. Kozlick, Adolf. "A Note on Consumer's Surplus." *Journal of Political Economy*, 49:754–762.

1942. Hicks, J.R. "Consumer's Surplus and Index-Numbers." *Review of Economic Studies*, 9:126–137.

1942. Samuelson, P.A. "Constancy of the Marginal Utility of Income." In O. Lange, et al. (eds), *Studies in Mathematical Economics and Econometrics*. Chicago.

1943. Hicks, J.R. "The Four Consumer's Surpluses." *Review of Economic Studies*, 11:31–41.

1943. Bishop, R.L. "Consumer's Surplus and Cardinal Utility." *Quarterly Journal of Economics*, 57:421–429.

1944. Knight, F.H. "Realism and Relevance in the Theory of Demand." *Journal of Political Economy*, 52:289–318.

1945. Boulding, K.E. "The Concept of Economic Surplus." *American Economic Review*, 35:851–869.

1946. Hicks, J.R. "The Generalised Theory of Consumer's Surplus." *Review of Economic Studies*, 13:68–74.

1946. Bishop, R.L. "Professor Knight and the Theory of Demand." *Journal of Political Economy*, 54:141–169.

1947. Mishan, E.J. "Realism and Relevance in Consumer's Surplus." *Review of Economic Studies*, 15:27–33.

1947. Samuelson, P.A. *Foundations of Economic Analysis*. Cambridge: Harvard University Press.

1948. Morgan, J.N. "The Measurement of Gains and Losses." *Quarterly Journal of Economics*, 62:287–308.

1949. Friedman, Milton. "The Marshallian Demand Curve." *Journal of Political Economy*, 57:463–495.

1950. Little, I.M.D. *A Critique of Welfare Economics*. Oxford: Oxford University Press.

1953. Ichimura, S. "A Note on the Concepts of Consumer's Surplus." *Econometrica*, 21:484–485.

1953. Pfouts, R.W. "A Critique of Some Recent Contributions to the Theory of Consumers' Surplus." *Southern Economic Journal*, 19:315–333.

1956. Hicks, J.R. *A Revision of Demand Theory*. Oxford: Oxford University Press.

1957. Graaff, J. de v. *Theoretical Welfare Economics*. Cambridge: Cambridge University Press.

1958. Houghton, R.W. "A Note on the Early History of Consumer's Surplus." *Economica*, N.S., 25: 49–57.

1960. Mishan, E.J. "A Survey of Welfare Economics, 1939–1959." *Economic Journal*, 70:197–256.

1963. Lerner, A.P. "Consumer's Surplus and Micro-Macro." *Journal of Political Economy*, 71:76–81.

1963. Patinkin, Don. "Demand Curves and Consumer's Surplus." In C. Christ, et al. (eds), *Measurement in Economics*. Stanford, Calif.

1965. Jaffé, William (ed.). *Correspondence of Léon Walras and Related Papers*, 3 vols. Amsterdam.

1965. Winch, D.M. "Consumer's Surplus and the Compensation Principle." *American Economic Review*, 55:395–423.

1966. Ahmed, Mohiuddin. "The Development of the Concept of Consumers' Surplus in Economic Theory and Policy." *Indian Economic Journal*, 13:647–666.

1966. Tipping, D.G. "Consumers' Surplus in Public Enterprise." *Manchester School of Economic and Social Studies*, 34: 221–245.

1969. Lindsay, C.M. "Option Demand and Consumer's Surplus." *Quarterly Journal of Economics*, 83:344–346.

1970. Piron, Robert. "Consumer's Surplus and Micro-Macro: Comment." *Journal of Political Economy*, 78:133–135.

1970. Lerner, A.P. "Consumer's Surplus and Micro-Macro: Reply." *Journal of Political Economy*, 78:135–136.

1970. Piron, Robert. "Consumer's Surplus and Micro-Macro: Rejoinder.' *Journal of Political Economy*, 78:137.

1970. Johnson, H.G. "Consumer's Surplus and Micro-Macro: Comment." *Journal of Political Economy*, 78:137–138.

1970. Lerner, A.P. "Consumer's Surplus and Micro-Macro: Methodological Epilogue." *Journal of Political Economy*, 78:138–139.

1971. Byerlee, D.R. "Option Demand and Consumer's Surplus: Comment." *Quarterly Journal of Economics*, 85:523–527.

1971. Cichetti, C.J., and Freeman, A.M. III. "Option Demand and Consumer Surplus: Further Comment." *Quarterly Journal of Economics*, 85:528–539.

1971. Currie, J.M., Murphy, J.A., and Schmitz, A. "The Concept of Economic Surplus and Its Use in Economic Analysis." *Economic Journal*, 81:741–799.

1971. Guillebaud, C.W. "Some Personal Reminiscences of Alfred Marshall." *History of Political Economy*, 3:1–8.

1971. Harberger, A.C. "Three Basic Postulates for Applied Welfare Economics: An Interpretive Essay." *Journal of Economic Literature*, 9:785–797.

1971. Mohring, Herbert. "Alternative Welfare Gains and Loss Measures." *Western Economic Journal*, 9:359–368.

1971. Schmalensee, Richard. "Consumer's Surplus and Producer's Goods." *American Economic Review*, 61:682–687.

1972. Jaffé, William. "Leon Walras's Role in the 'Marginal Revolution' of the 1870's." *History of Political Economy*, 4:379–405.

1972. Schmalensee, Richard. "Option Demand and Consumer's Surplus: Valuing Price Changes Under Uncertainty." *American Economic Review*, 62:813–824.

1972. Silberberg, Eugene. "Duality and the Many Consumer's Surpluses." *American Economic Review*, 62:942–952.

1973. Burns, M.E. "A Note on the Concept and Measure of Consumer's Surplus." *American Economic Review*, 63:335–344.

1973. Reaume, D.M. "Cost-Benefit Techniques and Consumer Surplus: A Clarificatory Analysis." *Public Finance*, 28:196–211.

1974. Arvidsson, Guy. "On Consumer's Surplus and Allied Concepts, Especially in Formulations of the Pareto Criterion." *Swedish Journal of Economics*, 76:285–307.

1974. Foster, C.D., and Neuburger, H.L.I. "The Ambiguity of the Consumer's Surplus Measure of Welfare Change." *Oxford Economic Papers*, 26:66–77.

1974. Glaister, Stephen. "Generalised Consumer Surplus and Public Transport Pricing." *Economic Journal*, 84:849–867.

1974. Soeria-Atmadja. "A Note on the Treatment of Consumer's Surplus with Related Goods." *Swedish Journal of Economics*, 76:332–347.

1974. Turvey, Ralph. "How to Judge When Price Changes Will Improve Resource Allocation." *Economic Journal*, 84:825–832.

1975. Bergson, Abram. "A Note on Consumer's Surplus." *Journal of Economic Literature*, 13:38–44.

1975. Bohm, Peter. "Option Demand and Consumer's Surplus: Comment." *American Economic Review*, 65:733–736.

1975. Schmalensee, Richard. "Option Demand and Consumer's Surplus: Reply." *American Economic Review*, 65:737–739.

1975. Mishan, E.J. "The Concept and Measure of Consumer's Surplus: Comment." *American Economic Review*, 65:708–709.

1975. Burns, M.E. "The Concept and Measure of Consumer's Surplus: Reply." *American Economic Review*, 65:710–711.

1975. Whitaker, J.K. *The Early Economic Writings of Alfred Marshall 1867–1890*, 2 vols. London.

1976. Chipman, J.S., and Moore, J.C. "The Scope of Consumer's Surplus Arguments." In A.M. Tang, et al. (eds), *Evolution, Welfare and Time in Economics: Essays in Honor of Nicholas Georgescu-Roegen*. Lexington, Mass.

1976. Rader, J. Trout III. "Equivalence of Consumer Surplus, the Divisia Index of Output, and Eisenberg's Addilog Social Utility." *Journal of Economic Theory*, 13:58–66.

1976. Willig, R.D. "Consumer's Surplus Without Apology." *American Economic Review*, 66:587–597.

1977. Bruce, Neil. "A Note on Consumer's Surplus, the Divisia Index, and the Measurement of Welfare Changes." *Econometrica*, 45:1033–1038.

1977. Burns, M.E. "On the Uniqueness of Consumer's Surplus and the Invariance of Economic Index Numbers." *Manchester School of Economic and Social Studies*, 45:41–61.

1977. Dahlby, B.G. "The Measurement of Consumer Surplus and the Path Dependence Problem.' *Public Finance*, 32:293–311.

1977. Dodgson, J.S. "Consumer Surplus and Compensation Tests." *Public Finance*, 32:312–320.

1977. Mishan, E.J. "The Plain Truth About Consumer Surplus." *Zeitschrift für Nationalökonomie*, 37:1–24.

1977. Pearce, I.F. "Demand Theory, Consumers' Surplus and Sovereignty." In S. Weintraub (ed.), *Modern Economic Thought*. Philadelphia.

1978. Foster, C.D., and Neuburger, H.L.I. "The Ugly Truth About Consumer's Surplus." *Zeitschrift für Nationalökonomie*, 38:379–388.

1978. Lyon, K.S. "Consumer's Surplus When Consumers Are Subject to a Time and Income Constraint." *Review of Economic Studies*, 45:37–380.

1978. Seade, James. "Consumer's Surplus and Linearity of Engel Curves." *Economic Journal*, 88:511–523.

1979. Button, K.J. "An Historical Survey of the Early Debate on Consumer's Surplus Theory." *Journal of Economic Studies*, 6:155–181.

1979. Hey, J.D. "A Note on Consumer Search and Consumer Surplus." *Bulletin of Economic Research*, 31:61–66.

1979. Cigno, A. "Search and Consumer's Surplus: A Generalization." *Bulletin of Economic Research*, 31:98–99.

1979. Dixit, A.K., and Weller, P.A. "The Three Consumer's Surpluses." *Economica*, 46:125–135.

1979. Sugden, Robert. "The Measurement of Consumers' Surplus in Practical Cost-Benefit Analysis." *Applied Economics*, 11:139–146.

1980. Bergson, Abram. "Consumer's Surplus and Income Redistribution." *Journal of Public Economics*, 14:31–47.

1980. Chipman, J.S., and Moore, J.C. "Compensating Variation, Consumer's Surplus and Welfare." *American Economic Review*, 70:933–949.

1980. O'Sullivan, P., and Ralston, B. "On the Equivalence of Consumer Surplus and von Thünian Rent." *Economic Geography*, 56:73–77.

1980. Randall, A., and Stoll, J.R. "Consumer's Surplus in Commodity Space." *American Economic Review*, 70:449–455.

1981. Hausman, J.A. "Exact Consumer's Surplus and Deadweight Loss." *American Economic Review*, 71:662–676.

1982. Abouchar, Alan. "Marshall, Consumer Surplus and the Marginal Utility of Money." *Eastern Economic Journal*, 8:79–82.

1982. McKenzie, G.W. and Pearce, I.F. "Welfare Measurement — A Synthesis." *American Economic Review*, 72:669–682.

1982. Macmillan, W.D. "On the Relationship Between Land Rent and Transport Market

Consumer Surplus." *Economic Geography*, 58:274–285.
1982. McClosky, D.N. *The Applied Theory of Price*. New York.
1982. O'Sullivan, P., and Ralston, B. "Reply to W.D. Macmillan." *Economic Geography*, 58:286–287.
1983. Dooley, P.C. "Consumer's Surplus: Marshall and His Critics." *Canadian Journal of Economics*, 16:26–37.

Notes

1. A deeper problem lurks in the conventional exposition of consumer surplus: the consumer is faced with a fixed budget; therefore he will not pay a higher price for 'earlier' units if he consumes up to the point where his demand curve meets the market price. This problem exercises modern welfare specialists, like Michael Burns (1973; 1975; 1977), who therefore tend to use consumer surplus in the context of a *market* demand curve, with each consumer taking only one unit.

2. In his review of consumer surplus theory, Houghton (1958) reviewed two of Bordas's criticisms, but ignored the 'income effects' passage. Furthermore, in referring to a like criticism made later by Walras, he makes a rather poor assessment of this point. According to Houghton (1958,52): "Dupuit's implied confusion [identification?] of demand and utility curves was of course a much less serious blunder [abstraction?] than Walras believed." This conclusion is untenable. The presence of a real-income effect and of a varying marginal utility of money expenditures puts an end to demand and utility curve identification and, therefore, to the use of demand curves to measure a 'utility' surplus. Since Dupuit did not hedge his theory with protective assumptions, his use of demand curves for such measurement is theoretically illegitimate, except in some rather restrictive circumstances.

3. Walras referred to both of Dupuit's major articles in his *Eléments*, but there is no indication that he was acquainted with Bordas's comment or the salient parts of Dupuit's rejoinder.

4. Jaffé (1972,395–96) notes that in his Geneva lectures of 1871, Walras taught Dupuit's doctrine of consumers' surplus, but without any mention of Dupuit. In view of his frequent and fervid denials of the practice of identifying demand curves with utility curves, this discovery means that an earlier "unregenerate" Walras was guilty of the same sin — even worse, since he identified the utility curve not with an individual's demand curve, but with a market demand curve.

5. Marshall wrote on the subject of consumer surplus as early as 1879, in his privately printed *Pure Theory of Domestic Values* (Whitaker 1975, 2:212–36), but Whitaker (1975, 2:279–83) found evidence that Marshall had mastered the concept sometime earlier, probably between 1867 and 1872. Pantaleoni (1889 [1898,78n.]) asserts that Marshall taught the theory of 'residual utility' [consumer surplus] at Cambridge as far back as 1869. Under these circumstances, it is hard to believe that Marshall first learned of the doctrine through Jevons. Moreover, the second of Marshall's examples [on tolls] from his mathematical notebook (Whitaker 1975, 2:281–83) is so like Dupuit's in both form and content that it is equally difficult to accept Marshall's express denial of Depuit's influence (see below). Still, the general view is that Dupuit's work was completely unknown in England until Jevons discovered it in the late 1870s.

6. Even before publication of the first edition of the Principles Marshall (1890 [1961, 2:260]) made it clear in a letter to J.N. Keynes that he regarded consumer surplus as a *sum of money*, not utility. He was very anxious that his doctrine not be confused with Jevons' notion of total utility. Nevertheless, Marshall did follow Dupuit's practice of identifying the demand curve with marginal utility, thereby inviting criticisms like Nicholson's.

At the same point, Marshall showed that he was aware of the income distribution problem, declaring to Keynes: "I can see no connection between the loss of Consumer's Rent and the loss of Total Utility resulting from a tax, unless it is known whether the commodity taxed is one consumed by the rich, by the poor, or by all classes alike."

7. A partial summary of Pareto's work was provided by Sanger (1895), whose review was

cited by Marshall (1890 [1961, 1:132n.]) in the third edition of the *Principles*. More recently, Abouchar (1982) has argued flatly that Marshall did not hold, and did not need, the assumption of constant marginal utility of money.

8. In the fourth edition of the *Principles* Marshall (1890 [1961, 1:463n]) publicly referred to Cunynghame's argument as "ingenious," whereas he (1890 [1961, 2:812; 810]) privately wrote to Edgeworth that Cunynghame's work was of "undergraduate rather than graduate" calibre, and that Cunynghame was "quick but impetuous; ... all through his life [he] has constantly supposed himself to know what he means when he does not."

9. On only one occasion did Marshall attempt to quantify consumer surplus — in a letter to the London *Times* (6 April 1891, p. 13), concerning his *bête noire*, the Post Office.

10. In his enthusiasm for the concept, Hicks (1941, 108) proclaimed that the theory Marshall unveiled in the *Principles* "was immediately recognized as the most striking novelty in the book." The early reviews of the *Principles*, however, do not support this assertion.

11. Hicks also extended his analysis to the case of an inferior good, but the normal good case is sufficient to illustrate why the Dupuit–Marshall triangle, except in unusual circumstances, cannot be used as a valid measure of consumer surplus.

12. Patinkin (1963) later maintained that Mishan's analysis holds only for perfectly competitive equilibrium situations.

90

On the 'Impossibility' of Hicks-neutral Technical Change*†

I. Steedman

Only a minority of economists would doubt that technical change is a major factor in economic growth; even fewer would deny that concepts of neutrality have occupied a central place in economic analyses of technical change. This is so whether the focus of attention be the effect on distributive shares (Hicks neutrality), the existence of steady growth (Harrod neutrality), or the possibility of 'capital aggregation' in vintage growth models (Solow neutrality). No less important, perhaps, has been the role of neutrality assumptions — usually Hicks neutrality — in the many attempts to estimate empirically the respective contributions of technical change and of the growth of inputs to the growth of output. In most cases, neutrality concepts have been defined at the aggregate, economy level and/or in terms of an overall relation between primary inputs and final outputs. Now, when one remembers both that actual technical change occurs at the level of the individual productive process and that the various industries are linked together by their use of produced means of production, one must inevitably be curious as to which particular process-level changes *can* give rise to the familiar kinds of neutral change at the more aggregated level. The principal purpose of this paper is to present a number of significant, alternative sufficient conditions under which Hicks neutral technical change is an *impossibility* (and is not merely empirically implausible). This result may be thought to be of some importance for the assessment of much recent neo-classical work on the measurement of technical progress and on the contribution of capital accumulation to the growth in labour productivity. Briefer remarks will also be made concerning Harrod neutrality and Solow neutrality.

Whilst neutrality concepts are usually defined with reference to production functions, we shall find it more convenient to use the 'dual' definitions; as Hahn and Matthews put it (1964, p. 830, no. 2), 'The three concepts of neutral technical progress can be shown in terms of the [wage-profit frontier]. Hicks-neutral technical progress causes the function to

---

†Source: *Economic Journal*, Vol. 95 (379), September 1985, pp. 746–58.

move outward in a constant proportion along rays through the origin; Harrod-neutral (= labour-augmenting) causes it to shift upwards in a constant proportion along the w-axis; capital-augmenting [i.e. Solow-neutral, I.S.] causes it to shift outwards in a constant proportion along the r-axis.' (In making these 'dual' translations of the neutrality concepts, Hahn and Matthews adopt the now conventional definition of Hicks neutrality as involving 'constant relative marginal products at constant factor proportions'; since we shall use the Hahn and Matthews definition, it is proper to note that Blackorby *et al.* (1976) have questioned whether this conventional definition is strictly equivalent to that originally given by Hicks in his *Theory of Wages* (1932).)

I. Preliminary Considerations

Our discussion of technical 'progress' will follow the conventional pattern of being couched in terms of a comparison between two different, stationary, constant returns to scale economies, to be called Advanced and Backward. Hicks neutral progress will thus be represented by the fact that the wage–profit frontier in Advanced is a radical expansion — by a factor $t > 1$ — of that in Backward. Our concern throughout will be with genuine 'input–output' economies, in which there are at least two produced commodities, in which produced inputs depreciate, and in which alternate techniques of production have at least some produced inputs in common (unlike the 'Samuelson Surrogate' type of economy); the discussion will, however, be confined to the case of single product systems, using only circulating capital.

It will be highly convenient — and involve no economically significant loss of generality — to rule out various special 'fluke' cases. It will thus be assumed throughout that our input–output matrices involve at least one basic commodity, that they have complete sets of distinct characteristic roots, and that no primary input vector is a characteristic vector of the related input–output matrix. Correspondingly, the composite commodity in terms of which wages and prices are measured, will be supposed not to be a characteristic vector of any relevant input–output matrix. And when a choice of technique is introduced, it will be assumed that the number of relevant alternatives is finite (although perhaps large) and that no change of technique involves a change in the process for more than one industry. (The contrary case is completely exceptional, as shown by Bruno *et al.* 1966.)

As was indicated above, we shall follow the example of Hahn and Matthews in representing Hicks neutral progress by a radial expansion of the wage–profit frontier. But in a multi-commodity economy there is in fact no such thing as 'the' wage-profit frontier. Rather there are as many such frontiers as there are ways of measuring real wages and until it is said *how* real wages are to be measured the definition of Hicks neutral progress is incomplete. Moreover, any proposal that Hicks neutrality be defined with respect to some particular measurement of real wages would require justification; 'why this measure and not that?' We shall sidestep these questions (which could easily generate futile controversy) by dividing our discussion into two parts. In the first we consider the conditions under which progress can be Hicks neutral for *all* possible measures of real wages; while in the second we consider the same question for any arbitrarily given standard of measurement of wages and prices.

II. Unambiguously Hicksian Progress

Consider first the simplest case, that in which there is only a single primary input-homogeneous labour — and in which the rate of profit is the same in all sectors. If **b**, **B** and *r* represent the labour input (row) vector, the input–output matrix and the rate of profit in Backward, then the (row) vector of labour-commanded prices in Backward will, if wages are paid ex-post, be given by

$$\mathbf{b}[\mathbf{I} - (1 + r)\mathbf{B}]^{-1}. \tag{1}$$

Let (**a**, **A**) represent the technical conditions in Advanced; if wages are again paid *ex-post*, labour-commanded prices at a profit rate of *tr* $(t > 1)$ will be given by

$$\mathbf{a}[\mathbf{I} - (1 + tr)\,\mathbf{A}]^{-1}. \tag{2}$$

But if there is to be Unambiguously Hicksian Progress (UHP) as between Backward and Advanced then the labour-commanded price vector given by (2) must equal only (t^{-1}) times that given by (1), even though the rate of profit is larger in (2) by the factor *t*. This precisely expresses the condition that the real wage–profit rate frontier in Advanced is a radical expansion — by the factor *t* — of that in Backward, *however* the real wage is measured. From (1) and (2), then, the condition for UHP is that

$$t\mathbf{a}[\mathbf{I} - (1 + tr)\,\mathbf{A}]^{-1} = \mathbf{b}[\mathbf{I} - (1 + r)\mathbf{B}]^{-1} \tag{3}$$

for all *r* not less than zero and not greater than the maximum rate of profit in Backward. This condition can be met, however, only if it holds for *all r*, so it will be more convenient to define $\rho \equiv (1 + tr)$, $s \equiv t^{-1}(t - 1)$, $\mathbf{c} \equiv t^{-1}\mathbf{b}(\mathbf{I} - s\mathbf{B})^{-1}$, $\mathbf{C} \equiv t^{-1}\mathbf{B}(\mathbf{I} - s\mathbf{B})^{-1}$ and to rewrite (3) as

$$\mathbf{a}(\mathbf{I} - \rho\mathbf{A})^{-1} = \mathbf{c}(\mathbf{I} - \rho\mathbf{C})^{-1} \tag{4}$$

for all ρ.

It will be apparent by inspection that (**a** = **c**, **A** = **C**) is a sufficient condition for the satisfaction of (4) and, on putting ρ = o, that (**a** = **c**) is a necessary condition. To show that **A** = **C** is also a necessary condition, we strengthen somewhat our assumption that no primary input vector is a characteristic vector of the related input–output matrix. Specifically, we suppose that the system $(\mathbf{b}, \mathbf{B})$ is 'regular' in the sense of Schefold (1976), i.e. that $(\mathbf{b}, \mathbf{bB}, \mathbf{bB}^2, \ldots, \mathbf{bB}^{n-1})$ are all linearly independent, where n is the number of produced commodities. (This is not a very restrictive assumption.) It is easily shown that the system $(\mathbf{c}, \mathbf{C})$ is then also regular (proof by contradiction). Now, with $\mathbf{a} = \mathbf{c}$, condition (4) can be written as

$$\mathbf{c}(\mathbf{I} - \rho\mathbf{C})^{-1} (\mathbf{A} - \mathbf{C}) = \mathbf{o}$$

for all ρ. But it is known that when $(\mathbf{c}, \mathbf{C})$ is a regular system, the vectors $\mathbf{c}(\mathbf{I} - \rho_i\mathbf{C})^{-1}$ are linearly independent for any n distinct values of ρ_i (Schefold, 1976). Hence $\mathbf{A} = \mathbf{C}$ is a necessary condition for UHP. In brief, $(\mathbf{a} = \mathbf{c}, \mathbf{A} = \mathbf{C})$ is both necessary and sufficient for UHP; that is, there is UHP if and only if

$$t\mathbf{A} = \mathbf{B}(\mathbf{I} - s\mathbf{B})^{-1} \tag{5}$$

$$t\mathbf{a} = \mathbf{b}(\mathbf{I} - s\mathbf{B})^{-1}. \tag{6}$$

Before discussing (5) and (6) we may quickly introduce the fact that there are many, heterogeneous primary inputs. For any given value of r, the frontier restricting real primary input 'wage rates' is linear, so that in order to ensure UHP with many primary inputs it suffices to ensure that, in addition to (5), there is a relation such as (6) for each primary input in turn. Thus replacing the vectors $(\mathbf{a}, \mathbf{b})$ by primary input matrices $(\mathbf{E}, \mathbf{F})$, our conditions for UHP become

$$t \begin{pmatrix} \mathbf{A} \\ \mathbf{E} \end{pmatrix} = \begin{pmatrix} \mathbf{B} \\ \mathbf{F} \end{pmatrix} (\mathbf{I} - s\mathbf{B})^{-1}. \tag{7}$$

(Note that $\mathbf{EB} = \mathbf{FA}$, which in the one commodity–one primary input case would say that the input *proportions* are the same in Advanced as in Backward. Note too that $\mathbf{A} \geqslant t^{-1}\mathbf{B}$ and $\mathbf{E} \geqslant t^{-1}\mathbf{F}$.)

Positivity

If $\mathbf{B}$ is irreducible, $(\mathbf{I} - s\mathbf{B})^{-1}$ is strictly positive. If $\mathbf{B}$ is reducible, number the commodities and industries so that 'Sraffa basics' appear in the upper-left part of $\mathbf{B}$; then the upper-left and upper-right parts of $(\mathbf{I} - s\mathbf{B})^{-1}$ are strictly positive. In either case, the upper part of $\mathbf{A}$, at least, is *strictly* positive. A necessary condition for UHP is thus that, in Advanced, *every* industry makes *direct* use of *every* basic commodity! Thus if it is excluded, for whatever reason, that every industry in Advanced makes such direct use of every basic commodity, UHP is impossible.

Similarly, from (7), the upper part of $\mathbf{E}$, at least, is *strictly* positive, if the primary inputs are so labelled that any primary input used (directly) in *no* basic industry appears in the lower part of $\mathbf{F}$ and of $\mathbf{E}$. Thus (7) states that *every* primary input used directly in *any* basic industry in Backward, must be used *directly* in *every* industry (basic or not) in Advanced. Thus if it is excluded, for whatever reason, that, say, hairdressing salons in Advanced employ directly the services of sheet-steel-rolling craftsmen, UHP is impossible.

The above considerations cannot, of course, force anyone to conclude that UHP is impossible, even in the type of economy considered here; it is impossible only on condition that we make utterly reasonable assumptions about the direct use of certain inputs, produced or primary, in certain industries.

Ex-ante wages

Return to the homogeneous labour case and suppose now that, in both Advanced and Backward, wages are advanced. Relation (3) must now be changed to

$$t(1 + tr)\, \mathbf{a}[\mathbf{I} - (1 + tr)\, \mathbf{A}] - 1 = (1 + r)\, \mathbf{b}[\mathbf{I} - (1 + r)\, \mathbf{B}]^{-1} \tag{3'}$$

and thus (4) to

$$\rho \mathbf{a}(\mathbf{I} - \rho \mathbf{A})^{-1} = (s + t^{-1}\rho)\, \mathbf{c}(\mathbf{I} - \rho \mathbf{C})^{-1}. \tag{4'}$$

Since $(s\mathbf{c})$ is strictly positive, $(4')$ *cannot* hold at $\rho = 0$. The *ex-ante* payment of wages makes UHP impossible. In the case of heterogeneous primary inputs, the *ex-ante* payment of even one 'wage' would render UHP impossible.

(Although we are not concerned with one-commodity models in this paper, it may be noted that *ex-ante* payment of wages makes a Hicks neutral shift of *the* wage–profit frontier quite impossible even in a one-commodity world, using only one primary input!)

Differential profit rates

Thus far we have assumed the existence of a uniform profit rate but it is often insisted, whether rightly or wrongly, that this is an arbitrary assumption. Suppose then that labour is homogeneous and paid *ex-post* but that (3) must be replaced by

$$t\mathbf{a}(\mathbf{I} - \mathbf{A} - t\mathbf{A}\hat{\mathbf{r}})^{-1} = \mathbf{b}(\mathbf{I} - \mathbf{B} - \mathbf{B}\hat{\mathbf{r}})^{-1} \tag{3''}$$

for all $\hat{\mathbf{r}}$, where $\hat{\mathbf{r}}$ is a diagonal matrix of profit rates. If $(3'')$ is to hold for all $\hat{\mathbf{r}}$ it must hold for all $\hat{\mathbf{r}} = r\mathbf{I}$, so that $(\mathbf{a} = \mathbf{c}, \mathbf{A} = \mathbf{C})$ is still a necessary condition for UHP. We therefore need to ask when

$$\mathbf{b}[\mathbf{I} - \mathbf{B} - \mathbf{B}(\mathbf{I} - s\mathbf{B})^{-1}\hat{\mathbf{r}}(\mathbf{I} - s\mathbf{B})]^{-1} = \mathbf{b}(\mathbf{I} - \mathbf{B} - \mathbf{B}\hat{\mathbf{r}})^{-1} \tag{8}$$

can hold for all $\hat{r}$. We need $(I - sB)^{-1}\hat{r}(I - sB) = \hat{r}$ or $\hat{r}B = B\hat{r}$ for all $\hat{r}$. Thus, *only* if **B** is diagonal can (8) hold for all $\hat{r}$.

To say that **A, B, C** are diagonal is, of course, to say that one is no longer considering a genuine input–output system. Hence if differential profit rates are to be allowed for, UHP is impossible.

Choice of technique

Suppose now that one basic industry in Backward has two alternative methods of production, that no other industry in Backward has any choice of methods, and that the two resulting techniques in backward are both used at some economically relevant level of the (again uniform) rate of profit. If the corresponding industries in Advanced face the same number of alternatives as those in Backward, the wage–profit frontier in each economy will consist of sections of the individual wage–profit frontiers for the two techniques in that economy. Hence there will be overall UHP if and only if the frontier for each technique exhibits UHP. (Note that it will be completely irrelevant to our argument whether there is or is not 'reswitching' between the two technique frontiers.)

Let $(\mathbf{A}, \mathbf{B})$ represent, as before, the Advanced and Backward produced input coefficients for one technique. Now let $(\mathbf{A}^*, \mathbf{B}^*)$ represent the corresponding coefficients for the alternative technique. Of course, each $\mathbf{M}^*$ differs from the corresponding $\mathbf{M}$ *in only one column*, say the first column so that industry 1 (a basic industry) is the one with a choice of methods.

For UHP overall we need *both*

$$t\mathbf{A} = \mathbf{B}(\mathbf{I} - s\mathbf{B})^{-1} \tag{9}$$

and

$$t\mathbf{A}^* = \mathbf{B}^*(\mathbf{I} - s\mathbf{B}^*)^{-1}. \tag{10}$$

Subtracting (10) from (9) we obtain

$$t(\mathbf{A} - \mathbf{A}^*) = (\mathbf{I} - s\mathbf{B})^{-1}\,\mathbf{B} - \mathbf{B}^*(\mathbf{I} - s\mathbf{B}^*)^{-1}$$
$$= (\mathbf{I} - s\mathbf{B})^{-1}[\mathbf{B}(\mathbf{I} - s\mathbf{B}^*) - (\mathbf{I} - s\mathbf{B})\,\mathbf{B}^*]\,(\mathbf{I} - s\mathbf{B}^*)^{-1}$$

or

$$t(\mathbf{A} - \mathbf{A}^*) = (\mathbf{I} - s\mathbf{B})^{-1}\,(\mathbf{B} - \mathbf{B}^*)\,(\mathbf{I} - s\mathbf{B}^*)^{-1}. \tag{11}$$

Since **B** and $\mathbf{B}^*$ differ only in the first column, the right-hand side of (11) is a matrix every one of whose rows is proportional to the top row of $(\mathbf{I} - s\mathbf{B}^*)^{-1}$. But that top row is strictly positive, so that every row on the right of (11) is strictly positive, or negative, or exactly zero. The matrix on the left of (11), however, is exactly zero everywhere other than in the first column and not exactly zero in that column. Thus (11) is self-contradictory; a choice of method in a basic industry makes UHP impossible.

It will be clear that the presence of a larger (but finite) number of alternative techniques will not alter the conclusion just reached.

Résumé

It has been shown that, in the type of economy discussed here, each of the following conditions is individually sufficient to render Unambiguously Hicksian Progress quite impossible:

(*a*) it is not the case that every industry in Advanced makes direct use of every basic commodity;

(*b*) it is not the case that every industry in Advanced makes direct use of every kind of primary input used in any basic industry in Backward;

(*c*) at least one kind of primary input is paid in advance;

(*d*) differential rates of profit must be allowed for;

(*e*) there is an economically relevant choice of method of production in at least one basic industry.

Of course, one can still make assumptions which allow UHP to be possible! But a more likely response to the above findings is perhaps the suggestion that UHP is too demanding an interpretation of Hicksian neutrality and that only one, or only some, wage–profit rate frontier(s) should be required to expand in a radial fashion. One might be allowed to wonder, in return, whether the need so to restrict Hicksian neutrality has always been made crystal clear and, if not, why not; and to ask *which* particular measure or measures of the real wage are required to exhibit neutral shifts and just *why* this measure (these measures) should be invoked and not others. Rather than ponder such (interesting) questions here, however, we turn to consider the conditions for such Ambiguously Hicksian Progress, in which only one particular frontier is required (or some particular frontiers are required) to expand radially.

III. Ambiguously Hicksian Progress

Suppose first that labour is homogeneous and paid ex-post, that the rate of profit is uniform and that a Hicks neutral expansion of the wage–profit frontier is required only in terms of the particular composite commodity given by the semi-positive (column) vector $\mathbf{z}$. Using our now familiar notation, we require

$$t\mathbf{a}[\mathbf{I} - (1 + tr)\,\mathbf{A}]^{-1}\mathbf{z} = \mathbf{b}[\mathbf{I} - (1 + r)\,\mathbf{B}]^{-1}\mathbf{z} \tag{12}$$

for all *r*, or

$$\mathbf{a}(\mathbf{I} - \rho\mathbf{A})^{-1}\mathbf{z} = \mathbf{c}(\mathbf{I} - \rho\mathbf{C})^{-1}\mathbf{z} \tag{13}$$

for all ρ.

A necessary condition for (13) to hold for all ρ is that both sides 'explode' at the same values of ρ — i.e. that $\mathbf{A}$ and $\mathbf{C}$ have a common set of characteristic roots. From the definition of $\mathbf{C}$, we have $\mathbf{C}[t\mathbf{I} - (t-1)\mathbf{B}] \equiv \mathbf{B}$, so that if $\mathbf{B}x_i = \lambda_i x_i$ ($i = 1, \ldots, n$) it follows at once that $[t - (t-1)\lambda_i]\mathbf{C}x_i \equiv \lambda_i x_i$. In other words, if the roots of $\mathbf{B}$ are $(\lambda_1, \ldots, \lambda_n)$ then those of $\mathbf{C}-$ and $\mathbf{A}-$ are given by

$$\mu_i = \left[\frac{\lambda_i}{t - (t-1)\lambda_i} \right]. \tag{14}$$

(One can show from (14), bearing in mind that $|\lambda_i| < 1$, that $|\mu_i| < |\lambda_i|$, for each i.) Whether in the form of (14) or — equivalently — in the form trace $\mathbf{A}$ = trace $\mathbf{C}$, …, det $\mathbf{A}$ = det $\mathbf{C}$, we now have n conditions on $\mathbf{A}$, which ensure that $\det(\mathbf{I} - \rho\mathbf{A}) = \det(\mathbf{I} - \rho\mathbf{C})$ for all ρ. But for any matrix $\mathbf{M}$ possessing an inverse, $\mathbf{M}^{-1} \equiv (\det \mathbf{M})^{-1}\mathrm{adj}\mathbf{M}$, so that (13) may be replaced by (14) *plus*

$$\mathbf{a} \text{ adj } (\mathbf{I} - \rho\mathbf{A})\mathbf{z} = \mathbf{c} \text{ adj } (\mathbf{I} - \rho\mathbf{C})\mathbf{z}. \tag{15}$$

Relation (15) is a polynominal in ρ of degree $(n - \mathrm{I})$, so that making it hold identically gives n conditions on $(\mathbf{a}, \mathbf{A})$ if $(\mathbf{b}, \mathbf{B})$ is regarded as known. Hence (13) places $2n$ restrictions on the $n(n + 1)$ elements of $(\mathbf{a}, \mathbf{A})$ — leaving aside any *a priori* knowledge that certain elements must be zero. If now it is required that (13) hold for m linearly independent $\mathbf{z}_i$ vectors (standards of value), (14) will apply in every case, while each $\mathbf{z}_i$ will generate a corresponding (15), so that we shall have a total of $(n + mn) = n(m + 1)$ conditions on the $n(n + 1)$ elements of $(\mathbf{a}, \mathbf{A})$. (The case of UHP, then, is just the case $m = n$.)

It will be clear enough that to require Ambiguously Hicksian Progress (AHP) is less demanding than to require UHP but it does not follow that there are no significant conditions sufficient to render AHP impossible, *even when* AHP is required in terms of only one standard of value. (And AHP naturally becomes increasingly demanding as it is required in terms of more standards, e.g. in terms of all consumption commodities.)

Positivity

It has already been noted that a necessary condition for AHP is that trace $\mathbf{A}$ = trace $\mathbf{C}$. But trace $\mathbf{C}$ is definitely positive, so that zero 'own use' in each industry in Advanced ($\mathbf{A}_{ii} = 0$ for all i) would suffice to render AHP impossible. More significantly, perhaps, allow for heterogeneous primary inputs, so that (13) must be replaced by

$$\mathbf{E}(\mathbf{I} - \rho\mathbf{A})^{-1}\mathbf{z} = \mathbf{G}(\mathbf{I} - \rho\mathbf{C})^{-1}\mathbf{z} \tag{16}$$

for all ρ, where $\mathbf{G} \equiv t^{-1}\mathbf{F}(\mathbf{I} - s\mathbf{B})^{-1}$. If (16) is to hold at $\rho = 0$, we require

$$\mathbf{Ez} = \mathbf{Gz} = t^{-1}\mathbf{F}(\mathbf{I} - s\mathbf{B})^{-1}\mathbf{z}. \tag{17}$$

The upper part, at least, of the matrix to the right of (17) is strictly positive. Thus if $\mathbf{z}$ is the ith unit vector — commodity i being the standardin which real wages are measured — (17) demands that the upper part, at least, of $\mathbf{E}_i$ is strictly positive; in Advanced, industry i must employ *directly* every kind of primary input used in any basic industry in Backward. Hence zero use, in Advanced's industry i, of any such primary input would make AHP (in terms of i) quite impossible.

Ex-ante wages

If labour is homogeneous and wages are paid *ex-ante* in both Advanced and Backward, AHP requires that

$$\rho\mathbf{a}(\mathbf{I} - \rho\mathbf{A})^{-1}\mathbf{z} = (s + t^{-1}\rho)\,\mathbf{c}(\mathbf{I} - \rho\mathbf{C})^{-1}\mathbf{z} \tag{18}$$

for all ρ. At $\rho = 0$, (18) becomes $0 = s(\mathbf{cz})$ or

$$0 = \mathbf{b}(\mathbf{I} - s\mathbf{B})^{-1}\mathbf{z}.$$

Hence *ex-ante* payment of wages renders AHP impossible.

Differential profit rates

Suppose that labour is homogeneous and paid *ex-post* and that $\mathbf{z}$ is the ith unit vector $\mathbf{e}_i$. With differential rates of profit, AHP then requires that

$$t\mathbf{a}(\mathbf{I} - \mathbf{A} - t\mathbf{A}\hat{\mathbf{r}})^{-1}\mathbf{e}_i = \mathbf{b}(\mathbf{I} - \mathbf{B} - \mathbf{B}\hat{\mathbf{r}})^{-1}\mathbf{e}_i \tag{19}$$

for all $\hat{\mathbf{r}}$. If $(1 + tr_i) = 0$, the left-hand side of (19) becomes simply $t(\mathbf{ae}_i)$, being independent of all the other $r_j\,(j \neq i)$. Hence a necessary condition for AHP is that the right-hand side of (19) be independent of all $r_j\,(j \neq i)$ when $(1 + tr_i) = 0$. But this can be so only if $B_{ji} = 0$ for all $j \neq i$ (see Appendix). Hence in a genuine input–output system, differential rates of profit make AHP impossible.

Choice of technique

Return to the simple case of a uniform rate of profit, with homogeneous labour paid *ex-post*, as represented by (13) for a particular technique. Suppose now that there is at least one more economically relevant technique in both Advanced and Backward, so that one or more points on each of the wage–profit frontiers shown in (13) is a switch-point. At a switch-point *all* relative prices must be the same in Advanced as in the hypo-thetical economy with 'technical coefficients' (**c**, **C**). (To keep the discussion simple, we suppose here that all commodities are basics.) It is thus 'as if' UHP were required *at* the switchpoint values of ρ and of real wage rate in terms of **z**. In addition to the $2n$ conditions which (13) places on (**a**, **A**), then, we have, at a switchpoint, a further $(n - I)$ conditions to make all relative prices the same and thus to ensure that the real wage in Advanced is equal to t times that in Backward *however* that real wage is measured, *i.e.* to ensure that it really is a switchpoint which is under con-sideration. If the frontiers represented by (13) have v switchpoints on them, we have a total of $[2n + v(n - I)]$ conditions on (**a**, **A**); and if $v = n$ we have $(n^2 + n)$ conditions on the $(n^2 + n)$ coefficients of (**a**, **A**), so that (**a** = **c**, **A** = **C**) is the only solution (in non-fluke cases). To put matters rather loosely, 'AHP with enough switchpoints is as demanding as UHP'. It is to be noted explicitly that in referring to the number of switchpoints on the frontiers represented by (13), we did *not* imply that the switches are (or are not) all with a single second technique frontier; that might or might not be the case, so that our argument involves no necessary reference to 'reswitching'.

Suppose now that the frontiers for two different techniques, between which there is at least one switchpoint, each have n switchpoints on them. Then in the notation used in our discussion of UHP, (**A** = **C**, **A*** = **C***) and that discussion can now be repeated to show that, in the sense just defined, in an economy with 'enough' switchpoints, AHP is impossible.

(It may be of interest to illustrate the above in terms of the much-loved but over-worked one capital good, one consumer good model. There is only one basic and thus the 'n' of the preceding paragraph is effectively unity (and not two). It is readily shown that if there is an economically rele-vant choice of method in the capital good sector then AHP, in terms of the consumer good, is impossible.)

It may be helpful, particularly to any reader unaccustomed to thinking in terms of the properties of switchpoints, to present the above argument in slightly different terms. Let $N_i \geqslant 1$ be the number of alternative processes available in industry i and used at some positive real wage rate, so that there are $(n + 1) \Sigma_1^n N_i$ technical coefficients to be determined. The number of alternative techniques in the economy is $\Pi_1^n N_i$. One cannot say on *a priori* grounds whether or not all these techniques will be used at some positive real wage rate; consider first the 'strong' case in which they are all used. In this case equation (13) yields a total of $(2n \Pi_1^n N_i)$ conditions on the $[(n + 1) \Sigma_1^n N_i]$ coefficients, so that AHP is impossible (except for flukes) if $(\Pi N_i / \Sigma N_i) > 0.5 (1 + n^{-1})$. With n reasonably large and even a moderate degree of choice in several industries, this condition is 'likely' to be met. (Purely as an illustration, suppose that each $N_i = v$; our con-dition becomes $v > [(n + 1)/2]^{[1/(n-1)]}$. The right hand side equals 1.5 when $n = 2$ and falls as n increases; for $n = 99$, it equals 1.04). Even if not all of the (ΠN_i) possible techniques are economically relevant, the point remains that, as the relevant choice of technique is extended, the number of conditions imposed by equation (13) is 'likely' to rise faster than the number of coefficients to be determined, with the result that, flukes aside, the choice of techniques renders even AHP impossible.

The above discussion has dealt with the homogeneous labour case but we now turn to the far more relevant case of many primary inputs. As was noted above, the condition

$$\mathbf{E}(\mathbf{I} - \rho\mathbf{A})^{-1}\mathbf{z} = \mathbf{G}(\mathbf{I} - \rho\mathbf{C})^{-1}\mathbf{z}$$

for all ρ suffices to ensure AHP, in terms of the standard $\mathbf{z}$, for a particular technique. Suppose now, however, that there is a choice of technique and that the surface $\mathbf{w}\mathbf{G}(\mathbf{I} - \rho\mathbf{C})^{-1}\mathbf{z} = 1$ — the frontier constraining r and the real 'wage rates' $\mathbf{w}$ — is thus cut by another such surface. At *all* the infinitely-many switching combinations of $(\mathbf{w}, \rho)$ thus defined, the actual technique $(\mathbf{E}, \mathbf{A})$ must generate exactly the same set of *all* relative prices as does the (hypothetical) technique $(\mathbf{G}, \mathbf{C})$. $(\mathbf{E} = \mathbf{G}, \mathbf{A} = \mathbf{C})$ is, obviously, a sufficient condition to ensure this. Suppose now that all the rows of $\mathbf{G}$ are linearly independent (or that n are if there are more than n) and that each row of $\mathbf{G}$ forms a 'regular' system with $\mathbf{C}$. If, as I conjecture, these conditions suffice to make $(\mathbf{E} = \mathbf{G}, \mathbf{A} = \mathbf{C})$ also a necessary condition for equal price vectors, at all switching $(\mathbf{w}, \rho)$, we can again, just as before, argue that a relevant choice of technique makes AHP impossible.

Résumé

It has been shown that, in the type of economy discussed here, each of the following conditions is individually sufficient to render even Ambiguously Hicksian Progress impossible:

(a) no industry in Advanced uses its own product as a direct input;
(b) the industry producing the standard of value commodity in Advanced does not employ directly every kind of primary input used in any basic industry in Backward;
(c) at least one primary input is paid *ex-ante*;
(d) differential rates of profit must be allowed for;
(e) the wage–profit frontiers for adjacent techniques (in a homogeneous labour economy) each have n switchpoints on the economy frontier.
It is probably also sufficient that:
(f) there is a relevant choice of technique in an economy with two or more primary inputs.

IV. Harrod and Solow Neutralities

It may be helpful to compare the conditions for Hicksian neutrality with those for Harrodian and for Solovian neutrality but, in the interests of brevity, this will be done here only in the context of 'unambiguously neutral' change; the interested reader can extend the argument to the 'ambiguously neutral' case.

Let $T >$ I represent the measure of (unambiguously) Harrod neutral progress as between Backward and Advanced; in our usual notation, if primary inputs are paid *ex-post* and the rate of profit is uniform, we require that

$$T\mathbf{E}[\mathbf{I} - (1 + r)\,\mathbf{A}]^{-1} = \mathbf{F}[\mathbf{I} - (1 + r)\,\mathbf{B}]^{-1} \tag{20}$$

for all r. Using arguments similar to those employed in relation to UHP, we find that

$$T\mathbf{E} = \mathbf{F} \quad \text{and} \quad \mathbf{A} = \mathbf{B}. \tag{21}$$

The material input–output coefficients must be the same in Advanced as in Backward, whilst the primary input coefficients must be uniformly smaller. Whilst $\mathbf{FA} = \mathbf{EB}$ in the case of UHP, we see from (21) that $\mathbf{FA} > \mathbf{EB}$ for unambiguously Harrodian progress.

It is clear from (21) that no *a priori* requirements that $\mathbf{E}$ and $\mathbf{A}$ should have the same patterns of zero elements as do $\mathbf{F}$ and $\mathbf{B}$, respectively, could cause any problems. Nor could *ex-ante* wage payments, for both sides of (20) would simply be multiplied by a common factor of $(1 + r)$. It can also be seen from (20) and (21) that differential rates of profit would make no difference. And nor, indeed, would the presence of a choice of technique — consider (21). Whilst unambiguously Harrodian progress is quite amazingly special — (21) — it is not vulnerable to the various kinds of 'impossibility' to which UHP has been shown to be liable.

While Solow introduced his concept of 'capital-augmenting' progress in the specific context of aggregating 'vintages' of machines, we shall treat it here in a more general way, as did Hahn and Matthews in the above-cited passage. If $\tau >$ I represents the measure of (unambiguously) Solow-neutral progress as between Backward and Advanced, we require that

$$\mathbf{E}[\mathbf{I} - (1 + \tau r)\mathbf{A}]^{-1} = \mathbf{F}[\mathbf{I} - (1 + r)\mathbf{B}]^{-1} \tag{22}$$

for all r. Define $\pi \equiv (1 + \tau r)$, $\sigma \equiv \tau^{-1}(\tau - 1)$, $\mathbf{H} \equiv \mathbf{F}(\mathbf{I} - \sigma\mathbf{B})^{-1}$, $\mathbf{D} \equiv \tau^{-1}\mathbf{B}(\mathbf{I} - \sigma\mathbf{B})^{-1}$ and rewrite (22) as

$$\mathbf{E}(\mathbf{I} - \pi\mathbf{A})^{-1} = \mathbf{H}(\mathbf{I} - \pi\mathbf{D})^{-1} \tag{23}$$

for all π. As with UHP, we require that $(\mathbf{E} = \mathbf{H}, \mathbf{A} = \mathbf{D})$, or

$$\mathbf{E} = \mathbf{F}(\mathbf{I} - \sigma\mathbf{B})^{-1} \tag{24}$$

$$\tau\mathbf{A} = \mathbf{B}(\mathbf{I} - \sigma\mathbf{B})^{-1}. \tag{25}$$

We notice, at once, from (24), that in their upper parts, at least, $\mathbf{E}$, is *strictly* greater than $\mathbf{F}$! Solow-neutral *progress* demands that all direct primary input coefficients are *worse* (greater) in Advanced than in Backward (at least with respect to those kinds of primary input used in some basic industry). It is only via such a deterioration in direct primary input efficiency that constant 'maximum wage rates' for a given technique can be reconciled with an improved 'maximum rate of profit' for that technique. While $\mathbf{FA} = \mathbf{EB}$ for UHP, and $\mathbf{FA} > \mathbf{EB}$ for Harrod neutrality, it follows from (24), (25) that $\mathbf{FA} < \mathbf{EB}$ for Solow neutrality.

It will be clear that the various conditions which were shown to suffice to render UHP impossible will, equally, render unambiguously Solovian progress impossible.

From the present perspective, then, Hicks and Solow neutralities have much in common, stemming from their difficulties in allowing for produced means of production, and the idea that Solow-neutral progress is 'the mirror-image of Harrod-neutral technical progress' (Hahn and Matthews, 1964, p. 830) needs to be interpreted with care, being itself a reflection of the treatment of 'capital' as a primary input.

V. Discussion

If the various results given above are logically valid, what is their significance? In the interests of brevity, and since our central focus of attention has been Hicks Neutrality, our discussion will be confined to that neutrality concept. At one level it is, of course, not very surprising that Hicksian neutrality should be 'unlikely'. It is, after all, a strict condition and Jones (1965), for example, pointed out twenty years ago that overall Hicksian neutrality is unlikely, even in a two-sector economy with each sector undergoing just such neutral progress. It may be noted that our emphasis has been distinctly different from that of Jones, who considered a model with *no* interindustry connections, *zero* profits and two *primary* inputs only; our stress has been on the way in which interconnectedness, through produced inputs, makes Hicks Neutral progress very difficult. More important than these differences from the argument of Jones, however, has been the demonstration that various very weak conditions — of 'positivity', of *ex-ante* wage payment, of differential profit rates, of sufficient choice of technique — suffice, independently, to render Hicks Neutrality not merely 'implausible' but *impossible*. It has been argued, that is, not that 'the numbers are unlikely to imply Hicks Neutrality' but rather that, unless one makes very strong *a priori* assumptions about 'positivity', the timing of all wage payments, etc. Hicks Neutrality is an internally inconsistent concept at the level of the economy, in the presence of produced inputs. Since no-one, we may suppose, will happily state that it is permissible to use internally inconsistent concepts, our results should be of interest to anyone not ready to defend the very strong assumptions which alone can render Hicks Neutrality free from such inconsistency. In the type of economic system discussed above, the concept of Hicks Neutral Progress is devoid of theoretical coherence and, therefore, of theoretical use.

The reader interested in employing the Hicksian neutrality concept in empirical work — on, say, income distribution and/or explaining economic growth — may nevertheless feel a slight impatience and may argue that, for the purposes of such work, an assumption of 'approximately' Hicksian neutrality may suffice — and this has not been shown above to be 'impossible'. It is not the place of the theorist to deny that, if empirical work is to be done at all, all sorts of aggregations, approximations and compromises will have to be made. Conversely, of course, good empirical workers attempt to stay as close to theoretical constraints and consistency requirements as they can. In relation to productivity, for example, there has been, since the days of the early 'residual' demonstrations, a growing insistence that productivity growth measurement *and explanation* should be based on a detailed theory of pricing relations. The welcome emphasis on the correct *theoretical* underpinnings of growth explanations and of attributions of output growth to technical progress and to input growth, naturally rests most comfortably with a *strict* interpretation of Hicks Neutrality. Would 'approximate' neutrality suffice for such attributions (which are indeed *theoretical* attributions)? Is UHP required or only AHP? If the latter, in terms of which standards of value is it required and why not others? Such questions, which arise directly from our preceding arguments, certainly ought to interest those engaged in empirical work using the Hicks Neutrality concept. For if UHP and AHP are generally 'impossible', it is for those who intend to use 'Approximate HP' to define it precisely, to show theoretically that it is adequate to their purpose and to show theoretically that it is not 'impossible'.

VI. Conclusion

This paper is already rather long and it would probably not be useful to repeat our earlier résumés. Suffice it to say here that, in the kind of production models discussed, various simple and significant conditions have been shown to be individually sufficient to make Hicks-neutral progress simply impossible. There may also be other such sufficient conditions, of course, but more useful than searching for them, probably, will be for someone to extend the present analysis to the case of joint production and fixed capital. To be valuable, the extension to the case of fixed capital will have to be within the von Neumann-Sraffa framework (and not within the rather silly radioactive depreciation one) and it will have to be decided whether the economic lifetime of a machine is or is not to be held constant, as between Backward and Advanced, in the definition of neutral progress.

It would be too strong to conclude here that Hicks Neutrality is never legitimately assumed, but it might not be unreasonable to suggest that those who do assume it — for example in estimating the separate contributions of technical progress and of input growth — are obliged to show explicitly that that assumption is compatible with their other assumptions.

Appendix

When $(1 + tr_i) = 0$, $(1 + r_i) = s$. The right-hand side of (19) in the text can then be written as

$$\mathbf{b}[\mathbf{I} + \mathbf{B}(\mathbf{I} + \hat{\mathbf{r}}) + \mathbf{B}(\mathbf{I} + \hat{\mathbf{r}})\,\mathbf{B}(\mathbf{I} + \hat{\mathbf{r}}) + \ldots]\,\mathbf{e}_i$$
$$= \mathbf{b}[\mathbf{e}_i + \mathbf{B}(\mathbf{e}_i + r_i\mathbf{e}_i) + \mathbf{B}(\mathbf{I} + \hat{\mathbf{r}})\,\mathbf{B}(\mathbf{e}_i + r_i\mathbf{e}_i) + \ldots]$$
$$= \mathbf{b}\{\mathbf{e}_i + s\mathbf{B}_i + s\mathbf{B}(\mathbf{I} + \hat{\mathbf{r}})\,\mathbf{B}_i + \ldots s[\mathbf{B}(\mathbf{I} + \hat{\mathbf{r}})]^n\,\mathbf{B}_i + \ldots\}$$
$$= \mathbf{b}_i + s\mathbf{b}\{\mathbf{I} + \mathbf{B}(\mathbf{I} + \hat{\mathbf{r}}) + \ldots [\mathbf{B}(\mathbf{I} + \hat{\mathbf{r}})]^n + \ldots\}\mathbf{B}_i$$
$$= \mathbf{b}_i + s\mathbf{b}[\mathbf{I} - \mathbf{B}(\mathbf{I} + \hat{\mathbf{r}})]^{-1}\mathbf{B}_i, \tag{A1}$$

where $\mathbf{b}_i$ and $\mathbf{B}_i$ are the ith 'columns' of $\mathbf{b}$ and $\mathbf{B}$. Suppose that $\mathbf{B}_{ji} > 0$ for some $j \neq i$. (A.1) will then depend on the jth column of $[\mathbf{I} - \mathbf{B}(\mathbf{I} + \hat{\mathbf{r}})]^{-1}$. But this *cannot* be independent of all r_j ($j \neq i$) when every industry uses some produced input(s). Hence $\mathbf{B}_{ji} = 0$ for all $j \neq i$ is necessary for AHP, in terms of i, with differential rates of profit.

References

Blackorby, C., Knox Lovell, C.A. and Thursby, M.C. (1976). 'Extended Hicks neutral technical change.' ECONOMIC JOURNAL, vol. 86, pp. 845–52.

Bruno, M., Burmeister, E. and Sheshinski, E. (1966). 'The nature and implications of the reswitching of techniques.' *Quarterly Journal of Economics*, vol. 80, pp. 526–53.

Hahn, F.H. and Matthews, R.C.O. (1964). 'The theory of economic growth: a survey.' ECONOMIC JOURNAL, vol. 74, pp. 779–902.

Hicks, J.R. (1932). *The Theory of Wages.* London: Macmillan.

Jones, R.W. (1965). 'The structure of simple general equilibrium models.' *Journal of Political Economy*, vol. 73, pp. 557–72.

Schefold, B. (1976). 'Relative prices as a function of the rate of profit: a mathematical note.' *Zeitschrift für Nationalökonomie*, vol. 36, pp. 21–48.

Note

*Earlier versions were presented to seminars at Manchester University, Trinity College, Dublin, the 1983 Trieste International Summer School and the 1984 Centro di Studi Economici Avanzati International Conference, Trieste. I am very grateful to C. Bidard, C. Birchenhall, P. Flaschel, U. Krause, H. Kurz, N. Salvadori, A. Villar, J. Woods and referees for very helpful discussion and comments.

91

Technology and Hedging Behavior: A Proof of Hicks' Conjecture[†]

M. O'Hara*

The idea that technology could lead to an imbalance in long and short hedging is due to John Hicks. He noted that:

> Technical conditions give the entrepreneur a much freer hand about the acquisition of inputs (which are largely needed to start a new process) than about the completion of outputs (whose process of production — in the ordinary business sense — may be already begun). If forward markets consisted entirely of hedgers, there would always be a tendency for a planned weakness on the demand side: a smaller proportion of planned purchases than of planned sales would be covered by forward contracts.

> [1946, p. 137]

It was this imbalance, Hicks conjectured, that would induce normal backwardation in forward prices.[1]

This paper provides a proof of Hicks' hedging conjecture. I demonstrate that, because of the properties of production functions and profit functions, long (or output) hedging may exceed short (or input) hedging *even if input and output decisions can be made at the same time*. The intuition behind this result is that the shape of a firm's technology may provide partial protection from price risks, but that this protection need not be symmetric with respect to input and output prices. To prove Hicks' conjecture, I develop a measure of the technology's price-risk sensitivity; this measure is similar to the Pratt–Arrow risk-aversion measure from utility theory. I then use this measure to indicate when producers will hedge input and output price-risks, and to provide sufficient conditions for Hicks' imbalance conjecture to hold.

That the technology per se, and not merely its timing, can lead to normal backwardation is the main contribution of this paper. My analysis can be viewed as a complement to the more extensive analyses of Hendrick

---

[†]Source: *The American Economic Review*, Vol. 75(5), December 1985, pp. 1186–90.

Houthakker (1968), David Newbery and Joseph Stiglitz (1981), and Ronald Anderson and Jean-Pierre Danthine (1983) on the existence of normal backwardation. Those authors demonstrate that forward prices can be influenced by a wide variety of factors such as storage, timing, and quantity uncertainty. My analysis suggests that technological conditions can also be important in influencing financial sector behavior.

I. Production, Profit, and Prices

To focus on the effect of technology on hedging, I consider a very simple model of the economy. I assume that production is non-stochastic, so a firm (or producer) faces no quantity uncertainty in output.[2] However, each producer does face price uncertainty as the output price, p, and the input price, w, both depend on the state of the world θ, $\theta \in [\underline{\theta}, \bar{\theta}]$. In the analysis that follows, I consider when a producer would prefer to "lock in" a price (either input or output) by entering a forward contract, or to wait and accept the uncertain price that will prevail in the spot market. Following Hicks, I define selling output via a forward contract to be long hedging; purchasing inputs via a forward contract to be short hedging.

Technology is given by $Y = g(X, Z)$ where Y is output, g is a production function, X is a variable input, and Z is a fixed input.[3] Initially, suppose that producers maximize expected profit. Then a producer selects X to maximize the expectation of the profit function.

$$(1) \qquad \pi(p, w) = p(\theta)g(X, Z) - w(\theta) X - Z$$

where the fixed input price is normalized to one. The following proposition characterizes the properties of this profit function.

PROPOSITION 1: *Let $g(X, Z)$ be strictly concave in X with $g'(X) > 0$, $g''(X) < 0$, and $g(0, Z) = 0$. Then*

(i) $\pi(p, w)$ is linear in p and linear in w if production decisions are made prior to the realization of $p(\theta)$, $w(\theta)$.

(ii) $\pi(p, w)$ is strictly convex in p and strictly convex in w if production decisions are made subsequent to the realization of $p(\theta)$, $w(\theta)$.

PROOF:
Given the timing of part (*i*), X is a number so $\pi(\cdot)$ is clearly linear in p and w. Part (*ii*) follows directly from Hal Varian (1978; Section 1.9).

Proposition 1 illustrates the relationship between prices and a producer's profitability. If producers cannot know the realizations of $p(\theta)$ and $w(\theta)$ before they produce, then (*i*) indicates that profit is linearly affected by price changes. This occurs because the producer's input and output amount is fixed; profit can vary only with price levels. If $p(\theta)$ and $w(\theta)$ are known, however, this simple relationship changes. Now the optimal amount to produce for each price realization can be selected; profit will vary because of quantity changes. As (*ii*) indicates, this quantity shifting means that different price levels have different, nonlinear effects on profit. The profit function becomes convex in input and output prices. The degree of convexity depends on the degree of concavity in the production function: the more concave the production function, the less convex the profit function.

The shape of the profit function has important implications for producers' forward market decisions. In case (*i*), the linearity of $\pi(p, w)$ means that an expected profit-maximizing producer would be indifferent between trading in the spot market at prevailing prices or trading in the forward market at the expected spot price. Since $\pi(p, w)$ is linear in both input and output prices, there is a symmetry in the forward demand to lock in these prices. This symmetry necessitates that the only forward market equilibrium has the forward price equal to the expected future spot price.

If the profit function is convex in prices, however, this is no longer the forward market equilibrium. The convexity of $\pi(p, w)$ means that producers actually *prefer* price variability. To induce producers to sell output forward, the forward price would have to exceed the expected future spot price. To induce producers to buy inputs forward, the forward price would have to be lower than the expected future spot price. No forward market composed only of hedgers could exist.

A forward market equilibrium characterized by normal backwardation, therefore, cannot occur if producers maximize expected profits. Since producers are, at worst, indifferent to price risk, they have no reason to "lock in" prices. This suggests that a necessary condition for Hicks' conjecture to hold is that (at least some) producers be averse to price risks. The analysis demonstrates that this aversion will not arise from the technology; if it arises at all, it must be because of producer risk preferences.

II. Utility, Technology, and Hedging

If producers are risk averse in profit, then their objective function is given by $E[U(\pi(p, w))]$, where U is a strictly concave utility function. Although $U(\cdot)$ is concave in profit, whether it is also concave in prices depends upon the relative shapes of the utility and profit functions. The shape of the utility function can be characterized by its measure of absolute risk aversion. The following proposition suggests a similar measure to characterize the shape of the profit function. These two measures provide a general rule for when risk aversion with respect to profit also implies risk aversion with respect to prices. If producers are averse to price risks, they will prefer to lock in prices in the forward market rather than accept the variable prices in the spot market.[4]

PROPOSITION 2: *Let $\pi(p, w)$ be the profit function, and $U(\pi(p, w))$ be the objective function. Let U denote a first derivative, $U_{\pi\pi}$ a second derivative (similarly for π). Then:*
   (i) A producer will hedge input price risks if in the absence of hedging

(2) $-U_{\pi\pi}/U_{\pi} > (1/\pi_w)\pi_{ww}/\pi_w.$

   (ii) A producer will hedge output price risks if in the absence of hedging

(3) $-U_{\pi\pi}/U_{\pi} > (1/\pi_p)\pi_{pp}/\pi_p.$

PROOF:
   Let $U(\pi(p, w)) \equiv V(p, w)$. Then to establish (2) note that $V_w = U_{\pi}\pi_w$ < 0 and $V_{ww} = U_{\pi\pi}(\pi_w)^2 + U_{\pi}\pi_{ww} \gtrless 0$. Concavity, or risk aversion in w, requires $V_{ww} < 0$. This implies $U_{\pi}\pi_{ww} < -U_{\pi\pi}(\pi_w)^2$ and the result follows. To establish (3) note that $V_p = U_{\pi}\pi_p > 0$ and $V_{pp} = U_{\pi\pi}p(\pi_p)^2 +$ $U_{\pi}\pi_{pp} \lessgtr 0$. Concavity, or risk aversion in p, requires $V_{pp} < 0$. This implies $U_{\pi}\pi_{pp} < -U_{\pi\pi}(\pi_p)^2$ and the result follows.
   The general rule stated above gives a simple way to characterize producers' forward market decisions. If a firm is risk neutral in profit, then $U_{\pi\pi} = 0$ and, as expected, the firm will not hedge. If the firm is risk averse, it will hedge if its absolute aversion to risk overwhelms the inherent convexity of the profit function. In the case of a linear profit function, π_{ww} and π_{pp} are zero, so hedging becomes attractive. This will occur, for example, when the firm's production decisions are made in advance of price realizations.If the profit function is strictly convex, however, even a very risk-averse producer may prefer not to hedge price risks.
   One implication of these conditions is that the timing of production may be sufficient to generate an imbalance in long and short hedging. If, as Hicks implies, input prices are more often known in advance of production than are output prices, then the profit function will be linear in p but convex in w. This means that producers will be more willing to hedge output prices than input prices. If only hedgers were present in forward markets, this imbalance would induce normal backwardation.
   Timing differences, however, are not necessary to generate this hedging imbalance. The technology itself may be sufficient to induce differential hedging. This can be demonstrated by incorporating some additional properties of profit functions and risk aversion measures into the analysis. To avoid timing complications, I assume that both input and output prices are known before production.[5] Then, from Hotelling's Lemma, $-\partial\pi(p, w)/\partial w = X$ and $\partial\pi(p, w)/\partial p = Y$ where X is the input demand and Y is output. Substituting for π_w and π_p in equations (2) and (3) and multiplying by π yields

(4) $-U_{\pi\pi}\pi/U_{\pi} > (-\pi/X)\pi_{ww}/\pi_w,$

(5) $-U_{\pi\pi}\pi/U_{\pi} > (\pi/Y)\pi_{pp}/\pi_p.$

   The left side of the expressions is the producer's relative risk-aversion measure. From (4), the producer's desire to hedge input price risks depends upon the relationship of both profit per unit of input and the technology to this relative risk-aversion measure. Equation (5) draws a similar comparison with profit per unit of output. One implication of this latter condition is that the higher the profit per unit of output, the more likely is the firm to hedge output price risks.

Equations (4) and (5) illustrate the interrelatedness of the hedging decision with technology. This linkage can be understood better by examining how the technology and profit function relate. Write the technology as $Y = g(X(p, w), Z)$ where $X(\cdot)$ is the input demand function. The profit function is then $\pi(p, w) = pg(X(p, w), Z) - wX(p, w)$. It is easy to show that

(6) $\pi_{ww} = pg''(X_w)^2 - 2X_w$

(7) $\pi_{pp} = pg''(X_p)^2 + 2g'X_p$

where primes denote derivatives of $g(\cdot)$ and subscripts denote derivatives of $X(\cdot)$.

Equations (6) and (7) can be simplified by realizing that, from the first-order conditions, profit maximization requires $pg'(X(p, w)) - w = 0$. This implies that $pg''X_x = 1$ and $pg''X_p = -g'$. It follows that

(8) $\pi_{ww}/\pi_w = 1/Xg''(\cdot)p$

(9) $\pi_{pp}/\pi = -(g'(\cdot))^2/g(\cdot)g''(\cdot)p.$

It is now easy to see how the shape of the technology influences the hedging conditions given by Proposition 2. As the technology becomes more linear, $g''(\cdot)$ goes to zero from below and both profit function conditions go to infinity. With the right sides of equations (2) and (3) infinite, even an extremely risk-averse producer will not hedge. As before, the intuition behind this result is that the shape of technology already provides insulation from price changes. The less concave this technology, the larger are the changes in X and Y for changes in p and w.

These price-induced changes in X and Y, however, need not be symmetric. As a result, the ability of the production process to limit input and output price risks may also not be symmetric. To see why, recall that $X_w = 1/pg''$ and $X_p = -g'/pg''$, and note that the output elasticity with respect to X, denoted η_x, is equal to $g'(\cdot)X/g(\cdot)$. Then equations (8) and (9) can be rewritten as

(10) $\pi_{ww}/\pi_w = X_w/X$

(11) $\pi_{pp}/\pi_p = \eta_X(X_p/X).$

The elasticity effect in equation (11) dictates that input and output prices affect the firm's production decisions in very different ways. While both price changes directly affect the input demand function, output price changes also have an indirect effect through the production function. The "warping" effect of the production function limits the technology's effectiveness in hedging output price risks. As the following proposition demonstrates, this implies that firms are more likely to hedge output price risks than input price risks.

PROPOSITION 3: *Given a strictly concave production function g(X) with g(0) = 0,*

$$(12) \quad (1/\pi_p)\pi_{pp}/\pi_p < (1/\pi_w)\pi_{ww}/\pi_w.$$

PROOF:

From equations (8), (9), and Hotelling's Lemma, this condition can be rewritten as

$$(-(g')^2/pgg'')1/g < 1/Xpg''(-1/X).$$

Simplifying yields

$$(g'/g)(g'/g) < (1/X)(1/X)$$

which is equivalent to

$$(g'X/g)(g'X/g) < 1.$$

But $(g'X/g)$ is η_X. Hence, we need $(\eta_X)^2 < 1$ to establish the claim. Since $\eta_X > 0$, it is sufficient to establish $\eta_X < 1$. Thus we need $Xg'/g < 1$, or $g' < g/X$. But this is equivalent to Marginal Product of $X <$ Average Product of X, which is always true if $g(\cdot)$ is strictly concave and $g(0) = 0$.

Proposition 3 provides an important result. If a firm will hedge input price risks, it will also hedge output price risks. However, a firm may hedge output prices *without* wanting to hedge input prices. As a result, the demand for "output price insurance" exceeds the demand for "input price insurance." As Hicks' conjectured, the technology induces an imbalance in long and short hedging. If forward markets were composed only of hedgers, then normal backwardation would result.

III. Concluding Remarks

This paper has examined the effect of technology on producers' forward market decisions. I have demonstrated that the technology itself may provide protection from price risks. This technological protection obviates the need for forward market protection, particularly in the case of input prices. This results in the imbalance of long and short hedging that Hicks conjectured would characterize forward market participation.

While I have demonstrated sufficient conditions for Hicks' conjecture to hold, it is certainly true that in other economic environments this hedging imbalance may not arise. As Anderson and Danthine have demonstrated, the presence of quantity uncertainty or storage can introduce other factors into producers' hedging decisions. Nevertheless, by focusing strictly on technology, this paper demonstrates the crucial link between technology and hedging behaviour.

References

Anderson, Ronald W. and Danthine, Jean-Pierre, "Hedger Diversity in Futures Markets," *Economic Journal*, June 1983, *93*, 370–89.

Hicks, John R., *Value and Capital*, 2nd ed., London: Oxford University Press, 1946.

Houthakker, Hendrick S., "Normal Backwardation," in J.N. Wolfe, ed., *Value and Growth*: *Papers in Honor of Sir John Hicks*, Edinburgh: Edinburgh University Press, 1968.

Newbery, David M. G. and Stiglitz, Joseph E., *The Theory of Commodity Price Stabilization*, Oxford: Oxford University Press, 1981.

Varian, Hal R., *Microeconomic Analysis*, New York: W.W. Norton, 1978.

Notes

*I thank Lawrence Blume, David Easley, and Robert Frank for helpful comments. I also thank the National Science Foundation, grant no. IST-8408770, for financial support.

1. Normal backwardation occurs when the forward price is less than the expected future spot price. Conversely, if the forward price exceeds the expected future spot price, this is referred to as contango.

2. The case of stochastic production is extensively analyzed in Anderson and Danthine. They demonstrate that quantity uncertainty can result in either normal backwardation or contango in forward prices. This leads them to conclude "it is not possible from a purely theoretical point of view to demonstrate conclusively the predominance of backwardation or contango" (p. 388). In this paper I demonstrate that with *non-stochastic* production this predominance of backwardation can occur.

3. In the analysis that follows, the concavity of $g(\cdot)$ in X plays an important role. However, this needed concavity is with respect to a specific input, and not necessarily with respect to total inputs. For example, a Cobb-Douglas technology of the form $Y = X_1{}^a X_2{}^b$ with $a + b = 1$ is linear in total inputs but is concave in specific inputs. For simplicity, the paper concentrates on the single-variable input case, but the analysis can easily be adapted to the multiple input case.

4. The decision to enter the forward market also depends upon the forward prices. In the analysis that follows, I evaluate forward demand and supply when the forward price is equal to the expected future spot price. If a producer's objective function is concave in prices, however, he would be willing to pay a premium to enter the forward contract. Hence, if long hedging exceeds short hedging, the forward price will fall, resulting in normal backwardation. If short hedging exceeds long hedging, the forward price will rise, resulting in contango.

5. With both input and output prices known before production, the producer has the maximum amount of production flexibility. This allows the producer to partially offset unfavorable price conditions, and thus reduces his incentives to hedge. By focusing on this case, the analysis examines the interaction between production flexibility and hedging when production flexibility is at its greatest. Certainly, if the producer must take production decisions before prices are known, his hedging decisions may differ.

92

Limits on Growth*†

N. Kaldor

I regard it as a great privilege to have been asked to give the second of the Special Lectures which the University of Oxford arranged as an annual event in honour of Professor Sir John Hicks. I do so for both personal and professional reasons.

For convenience of exposition, though not on account of its prime importance, I should like to speak of my personal reasons first. Sir John Hicks is one of my oldest friends in England, and I owe him an immense debt for all that he taught me at the time when my knowledge of economics was very rudimentary. He is four years my senior — a difference which is hardly worth a mention now, but was of enormous significance when we were both young and he was a fully qualified teacher in economics when I was a first year undergraduate. John Hicks first came to the L.S.E. from Oxford as a lecturer in 1926. I arrived a year later, and began as a first-year student reading for an economics degree in October 1927.

I first got to know him when I attended his lectures on Advanced Economic Theory. I remember a great deal of that course since it gave an exposition of the theories of Walras and Pareto and how they compared with the partial equilibrium method of Marshall. After my graduation I was awarded a Research Studentship and I moved into a small unfurnished flat in Bloomsbury which, as it happened, was next door to the one occupied by John Hicks. It did not take long before we saw each other frequently — indeed almost daily, for meals in small Italian restaurants, and talked about economics incessantly. There was at least one occasion when we went on a joint continental holiday. This, in some ways idyllic, arrangement came to a halt (though only temporarily) with my marriage, closely followed by a Rockefeller Fellowship in the United States, while Hicks married a close L.S.E. friend and fellow graduate student, Ursula K. Webb (who died recently) who was the real founder of the *Review of Economic Studies*. When the *Review* first appeared it was treated by the professionals with considerable scorn. Hayek thought it could not last for more than a year. Keynes thought there was no real need for it since, as the editor of the *Economic Journal*, he believed he had never had to turn down an article

†Source: *Oxford Economic Papers*, Vol. 38, November 1986, pp. 187–98.

that was worthy of publication on account of pressure on space. Fifty years later the *Review* is still going strong and nobody would say now that its existence has not been justified.

Though we never shared a university again, and lived in different cities and hence saw each other much less frequently our mutual friendship was never in question — even though the gaps in erudition between us, though they may have narrowed in the course of the years, were never closed. I never had the patience to learn mathematics; Hicks got a first in Maths Mods at Oxford, and taught himself a number of foreign languages sufficiently well to be able to read and enjoy treatises on economics that were not available in English. As a result he was able to cut himself loose from the narrow dogmatism of Robbins and Hayek, and in this I followed him eagerly. He recommended that I should read Wicksell and Myrdal as an antidote to Hayek. But I learnt most from him in connection with his early work on Money and on general equilibrium economics; and I believe I was allowed to read *Value and Capital* almost chapter by chapter as it was written.

Now, coming to the professional reasons, which are far more important, John Hicks is an economist in the great classical tradition: undoubtedly one of the greatest now living, not just in this country but in the Western World. He is a pure economist in the sense that his interest is in developing general economic theory by improving the framework of assumptions whenever the case for such an improvement is established, and in exploring their implications as fully as logical reasoning, aided by mathematics, makes possible. Unlike others, whose interest in economics is more pedestrian, Hicks' main aim is the pursuit of knowledge as such. He is not an advocate of particular economic policies: he allows his readers to make up their minds on such matters — his own views and preferences are on most occasions kept firmly in the background. In this he differs from some other famous economists who developed the subject for the sake of finding better arguments for their preferred policies for improving the performance of the economy.

Hicks of course is also primarily interested in exploring the limits on production and growth but without any preconceived objectives of supporting one particular set of policies as against others. In this respect Hicks is nearer to the grand tradition of the Lausanne School of Walras and Pareto than to that of the English classical economists.

His main virtues are the virtues of the intellectual — they are found in the thoroughness and patience with which he explores the implications of particular assumptions to the last detail — I would almost say, to the "last unsuspected detail". Indeed the feature that impresses me most in reading his works is the scrupulousness with which he pursues the numerous aspects of a problem — aspects the existence of which would not have been suspected by a more impatient and less intellectually thorough economist like myself.

But the most impressive thing about Sir John Hicks is the sheer magnitude, I would indeed say, the incredible magnitude, of his written record. He is the author of three major treatises — *Value and Capital, Capital and*

Growth, and *Capital and Time*, any one of which could be regarded as an ample testimony of the concentrated effort of a life-time. But in addition to these three treatises Hicks published a large number of important and famous books on particular topics, beginning with the *Theory of Wages* in 1932, his *Contribution to the Theory of the Trade Cycle* in 1950, the *Theory of Economic History* (which is my personal favourite), and various books on monetary economics down to his most admirable, though difficult, methodological essay on *Casuality in Economics* published in 1979, or 47 years after the appearance of his first book. In between he published at least three books containing papers on monetary theory, and this was followed by three large volumes of Collected Essays on Economic Theory which appeared in the last few years. I cannot say that I have read everything which Hicks has written, though in relation to any other author (with the possible exception of Keynes) my score of having read and studied Hicks is rather a high one, and the more one considers his books the more one marvels how one man could have accomplished all this, and at the same time made such an extensive and continuing study of the works of others, as is evidenced by the broad variety of his references in the footnotes which are adduced to support particular points in the text.

One of Hicks' most engaging qualities and a rare one among academics, is the readiness with which he is prepared to set aside his previous writings if in the light of further thought he sees a problem differently from the way he approached it before. Unlike lesser men, he never feels constrained by his past utterances. As he put it in the Introduction to *Capital and Time*, "it is just as if one were making pictures of a building; though it is the same building, it looks quite different from different angles. As I now realise, I have been walking round my subject, taking different views of it." (No such sentiments could be expressed by an author who writes a treatise entitled *Principles of Economics*.)

As John Hicks argues in his latest book, economics is on the edge of the sciences and also on the edge of history — it is on the borderline of both. The economist, unlike the historian, is primarily concerned with the present, and for the sake of the present, is also concerned with the past — with the historian it is the other way round. More generally I would say that economic theory embodying hypotheses concerning the causal relationship between events should help us to understand the forces which shape historical developments. Ideally one would like to see induction and deduction closely interwoven. This however is not generally possible. The main reason, I think, is that the results derived by deductive reasoning necessarily presuppose a whole framework of assumptions, some of which may be supported by empirical investigations, while others may turn out to be immaterial.

However, the critical assumptions underlying theoretical propositions are not known in advance; hence the applicability of a theory, its explanatory power, can only be properly gauged after the deductive process is completed.

I shall choose as the main theme today Hicks' interpretation of the prolonged post-war boom, and the causes of its breakdown after 1973. It is found in a long essay on "Monetary Experience and the Theory of Money" which first appeared in a volume of essays on *Economic Perspectives* in 1977, though it may have been written sometime before that. The main purpose of Hicks' paper is a review of monetary theories from Hume to Wicksell and to Keynes and to deal with the slow and uninterrupted inflation which characterised the whole of the post-war period but which proceeded at a moderate pace — the so-called "creeping inflation" — of the 1950s and 1960s. It only became more violent (in all industrialised countries and not just in Britain) in the mid-seventies. After showing that the long post-war inflation — the *moderate* inflation — was an indispensable prerequisite of fast economic growth and universal full employment (since it made it possible for the slow growing countries to prosper provided that inflation was large enough in the fast growing countries), the maintenance of full employment in the industrial or so-called "secondary" sectors of the world economy (and as Hicks says, it is this sector which Keynes in the *General Theory* mainly had in mind) critically depended on an adequate growth in supplies in the "primary" sector (i.e., in agriculture and mining) which provide the indispensable inputs for the secondary sector. The classical economists were well aware of this; the Law of Diminishing Returns is a consequence of the fact that land is in fixed supply, and "land" (meaning the natural environment) is the critical factor both in the production of food and in the provision of raw materials of all kinds as well as of sources of energy. Hence the basic pessimism of all classical economists concerning the long-term possibilities of economic growth. The accumulation of capital, in the classical view, is a necessary but not a sufficient condition for growth. The growth of production will be less than in proportion to the increase in 'resources' (meaning both capital and labour), it must therefore involve (given the level of wages as determined by the costs of subsistence) a falling rate of profit which is indeed (I am here quoting Ricardo) "checked at repeated intervals by the improvements in machinery, connected with the production of necessaries, as well as by discoveries in the science of agriculture". However, sooner or later the Law of Diminishing Returns must reassert itself. The motive for accumulation (I am quoting Ricardo again) "will diminish with every diminution of profit and will cease altogether when profits are so low as not to afford them [the manufacturers] an adequate compensation for their trouble and for the risks which they must necessarily encounter in employing their capital productively".[1] Sooner or later all avenues will inevitably lead to the long run equilibrium of the Stationary State. And on the way to it, it appeared inevitable that a steadily rising proportion of resources should be absorbed in the procurement of food, leaving less available for everything else. This was the main lesson to be derived from the Law of Diminishing Returns.

As is the case with many of the long term predictions of economists, subsequent history not only failed to support the predictions but led quite universally in the opposite direction. The proportion of resources of the world economy (or the world *trading* economy — as Hicks prefers to regard the real-world equivalent of the economist's motion of a "closed economy") which was required for the primary sector of production has steadily diminished with economic progress — indeed in the views of some it was the steady fall in the proportion of resources required for satisfying primary needs which made possible economic progress and rising living standards in a steadily growing number of countries or areas. The proportion of the annual labour force occupied in agriculture in Britain is estimated to have been around 50 per cent in the 17th century but less than 36 per cent in the early 19th century; 20 per cent by the middle of that century, 8 per cent by 1900 and only 2.5 per cent today. (Even the earliest figure — 50% — is much lower than that of other European countries of the period, e.g. France. This indicates that even prior to the Industrial Revolution England was a relatively rich country in Europe, the reasons for which would deserve closer investigation than they have yet received.)

It is true that today home production covers only around 60 per cent of our food requirements (this is a higher figure than that of the early decades of this century). But even so, the proportion of labour and capital resources needed to provide food for the whole of the population is 5 per cent or less — less than one twentieth. This is consistent with the figures for other countries having a modern, commercialised agriculture — for example, in Australia the proportion of the labour force in agriculture is around $6\frac{1}{2}$ per cent, but two thirds of the output is exported, so the proportion required to provide food for the indigenous population is only around 2 per cent. This may be lower, but not much lower, than the figures for Western European countries as well as America, in all of which the agricultural work force fell dramatically since the Second World War. As far as one can tell, this process is by no means at an end.

But this is only the labour-saving measure of technical progress in agriculture, which tells us nothing of the rate of growth of output, and how it compares with the rate of growth of demand for primary products. For that we need another measure of technical progress, looked at from the "land-saving" or "natural resource saving" aspect. It is the latter aspect which is crucial for growth. I define a land-saving innovation as anything which increases the total yield of a given area, whether agricultural or mineral (including sources of energy), though it is impossible to say whether the innovation is the result of new knowledge or merely newly adopted knowledge. The same kind of haziness which Sir John Hicks found in the notion of an industrial production frontier which depended on capital and labour resources, also applies to the production frontier for primary products — we cannot really distinguish movements along the curve from outward shifts of the curve. Anyhow, the real issue is whether the growth of labour productivity in industry and services and the growth of land productivity in agriculture and mining (the latter including oil-extraction) are in an *appropriate relationship* to one another (which need not imply proportionality).[2]

As Hicks says, from the early 1970s on "the Keynesian identification of the limit to growth with Full Employment of Labour is called into question".[3] During the Bretton Woods period full employment was the effective barrier but since then, the effective barrier has been different (quoting Hicks), "full employment cannot now be reached since the supplies of primary products that would be needed to support it are not available".[4] As my lecture is mainly intended to cast doubt on this proposition, I think I ought to add that I was just as convinced of this as Hicks was[5] — indeed more convinced, since Hicks went on immediately to qualify his statement by saying that the experience of the early 1970s may have been a temporary one due to "the exceptional expansion of 1972–3 which imposed an exceptional strain". (This resulted, I presume, from the sudden relaxation or disappearance of the balance of payment constraint in a number of countries which followed the abandonment of Bretton Woods.)

Indeed, the year 1973 was unique for its fast economic growth — which was higher in that year in *all* industrial countries than in any previous year or any of the subsequent years. Manufacturing output rose by 9.5 per cent in the U.K. by 10.3 per cent in the seven main industrial countries (including the U.S.) and by 10 per cent in the OECD countries as a whole. These rates were at least 50 per cent higher than the average rate of growth of industrial production in the previous 25 years, and while it can readily be granted that they were not sustainable, given the rate of growth of the output of primary products, the shortage of primary products certainly cannot explain why the rate of growth of industrial production in subsequent years — that is to say, in the years 1973–1984 — should have fallen so low — to $1^3/_4$ per cent a year in the European OECD countries as a group, as against the growth rate of $5^3/_4$ per cent a year achieved in the previous 25 years. Indeed, in the light of these figures it is in my view impossible to maintain that the Depression of the Seventies (and after), with the reappearance of heavy unemployment in the industrial countries, was a consequence of *supply constraints*, the effects of which would have been aggravated, not alleviated — as many people maintained at the time on both sides of the Atlantic — by the more deliberate use of Keynesian policies acting on effective demand. The most one can say is that uncoordinated measures of expansion by individual countries would have tended to aggravate the imbalances in international trade and payments. Indeed it was the disproportionality between import and export propensities of individual countries under conditions of fully liberalized trade which was the major cause of the well-nigh universal state of recession.

I think it is in this context that Sir John Hicks' distinction between fix-price and flex-price markers is important. The manufacturing sector is the archetypal case of fix-price market — at least in the present century — when manufacturers are almost invariably price-*makers* and quantity-*takers*, and not the other way round. The working of this system is by no means fully clarified. It generally involves some firm, or firms, assuming the role of a price leader which other manufacturers follow — hence from the consumers' point of view, there is not much difference whether he buys from a high cost firm or a low cost firm, the differences in efficiency are reflected, not in a difference in prices (for goods of the *same* quality), but in differences in profits per unit of sale of different producers which, as we know from various kinds of statistics, are very large indeed.

Everybody practices mark-up pricing, but it is the price-leaders' costs and mark-up which determines the permissible, or viable, mark-up of the others. In such markets supply tends to equal demand in the sense that the flow of actual production tends to approximate actual take-up, or consumption, but this is not "market clearing" in the economists' sense, since the actual production of the representative seller is below his optimum production at the prevailing price — below the level of production that would maximise his profits. Differences between demand and supply in this sense are mainly reflected in stock changes; a fall in demand leads to an undesired (or involuntary, as the Keynesian term goes) accumulation of stocks, and *vice versa* if demand exceeds supply. The market operates via changes in quantities rather than in prices; in the relation of actual stocks to desired stocks, which tend to get eliminated through the operation of the stock adjustment principle. In markets of this type uncertainties concerning the future growth of demand mainly affect the degree of utilization of capacity; it pays the manufacturers to maintain capacity in excess of demand and keep the growth of capacity in line with the growth of demand. They are in a position to do this precisely because in the absence of keen price competition their profits will be large enough to finance new investment on a continuing basis. Prices are changed too, but these happen mainly as a result of changes in costs, either of raw materials or of labour, or both.

In flex-price markets, on the other hand, markets operate far more closely to the text book manner; the individual producer has no control over prices and cannot benefit from withholding supplies. Prices *fall* when supply (in this case it is the true supply, which means the *maximum* amount that sellers are prepared to sell at any particular price) exceeds demand and *vice versa*. In these markets short-term stock changes are also important and they can exert an influence both in a price-stabilizing and also a price-destabilizing direction. The stocks are held, not just by producers and consumers but mainly by market dealers (intermediaries) who maintain "buffer stocks" to be able to buy or sell to their customers at any time they desire even if the timing of purchases and sales is not perfectly synchronised. They make their money on the "dealers' turn" between their buying and selling prices, which are both varied simultaneously according as they perceive that their stocks are changing in one direction or another, contrary to the desired norm.

In performing these functions the dealers almost inevitably become speculators as well, who increase stocks on their own initiative when they expect prices to rise, and *vice versa* when they expect prices to fall. While their normal functions as dealers operate in a price-stabilizing direction, their speculative transactions have the opposite effect. As a combined result price movements normally continue until a point is reached when traders feel that prices are abnormally low (or high as the case may be), in which case their policy goes into reverse (they buy in the expectation of a rise, when they consider that prices have fallen "too far", and so on) which creates a turning point, followed by an equally rapid movement of prices in the opposite direction. So commodity prices in unregulated markets behave like a yo-yo, they move up and down by very large amounts, normally within a period of a year or less. Keynes, writing in 1938, calculated that the *average* annual difference between the highest and a lowest price, over a ten-year period, amounted to 67 per cent in the case of four commodities (rubber, cotton, wheat and lead).[6] After 1945 the same kind of fluctuations continued, according to some authorities on an even larger scale, particularly after 1971,[7] and rising and falling prices tended to alternate in two-year periods more often than within a single year. Thus the sharp rise in prices in 1972–73 (by 150 per cent in terms of the index of commodity prices) was followed by a sharp fall of the order of 25 per cent in 1974–75, and a sharp rise in prices in 1976 (by over 40 per cent), followed by a fall in 1977; a rise in 1978–79 of over 30 per cent followed by a sharp fall of 26 per cent in 1980–82, and again by a further 20 per cent in 1984–85.[8]

The working of flex-price markets is thus in fact very inefficient — it is attended by large fluctuations in prices which are not regular enough to be predictable in extent or timing, and which generate risks that act as a drag on production.[9] Hence whether a stabilization scheme succeeds, it is soon followed by a rise in production which brings about a large accumulation of stocks (butter mountains or cocoa mountains) which give the impression to consuming countries that they are made to pay too high a price as a result of the price stabilization scheme, whereas the presumption is that *without* price stabilization the effective price paid for commodities over the average of high and low periods would have been considerably more and not less.

If the prices in commodity markets could be stabilized through international commodity price stabilization schemes, as Keynes advocated strongly (though unsuccessfully) during the War, it is highly probable that the long-term rate of growth of output of primary commodities would be sufficiently enhanced to equal or to exceed the requirements arising from any *feasible* rate of growth of industrial output.[10] For while there is no *ultimate* limit to industrial production in a world context, there is a limit to the rate at which output can grow, a limit given by the sequential character of production, as analysed in *Capital and Time*. Just as it takes nine months to produce a baby, and it cannot be done in less, so in a world where it needs steel to make machinery and iron and coal to make steel, and each of these processes takes time, there is a limit to the rate at which additional labour can be absorbed in productive activities.

In agriculture, or in primary production as a whole, the same limitation due to the sequential character of production applies but it need not impose any *narrower* limit provided that adequate stocks are carried to ensure the success of the price-stabilisation scheme. For the real difference between primary production and secondary production (that is to say, between agriculture and mining on the one hand and industrial production on the other hand) resides in the short term elasticities of supply. In industry, on account of the nature of competition and marketing, an increase in demand is likely to call forth an increase in output fairly smoothly without much delay or impediment. In agriculture and mining on the other hand production normally responds to increased demand with some delay, particularly in the case of minerals where increased capacity may require the sinking of new shafts, etc. Over a longer period, on the other hand, there is no reason to suppose that the elasticity of supply of primary products be any less — indeed, historical experience shows the opposite, since the prior requirements for primary products could be satisfied with a *steadily falling proportion* of labour and capital devoted to the primary sector. This is despite the fact that technological progress involves the substitution of primary products for labour — in the form of energy generated by fossil fuels in place of human muscle power — as well as the substitution of manufactured goods (machinery) for labour.[11]

The basic requirement of continued economic growth is that the various complementary sectors expand in due relationship with each other — that is to say that general expansion is not held up by "bottlenecks" in key sectors. However, in the course of time, under the influence of technical progress, both of the natural-resource saving and labour-saving kind, the requirements of expansion may become considerably modified. In the manufacturing sector which becomes more important as real incomes rise, there are considerable economies of scale, as a result of which manufacturing activities are subject to a *"polarisation process"* — they are likely to develop in a few successful centres, and their success has an inhibiting effect on similar developments in other areas. The realisation of these economies of scale normally requires also that numerous processes of production which are related to each other are carried out in close geographical proximity.

As a result different regions experience unequal rates of growth of output and of population. The industrial areas experience a growing demand for labour which may involve immigration from other areas once their own surplus labour is exhausted. Technological development in primary production on the other hand, tends to be more labour-saving than land-saving, so that the growth of output may go hand in hand with a falling demand for labour; and though output per head may grow fast in real terms, the level of wages will tend to remain low (and may even be falling)[12] as a result of a growing surplus population. Since labour cost per unit of output is the most important factor in determining selling prices (at any rate under competitive conditions) the low wages prevailing, in terms of *industrial* products, will mean that the terms of trade will move unfavourably to primary producers, which may be the main factor, along with the low coefficient of labour utilisation, for their state of "underdevelopment" characterised by low standards of living.

The important contrast — which I regard as a major factor in the growing inequality of incomes between rich and poor countries — resides in the fact that the benefit of labour saving technical progress in the primary sector tends to get passed on to the consumers in the secondary sector in lower prices, whereas in the industrial sector its benefits are retained *within* the sector through higher wages and profits. (The main reason for this difference lies in the differing manner of operation of perfect and imperfect competition.)

Industrial growth leads to both higher real wages and a higher volume of employment, which will mean a higher concentration of the population in urban areas. This may entail cumulative advantages through the spread of knowledge and education with favourable repercussions on progress through the application of scientific knowledge to industry. These go well beyond the economies of large-scale production, though these economies, through their need for geographic concentration, may have been instrumental in creating them. The reverse side of this (of which we have heard much recently) is found when the industrial sector, due to falling market shares in relation to other centres, becomes stagnant and then goes into a decline, causing unemployment which tends to be concentrated in the inner cities of large towns which fall into decay.

In the primary producing regions, by contrast, technical progress involves a combination of rising production and of falling demand for labour, resulting in both open and disguised unemployment, the natural corrective for which is the movement of populations from agricultural to industrial areas. However, actual mobility has never been large enough to even out the differences in the level and the rate of growth of real wages between agriculture and industry — not even within the same country, and much less so when the required movement is across political boundaries.

There is thus no effective tendency to level out the differences between the advanced industrial areas and the surplus-labour agricultural areas; on the contrary, if our analysis is correct, the benefits of technical progress of *both* sectors tend to accrue to the *industrial* sector. This means that the faster the growth of technical knowledge the more "the terms of trade" will turn against the primary producing areas and the greater will be the inequality between rich and poor countries.

Hence contrary to the view expressed at the beginning, the fall in growth rates and the rise in unemployment levels in the advanced industrial countries after 1973 was not the inevitable consequence of shortages in primary products — the indications are that the supplies of food, raw materials and energy would have proved adequate to the needs of the advanced industrial countries — particularly so if their prices had been kept steady by stabilisation schemes, instead of showing the sharp movements due to changes in short-term market expectations, and if there had not been the rise in prices due to monopolistic restrictions such as the creation of the oil cartel.

Thus the physical limits on growth (as distinct from the actual limits which became increasingly dependent on a complex of policy objectives) have continued to be set by the availabilities of labour in the advanced industrial countries — just as was the case in the first 25 years after the Second World War. If the maintenance of full employment in the industrial countries came under increasing strain it was as a result of accelerated inflationary trends caused by the sharp rise in commodity prices after 1971 — which are likely to have been largely speculative in origin, following America's abandonment of the gold standard. (This is shown by the fact that the movement of commodity prices closely followed the movement of the gold price[13] and the repercussions of this on the cost of living and hence on the rate of money-wage increases which aggravated the process.) The reaction, almost universally, was to deal with the problem as if it had been caused by demand inflation, not by cost inflation — in other words, by tightening fiscal and monetary policies (though for reasons that are evident, it is very difficult for any single country to stand out against the prevailing trend — unless it isolates itself by quantitative controls over trade as well as strict control of foreign payments).

For Britain the lower growth rate of the world economy meant an actual fall in industrial production after 1973, the level of which has still not been regained. Despite recent Ministerial claims of five years of uninterrupted growth, current manufacturing output is still 12 per cent below 1973 and 7 per cent below 1979. The counterpoint to this was a heavy increase in unemployment, the incidence of which was concentrated in old areas of manufacturing industry, which are often found in the decaying inner city areas of large towns, where prospects of finding alternative employment opportunities are virtually non-existent. Twelve years of industrial decline has thus created *within* Britain the same kind of contrasts between prosperous and depressed areas as exist in the world at large between developed and under-developed countries.

Notes

*The second annual Hicks Lecture, delivered in Oxford on November 28th, 1985.

1. *Principles*, Sraffa edition, pp. 120 and 122.

2. Strict numerical proportionality is not of course what is required, since the income elasticity of consumption demand for foodstuffs is less than unity and that for manufactures and services greater than unity — but the main point made in the text is valid in the sense that there is a "warranted" relationship between them at any particular level of real income.

3. *Economic Perspectives*, p. 98.

4. *Ibid.*, p. 99.

5. Cf., "Inflation and Recession in the World Economy", *Economic Journal*, December 1976, pp. 704–708.

6. "The Policy of Government Storage of Foodstuffs and Raw Materials", *Economic Journal*, 1938.

7. According to Prof. Sylos Labini, the variations in raw material prices were three times as large in relation to changes in world industrial production, than before 1971. Cf., Sylos Labini, *On the Instability of Commodity Prices and the Problem of Gold*; cf., also the graph in *Lloyds Bank Review*, July 1983, p. 25.

8. These figures relate to an index number of 12 commodities — they are not comparable therefore with Keynes' figures which related to a group of four commodities only.

9. It could be argued that competitive markets would be far less inefficient if dealers carried much larger stocks in relation to turnover as this would enable them to exert a far greater price-stabilising influence as part of their actual business. However, the stocks which they find profitable to carry are themselves related to the profit made on the "dealers' turn" which is itself kept down by competition. Thus the same forces of competition which made intermediation relatively costless are in part responsible also for the large fluctuation of prices.

10. As was found with the pre-war "marketing boards" in African countries, the introduction of an assured price gave a very large encouragement to peasant production.

11. I am ignoring in the context of this lecture the truly long-term problem created by the exhaustion of reserves of non-renewable sources of energy and minerals which agitated some scientists (Meadows and Co. and the Club of Rome) some 15 years ago. The uncertainties surrounding this question are too large to enable worthwhile consideration of this problem. For one thing, *known* reserves are no indication of total available reserves, since it becomes totally uneconomic to search for reserves where known reserves exceed 30–40 years current consumption. It must also be borne in mind that technical progress has generally succeeded in circumventing scarcities arising from the shortage or insufficiency of particular commodities (the best known example is Darby's invention of the coking of coal which made iron production independent of timber supplies at a stage when deforestation caused an acute shortage

of timber) and there is no reason why this process should come to a halt. (Cf. W. Beckerman, 'Economists, Scientists and Environmental Catastrophe', *Oxford Economic Papers*, November 1972).

12. Sir Arthur Lewis had shown that the spectacular increase in both labour and land productivity in sugar production over 40 years coincided with a fall in wages in sugar plantations.

13. Cf. the graph in OECD *Economic Outlook*, December 1973, p. 106.

93

Reflecting on the Theory of Capital and Growth[†]

E. Malinvaud[1]

Improving the understanding and theoretical analysis of economic growth has been one of the main motivations of Sir John Hicks through many of his writings. Since this is also for me a strong motivation, I find it proper on this occasion to discuss the full range of theories in which the essential role of time is recognized.

One may say that these theories aim at providing a conceptual system that should permit rigorous study of the reasons why some economies grow faster and perform better than others, or than the same economies in different historical phases. Experience has taught us the difficulty of such an ambitious aim. This is why we often view the theory of capital and growth as dealing more modestly with the representation of medium and long term economic evolution under steady conditions.

Even when its scope is so limited, the ideal theory is not available today. We have some notions on what it should be; but we do not hope to be able to specify it properly right away. We are rather striving to make some sure steps toward its construction. Hence, two questions: are the steps sure? Do they go in the right direction?

The whole of Hicks' research applies this strategy. He made some important steps, probed their reliability, argued for their significance. Since I walked behind him, but sometimes stepping a few feet out of his way in the hope of finding a better path, I may sit down today, look around and wonder where he and his colleages or students have led us on the way toward this ideal theory that appears in the far distance, still quite fuzzy for our eyes.

While I do so, you will notice a difference in style, since you are all faithful readers of Hicks. I am indeed unable to convey, as well as he does in his writings, the feeling that the choice of the best specification for the theoretical analysis of complex phenomena is a very delicate problem, the solution of which can always be questioned. As for me, I like to stress the parts that I think to have been firmly established, often fooling myself in behaving as if these parts at least were unquestionable.

The first phase in our search for the theory of growth has been to reach

[†]Source: *Oxford Economic Papers*, Vol. 38, November 1986, pp. 367–85.

a clear understanding on what would be a stationary equilibrium. I shall have relatively little to say on the microeconomic field of this well explored area. But it also contains macroeconomic bushes and swamps, through which the best way to choose is less apparent. Later, our discussion will concern whether and how, starting from a given initial situation, but still operating under stationary conditions, economic growth will reach an equilibrium: what Hicks called "the traverse". From there on, we shall have to explore a few tentative ways to go over the many difficulties of the study of growth under disequilibrium prices.

1. Microeconomic Equilibrium Theories

The ultimate aims of theories of capital and growth are the understanding and analysis of macroeconomic phenomena. But solid foundations are mainly microeconomic. I am one of those who think that macroeconomic specifications do not arise only from abstract reflection but also from econometric induction (even though this induction is often at present not formalized and quite loose; even though it will seldom be quite conclusive and never be easy). Nevertheless even simply embedding econometric results within the main theories requires a careful study of their relations to the microeconomic environment from which they come and of the various aspects of aggregation.

Microeconomic theories providing the required foundations must then be general. Of course, this does not mean that general models only are admissible in the research process on microeconomic theory. Quite the contrary, the building of present theories of capital and growth most often proceeded from the careful study of special models: the point-input point-output case of the exploitation of growing forests, the "Akerman problem", Samuelson's chocolate economy, and so on. But those must in the end be viewed as intermediate steps toward the derivation of general microeconomic theories, from which macroeconomic theories ought to be derived by a process of aggregation and econometric selection.

In other words, research typically moves to and fro. It does not need to, and in fact cannot, specify from the beginning the appropriate general fundamental models that will later be accepted. But we must from time to time try to be precise on our general theories. This is why I want to stress here the two features of these theories that I consider as being essential: economic activity proceeds recursively, growth results from a sequence of temporary equilibria.

But before I do so, I should like to draw your attention to two somewhat puzzling sections at the beginning of *Capital and Time* (I.3 and I.4), where Hicks discusses what he calls "the *disintegration* of the productive process". Considering how we can represent production in our theories of capital and growth, he there distinguishes three methods, which he respectively calls the "method of sectoral disintegration" (some firms produce capital goods, others use these goods), the "method of von Neumann" (production lasts just one period, inputs occurring at the beginning, outputs at the end), the "method of separable elementary processes" (a process uses only primary inputs and produces only outputs directly used in consumption). We there have the vision of production taking place before us in the economy, like in a living organism. Hicks asks us to wonder how we should disintegrate this organism so as to understand how it functions.

If I am drawing your attention to these sections, it is because they seem to suggest that, in contradiction to what I shall assume here, micro-economic concepts may not be the most fundamental ones. They may already be the result of simplifications, abstracting from important features of a reality that might better be described with less disintegration. Let us keep this query in mind for future research.

Without now choosing between Hicks' three methods, I want to stress here that they have in common two features. First, the notions of goods and commodities are the same in the three cases. They accept the idea, clearly expressed for instance by Debreu, that two equal quantities of the same physical good are not fully substitutable for one another if they are available at different times; these two quantities then correspond to different commodities. But, when listing the commodities, the specifications keep the notion of goods that remain physically the same through time. The index of a commodity specifies the good as well as the time concerned. Indeed, the very concept of growth requires that some things are directly comparable from one period to the next, and it seems to be admissible for general theories that all goods (and services) keep a constant meaning through time.

The second common feature is that, in all three methods, each elementary productive operation only concerns a finite number of periods, although production can proceed for ever into the future, although the periods of elementary operations can overlap. This is what I mean when I say that production proceeds recursively. But our general theories must recognize that this feature does not apply only to production but to any economic activity; generations of consumers also live finite times. This is why the recent study of overlapping generation models has been a major achievement of the last three decades for the development of the general microeconomic theories of capital and growth. I am sure that this specifi-cation with overlapping generations will more and more be recognized as the proper one.[2]

These theories have used two equilibrium concepts. One, the "full general equilibrium" concept, simply generalizes the corresponding concept of static timeless theories. The identity of individual goods then matters very little; but a high degree of consistency is required from the full set of individual plans, no matter how remote in the future they may be. The alternative concept, the "temporary general equilibrium" was lucidly discussed in *Value and Capital* (in particular chap. 9), transposing to general equilibrium the analysis of Alfred Marshall; its exact definition, involving in particular expectations of agents as to future prices and other conditions, is familiar and will not be repeated here. Clearly this second concept is much better suited than the first one for positive theories of capital and growth. But the distinction is sometimes forgotten.

This may result from the fact that the two concepts happen to coincide for stationary economies, in which expectations not only keep constant values, as all other variables do, but are quite naturally assumed to be also exact. The coincidence even extends to proportionally growing economies, which are hardly different from stationary ones, but were often considered during these past decades as providing a better reference. The coincidence may seem trivial; it requires however the proof of a stationarity property for the structure of the full general equilibrium price system of a stationary economy. This proof actually gave me a hard time when I worked at it thirty-five years ago.[3]

But the coincidence is not always a blessing, because it may lead the theorist to overlook the distinction between the two concepts of equilibrium and therefore to pay too little attention to some special features of the temporary equilibrium definition.

I must now turn attention to the distinction between Hicks' three methods of disintegration for the representation of the productive system. I shall not quarrel with him by arguing that the first method, at least in the way it was used so far, is a particular case of the second. The important point is to discuss the role of the third method, by comparison with the second. Clearly, Hicks likes it and I do as well. But what are his reasons, before I give mine?

In chapter I of *Capital and Time*, he gives two reasons. In section I.3, speaking of the second method, he says: "the categories with which it works are not very recognizable as economic categories"; then at the beginning of the following section: "Thus there should be room for a third method, expressible more naturally in economic terms". The argument is surprising: since the second method is quite flexible in its definition of goods, it can be applied to all conceivable cases, even though it may be cumbersome when it has to identify many kinds of more or less used equipment goods; on the contrary by limiting itself to primary factors and consumption goods, the third method forces the analyst to simplifications that are not so natural.

But Hicks goes on to argue, in section I.6, that the special usefulness of the third method is for the analysis of "the traverse", i.e. for growth outside of the steady state.[4] The main feature that ought to appear is "extensive *complementarities over time*" (italics in the text); the second method would make "the economy too flexible", whereas the third would recognize its inflexibility. This is an interesting point, but so far only based on intuition. I do not think it has ever been proved; it would certainly be a worthwhile question to clear up for a mathematical economist. My own guess is that no general formal proof of the difference will be found; it is indeed known that, within the second method, the putty-clay specification (not to speak of the clay-clay) introduces a good deal of complementarity over time.

Actually, if Hicks asserts the third method to be particularly appropriate for the study of the traverse, it is because he is becoming more and more motivated by a particular issue in this study, namely what I shall call the "Impulse problem"; how does a technical innovation change the structure of production and consumption, as well as the price structure, this change being traced from the initial introduction of the innovation to its exclusive use. A number of Hicks' writings reveal the importance he gave to this problem after 1970. I shall come back to it. Whenever the innovation amounts to the discovery of a new elementary process for transforming primary factors into consumption goods, then clearly the third method has a definite advantage.

Beyond these two reasons there may also be a sentimental attachment of Hicks for the third method which, after Böhm-Bawerk and Wicksell, he extended in *Value and Capital* ("in one of the less read chapters" as he revealingly writes in "Time in Economics", op. cit.). It may moreover be that Hicks will agree with me when I give my own argument as follows: as an alternative analyzing to the second method, the third one provides a different way of analyzing the same basic issues; its occasional use should be recommended because it may lead us to see better some important points. In theoretical analysis it is indeed often rewarding to look at the same questions through different glasses. The main reason for arguing in favour of the third method may then simply be that it is too neglected nowadays.[5]

2. Macroeconomic Analysis

After this initial discussion on methods, let me come closer to the substance of the theories of capital and growth. We cannot do so without often speaking in macroeconomic terms. Indeed, the largest part in the content of these theories is macro. A good deal of the irritation that participants in, and observers of, debates on these theories suffered, could have been avoided if the conditions applying to the edification of macroeconomic theory had been better recognized from the beginning. Here, I shall express agreement with Hicks on his main statements but I may appear to be more dogmatic in my assessment of fundamental difficulties.

Let me first quote an important excerpt from "Methods of dynamic analysis", an article presented by Hicks in his collected essays as being particularly important but hardly even read (essay number 18 in volume II). Evaluating the relative merits and conditions of static and dynamic analyses, he there makes a comparison with economic history, which has both to survey the state of a given economy at a given epoch, stressing differences with other economies or epochs, and to present a narrative of some process of economic change. He then writes: "it is in fact exceedingly difficult to cast economic history into a narrative form without becoming *more* abstract than one has to be on the survey method; greater realism in the matter of time-sequence has to be purchased by a higher level of abstraction in most other respects. We are, I believe, in substantially the same case in economic theory ... It is no accident that dynamic theory tends so largely to run in terms of simple aggregate models".

Before we discuss some of these models, it is worth considering briefly the mere definition of the main concepts of macroeconomic analysis. By doing so we are faithful to Hicks, who very substantially contributed to the subject.

I shall submit here that the main point is to decide whether a capital aggregate is a different kind of animal from a production aggregate. As soon as the question is phrased in this way, the answer is obvious: it is not a different kind of animal, but simply a more difficult animal.

The production flow and the capital stock are both made up of many different goods. Speaking in macroeconomic terms we aggregate these many goods; the only way we do it in practice is by valuing them with prices. They may be prices varying through time; we then speak of value aggregates. They may be fixed prices resulting in volume aggregates. (In order to avoid complications, I shall limit attention here to two periods, and hence neglect volume aggregates defined from chain indices.) The problems begin when we try to be precise on what are these prices. Statisticians would like them to be actual prices, current prices for value aggregates, average prices of a given period for volume aggregates. Theoreticians would moreover like these prices to correspond to those of their theories, most often to be purely competitive prices. Both must recognize that some prices have to be imputed because some goods in the production flow and still more in the capital stock are not actually traded.

It is, of course, an important question to decide about the principles that may lie behind the determination of these imputed prices, in particular behind the choice of prices to be applied to old equipment. Similarly it is important, for capital still more than for production, to deal clearly with the treatment of new goods and to know which base period prices will be given to them in the computation of volume aggregates. Economic statisticians have discussed these issues many times, using in particular Hicks' lucid writings on the subject.[6] A simple reason explains why the discussion is neither very convincing, not even always conclusive: indeed the problems, as they are posed, have no good solution; capital aggregates, but also production aggregates, will never be rigorously defined in such a way that, in all conceivable applications, they can perfectly replace the microeconomic entities that they represent.

It is my view that, in order to be useful, the study of these questions must be fully reoriented. We need as many theories of aggregation as we have types of macroeconomic analysis and each one of these theories must consider several cases of microeconomic environment, in each case clarifying the meaning of macroeconomic results and the errors to which they may be exposed. Some general principles may help in the building of these theories. I considered them long ago[7] and stressed in particular the role of aggregate quantities, seen as imperfect representations of corresponding microeconomic quantities. But a general study of aggregation can only be a first step, without much interest if other steps are not made.

This being my position, let me consider for instance one type of macroeconomic analysis that plays an important role in the study of economic growth: the analysis of productivity trends. Whenever we assess the past, present or future role of capital accumulation on productivity trends, we are using some sort of capital volume aggregate and some sort of macroeconomic production function, whether explicitly or implicitly. Those who objected to the use of such tools had no impact on actual macroeconomic analyses because they neither proved that we need not study the role of capital accumulation on productivity trends, or found out another way of doing it. On the contrary a careful and positive study of the aggregation problems in this context will improve the methodology actually used and throw light on the significance and pitfalls of the results.

There is a literature on this problem. Indeed, the irritating debates between the two Cambridges can coolly be read again with benefit as a contribution to the problem (if one has the time necessary to read it again). Cases have been found in which the use of proper aggregates does not run the risk of erroneous assessments, such as the case discussed by Samuelson in his 1962 article on "the surrogate production function".[8] But other cases have also been found in which no technical change occurs and the set of competitive stationary states has a different structure from the one that could be derived from a sensible aggregate production function.

Actually, these latter cases are better understood if one refers to the technical literature on the aggregation of production functions.[9] It dealt rather fully with the situation of a competitive environment, labour inputs being perfectly mobile and capital inputs immobile. But in macroeconomic analysis, other situations have also to be considered, whether perfect competition does not apply or labor is not perfectly mobile. Hence, other significant aggregation problems have to be discussed.[10]

3. Comparative Dynamics

Some important conjectures concerning macroeconomic properties must also be studied by what Hicks called "comparative dynamics".[11] Two such properties have a long history in economic theory, technology being assumed fixed in the two cases and perfect competition assumed to prevail: a higher capital per unit of labour input requires a lower real interest rate; a lower real interest rate implies a longer production process. Both properties associate capital deepening with a falling interest rate (or a falling rate of profit, if the two rates are identified). The first property often was in the background of the debates between the two Cambridges and the second property was discussed by Hicks several times, notably in *Value and Capital* and *Capital and Time*. The properties hold in the most aggregated models: the case of a single produced good serving both as capital in a one period production function and for consumption, or the case of a single final good obtained from labour by a point-input point-output process. The problem is to know whether they are generally valid.

The first source of confusion concerns the way in which the properties ought to be specified in general, when the relative prices of the various goods are not the same in the two hypothetical situations to be compared (stationary states or proportional growth paths). Speaking in broad terms, one may say that, when comparing the capital aggregates or the average periods of production in the two situations, these aggregate quantities should be computed with the same prices. If not, the properties would have an ambiguous meaning with respect to the notion of capital deepening. The confusion arose time and again about the capital aggregate, changes in the value of capital being mistakenly considered when changes in the volume really mattered. The same confusion would undoubtedly arise, if the average period of production became more familiar, for instance as a result of wide adoption of Hicks' third method. In other words, the capital aggregate and the average period of production are considered as reflecting quantitative features of production, but their measures also imply prices used as weights; when comparisons are aimed at revealing quantitative changes associated with a change in interest rate, the prices used for the aggregate measure of quantities must be kept fixed.[12]

But even when they are adequately specified, the two properties cannot be proved to hold in full generality. The theoretical work of the last thirty years has shown that the interest rate is related in a very complex way to the many exogenous determinants of equilibrium and that changes of relative prices, which are associated with changes of interest, may be responsible for paradoxical effects in the simultaneous variations of the interest rate and of quantitative characteristics of the equilibrium.

For the relation between the volume of capital and the interest rate, I may first refer here to the article I wrote on the occasion of my 1959 visit to Professor Hicks at Oxford, where I showed that a general comparative dynamics approach did not lead to the conjectured property, even simply in a three commodity world.[13] Later, some counterexamples to the property were explicitly worked out. Finally, the conditions under which the conjectured "capital deepening response" to changes in interest rate held were greatly clarified in E. Burmeister and J. Turnovsky.[14]

All this work concerned what Hicks calls "the second method of disintegration". What about the changes in the length of the production process? The question has been seriously concerning Hicks. He dealt with it in *Value and Capital* (chapter 17) and discussed it again in *Capital and Time* (chapter 12), essentially restating more neatly the results established more than thirty years earlier. I read his contribution as having been to make rigorous a property that previously was loosely stated, or proved only in very special cases. He showed that, for the conjectured property to apply, one needed to define the average period of production properly, each lag being weighted not exactly by the net input that it concerned, but by this input capitalized at the current rate of interest; moreover when the impact of a change in interest on the timing and quantity of net inputs was being considered, one needed to maintain fixed, in the measurement of the average period of production, the coefficients by which inputs were capitalized.

However, his proof concerned only the case in which there would exist just one primary factor and one final good. It is legitimate to ask whether the property generalizes to several primary factors and final goods. Since the question has not been extensively studied, I cannot be absolutely sure, but I feel quite confident that no generalization of the property will be found: the "capital deepening response" to change of the interest rate ought to be subject, in this formulation, to the same kind of limitations that appeared with the second method. If I am rather confident in this statement, it is because I looked carefully at a completely neglected article by John Sargan, who seriously tried to apply the third method in the general case of several primary factors and final goods and to derive comparative dynamics properties.[15]

What are the implications of these theoretical developments for applied macroeconomic analysis? At this point, it is natural to wonder whether any use should be made in applications of the average period of production. Hicks never suggested it; his earlier writings may already have led readers to conclude that he considered his third method as being appropriate only for theoretical exploration. This conclusion was later made explicit in *Capital and Time* or still better in an article published at about the same time, where it is explained that the joint production resulting from the durable use of fixed capital makes roundaboutness a confusing concept: "There is no period of production", he writes.[16] Indeed, attempts at direct determination of the average period of production by statisticians would meet insuperable difficulties, since it would require detailed data on the use of old equipment, data that are not available, even simply within the firms. Indirectly, one could use the approximation derived by Maurice Allais, according to whom, under perfect competition, the average period of production may be approximated by the ratio between the value of productive capital and the income earned by primary factors of production.[17] But this would mean only another way of looking at essentially the same macroeconomic variables, and with little benefit since it would require an increased degree of abstraction.

More usefully, we must wonder whether the lapses from the conjectured capital deepening response, whatever the approach from which it is specified, have real significance. For lack of accurate econometric evidence the question must be left open. In my work as an applied macroeconomist, whenever this capital deepening response is assumed, I am, however, not really disturbed. My subjective evaluation gives very low probability to the risk of mistakes resulting from the assumption. I know of too many other cases of theoretical possibilities, such as upward sloping demand curves, that have little bearing on actual phenomena. But of course this intuition of mine ought to be substantiated, for instance by an approach similar to the one used by W. Hildenbrand to demonstrate that aggregate demand curves are downward sloping.[18]

4. Proportional Growth and the Traverse

When attention turns from stationary equilibria or proportional growth paths to less special evolutions, we must on this occasion speak of "the traverse", the denomination used by Hicks. My first reflection will then be to wonder whether this is such a good word that we should always use it in preference to any other.

So far as I understand, it evokes a path that permits us to reach, rather directly, a main road. If so, its exclusive usage may convey a misleading image because, even in a stationary environment, evolution outside the feasible stationary equilibrium may fail to converge with it and may indeed not be geared to join it.

Actually, Hicks was clear on the limitations of the concept. For instance, in *Capital and Time*, when introducing the study of cases in which the economy is not in a steady state, he writes: "In most of the cases which we shall examine there will prove to be a tendency to equilibrium; so that our sequence can properly be considered as a *Traverse* from one steady state to another. But, as we shall see, it is far from clear that this is generally true. There are other possibilities" (p. 82).

But another aspect of the concept is also disturbing me. Taking a traverse implies the intention to join a main road. Is economic growth far sighted enough to make the image appropriate in this respect? The question actually raises an issue which is at the core of a conflict of opinions concerning the operation of our economic system. Some economists claim that, when proper account of expectations and market forces is taken, the economy is stable and naturally finds the efficient growth path; a good model should then be one of competitive growth with perfect foresight; the image of a traverse should well suit these economists. But other economists do not share this optimistic thesis. I find it a bit troublesome that our vocabulary may seem to prejudice the solution of this big unsolved issue.

In fact, it is curious to note that, for the study of the traverse, Hicks only considers models in which economic growth is absolutely myopic, even blind: the conditions of the current period fully determine investment, without conditions in subsequent periods playing any role, expectations being assumed static when they have to occur. Hicks even says that a theory with correct expectations is not "the kind we are here endeavouring to construct" (CT, p. 56). Convergence to the steady state may then perhaps better be described as a situation in which the forest, through which the blind walker moves, gently slopes down to an unexpected main road.

Let us, however, speak of the traverse, since it is a handy short expression for economic growth outside the steady state. I see the study of the traverse as having three possible objectives; (i) description of qualitative features of economic growth, after the steady state has been disturbed, (ii) convergence to a steady state, (iii) possibility of overcapitalization or of overexhaustion of resources. The available literature mainly concentrates on problem (ii), whereas Hicks is also quite interested in problem (i) and I think problem (iii) ought not to be neglected.

For the organization of what I should like to say, I find it convenient to sharply distinguish between the flexprice case, which is going to be the subject of this part, and the fixprice case, which I shall consider only in the following and last part of my talk. Let us then now discuss the properties of a full employment growth path made of a sequence of competitive temporary equilibria.

What is the ultimate aim of this discussion? Can it be to sharpen our intuition about the evolution of quantities and prices in a real economy? Such was certainly the aim of Ricardo and other great economists of the nineteenth century. Such is also one important motivation of Hicks. Indeed, he often presented his study of the traverse as being intended to provide the missing last chapter of his book *A Theory of Economic History*.[19] Since he sees the "mainspring of economic growth" as being technical progress, he wants to study how, after each invention, resource allocation and relative prices change and evolve. This is a main theme in the second part of *Capital and Time*.

So far as I know, no other mathematical economist today entertains the same hope of being able to trace through time the impact of each new change in economic environment on equilibrium prices and quantities. We have become more modest. When we want to know the effects of technical progress, increased scarcity of some resources and other changes, we most often neglect to consider transitory phases.

Indeed, the theoretical answers that we are deriving at present come most often from the comparative dynamics of steady states, either stationary states or rather proportional growth paths in which some form of technical progress is recognized. The answers precisely follow from the kind of properties that I examined in the preceding section. Considering what can be, and cannot be, achieved by a purely theoretical analysis, I indeed think the comparative dynamics of steady states essentially provides the proper background for our intuition on such issues. I do not expect many extra insights resulting from attempts at precisely studying flexprice growth out of the steady states, which would then have to be in an evolving environment.

The ultimate aim of the discussion of the traverse in a flexprice setting is rather, I believe, a better understanding of the role of the price system in our economies, a better understanding of whether and why it has, or ought, to be supplemented by other guides for long term decisions. My own conclusion of what I learned from this theory can be stated as follows: orderly convergence of economic growth to a steady, sustainable and efficient path could not be taken for granted, and would even appear unlikely, if the price system alone was operating. I think I then see a little better the meaning of the following questions: why is the price system not alone to operate? Which ones of the many mechanisms, that operate besides it and interfere with it, play a useful role? Which ones ought to be removed and which ones maintained, reactivated or even added?

With this concern in mind, we cannot but be impressed by the complexity of the model to be tackled by a fully convincing theory. "The task thus outlined is formidable", writes Hicks (CT, p. 82); and I can paraphrase one of its following sentences by saying: "most of what we theorists can offer is not more than solutions for quite special cases".

But when clearcut results in favor of one thesis fail to be obtained on most of the special cases studied, we at least know that truth of the thesis in the complex conditions of the real world is unlikely. This is precisely the situation we are facing about the convergence hypothesis. Without attempting to survey the relevant literature on this hypothesis, I may briefly recall some of its main findings.

The mathematical exploration of the problem is fairly advanced for one case, which makes the recursive structure of economic growth quite simple, the case in which the value of consumption is assumed to be equal to wages and in which labor is the unique primary factor of production (I suppose the hypothesis made in *Capital and Time*, according to which wages are consumed and consumption out of profits is constant, makes little difference.) In the classical two sector model, with one consumption good and one capital good, one knows, in particular from Hicks' discussion in *Capital and Growth*, that converge may fail to hold if production of the capital good is more capital intensive than production of the consumption good. Taking the multiplicity of capital goods into account requires an hypothesis about expectations, the easiest one being perfect myopic forecast: the instantaneous changes in the prices of the various capital goods are correctly expected. Since the initial work of F. Hahn on this model,[20] it is known that dynamics in the neighbourhood of the steady state usually has the saddle-point property, which means that convergence requires very particular and unlikely initial conditions. The joint production case, which would properly deal with complementarity over time, has, however, been little studied in the framework of this model, which applies the second "method of disintegration".

More generally, convergence depends on what are the characteristics of technological constraints, of saving behavior and of expectations formation. But introduction of alternative hypotheses, concerning in particular savings, does not make convergence more likely than in the case I just discussed. This conclusion applies for instance when one studies the implications of the two main theories of saving: the permanent income hypothesis[21] and the life cycle hypothesis embedded in the overlapping generation model.[22]

Considering the aim I attribute to the study of convergence, one understands why I insist also on the study of questions that more explicitly belong to the welfare economics of growth, even though one might dispute their classification under the heading of the traverse problem. Overcapitalization could occur in a proportional growth path. Even though consideration of exhaustible resources rules out proportional growth, it can still be conceived in the framework of a regular and typical pattern playing the same role in the theoretical elaboration as does the steady state. But the possibility of overcapitalization or overexhaustion fundamentally concerns efficiency of the price system, in the same way as possible lack of convergence.

Actually, the two possibilities of overcapitalization and overexhaustion raise different problems. Overcapitalization is well defined now, after the success of the golden rule literature. The question of knowing whether it occurs is mainly econometric. Theory can, however, clear the ground and help in the specification of the hypothesis to be tested. It can study under which conditions overcapitalization might result from too high saving propensities, from the high pure profit rates that risk taking in business may require, or from non competitive market structures and behavior. I believe this study does not attract the attention it deserves.[23]

Overexhaustion may on the contrary appear to be an elusive concept. Its study requires a rigorous definition of the efficient speed of exhaustion of natural resources. If a formal definition can be derived from macro-economic specifications that are similar to those used in the optimal growth literature, one may feel that these specifications assume as given some parameters whose determination precisely is at the root of the problem, such as the rate at which utilities of future generations should be discounted. However, an elusive concept is not necessarily a void concept. In this instance public interest, as well as reflection, proves that it is not void. I believe this theory should aim at making it less elusive and at study-ing the conditions of its actual occurrence.

5. Growth Under Sticky Prices

We owe the distinction flexprice–fixprice to Hicks. Was it pure coincidence if the distinction was first clearly introduced and discussed in *Capital and Growth*? Few economists share the extreme view according to which a fixprice theory cannot teach anything that would be relevant to the real world. On the other hand, few economists believe that the fixprice hypo-thesis can be appropriate anywhere in a theory of economic growth. Hicks is, however, among those few since in *Capital and Time*, published eight years later, he again treats on a par the two fixprice and flexprice cases.

I am also among those few. More precisely, in what would, I believe, be an appropriate theory, the temporary equilibrium would assume most prices to be fixed, i.e. exogenous; prices would then move from one temporary equilibrium to the next, but not by the full extent that would have been required to clear all excess demands and supplies; moreover, they would be subject to autonomous trends and shocks. Such an appro-priate growth theory is, however, quite complex to deal with and has many degrees of freedom; hypotheses intended to make it simpler or more precise can seldom avoid the criticism of being "*ad hoc*". Under these circumstances, I see the two growth theories, built respectively under the flexprice and the fixprice assumptions, as playing complementary roles and as enlightening two sides of the same reality. This is probably also the view held by Hicks who wrote in *Capital and Growth*, p. 77: "Though our ultimate preference may be for something which lies between [flexprice and fixprice], anything which does so must partake to some extent of the difficulties of both. It is the extremes which are (relatively) simple, so that it is with them that it is best to begin".

One must recognize, however, that they apply to different time per-spectives: the real long run for the flexprice growth theory, the transition from the short to the medium run for the fixprice. One might even enter-tain a synthesis, according to which the flexprice theory would provide the relevant reference for long run growth, whereas evolution around this long term trend would be properly understood by reference to the fixprice theory. Although at some places, for instance when he considers the traverse as "the passage to equilibrium", Hicks might be understood as accepting this synthesis, a careful reader will probably conclude that he does not. For instance on page 131 of *Capital and Growth*, he writes: "It is essentially this method [of endogenous determination of prices] which is the basis for what has been presented by a number of economists ... as *Growth Theory*: a general theory ... of long-term Economic Growth. I would not myself claim for it that it is a theory of Economic Growth, if by that one means a theory that can hope to give at all an adequate explanation of actual Growth phenomena".

Now, I think we have to be more clear. Either we completely discard the flexprice growth theory as empirically irrelevant, as some radical economists undoubtedly do, and then we should no longer pay any attention to it in our reflections. Or we believe that it provides a useful first approximation for some phenomena, and then we ought to say which phenomena. As for me, I am confident that the flexprice theory gives us the adequate framework for the explanation of most long term trends of relative prices, as I already hinted earlier. Therefore it is also reliable when we want to understand such things as long term changes in consumption patterns, or to discuss at least some of the likely impacts of such institutional changes as fiscal reforms or trade liberalization.

On the other hand, I do not find in this flexprice theory some of the ingredients that seem to be required for the understanding of relative growth performances of various industrial countries, for instance of England and France through the eighteenth, nineteenth and twentieth centuries. Why is it so? Because I agree with economic historians in thinking that an essential element in the explanation is the course of business profitability, while this latter is precisely a deviation from the flexprice equilibrium.

Business profitability may be characterized by the anticipated marginal pure profit rate (excess over the real interest rate or, if I may use this word in order to avoid being misunderstood, excess over the marginal productivity of capital). Over decades and excepting cases of major shocks, this can be properly measured by the mean realized pure profit rate. So far as we now know, such a measure shows substantial differences from one economy to another, from one decade to another. The existence of a non-zero pure profit rate is inconsistent with existing flexprice growth theories. Taking explicit account of uncertainties and of risk aversion into account, one could certainly build a flexprice theory that would explain a positive pure profit rate. But this would still not suffice for the explanation of some growth phenomena, since the observed differences, with at some times and places negative, at others high pure profit rates, cannot be mainly explained by differences in risk exposure or business attitudes toward risk. They truly reveal what is best interpreted as disequilibria of the price system.

It is common sense to believe that these disequilibria play an important role in explaining relative growth performances. They may themselves result from inadequate economic policies or from the working of the socio-economic system, for instance along lines stressed by M. Olson.[24] But they certainly also have to do with the institutional changes that Hicks emphasized in his book, *A Theory of Economic History*. More precisely, a good understanding of the interplay between the institutional environment and economic performances requires consideration of business profitability, which is a very important link between the two.[25]

The existence of disequilibria, leading to durable differences in profitability conditions, shows that something else than our present flexprice growth theories is required. Fixprice growth theories offer an alternative view. I agree with Hicks in thinking that, at the present phase of development of our economic theories, a research programme on economic growth under the fixprice hypothesis is quite warranted. Indeed, I like to think that I am taking part in this programme. But I certainly would not claim that it will be the end of our efforts. Even if purely real and wholly aggregated, consisting only of one real wage rate and one real interest rate, the price system has, according to the fixprice hypothesis, full exogeneity, which is difficult to swallow within a theory of economic growth and can be maintained only for some limited purpose. Intermediate specifications will have to be found and worked out.

I also agree with Hicks in thinking that "the traverse" may be the domain of questions for which we shall most often refer to the fixprice kind of growth theory. Keynesian long term stationary equilibria are also relevant. But if a change is being brought to their determinants, for instance a change in the real wage rate, it is interesting to study not only the long term effect and its stability, but also the path through which it is achieved, and in particular the short term effect, which may go in the reverse direction. This is precisely the study I tried to present in "Wages and Unemployment".[26] The same framework may be used in order to understand why a deliberate policy of low real interest rates should be favourable to economic growth, but not always in the long run to employment.

Rather than considering shifts of the fixed prices, Hicks focused his attention on changes in the physical determinants of growth, and in particular on technical progress. In *Capital and Time* he took again the old but still significant problem studied by Ricardo, namely whether technical progress may result in unemployment. Another similar problem is to know whether an acceleration of participation to the labour force may induce some increase in unemployment. The popular belief, and even the intuition of some economists, is indeed that such an effect should occur. Hence, a careful study makes sense. Using the flexprice, and therefore full employment, hypothesis cannot be appropriate. Therefore one should, at least for the time being, use the alternative fixprice hypothesis

The answer given by Hicks is that, if the real wage rate remains fixed, the introduction of new machines could induce a temporary surge of unemployment, but that eventually employment will on the contrary increase faster. One should, however, remember that this is proved within a model of capital shortage, whose relevance has to be assessed in actual economies to which the conclusion would be applied: employment is a function of existing productive capacities, which depend on capital accumulation, hence on profit margin. The introduction of a new more efficient process of production both decreases the labour requirement per unit of capacity and increases the profit margin. The first effect may dominate in the short run, but will eventually be superseded by the second.

Clearly the examples that I have just considered, namely the effect of an exogenous change in real wages and the unemployment that can result from inventions, are only two among the many questions to be clarified by the theory of growth under imperfectly flexible prices. In order to emphasize the point at the end of this talk, let me consider briefly Hicks's vision about the driving force of the actual modern growth process. This is presented at the end of his Nobel lecture[27] and developed more fully in an essay published a little later.[28] The intention there is to supplement the book *A Theory of Economic History* which, stressing the role of the merchants in the emergence of a market system, was mainly addressed to growth before the Industrial Revolution.

The mainspring of industrialism is "science-based technical progress embodied in physical equipment". Each new invention gives an Impulse that works through a temporary rise in the rate of profit, the latter generating the necessary saving for implementation of the invention. The Impulse eventually peters out because of scarcity of primary resources, most often in modern times scarcity of labour. But new inventions, some of them induced, come in and maintain economic growth.

This process does not work as well in all times and places. "The individual Impulse has two dimensions, since it is spread out over time. Its size and its time-shape depend partly upon the nature of the improvement which has initiated it, partly on the characteristics of the economy in which it is carried through" (p. 31 of the 1977 reprint of "Industrialism"). Where the "English sickness" prevails, technical progress is threatened or twisted, by a "sectional struggle" of each industry trying to gain against the others, by improving its terms of trade (p. 38). In such distortions of the price system with respect to what "economic criteria" would require, the formation of wages plays a special role. Not only are wages to a large extent protected against the ups and downs that the law of supply and demand would imply, but they are also subject to a "social spreading" (p. 41).

I do not want to comment here on this vision of modern economic growth and to compare it with the ones proposed by others (actually many economists do accept it). I should just like to stress that it raises a large number of theoretical questions if we begin to look at it closely. It recognizes the existence of some disequilibria between demands and supplies, or within the price structure, but it does not make them fully explicit, neither does it study under which conditions the conjectured effects of these disequilibria will occur. Hence, it suggests an important research programme for the theory of capital and growth.

In the Preface of *Economic Perspectives* Hicks explains that *Capital and Time* was the ladder by which he climbed to his present point of view; it provided the formal argument; but before the point of view could be stated clearly, he had to diminish his dependence on the formal argument. "In the essay on "Industrialism" the ladder has finally been kicked down" he wrote (p. xvi). I would like to conclude this talk in announcing that many of us are now putting our own ladders up around the tree on top of which Sir John is sitting.

Notes

1. Text of the Hicks Lecture, given on May 1st, 1986.

2. The first introduction of overlapping generation models is usually attributed to P. Samuelson (*Journal of Political Economy*, December 1958). I recently discovered that it may be found in M. Allais (*Economie et Intérêt*, Imprimerie Nationale, Paris 1947).

3. *Econometrica*, April 1953. The proof was not even quite complete, as was later pointed out in D. Gale and R. Rockwell, "On the interest rate theorems of Malinvaud and Starrett", *Econometrica*, March 1975.

4. This second argument, but not the first one, is repeated in "Time in Economics", published in 1976, and appearing as essay 21 in John Hicks, *Collected Essays on Economic Theory*, Vol. II, Basil Blackwell, Oxford 1982.

5. A careful reader of my writings may note that I was less favourable to the method in the last sentences of my 1960 *Review of Economic Studies* article. Age may make me less dogmatic.

6. After his important writings on the definition and measurement of social income, those on capital appear as essays 8 and 9, published respectively in 1958 and 1969, in *Collected Essays on Economic Theory*, Volume I. See also chapter 13, in *Capital and Time*, 1973.

7. E. Malinvaud, "L'agrégation dans les modèles économiques", *Cahiers du Séminaire d'Econométrie*, No. 4, 1956, Paris, C.N.R.S.

8. P.A. Samuelson, "Parable and realism in capital theory, the surrogate production function", *Review of Economic Studies*, June 1962.

9. See F. Fisher, "The existence of aggregate production functions", *Econometrica*, October 1969; L. Johansen, *Production Functions: an Integration of Micro and Macro, Short Run and Long Run Aspects*, North Holland Pub. Co., Amsterdam 1972; F. Fisher, R. Solow and J. Kearl, "Aggregate production functions: some CES experiments", *Review of Economic Studies*, June 1977.

10. I have tried to discuss a wide range of situations in section 5, chapter 4 of *Théorie Macroéconomique*, vol. I, Dunod, Paris 1981.

11. J. Hicks, "'A Value and Capital' growth model", *Review of Economic Studies*, June 1959.

12. I may mention in passing that the same kind of confusion nowadays threatens comparative statements involving Tobin's q indicator in theoretical disequilibrium economics, since computation of this indicator involves quantities as well as prices. When its changes are considered as reflecting changes of relative prices, quantities must be kept fixed.

13. E. Malinvaud, "The analogy between atemporal and intertemporal theories of resource allocation", *Review of Economic Studies*, vol. XXVII, no. 3, 1961.

14. E. Burmeister and J. Turnovsky, "Capital deepening response in an economy with heterogeneous capital goods", *American Economic Review*, December 1972.

15. J. Sargan, "The period of production", *Econometrica*, April 1955.

16. "The Austrian theory of capital and its re-birth in modern economics", essay No. 8 in volume III of *Collected Essays on Economic Theory*.

17. M. Allais, *Economie et Intérêt*, Paris, Imprimerie Nationale, 1947. The approximation is given on page 132 for a stationary economy. It holds for proportional growth as well, if the interest rate is not very different from the growth rate.

18. W. Hildenbrand, "On the law of demand", *Econometrica*, 1983, 997–1019; K. and W. Hildenbrand, "On the mean income effect: a data analysis of the U.K. family expenditure survey", Bonn discussion paper, November 1985.

19. See for instance page xvii in the Preface of J. Hicks, *Economic Perspectives, Further Essays on Money and Growth*, Clarendon Press, Oxford 1977.

20. F. Hahn, "On warranted growth paths", *Review of Economic Studies*, 1968.

21. T. Bewley, "The permanent income hypothesis and long-run economic stability", *Journal of Economic Theory*, June 1980.

22. I discussed this case in *Théorie Macroéconomique*, chap. 6, Dunod, Paris 1981.

23. I devoted a few pages to it in *Théorie Macroéconomique*, op. cit.

24. M. Olsen, *The Rise and Decline of Nations*, Yale University Press, 1982.

25. So far as I can see, Hicks never explicitly stressed in his writings the importance of profitability as a driving force of economic growth. Considering both his role in promoting the

fixprice approach and his vision about the driving force of modern economic growth, I find this lack of interest curious.

26. *Economic Journal*, March 1982.

27. "The mainspring of economic growth", *Swedish Journal of Economic*, 1973, reprinted in *American Economic Review*, December 1981.

28. "Industrialism", *International Affairs*, April 1974, reprinted in J. Hicks, *Economic Perspectives: Further Essays on Money and Growth*, Clarendon Press, Oxford, 1977.

94

Book Review: *The Economics of John Hicks* [†]

E. Beach

The Economics of John Hicks. Edited by Dieter Helm. Oxford and New York: Basil Blackwell, 1984. Pp. 304.

This small collection of Hicks's works, with a 20-page introduction by the editor and an 11-page list of Hicks's publications, is aimed at "the economics undergraduate" of the U.K. The first and longest Part I consists of the 1934 paper on value, and three other chapters on income and its measurement. Parts II–IV, of about equal length, are devoted to welfare economics, macroeconomics and money, and methods. In Part IV there is a survey of the history of economic thought, a chapter on history, the 1976 paper on time, and a chapter on Hicks's "formation." There is nothing on growth theory, to which Hicks devoted two books (1965 and 1973).

The Introduction refers to "the Hicksian method" as "a shaping of tools to be specific to the problem at hand" (p. 1). Despite the editor's feeling that (p. 2) "it is too early to place Hicks within the framework of the history of economic thought," this reviewer offers an assessment. Hicks's work on value theory and on index numbers has been outstanding. His monetary theory has been notable. His macro theory contains some remarkable work. His treatment of history does not stand up well in comparison, say, with Marshall. His struggle with 'dynamics' over the years has been a failure. Based so firmly on the Swedish model of periods, it does not show a comprehension of continuing change and growth.

Hicks's understanding of economics as a whole may be tested by an examination of his survey of the history of thought (chapter 12). Covering two centuries, it contains one very insignificant reference to Marshall (p. 244), who was central to the development of economic theory in a number of ways. Living near the middle of this long period, his reputation, in his lifetime, reached a prominence that few could match. He has been praised for his integration of supply and demand into a theory of value that was the foundation of neoclassical work, even more than that of Menger, Jevons, or Walras, to whom Hicks gives credit for the shifting of interest to exchange theory. Marshallian tools became important for much later work.

[†]Source: *History of Political Economy*, Vol. 18(2), Summer 1986, pp. 351–2.

Marshall shared the "vision of the economic process" (p. 247) of the classical political economist, because value theory, essential as it is, is but a step along the way to "the high theme of economic progress." Marshall was the bridge between the two centuries, between classical political economy and the technique of neoclassicals. Hicks seems to have missed all of this because he seems not to have gotten "much out of Marshall" (p. 282). The result is a portrayal of Hicks's own interests and perceptions, which is useful, but not to be taken as a reliable statement of the evolution of economic thought.

Chapter 13 is an extract from the first chapter of *A Theory of Economic History* (1969). It appears that he wishes to formulate a way of understanding historical events from an understanding of social, particularly economic, ideas. These ideas appear to be relatively fixed, to be used to illuminate history. How much more helpful is the approach that induction and deduction help each other! So that, as Schmoller suggested, we walk on two legs.

Hicks's 1937 paper on Keynesian theory is one of his best and best-known (chapter 8). The 'Explanation' (1980; here chapter 10) is less happy. The intervening chapter, the 1956 paper, 'Methods of dynamic analysis,' is helpful in explaining why. The use of periods in which variables are required to reach equilibrium implies that they can be subsequently moved only by exogenous forces. Continuing endogenous movement is ruled out.

In contrast Marshall allows his variables to reach equilibrium only in the 'auxiliary' models, but not in his realistic theory of continuing change. Strong equilibration forces operate, producing endogenous change, as seen in Book V, chapter 12, of the *Principles*.

A part of the problem lies in Hicks's distinction between stock and flow variables (p. 207). He does not realize that a particular variable, like output, may be handled in two different ways — as a rate of flow and as a quantum accumulated over a period of time.

Hicks's misreading of Marshall is illustrated on p. 6: "Marshall ... took them into account only with reference to a single industry." Marshall's basic model was that of an industry producing a single commodity, but chapter 6 of Book V explains interrelations of industries and commodities more adequately than Walras did.

Hicks's difficulties are quite common to the profession. Hicks realized that his models — say the fixprice and the flexprice models — are but partial explanations of reality. It is not possible, however, to get very much from a particular model. Marshall's method, so generally misunderstood, is different. He has a number of "auxiliary" models — a supply curve, a demand curve, a market model, etc.; but he also has a model of continuing activity of a particular industry. It is, in effect, a two-tiered approach. The first tier contains partial, highly abstract models. The second is much less abstract, more realistic, weaving the partial models into a useful whole. The partial models illustrate the working of a particular aspect of the more complete and realistic model.

A statement at the beginning of the essay under review (p. 200) is revealing: "One of the greatest changes which has come over economic theory in the last thirty years (1926–55) is the transformation of economic dynamics from a pious aspiration into a respectable body of principles." This reviewer feels strongly that there was more practical, realistic, substantial dynamic theory developed before 1926 than has been produced since that time. The more elaborate, later models have been more abstract, with limited application, and are questionable for policy recommendations.

95

Early Hicks and Keynesian Monetary Theory: Different Views on Liquidity Preference[†]

J. Pekkarinen

I

The last fifteen years have been a period of theoretical self-criticism for the Keynesian tradition. It started as a discussion of whether the Keynesian theory represents what Keynes really said and whether, for example, the ideas of the *Treatise on money* have been forgotten. Subsequently, Keynes's multiplier theory has been given a new theoretical interpretation in terms of disequilibrium theory.

In this whole debate, Keynes's monetary theory has been left in the background. In fact, it seems that his contributions in this field have been accepted by a great majority of Keynesians and monetarists alike. Essentially, these amount to the *portfolio approach*, which analyzes the role of money on the basis of optimal choice of the composition of assets.

One of the few deviants in this respect is Sir John Hicks, who himself contributed to the theoretical developments in the 1930s. In his later writings on monetary theory, he has expressed his dissatisfaction with the way liquidity is analyzed in the *general theory*. In the same vein, he has argued that his own writings in monetary theory in the early 1930s, 'A suggestion for simplifying the theory of money' in particular, "was a Declaration of Independence, not only from the 'free market' school from which I was expressly liberating myself, but also from what came to pass as Keynesian economics" (1982, 10).

Hicks's claim stands in a clear contrast to the standard interpretation, as represented by e.g. Patinkin 1974, which maintains that Hicks's early contributions represented a line of development parallel to Keynes.[1] In fact, it has even been generally thought that Hicks's writings, such as his 'Suggestion' of 1935 and 'Mr Keynes and the Classics' of 1937, represent in some respects a clearer statement of the Keynesian approach to money than Keynes's *General theory* itself (cf. Patinkin 1974, 9).

In what follows we shall examine Hicks's recent claims. We shall show, first, that Keynes in the *General theory* and Hicks in the early 1930s

[†]Source: *History of Political Economy*, Vol. 18 (2), Fall 1986, pp. 335–49.

emphasized the nature of the demand for money and the related liquidity problem in different ways, and, second, that as a consequence of this, the transmission mechanism of monetary influences sketched by Hicks was different from that in Keynes. Hicks took account of liquidity at several stages of the transmission nexus. It is in the nature of our approach that we shall look at Keynes through the *General theory*. Moreover, we shall for the most part be satisfied with the standard IS–LM-interpretation of that work. We are not concerned with whether this represents the 'true' Keynes.

The standard interpretation of the *General theory* is in itself to a great extent Hicks's creature. Since we shall argue that Hicks's writings in monetary theory in the early 1930s differ from this interpretation of Keynes, it follows that there is a change in emphasis in Hicks's own monetary writings after the publication of the *General Theory*. Instead of arguing for his own views, Hicks now became an interpreter of Keynes. This change, which can be placed between 'A suggestion ...' (1935) and 'Mr Keynes' theory of employment' (1936), is also noted by Hicks (cf., e.g. Hicks 1977, 146). In what follows we shall not concern ourselves with Hicks's writings in the latter part of the 1930s. They are only implicitly present in the standard interpretation of the *General theory*. In our interpretation, we shall also utilize Hicks's recent writings, in which he has returned to his early views on money. We shall show that his present emphasis is indeed to be found in his early work.

As it turns out, early Hicks built extensively on the various schools in monetary theory in the 1930s: the Austrians, the Swedes, and the Cambridge School, including Keynes's *Treatise*. As such, his writings can be regarded as a challenge to modern theory as well, since this, to a large extent, stems from the *General Theory*. Hicks himself, in his recent writings, has taken up this challenge by indicating the direction in which his views would lead. We shall also indicate how the Hicksian perspective might complement the standard Keynesian analysis.

Our discussion is organized as follows. The next two sections are concerned with the main differences between early Hicks and the *General theory*. Section II points out the differences in the determinants of the demand for money or the liquidity-preference relation. This, in turn, will lead us to discuss, in Section III, differences in the link between the demand for money and commodity markets, which in the *General theory* consists of the nexus between the rate of interest and the marginal efficiency of capital. Section IV looks at early Hicks as a synthesizer of the different approaches in contemporary monetary theory. Finally, we conclude in Section V by briefly considering Hicks's work as a challenge to present-day discussion.

II

As far as the demand for money is concerned, Keynesian theory chooses as its frame of reference stock equilibrium between money and other assets. It stresses the role of expected capital values in the demand-for-money function. In the *General theory,* Keynes almost exclusively discussed liquidity under the heading of *price uncertainty,* and so it is in this way that mainstream Keynesian tradition has interpreted his message.

Hicks, in his 'Suggestion' article, conceived the role of this analysis of stock equilibrium and asset prices differently insofar as the determinants of the demand for money are concerned. There is no doubt that he clearly recognized expected capital gains or losses as *one* factor, but we shall argue that in Hicks's analysis it is not regarded as the main factor in the demand for money. He took a more general view.

This is perhaps most clearly evident in Hicks's writings on money before the 'Suggestion' article, which are published in volume 2 of his *Collected essays* (1982). In his essay 'Equilibrium and the cycle,' originally published in German in 1933, he puts forward the by now familiar question of why people should hold money which yields no interest revenue. His proposed solution to this problem is particularly relevant in this context:

> Suppose we have a community which possesses a given volume of money ... Then it is necessary that at any moment the money should be divided among the individuals composing the community in proportion to their demand for it. But what governs their demand for it? *Only their need to use it for making future payments* ... But now it must be observed that it is only for *future payments that are uncertain* that it is absolutely necessary to hold money [translation from Hicks 1977, 138–39; italics added].

The emphasis in this passage is on expected uncertain transaction requirements, not on expected capital values. In terms of Keynes's analysis, Hicks would have given a prominent role to the precautionary motive.

The same conceptual structure can also be identified in the final form of the 'Suggestion' article. There Hicks's analysis starts from the old notion of 'friction' as an unexplained element in monetary analysis and he sets out to analyze it more closely in terms of marginal analysis (1982, 51). He then describes *transactions costs* as the "most obvious" and "undoubtedly one of the most important" kinds of friction. It is clear that he now takes expected capital gains or losses more explicitly into account than in the earlier version. They are connected with the risk factor; but the latter is still linked with transaction requirements as well through *uncertainty over the time of realization* of assets:

> The risk-factor comes into our problem in two ways: first, as affecting the expected period of investment; and second, as affecting the expected net yield of investment. There are certain differences between its way of operation on these two lines; but ... the resultant effects are broadly similar [1982, 53].

Hicks conceived the determinants of the demand for money more broadly than Keynes in the General theory. Expected capital gains or losses are only one factor, and perhaps not the most important one. That Hicks has been consistent in his emphasis in this respect is shown by his later writings — e.g., by the 'two triads' lectures (1967, 1–60), where he attempts to rehabilitate the *precautionary motive*. There he also clearly indicates that he regards Keynes's theory as a special case of a broader notion:

> What he is there [i.e. in the *General theory*] contemplating is the limiting case in which costs of investment and disinvestment are negligible, so that the only thing which matters to the rational investor is the value of his portfolio in the near future ... Once this point is reached, it becomes possible that a non-interest bearing money will be held for the Speculative Motive [1967, 45].

To emphasize this difference, we may say that Hicks discussed liquidity not exclusively in terms of safe capital values, as Keynes tended to do in the *General theory*, but in terms of a more general concept of freedom of action. This may be called *sequential liquidity*, because according to this notion it "is not a matter of a single choice; it is a matter of a sequence of choices, a related sequence" (Hicks 1974, 38). It is through this notion of liquidity that transactions costs become important. (Of course safe capital values are also essential for sequential liquidity.) Sequential liquidity has not been made explicit until Hicks's recent writings. Yet its antecedents can be traced back to the emphasis on transactions costs and on the uncertainty over the time of realization in his early writings.

A further difference lies in the fact that Hicks explicitly argued in terms of a *spectrum* of assets in a descending order of liquidity, not just money and bonds as in the simplest Keynesian model. The latter might be taken merely as an analytical simplification. Yet in Hicks's case a crucial implication of the existence of different degrees of liquidity is explicitly recognized. Since transactions costs that tend to keep one's portfolio frozen depend on the state of development of the financial system, Keynes-like price speculation is apt to be the more important the more highly developed the financial sector of the economy is. Hicks has perhaps stated this most clearly in his more recent writings: "the rise in the importance of the speculative motive is a consequence of the rise of financial markets" (1967, 47). Hicks in his 'Suggestion' article draws the same distinction between *different types of economic agents* in the same economy. He distinguishes between "insensitive" people for whom "the costs of transferring assets are large relative to the amount of assets they control" (1982, 63), and "sensitive" ones who can continuously adjust the composition of their portfolios in accordance with changes in their expectations. Thus the Keynesian framework is more applicable to the latter, relatively wealthy and liquid sector. Indeed, Keynes in his writings paid most attention to an economy with well-developed financial markets.[2]

In the monetary tradition Hicks first got acquainted with, monetary stability was conceived as the main problem. He also attributes the maintenance of a reasonable price stability of asset prices to the slow reactions of the insensitive sector. As a consequence, the development of capitalism, by decreasing transactions costs, "is its own enemy, for it imperils that stability without which it breaks down" (1982, 63). In fact, both Hicks and Keynes were much concerned with short-run changes in the demand-for-money function and the resultant instability. But differently from Keynes, Hicks places the uncertainty concerning *future transaction requirements* on an equal footing:

> So far the effect of risk seems fairly simple; an increase in the risk of investment will act like a fall in the expected rate of net yield; an increase in the uncertainty of future outpayments will act like a shortening of the time which is expected to elapse before those outpayments; and all will ordinarily tend to increase the demand for money [Hicks 1982, 54].

As a matter of fact, after the *General theory*, Keynes made a concession to his critics by admitting that he had misspecified the demand for money in the *General theory*:

> I allowed, it is true, for the effect of an increase in actual activity on the demand for money. But I did not allow for the effect of an increase in *planned* activity, which is superimposed on the former [Keynes 1937, 667].

In order to alleviate this defect, Keynes introduced the concept of the *finance motive* for the demand for money, which has not been incorporated in the standard Keynesian system. It seems that in Hicks's theory it had a more developed counterpart from the start.

III

Next, we turn to the second main part of our argument, i.e., to a closer examination of the link between money and economic activity.

In fact, in the case of the standard Keynesian approach, the same basic principle of optimal portfolio choice is applied to the demand for both money and real assets. It determines the optimal stock of real capital as the starting point for determining the investment flow. This is often regarded as the hallmark of the Keynesian approach in contrast to older approaches.[3] In Hicks's 'Suggestion' article it is also possible to discern a clear analysis of how portfolio selection affects asset prices. So is there after all really any need for distinguishing between Keynes's and Hicks's analyses?

We shall argue that there is. That this might be so is suggested by a general feature of the 'Suggestion' article which strikes a modern reader. The article makes only a few passing comments on changes in the level of activity; its basic concern seems to be with prices. One obvious way to explain this emphasis might be to attribute to the article the same old view of the scope of monetary theory that is still attributed to, say, Keynes's *Treatise*. Old monetary theory conceived the role of monetary theory as explaining the price level, while the task of explaining activity was usually left beyond the scope of one's analysis. On this basis, it was Keynes's *General theory* which explicitly widened the scope of monetary theory.

However, we shall next show that careful reading of the 'Suggestion' article, and of Hicks's more recent writings in particular, lends support to an alternative more substantial explanation of this difference in emphasis between Hicks's approach and that of the *General theory*. Hicks deliberately conceived the scope of the portfolio-selection approach differently and more narrowly than the latter. The portfolio-selection approach was primarily used by Hicks to explain choice among (relatively liquid) *financial* assets. As we shall see, the nexus between these and (relatively illiquid) *real* assets, in turn, was to be explained by different principles. These would take liquidity considerations into account from a different perspective not discussed by Keynes.

As far as the 'Suggestion' article itself is concerned, there are at least some clues pointing in this direction. First, although Hicks apparently incorporates the balance sheet as a whole in his analysis, i.e., by including real as well as financial assets (1982, 58), in most of his portfolio analysis the real side of it is kept 'frozen.' Furthermore, there is a wealth of indirect evidence indicating that the distinction between real and financial assets plays a crucial, although frequently unexplained, background role in the analysis. Recalling that Hicks channels the influence of risk through price uncertainty as well as uncertainty over the point of time of realization of assets, it appears that an economics agent primarily operating in real assets, e.g., an industrial firm, is particularly influenced by the latter kind of uncertainty:

> in the case of that kind of investment which consists in the starting of actual processes of production, the yield which is expected if the process can be carried through may be considerable; but the yield which is expected if the process has to be interrupted will be large and negative. Uncertainty of the period for which resources are free will therefore have a very powerful effect in interrupting production [1982, 58n.].

To indicate the direction Hicks was striving for, one may also recall Hicks's distinction between "sensitive" and "insensitive" groups in asset behavior. In the case of the latter group, relatively large transactions costs inhibit them from adjusting the composition of their wealth to transitory changes in yield expectations. It might be argued that industrial enterprises the bulk of whose assets are locked up in productive equipment belong to the insensitive group falling outside the main focus of the 'Suggestion' article, which is much concerned with the instability caused by sensitive portfolio behavior. Indeed, foreseeing the Keynesian doubts on the interest elasticity of investment, Hicks notes:

> Short-run optimism will usually be enough to start a Stock Exchange boom; but to start an industrial boom relatively long-run optimism is necessary [1982, 58n.].

This same difference between industry and finance in terms of sensitivity is also noted towards the end of the article:

> Stock exchange booms will pass over into industrial booms, if industrial entrepreneurs are also fairly sensitive ... But the insensitive are always there to act as a flywheel, defeating by their insensitivity both the exaggerated optimism and the exaggerated pessimism of the sensitive class [1982, 62–63].

And then, recalling the contemporary trade-cycles theories of von Hayek, he passes over the problem:

> How this comes about I cannot attempt to explain in detail, though it would be an interesting job, for one might be able to reconcile a good many apparently divergent theories. But it would lead us too deeply into Cycle theory — I will only say that I think the period of fluctuation turns out to depend, in rather complex fashion, upon the distribution of sensitivity and the distribution of production periods between industrial units [1982, 63]

So it turns out that the link between the prices of financial assets and real investments is abstracted from in the 'Suggestion' article. It is indicated that explaining this link would require much stronger emphasis on sequential liquidity than is needed to explain the asset behavior of the sensitive sector.

Substantiation for this claim is given by Hicks's more recent writings. In these he has repeatedly insisted that Keynes's theory of liquidity is a special case applicable to financial markets only:

> the way in which liquidity appears in the formal Keynes theory, as a relation between 'supply of money' and the 'rate of interest' is no more than a special case. That is the way in which liquidity appears on financial markets; but the general concept of liquidity is much broader [Hicks 1979, 94].

This broader notion of liquidity, we shall argue, is the concept of sequential liquidity, which the 'Suggestion' article analyzed primarily and tentatively in the context of financial markets.

Furthermore, Hicks now insists that it is in the non-financial sphere that the liquidity problem is more acute:

> I have myself become convinced that it is outside the financial sphere (very inadequately considered, in relation to liquidity, by Keynes) that liquidity is potentially of the greater importance.
>
> This is because the decisions that affect the liquidity of the non-financial firm are larger relative to its business than those that affect the liquidity of the financial firm ... The financial firm ... is continually acting in such a way as to diminish or to increase its liquidity by small amounts. Liquidity preference, for the financial firm, is a matter of

marginal adjustments, as Keynes very rightly saw. But the liquidity problem of the non-financial firm is not, as a rule, a matter of marginal adjustment [1979, 95].

Yet it is largely an open question how sequential liquidity affects non-financial decisions and how monetary forces exercise their influence by means of it. It seems that there exists *complementarity* between (illiquid) real assets and liquid assets: "the liquidity problem of the financial firm is a question of the relative liquidity of its financial assets ... the liquidity problem of the non-financial firm is a matter of the relation between its real assets, on the one hand, and its financial assets (and liabilities), on the other" (1979, 94). Substitutability between them, stressed by the standard Keynesian tradition, is pushed into the background.

As a crude simplification, one may also illustrate the relation between liquid and illiquid assets by using the terms of production theory. Money and other relatively liquid assets can be regarded as an input in the productive process operating on illiquid real assets. This input coefficient is liable to shifts through changes in the risk factor as already emphasized by the 'Suggestion' article. Nevertheless, at a given point of time with given expectations, this input coefficient is relatively fixed.[4] Consequently, the role of the rate of interest is changed as well. It no longer sets the yield standard for real investment, as in Keynes's *General theory* framework. Instead, in imperfect markets,

> it is a great mistake to think of the liquidity of the producer purely in terms of profit and loss. It is here, I think, that Keynes went most seriously wrong. It was very wrong to think that investment is governed by the rate of interest, as if any concern that wanted to invest could always raise as much capital as it required at a ruling rate of interest. Rates of interest, at the most, are an index of liquidity; they are not by any means always a perfect index [Hicks 1979, 50].

Statements like this are nothing new. Practically oriented macroeconomists, those of the Keynesian inclination in particular, have always insisted on the importance of market imperfections when considering the efficacy of monetary policy. What is new in Hicks's case is that he is trying to develop apparently diverse notions into a coherent conceptual structure.

What Hicks himself seems to be particularly endeavouring to do through his general notion of liquidity is to intimately link the explanation of economic events with time. In the sequence of economic events over time, liquidity can, for example, affect the lags in reactions so that the better one's liquidity, the quicker one is able to utilize advantageous opportunities.

IV

One outstanding feature of Hicks as an economist is that he synthesized different traditions in his own analysis. He made his breakthrough as an economist at The London School of Economics, at that time strongly influenced by Hayek and the Austrian school. From continental economic thought he also adopted the Walrasian approach and, what is important here, the basic ideas of the Swedish school. In his "Recollections and documents" (Hicks 1977, 134–38) and Introduction to Hicks 1982, Hicks recalls how he, originally under Knightian and later Hayekian influence, gradually in the first half of the 1930s came under the influence of Walrasian, Swedish, and Cambridge economists. It is important to note, however, that his first contacts in Cambridge were not with Keynes but with Dennis Robertson. Indeed, Hicks later occupied a kind of intermediate position between the two competing camps.

These various influences can also be distilled from Hicks's early writings. Thus, in the first instance, there is the influence of Knight, Hayek, and the Austrian school. Hicks's emphasis on the time structure of production can be regarded as a reflection of these influences. But his contribution was to stress its relevance for the analysis of liquidity. Furthermore, the whole analysis of 'Suggestion' is taken up with the threat of instability to which a monetary economy is subject. Hicks arrived at this issue, as the essays of the early 1930s, collected in Hicks 1982, 3–79, clearly indicate, from Hayek's problem of monetary equilibrium. Hicks went beyond Hayek by noticing that monetary shocks are not the only factor disturbing a monetary equilibrium. Indeed, a sensitive monetary equilibrium is inherently unstable. This is the message clearly conveyed by 'Suggestion.' But it was also the question that occupied Wicksell and his Swedish followers in their analysis of a credit economy. Indeed, at the time of 'Suggestion,' Hicks had already acquainted himself with the Stockholm School. Two examples serve to illustrate this.

First, a contemporary counterpart to 'Suggestion' was the German version of Myrdal's *Monetary equilibrium*, which Hicks reviewed in *Economica* in 1934 (Hicks 1982, 42–45). Myrdal, like Hicks, was also concerned with the instability of a monetary economy. In this respect there seems to be a difference in emphasis, however. While Hicks stresses the role of transactions costs and the 'locked' position of the insensitive sectors in maintaining stability, Myrdal gives more attention to *wages* as sticky prices (in fact, in this respect he may be said to anticipate incomes policy). In other words, Myrdal in a way anticipated the distinction between "fixprices" and "flexprices" which came to play such a large role in Hicks's own later work (on this cf. Hicks 1982, xiii, 8).

Second, Hicks, like the Swedish writers, emphasized the role of *expectations* and was much concerned with explaining causes and consequences of changes in expectations. Indeed, it seems that in his first review of the *General theory for the Economic Journal* (Hicks 1936), he was prepared to perceive Keynes's analysis as a more thoroughgoing and precise explanation of expectations than is perhaps warranted, given the aims of the book.

Apart from Hayek and the Stockholm School, Hicks's early monetary essay was also influenced by the Cambridge monetary tradition. Thus, in the first place, one may note that various writers of the Cambridge School anticipated the idea of sequential liquidity as freedom of action which was discussed above. The clearest example of this is perhaps F. Lavington, who writes:

> In order to carry through his payments quickly and conveniently each person holds a part of his resources in the form of a stock of money. The size of that part of this stock which he holds to carry through current transactions depends directly upon the volume of his payments; ... But the size of that part of this stock which he holds as a first line of defence against emergencies depends less directly upon the volume of his payments; it depends upon his *estimate* of contingent payments, and consequently varies with his state of mind, or, more correctly, with the business outlook [Lavington 1921, quoted in Patinkin 1974, 26].

But also D.H. Robertson notes:

> it is necessary to distinguish between Keynes's own interpretations of 'liquidity preference' in terms of his speculative motive, and that broader interpretation in terms of desire for protection against general uncertainties of business life, which I have attributed to certain pre-Keynesian writers [Robertson 1959, 72].

As the second indication of the Cambridge tradition, one may refer to the idea of complementarity between liquid and real assets and the view of money and liquid assets as an input in production processes, discussed in Section III above. It seems that they share a common starting point with the Cambridge cash-balance equation and can be seen as a further development of it. Thus, for instance, Lavington writes:

> In a modern community each person with resources at his disposal needs some means by which he can employ these resources in order to obtain goods from other parties ... Each therefore will find it convenient to hold part of his resources in the form of a stock of something, which, being generally acceptable and easily transferable, serves as general purchasing power [Lavington 1922, 29]

In view of these close similarities between Hicks's early writings and several contemporary approaches, they can be said to represent a kind of a synthesis of the monetary theory of the 1930s before the *General theory*. But the question then arises as to what the role of Keynes's *Treatise on money* is as a source of Hicks's inspiration. Should it be regarded more as a preliminary to the General theory, or does it instead represent a line of development parallel to early Hicks, to be rejected by Keynes himself later on?

An extensive discussion of the relation between the *Treatise* and the *General theory* would take us too far into the Keynes exegetics, so that only a few remarks are in order here. Hicks himself maintains that the influence of the *Treatise* on his early analysis was scant, and that the references to it in his early writings were secondary (Hicks 1982, 8). Be it as it may, this is not of decisive importance, because both Hicks and Keynes in the *Treatise* drew from the same sources of monetary theorizing and may have independently come to the same ideas. Furthermore, it is generally acknowledged that Keynes's *Treatise* is in many ways richer in its monetary analysis than the *General theory*. Coming to the latter book, Keynes, in addition to opening some new routes, closed many old ones. The analysis of the *General theory* is also much more condensed than that of the *Treatise*. Consequently, it comes as no surprise that many of the notions we have attributed to Hicks's early writings above can be found in the *Treatise* as well. This applies, for example, to the idea of a *spectrum* of assets of different degrees of liquidity. In the same context the *Treatise* also notes the role of transactions costs in its definition of liquid assets which are "realizable at short notice without loss" (Keynes 1972, 59). The *Treatise* and early Hicks also share with contemporary monetary theory the feature that the price level and, in connection with this, the level of asset prices are regarded as the problem of monetary analysis, while the determination of the level of activity is left in the background.

These similarities may be enough to place early Hicks and the *Treatise* in the same category. There are some objections to this, however. First, apart from the definitions, the analysis in the *Treatise*, like that in the *General theory*, stresses price uncertainty and the liquidity problem of a financial investor rather than transactions costs and the liquidity problem of an industrial enterprise, and thus differs from Hicks. Secondly, in accordance with the *General theory*, the *Treatise* is also mostly concerned with well-developed financial markets where "securities" (corresponding to the bonds of the *General theory*) represent the main alternative assets to money. Thirdly, from the point of view of determination of investment, the *Treatise* also tends to look at real and financial investments as compatible substitutes in portfolio allocation. Indeed, the whole distinction between investment in securities and real investment is not clearly made in it.[5] In these respects, the *Treatise* can be seen as an antecedent to the *General theory*, whereas these kinds of factors receive a different treatment in early Hicks, as we have seen.

One should note, however, that interpreting Keynes's theory is problematic. As has often been argued, Keynes was basically an applied economist in the sense that he used and devised analytical weapons in order to find an answer to a certain concrete historical problem. It is this historical context which determines the main emphasis of his analytical efforts and the change in which may cause changes in his theoretical weapons. One can argue that from this point of view it was precisely the speculative demand for money by *rentiers* which was important to Keynes in the *General theory*. In the 1930s it prevented, in Keynes's view, the badly needed decline in the long-term rate of interest. The analysis of liquidity preference and the rate of interest in the *General theory* highlights this problem. The IS-LM model has well preserved this part of Keynes's analysis.

To say this is not to deny that the *General theory*, and even more the *Treatise on money* or Keynes's other works, involve elements which come close to the interpretation we have given to Hicks's early writings above. But in the *General theory* they played a subsidiary role at best and consequently have been neglected by the later Keynesian tradition. Yet Keynes's multiformity suggests that it is better not to regard Keynes and early Hicks primarily as rivals. Rather, they complement each other, and early Hicks offers an analytical starting point the emphasis of which is different from Keynes's.

V

We have argued that early Hicks differs from Keynes, and from the *General theory* in particular, both in its conception of liquidity and, as a consequence of this, in its analysis of the transmission of monetary influences. The role of transactions costs and the flexibility aspect of liquidity are given much more stress by Hicks. In stressing these he draws attention to various kinds of frictions which are not emphasized by Keynes. These frictions can be utilized, as early Hicks utilized them, to analyze the price stability of a monetary economy; or perhaps more interestingly in comparison with Keynesian analysis, their role in the behavior of economic agents can be taken as the starting point for analyzing the influence of money on the real economy. Early Hicks, however, gives only hints in these respects.

One may also ask in what respects Hicks's way of looking at liquidity as flexibility calls into question the standard Keynesian monetary analysis, which closely follows the *General theory*. One might say that the more imperfect the markets are, the more relevant is Hicks's liquidity. From this point of view the development of the financial system might also be fruitfully analyzed. Hicks's emphasis on expected transactions and flexibility requirements also offers a perspective of the formation of expectations. This might also help in accounting for shifts in the demand for money function which have sometimes formed a puzzle for the standard analysis. On the other hand, there are cases where Hicksian liquidity might offer a theoretical perspective of certain Keynesian policy views which have been left without theoretical support by the portfolio approach. The low interest-rate elasticity of investment, for instance, can be taken as an outcome of the specific type of liquidity problem of an industrial enterprise analyzed by early Hicks. But it is too early to indicate the implications of the Hicksian perspective because it has been left undeveloped in monetary theory after the Second World War. The exceptions are few.[6] We have already shown how Hicks himself in his recent writings has returned to his early work and how he has made some progress in its further development.

One could perhaps also point out some lines of thought in the present debate which come quite close to early Hicks in their emphasis, although the similarities have not been noticed. Thus we have noted that Hicksian liquidity may provide a theoretical background to those Keynesian views which stress the importance of market imperfections for the efficacy of monetary policy. Keynesian elasticity pessimism might be viewed in this

light. Furthermore, the American *post-Keynesians*, despite their willingness to perform as the true followers of Keynes, might do better to choose
early Hicks as their authority. They have stressed Keynes's *finance motive*
for holding money as the link through which the planned level of activity
affects the demand for money (cf. Davidson 1978). In Keynes's case,
however, this remained as a loose attempt to meet Ohlin's critique, while,
as we have seen, it constitutes a central element in early Hicks. Furthermore, the post-Keynesians share with early Hicks the view, discussed in
Section III above, that substitutability between liquid assets and real assets
is low.[7] While this again is a central issue in Hicks, it appears in the
General theory only in the controversial chapter 17. The post-Keynesians
have analyzed cyclical financial instability (cf. Minsky 1977), which early
Hicks also stressed, while Keynes in the *General theory*, although recognizing it, was more occupied by the fear that speculation locks the long-
term rate of interest persistently at a high level.

All in all, we have shown that Hicks's rich analysis of liquidity and the
monetary tradition underlying it are not merely minor steps on the road to
the *General theory* and to its IS-LM interpretation, but are also worth
pursuing on their own account. In their further articulation much still
remains to be done.

I am grateful to two anonymous referees for their helpful comments.

References

Davidson, Paul 1977. 'Post-Keynesian monetary theory and inflation.' In Weintroub, ed.,
    Modern economic thought (Philadelphia), 275–93.
—— 1978. 'Why money matters: lessons from experience from a half-century of monetary
    theory.' *Journal of Post-Keynesian Economics*, Fall 1978, 46–70.
Hicks, John 1935. 'A suggestion for simplifying the theory of money.' *Economica*, Feb.
    1935.
—— 1936. 'Mr Keynes' theory of employment.' *Economic Journal*, June 1936, 338–53.
—— 1937. 'Mr Keynes and the classics.' *Econometrica*, April 1937.
—— 1967. *Critical essays in monetary theory*. London.
—— 1974. *Crisis in Keynesian economics*. Oxford.
—— 1977. *Economic perspectives*, Oxford.
—— 1979. *Causality in economics*. Oxford.
—— 1982. *Money, interest and wages: collected essays on economic theory*, vol. 2. Oxford.
Keynes, John Maynard 1937. 'The *ex-ante* theory of the rate of interest.' *Economic Journal*,
    Dec.
—— 1971. *The collected writings of John Maynard Keynes*, vol. 5. London.
—— 1972. *The collected writings of John Maynard Keynes*, vol. 6. London.
Lavington, F. 1922. *The English capital market*. London.
Minsky, Hyman P. 1977. 'An "Economics of Keynes" perspective on money.' In Weintraub
    ed., *Modern Economic thought* (Philadelphia), 295–307.
Patinkin, Don 1974. 'Keynesian monetary theory and the Cambridge School.' In Johnson and
    Nobay, eds., *Issues in monetary economics* (London).
—— (1976). *Keynes' monetary thought*. Durham, N.C.
Radcliffe Committee on the Workings of the Monetary System 1959. *Radcliffe Report*.
    London.
Robertson, D.H. 1959. *Lectures on economic principles*. London.
Smith, V. Kerry 1980. 'Money as a factor of production: ultimate neoclassical heresy or
    Keynesian insight?' *Journal of Post-Keynesian Economics*, Winter 1979/80, 273–80.

Notes

1. G.L.S. Shackle, however, is an exception. He maintains, quite in line with our own argument below, that there are crucial differences between Keynes and Hicks (Shackle 1978, 225).

2. This suggests that the standard Keynesian framework may be particularly inappropriate when considering money in an economy with rudimentary financial markets. Account must be taken, however, of the fact that Keynes himself argued in chapter 17 of the *General theory* that the notion of what is liquid depends on social practices and institutions. He indicated that in certain historic environments land may have assumed the role of money in carrying a high liquidity premium.

3. Cf., e.g., Patinkin 1974, 10.

4. But one has to be careful. Taken literally, this simplification amounts to a view quite similar to the crude quantity theory of money: output is a function of liquidity which is determined by monetary policy.

5. "The decision as to the volume of saving, and also the decision relating to the volume of new investment, relate wholly to current activities. But the decision as to holding bank deposits or securities relates, not only to the current increment to the wealth of individuals, but also to the whole block of their existing capital. Indeed, since the current increment is but a trifling proportion of the block of existing wealth, it is but a minor element in the matter" (Keynes 1971, 127).

6. It is interesting to note that the Radcliffe Committee on the Workings of the Monetary System (*Radcliffe Report*, 1959) bears close similarity to Hicks in its view on liquidity.

7. "another fundamental conceptual difference between Keynes, on the one hand, and Friedman and neoclassical Keynesians such as Tobin who emphasize portfolio balance, on the other, is the magnitude of the elasticity of substitution between money (and financial assets) and *resource-using reproducible durables* as vehicles for transferring purchasing power to the uncertain future" (Davidson 1977, 292; cf. also Davidson 1978 and 1980, and V. Kerry Smith 1980).